D0793726

American Frontiersmen
on Film and Television

ALSO BY ED ANDREYCHUK
AND FROM McFARLAND

Burt Lancaster: A Filmography and Biography
(2000; paperback 2005)

*The Golden Corral: A Roundup
of Magnificent Western Films* (1997)

American Frontiersmen on Film and Television

Boone, Crockett, Bowie, Houston, Bridger and Carson

by ED ANDREYCHUK

McFarland & Company, Inc., Publishers
Jefferson, North Carolina, and London

Library of Congress Cataloguing-in-Publication Data

Andreychuk, Ed.
American frontiersmen on film and television : Boone, Crockett,
Bowie, Houston, Bridger and Carson / by Ed Andreychuk
p.   cm.
Includes filmographies.
Includes bibliographical references and index.

ISBN 0-7864-2132-0 (illustrated case binding : 50# alkaline paper) ∞

1. Pioneers in motion pictures.
2. Pioneers on television.
3. Pioneers—United States—Biography.
4. Motion pictures—United States—Catalogs.
I. Title.
PN1995.9.P487A53   2005
791.43'652—dc22
2005000092

British Library cataloguing data are available

©2005 Ed Andreychuk. All rights reserved

*No part of this book may be reproduced or transmitted in any form
or by any means, electronic or mechanical, including photocopying
or recording, or by any information storage and retrieval system,
without permission in writing from the publisher.*

On the cover: John Miljan as Daniel Boone in *The Great Meadow* (1931)

Manufactured in the United States of America

*McFarland & Company, Inc., Publishers
Box 611, Jefferson, North Carolina 28640
www.mcfarlandpub.com*

To the memories of these six men
who explored the American frontier
and to the filmmakers
who were inspired by their deeds

ACKNOWLEDGMENTS

My many thanks to all those who have helped me in gathering information and materials in order to complete this book.

Included are: Daughters of the Republic of Texas Library; David Crockett State Park; Eddie Brandt's Saturday Matinee; Enoch Pratt Library (Central Branch); Filson Historical Society; Fort Boonesborough; Fort Bridger Historic Site; Greater Bridger Valley Chamber of Commerce; Jerry Ohlinger's Movie Material Store; Larry Edmunds Bookshop; Library of Congress; Mary L. Martin Postcards; Museum Association of Taos; and the Smithsonian Institution.

I especially want to thank my wife and daughter for enduring my typing and research.

TABLE OF CONTENTS

PREFACE

American Frontiersmen on Film and Television focuses not on every single frontier figure but on six in particular — six of the boldest and certainly among the most famous. Their names are Daniel Boone, Davy Crockett, Jim Bowie, Sam Houston, Jim Bridger and Kit Carson.

Well over 100 years of American history is reflected through the lives of these men. From the French and Indian War to the Civil War, their lives are explored as are their legends.

The dominant characteristic shared by all of them is that great pioneer spirit. This spirit is extended through the many film and television depictions, from the silent film era and into the 21st century.

Each frontiersman has a biography and overview along with a filmography. Pictures and photographs help to give a glimpse into their history and a glimpse of those performers who recreated their adventures.

While an exhaustive attempt was made to reflect as many film and television entries as could be found, undoubtedly there will be some titles that were overlooked. For this, I extend any apologies which are necessary.

Also, one of the most colorful of all frontier figures, Buffalo Bill Cody, has not been purposefully slighted. Cody is reflective of that period in history not covered in this book, and which follows the Civil War and continues into the 20th century. Surely a separate book would be needed to cover Cody and other such frontier figures of his day as Wyatt Earp, George Armstrong Custer, Wild Bill Hickok, Bat Masterson and Tom Horn.

Of all the frontiersmen in this current book, Davy Crockett remains my own personal favorite. Perhaps this is due more than anything else to my cherished memories from childhood, when I was caught up in that fabulous Walt Disney–inspired Crockett craze.

During that time in the 1950s, I remember getting a Disney Alamo playset one Christmas (with a picture of Fess Parker); and I remember my dad, caught up in my enthusiasm as well, buying me a whole box of Crockett trading cards (again of Parker) one afternoon when he intended to buy only a pack.

Despite any favoritism, or bias, I may have shown about Crockett or the others in writing this book, hopefully I have shared a reflection of both good and bad traits. Most importantly, I hope their legends have not been tarnished by my hand.

One

DANIEL BOONE

Biography and Overview

In 1713, Daniel Boone's father, Squire, was 17 when he emigrated to Pennsylvania from England. Accompanying him were two older siblings, George IV (23) and Sarah (22). Their father, George III, brought the rest of the family over almost four years later. They followed the Quaker faith of William Penn, who had founded Pennsylvania in 1682.

When he was 25, Squire married 20-year-old Sarah Morgan. He made his living as a weaver, farmer, and blacksmith. By age 46, she had given birth to their 11 children. Son Daniel was born in a single-room log cabin in the township of Exeter, near what is today Reading, Pennsylvania, on October 22, 1734 (by the old Julian calendar or November 2 by the new Gregorian calendar).

As a boy in Pennsylvania, Daniel became enthralled with the Delaware Indians who came to trade their furs. From them he discovered how to fend for himself in the wilderness such as by erecting a shelter or tracking animals over the hardest terrain.

Squire gave Daniel his first rifle in 1747 when he was not yet 13. It wasn't long before Daniel was the provider of meat for his family. Sometimes he would be gone a few days hunting deer, turkey and even bear.

Young Daniel preferred this independent lifestyle in the wilderness, especially over sitting down to any schooling. Yet as a teenager he did learn how to read and write from Sarah Day Boone, his older brother Samuel's wife.

By 1750, Squire Boone had been expelled from the Quaker order, the Society of Friends, after eldest son Israel married outside the faith (and there was an earlier issue when Sarah, his oldest child, did the same thing). Discouraged and concerned as well that good farmland would not be abundant in the years ahead, Squire set out with the family for a new home.

Only 15, Daniel guided the group, including his friend Henry Miller, to the Susquehanna River and onto the Virginia Road. Along the way, Daniel enjoyed his first long hunt; it was with Henry in the Shenandoah Mountains and along the Roanoke River.

The Boone family settled in North Carolina's Rowan County on the Yadkin River in 1751. Daniel spent a few years helping his father farm the land although his heart was never in it. But he did have the chance to hunt and was regarded as one of the best marksmen in the county.

Out of the 20 entries in the Daniel Boone filmography, only one deals with his being a teenager. It is the only animated entry—1981's *Daniel Boone* (Hanna-Barbera)—and for television. Ironically, it is the only one as well to try to cover aspects of his entire life.

However, there are at least a couple of films which take place during the French and Indian War in 1755 (in which Boone was involved). They are 1923's silent 15-chapter *In the Days of Daniel Boone* (Universal), and a film made in 1950, *Young Daniel Boone* (Monogram). Unlike this similar titled film, the 1977 four-episode television series, *Young Dan'l Boone* (20th Century-Fox), had him just exploring Tennessee on the way to Kentucky.

When Daniel Boone was almost 20, in 1754, the French and British were fighting for control of various territories. In what was then the West it was for the Forks of the Ohio, where the Ohio River was joined by the Allegheny and Monongahela rivers. On this site was the French-held Fort Duquesne (where Pittsburgh, Pennsylvania, would be in time). Col. George Washington of Virginia led a colonial force of 150 men to take the fort; although he did defeat a French exploratory force, his mission failed and he had to surrender to the enemy his own frontier outpost, Fort Necessity.

The British then made Washington a commander in Gen. Edward Braddock's 1,850-man army (of which 1,400 were British soldiers and 450 were colonials) in the next attempt to take Fort Duquesne away from the French. Although outnumbering the enemy, Braddock's strategy to march his troops in rigid and open formation proved fatal. On July 9, 1755, they were defeated by the French soldiers and their Indian allies, attacking not only from the road but also from the cover of the forest.

Braddock was mortally wounded and 977 of his men were either wounded or killed (with only 50 casualties for the enemy). Washington led the survivors to safety. Boone was among the colonial volunteers, as a supply wagon driver, under the supervision of Maj. Edward Brice Dobbs. By cutting his lead horse free during the battle, Daniel was able to ride away and avoid capture.

Homeward bound in North Carolina, Boone's life was threatened by a knife-wielding Indian over a gorge on the Juniata River. Unarmed, Daniel rushed at his assailant and threw him to his death on the rocks 40 feet below.

The courtship of Rebecca Bryan soon followed for Daniel. On August 14, 1756, when she was 17 and Daniel 21, they were married by his own father. Squire just happened to be the justice of the county court.

There was no honeymoon for the newlyweds, however, for Rebecca set right off to help Daniel raise Jesse and Jonathan, the sons of his brother Israel (who died of tuberculosis, as had his wife before him and two daughters after). Between 1757 and 1780, Rebecca gave birth to six boys and four girls.

Daughter Jemima was allegedly fathered by Daniel's younger brother, Edward (or Ned as he was mostly called). This happened when Ned was helping to take care of Daniel's family, which was then living in Culpeper County, Virginia, because of Cherokee Indian uprisings in North Carolina.

During this time between 1760 and 1762, Daniel was gone and Rebecca believed he might be dead. He supposedly served as a volunteer with Maj. Hugh Waddell's militia against the Cherokee in North Carolina, and also took part in a long hunt which comprised that area as well as Virginia and Tennessee.

Daniel apparently overlooked the indiscretion between Ned and Rebecca. Raising Jemima as his own daughter, Daniel was perhaps closer to her than any of his girls. Ned later married Rebecca's sister, Martha.

The Boone family returned to live in North Carolina in 1762. More settlers were coming in and driving away the game. This affected Daniel's livelihood as a hunter to bring in furs and skins. Debts for his hunting supplies were mounting up.

Within two years, Boone found himself in the Rowan County Court to face a judgment against him for his debt. The problem was apparently handled in this instance by selling off the 640 acres of land he had bought several years earlier from his father.

A portrait of Daniel Boone as an older man.

On January 2, 1765, patriarch Squire Boone died at age 69. Daniel and his youngest brother, Squire Jr., were among a group of friends that journeyed to Florida later that year; they had a look-see at the hunting and settling prospects. Although Daniel bought a lot there, Rebecca would not consider moving so far away from everything and everyone.

In the winter of 1767-68, Daniel, brother Squire, and a friend, William Hill, went out on a long hunt. They found their way across the Appalachian ridge to the Big Sandy River. Daniel hunted his first buffalo in this strange land. Caught there by a snowstorm until spring, they returned home not realizing that this was Kentucky.

John Findley, a trader and peddler, initially sparked Daniel Boone's fascination about Kentucky, with its tall canebrakes, fertile valleys and abundant wildlife. This was when they met as wagon drivers during the French and Indian War, which was won by England in 1763 (but before this, in 1752, from his trading post at the Forks of the Ohio, Findley canoed down the Ohio River into Kentucky). When

Boone and Findley's paths crossed again, in 1768, Daniel's fascination for Kentucky was rekindled.

Boone and his brother-in-law, John Stewart (married to Daniel's youngest sibling, Hannah), joined Findley and three friends for a long hunt to Kentucky on May 1, 1769. But a better route was chosen — across the Appalachian region and through the Cumberland Gap mountain pass, on the Warrior's Path (named after the Cherokee Indians who journeyed to fight other tribes).

Station Camp was the initial base of operations set up by Boone and his companions for their hunting and trapping. In December 1769, Boone and Stewart were hunting together when their animal skins and horses were stolen by Shawnee Indians.

Following the Indians, Stewart and Boone took back their property as the enemy slept. But the Shawnee gave chase and held them captive for seven days. Escaping, the two hunters returned to camp and found Squire and another friend, Alexander Neeley, there with more supplies and horses.

However, Findley and the first three friends soon departed; as would Neeley after Stewart disappeared while checking beaver traps alone. John Stewart's skeleton was found some five years later in a hollow tree (Daniel believed he hid there after being attacked and wounded by Indians).

In the spring of 1770, Squire went back to sell their furs and left Daniel alone in the Kentucky wilderness for three months. Squire returned and went back with a second load before Daniel decided to go home with him. En route, the Boone brothers' beaver skins and horses were stolen, again by Indians. When he arrived home in May 1771, Rebecca at first did not recognize Daniel because of the long hair and beard which had grown.

The Proclamation of 1763, signed by England's King George III, forbade any colonization west of the Appalachian Mountains. Yet this didn't stop colonists like Daniel Boone, who were tired of the unfair taxes levied against them by the king, from venturing onward to possible better lives for their families.

The first attempt to begin a Kentucky settlement was by Virginian William Russell and Boone. From Russell's settlement of Castle's Wood, a party of between 40 and 50 people were led toward Kentucky by Daniel on September 25, 1773. Included were Rebecca and their children — James, Israel, Susannah, Jemima, Levina, Rebecca, Daniel Morgan and Jesse Bryan. Daniel's mother had stayed behind; their farewell at the Forks of the Yadkin was the last time he saw her (for Sarah Morgan Boone died in 1777).

During the trek, Daniel sent his 16-year-old son, James, back with a small party for additional supplies from Russell following behind. Returning on October 9, and not realizing they were only three miles from Daniel, the supply party bedded down in the Powell Valley (where Daniel and Squire were earlier robbed). The group was attacked by 15 Indians (Delaware, Shawnee and Cherokee), and James and Russell's own son, Henry, were among the fatalities. Each boy was shot in the hip and then tortured.

The Indians succeeded in preventing the first settlement of Kentucky when the others decided to turn back. Although Daniel wanted to go on, he accepted an offer to use a cabin on Tennessee's Clinch River for his family.

Various entries in the Boone filmography deal with aspects of settling in Kentucky and the ensuing Indian conflict. Included are the last silent film entry, 1926's *Daniel Boone Thru the Wilderness* (Sunset), and the first sound entry, 1931's *The Great Meadow* (MGM). Perhaps covering the earliest period of Kentucky settlement is the four-part television show, 1960-61's *Daniel Boone* (Walt Disney).

In 1774, Lord John Dunmore, Virginia's royal governor, was disturbed by the continued attacks upon settlers by the Indians. Boone and Michael Stoner were sent by William Russell back to Kentucky to try to warn the surveyors there of the impending conflict soon known as Dunmore's War.

One Indian attack, at Fort Blackmore on September 23, was just 20 miles from Daniel's home. Daniel became a captain in the local militia against the Indians (who were not only attacking settlers for intrusion on their hunting grounds, but also for attacks on their own people as well).

Following their defeat on October 10 by Virginia forces at Point Pleasant, the Delaware and Shawnee signed a peace treaty. This lost them their rights to hunt in Kentucky; apparently overlooking the Proclamation of 1763, Lord Dunmore told the Indians that the settlers would now stay south of their homes across the Ohio River from Kentucky.

As 1774 drew to a close, North Carolina justice Richard Henderson arranged for Daniel Boone to contact the Cherokee about purchasing their part of Kentucky. While Henderson didn't have the authority to make transactions at all (for the earlier proclamation also forbade private sales with the Indians), neither did the Cherokee supposedly have any legal rights to the land. Kentucky, still a colony of Virginia, was under England's ownership based on a 1609 charter by King James I.

Nonetheless, a sale between the Cherokee and Henderson's Transylvania Land Company was signed on March 17, 1775. At Sycamore Shoals in Tennessee, 200,000 acres of land were sold for $10,000 worth of goods (including guns, clothing, trinkets and liquor). Some Indians predicted that with the new land would come bloodshed.

A week before the sale, Henderson had Boone take about 30 men to build a road for traveling to Kentucky. Just eight days after the sale, Indians attacked the road builders, killing two of them. The bloodshed continued.

However, the building of the Wilderness Road would not be deterred. Boone was not only the leader, he was also the hunter for the men whose work consisted of removing all obstructions, such as brush, branches, logs and more. The road, which included the widening of the Warrior's Path, went from Tennessee (where Kingsport now sits), through the Cumberland Gap, and to the Kentucky River.

A settlement site was then chosen near the banks of the river, initially called Fort Boone; it was changed to Boonesborough by Henderson after he arrived there in April. As did other men before Boone pass through the Cumberland Gap (like Gabriel Arthur, returning to Virginia from Indian captivity), so too did other entrepreneurs besides Henderson form land companies (like William Preston, who sent James Harrod to actually start the first Kentucky settlement, Harrodsburg).

In April 1775, the same month and year as the founding of Boonesborough, the American Revolution began in Lexington, Massachusetts, between England and her colonies. Many colonists were disheartened by the unfair taxes and restrictions imposed on them, and it finally induced warfare.

By September, Richard Henderson's land company lost support because of its own unfair practices (like doubling land prices for new settlers and lowering them for friends), and Daniel Boone had brought his family and 17 others to live at Boonesborough. Others soon followed, including Squire Boone.

On July 4, 1776, and supported by 12 of the 13 colonies (with New York's support a few days later), the Declaration of Independence was signed in Philadelphia, Pennsylvania. But it took until August before word of it reach Boonesborough.

Meanwhile, on July 14 (just 10 days after the signing), 13-year-old Jemima Boone and two other teenaged girls were kidnapped by three Shawnee and two Cherokee. The other girls, daughters of Boonesborough colonist Richard Callaway, were named Elizabeth (or Betsy) and Frances (or Fanny).

Canoeing on the river alongside Boonesborough, the girls were taken into the forest on the far shore and carried off. Yet their screams were heard, and Boone (running out barefoot), Callaway and others followed as quickly as possible. The rescuers were still outdistanced.

Daniel believed the Indians were taking the girls north to the Ohio River. While Callaway and a party of horseback riders were dispatched in one direction (with hopes of cutting off the kidnappers at the Licking River), Boone and his group followed the trail on foot through the forest.

The first night out, a lad, John Gass, was sent back for provisions (including moccasins). The pursuit was slower than anticipated, and so Boone led his party off the trail to cut through the woods (thereby coming out on the trail further ahead and saving time).

During the third day of pursuit, Boone's group came upon the kidnappers and their victims. The Indians were fired at and they fled; all three girls were saved (and later on it was ascertained that two of the Shawnee had been mortally wounded).

This famous episode in Daniel Boone's history has been reflected in at least two motion pictures—both silent—1907's *Daniel Boone, or Pioneer Days in America* (Edison), and 1911's *The Chief's Daughter* (Selig). However, the 165-episode television show 1964–70, *Daniel Boone* (20th Century-Fox), had elements of the frontiersman's life, including Jemima's kidnapping

(and Boonesborough's founding, as well as the later capture of Daniel and attack on the frontier fort by Indians). Another silent film entry from 1911, *Daniel Boone's Bravery* (Kalem), also had him captured by Indians.

One of the Indians reputedly killed while trying to kidnap Jemima and the Callaway sisters was the son of Blackfish, a Shawnee chief. Indian attacks against Boonesborough (and other forts in the area) were later led by Blackfish, including one on April 24, 1777. When settler Daniel Goodman was fired at and scalped just outside the fort, scout Simon Kenton came out and shot down his assailant.

Boone and others then ran out to join Kenton. A Shawnee fired at Boone, breaking his ankle. Lying stunned on the ground, Daniel was expecting to be tomahawked when Simon shot down that Indian. Standing over Daniel to protect him, Simon downed still another assailant using his rifle as a club. Then carrying Boone over his shoulder, Kenton ran to the safety of Boonesborough where Jemima stood waiting. Boone's broken ankle mended in about six weeks, but pain from it continued to bother him over the years.

The Boonesborough colonists found themselves, by year's end, nearly out of salt (which they used to preserve meat). In January 1778, Daniel led 28 men to make more of it from the salt springs 50 miles away on the Lower Blue Licks. Boone hunted and scouted for the men, as did Thomas Brooks and Flanders Callaway (the latter being not only Richard Callaway's nephew, but also Daniel's son-in-law after marrying Jemima).

On February 7, Daniel was returning to the salt makers' camp with a few hundred pounds of buffalo meat strapped to his horse when he was confronted by four Shawnee warriors. As his knife was frozen in its sheath, he could not cut loose the meat to escape on horseback; instead he tried to run but was soon captured.

Chief Blackfish was on the warpath with over 100 warriors—intent on killing the salt makers and taking Boonesborough—as revenge for the murder of another chief, Cornstalk, by frontiersmen at Point Pleasant. Taken before Blackfish and his men, Boone learned of this from their translator, Pompey (a black man raised by the Shawnee). Using his cunning, Boone was just able to convince the Indians to take the salt makers as prisoners (to replace their dead as warriors), and to refrain from attacking Boonesborough until warm weather set in (when the captive women and children could then handle the long trek to the Indian towns across the Ohio River).

Boone and his comrades (except for hunters Callaway and Brooks, who avoided capture by being away from camp), were marched 100 miles to the Shawnee town of Chillicothe. On the way, the Shawnee had Daniel Boone run the gauntlet, between two rows of warriors wielding sticks and clubs. Racing from side to side, and then knocking over a warrior blocking his path, Boone escaped serious injury and was met with hearty approval from both his comrades and the Indians.

To replace their dead husbands and sons, the Shawnee did adopt around 10 of the captive salt makers. Blackfish adopted Boone into his family as a son, and called him Sheltowee (meaning "Big Turtle"). Daniel was still a captive but he grew close to his Indian parents and two little sisters, and he might have even had a relationship with an Indian woman during this period.

The rest of the captives were taken in March, by Blackfish and 40 Shawnee (accompanied by Daniel), to the British outpost at Detroit (for the Revolutionary War was being fought in many territories, and various Indian tribes allied themselves with the British). Hard labor and imprisonment awaited these captives, as the Shawnee collected the bounty offered for them by the British lieutenant governor, Henry Hamilton.

Adopted captive Andy Johnson escaped in April from Chillicothe, and fled back across the Ohio to Harrodsburg. He soon led a raid against the Shawnee towns. Johnson furthermore accused Daniel of both surrendering the salt makers without a fight (when Boone knew that resistance would have gotten them all killed), and of being a British sympathizer (when Daniel was just trying to use his wiles to deceive the enemy).

By June 1778, Blackfish was trying to recruit Indians along the Scioto River for the delayed assault on Boonesborough. Realizing he had to warn the fort, Boone escaped from his captor on the 16th with a horse, a little food and a rifle he built from salvaged parts.

Riding as fast as he could until his horse could not go any further, Daniel then ran on foot and crossed the Ohio holding onto a log. The Shawnee chased after Boone but failed to catch him. He killed a buffalo for more food during the 160-mile journey, and on June 20 Daniel Boone reached Boonesborough.

Jemima Boone soon greeted her father, but Rebecca and the rest of the family had returned to North Carolina. The question of Daniel's loyalty, fueled by Andy Johnson, left some apprehensive in the fort. Nonetheless, they all followed Boone in his actions to strengthen their defenses.

When another captive, William Hancock, escaped from the Indians in July, he cast suspicion as well on Daniel as a British sympathizer (or Tory). By late August, with no attack from the Indians yet and with suspicion about Boone becoming stronger, he led a raid back across the Ohio.

Simon Kenton was scouting ahead and was soon fighting a Shawnee war party. Boone and 18 other men came to Simon's aid and ran the Indians off.

Finding the Indian village of Paint

Creek abandoned, Boone reasoned that perhaps now the Indians were on their way to take Boonesborough. Except for Kenton and Alexander Montgomery (who remained behind to recover stolen horses belonging to the Kentucky settlement, Logan's Fort), Boone's raiders made it back to their settlement on September 6. This was just the day before Blackfish and 400 Indians did; and with the Indians were Pompey and a British militia company from Detroit.

Daniel Boone confronted the enemy alone outside the fort. Blackfish gave him a letter from Hamilton in Detroit, a reminder of an earlier promise to surrender the fort peacefully (but again this was a deception on Daniel's part). The situation, Boone related to Blackfish, involved others in the fort as well who had to decide on surrendering.

Richard Callaway (who felt Daniel's raid into Indian territory was foolish, since it depleted the already small force of 50 men at Boonesborough) now believed that any prior promises to the British made Boone a traitor. The men in the fort weighed the impending situation, including Squire and Daniel Boone, and the decision was to fight and die if necessary.

The enemy forces were informed the following day of Boonesborough's decision. Blackfish then agreed to put off any attack, while another day was spent devising a supposed peace treaty. But Blackfish proved as wily as Boone; the treaty signing was just a diversion to lure nine delegates outside the fort (and they included Daniel and Squire Boone, and both Richard and Flanders Callaway).

When the Indians surrounded the delegates and tried to drag them away, riflemen shooting from the fort's bastions allowed the delegation to escape back inside. In the process, the enemy struck back and Daniel was cut superficially on the head and across the shoulders by a tomahawk blow, and

Squire was shot in the shoulder. The attack on Boonesborough had begun.

This conflict, undoubtedly the most famous chapter in Boone's life, played the biggest part (along with the fort's actual settlement) in the frontiersman's filmography. The first silent entry from 1906 is called *Attack on Fort Boonesboro* (American Mutoscope and Biograph). Other silent films on the siege included 1912's *Life of Daniel Boone* (Republic), and 1923's *Daniel Boone* (Yale University). The two big sound films—1936's *Daniel Boone* (RKO), and 1956's *Daniel Boone, Trail Blazer* (Republic)—contain attacks against Boonesborough (along with aspects of its settlement).

In the 10-day battle, firing continued daily between both sides. On the first day, the Indians tried to storm the gate but were driven back by the marksmen. And Daniel removed the bullet from his brother's shoulder.

During the second night, a supply of flax, leaning against the outside of the fort, was set afire by the Indians; a defender, John Holder, rushed out and extinguished the blaze. Torches were thrown over the fort's walls starting the third night by the Indians. While some of the torches did land on cabin rooftops, they were quickly knocked off with poles by the women.

Although the Indians running to throw torches provided easy targets for the marksmen, this tactic was attempted each night for the next week. But during the day the enemy forces also were building a tunnel from the steep banks on the Kentucky River toward the fort.

There was no artillery brought against Boonesborough, so the Detroit militia conceived the tunnel as a way to possibly get close enough to be able to plant a powder charge. This threat was met by Daniel with a trench dug parallel to the fort's rear wall, so as to meet the enemy if they should break through.

On September 17, it began to rain

heavily. This not only put out any torch fires, but the next day the defenders (after only a brief exchange of gunfire) discovered the tunnel had collapsed. And the militia and Indian forces were gone as well.

Daniel received another superficial wound during the siege, with a grazing shot to the neck. Only two defenders were killed — a slave, London, and David Boudrun. Pompey was among the enemy killed, which Boone believed was around 37 in number.

Following the siege, a court-martial against Captain Daniel Boone was held at Benjamin Logan's settlement of Logan's Fort (or Station). Instigated by Richard Callaway's accusation that Boone was a traitor, testimony against him also came from the two prior captives, Andy Johnson and William Hancock.

Yet Boone's eloquent and quiet defense reminded everyone once more that his dealings with the Indians and British, while in captivity and afterwards, were deceptions and plans to save lives and to keep Boonesborough safe. Boone even made the point that Callaway was party to deception (as were all nine delegates), when they willingly left the fort to sign the treaty which included an agreement to bear allegiance to the British crown.

It took only a short time for Boone to be acquitted of four actual charges of treason — regarding the surrender of the salt makers, the promise to surrender Boonesborough, the raid in Indian territory, and taking the delegates to the treaty signing. Daniel was immediately promoted to major in the local militia.

Despite the vindication, Daniel was hurt that his loyalty had to endure such humiliation. In November 1778, he was back with Rebecca and their family in North Carolina. With him were Jemima and Flanders.

Yet Daniel Boone and his family returned to Boonesborough in October 1779.

He brought 100 people with him, which was then the largest group of settlers to travel together to Kentucky.

Daniel, however, did not stay at Boonesborough for long. When a claim was approved by the land commission just six miles away, he started a new settlement called Boone's Station. And afterward he had a farm on nearby Marble Creek.

With an interest in acquiring more real estate, Daniel offered his services to seek out claims for others as well (and thereby earn the funds needed for his own transactions). His work included being entrusted by various land speculators with $20,000 in currency to take to Virginia in February 1780 to buy land warrants.

En route, Daniel was robbed at a Virginia inn where he stayed the night. Boone believed the landlord was somehow responsible, but it was never proven.

Back in Kentucky, some of those who lost their money forgave Daniel. Yet others did not, and even feeling he had stolen it. Boone eventually paid back those who held him responsible.

Most settlers knew Daniel was of upstanding character. Late in 1780, he was given another promotion, to lieutenant colonel, in the militia of Fayette County (one of the three counties in Kentucky).

In October 1780, Daniel and brother Ned were returning from hunting near the Blue Licks. About 20 miles from Boone's Station, a Shawnee war party attacked them; Ned was shot and killed, and Daniel escaped into the canebrakes. When Daniel came back with help, he found Ned beheaded.

This incident was another brutal act in the ongoing warfare between the Indians and colonists. Included was a strike that summer by 1,100 militia men, led by Gen. George Rogers Clark (and for whom Boone served as a scout), against the Shawnee across the Ohio. Also, the year before, Chief Blackfish died of an infection from a wound sustained in a raid against Chillicothe by 300 Kentuckians led by Col. John Bowman.

England's chances for victory in the American Revolution were ended with the surrender of Gen. Charles Cornwallis to Gen. George Washington. It happened on October 19, 1781, at Yorktown, Virginia; Washington's 9,000 Americans, allied with 7,000 French soldiers, had defeated 8,000 British soldiers under Cornwallis.

A preliminary peace treaty between England and the United States of America was not signed until November 1782. Meanwhile, British forces and their Indian allies continued the warfare, including a victory in what was considered the final battle of the Revolutionary War.

This took place on August 19, 1782, near Kentucky's Lower Blue Licks (where the salt makers had earlier on been taken captive). Tory renegade Simon Girty, with 300 or so Wyandot Indians, and British Capt. William Caldwell, with 50 soldiers, ambushed 182 Kentuckians.

After a previous attack on the Kentucky settlement of Bryan's Station (founded by Rebecca Boone's kinfolk), Col. John Todd then led the Kentuckians against those enemy forces responsible. Girty's Indians and the British were hiding in wooded ravines across the Licking River.

Daniel Boone had 45 militia men from Fayette County with him, including his 23-year-old son, Israel. A trap seemed evident (for the enemy tracks were just too easy to follow), and Daniel shared these feelings with his commander. But Todd and another officer, Maj. Hugh McGary, were bent on continuing instead of waiting for the 500-man force under Col. Benjamin Logan to join them.

The Kentucky militia made a valiant effort but were overwhelmed within moments by the enemy and driven back into the Licking River. Todd and Israel (both shot in the chest) were among the 77 slain; the others were forced to retreat from their assailants. Daniel had tried to get his son to escape on a horse before he was killed, but Israel wouldn't leave his father's side.

Indian attacks led by Simon Girty are part of the Boone filmography. Included are the aforementioned films *Daniel Boone, Trail Blazer* (in 1956), *Daniel Boone* (in 1936), and *Daniel Boone Thru the Wilderness* (in 1926).

Along with the violent deaths of James and Israel Boone, another son, William, was sickly and died as an infant (shortly before Daniel brought the family to Boonesborough for the first time). Rebecca and Daniel's last child, Nathan, was the only one born in Kentucky.

The fighting between the Indians and settlers seemed to be retaliatory strikes. In the fall of 1782, for the tragedy of the Battle of Blue Licks, at least 1,000 men followed George Rogers Clark back across the Ohio. With Clark were Logan and Boone; Shawnee crops and villages were burned, forcing the Indians to flee further north.

In 1783, Daniel moved his family north to live along the Kentucky side of the Ohio River. There in the port town of Limestone (incorporated in time into the town of Maysville), the Boones lived in a boat turned into a cabin. Daniel ran a tavern and a supply warehouse. Rebecca handled the kitchen duties in the tavern with the help of several slaves the Boones owned.

Having been made a deputy surveyor in late 1782, Boone became involved in land surveying and speculation. He located and entered claims with the help of son-in-law Will Hays (married to daughter Susannah), who also kept the records.

Surveying included the laying out of marks and measuring chains, and others in the Boone clan were involved too. Sons Jesse Bryan and Daniel Morgan were chainmen, while Flanders Callaway and yet another son-in-law (daughter Levina's husband), Joseph Scholl, were markers.

The land business was speculative, with funds invested in surveying and obtaining the warrants often at risk. Properties could be overlapped or already claimed. Fraud went on as well (but not with Daniel Boone). Lawsuits readily occurred; one of the earliest in Kentucky was the case of *Boofman v. Hickman* (which did involve Daniel).

It was Boone, back in 1776, who located the land for James Hickman, which covered an area on both sides of Boone's Creek. John Floyd, Hickman's surveyor at the time, wanted the western side for Jacob Boofman and claimed the eastern side only for Hickman. By 1785, both Floyd and Boofman were deceased. Hickman then sued Boofman's heirs to acquire the land; however, the case took over 20 years to be resolved.

For a short time Boone was among the biggest land speculators in Kentucky. While surviving records reflected his land holdings to around 39,000 acres, son Nathan in later years believed the amount was some 100,000 acres because of the records which did not survive.

Any wealth from the speculation was soon depleted. Boone gave portions of his holdings to family members, and lent money to others without compensation. Lawsuits were lost to sharper businessmen who utilized the often underhanded tactics needed (and which Daniel would not use) to win out in the surge of faulty claims and surveys that abounded due in large part to more land warrants being issued than land existed for.

One underhanded speculator, Gilbert Imlay, signed an agreement with Daniel to buy 10,000 acres of land from him. Daniel filed the survey in Imlay's name, but never received any payment. The apparent rights to the land were given over to Imlay with the survey; Boone later discovered, after Imlay had left Kentucky, that Imlay sold the land out from under Boone.

Some justice may have come from the association with Imlay. He supposedly went overseas to England and France and spread word on Boone's fame, as well as bringing the frontiersman's exploits to bear in America with writer John Filson.

With Daniel's 50th birthday came the book *The Discovery, Settlement and Present State of Kentucke … To Which is added An Appendix, Containing the Adventures of Col. Daniel Boon.* During 1783, Daniel indeed shared his time and life's adventures with Filson. The results of Filson's book proved popular (with some 33 pages about Boone), and only enhanced the legend.

The end of the American Revolution certainly did not mean an end to the Indian problems. There was a treaty in January 1785 with several tribes (including the Delaware and Wyandot), but it gave up most of the Ohio lands to white emigration. Another attack on the Shawnee there occurred in the fall of 1786, with Boone joining Col. Logan's militia of 800 men, to rout and capture Indians. It helped to bring about the exchange of captives.

But Maj. McGary, still fuming over the Blue Licks tragedy, killed Chief Moluntha (who had been with Blackfish at the siege of Boonesborough). Another Indian, a Cherokee called Big Jim, was attacked and killed by the Kentuckians (for he was recognized by Boone as one of those who killed son James).

Daniel Boone fed and housed the Indian prisoners at Limestone. He helped free Nohelema, another Shawnee chief (and the late Cornstalk's sister). The Boones took care of a freed white captive, a little girl named Chloe Flinn, until her relatives were found.

Later on, Daniel may even have helped a chief escape from captivity, Blue Jacket, who had helped to free another white captive. Captured first by the Shawnee, during the Revolutionary War, Blue Jacket was actually a white man turned Indian leader (and whose name had been Marmaduke Van Sweringen).

Between the prisoner exchange in 1787 and Blue Jacket's escape in 1788, Boone served in the Virginia Assembly in Richmond (from October '87 to January '88). Elected to the assembly for the first time in 1781 (prior to Cornwallis' surrender), he was then briefly arrested by the British. In 1791, he was again a member of the assembly.

Daniel had moved his family in 1789 further east on the Ohio River, to Point Pleasant (now part of West Virginia). Among his ventures, he was involved in shipping cargo along the Ohio and its tributaries; the Boones lived in a cabin off one called the Kanawha River.

Some time was spent too in surveying and speculation there in Point Pleasant. But in 1794, Boone's land problems continued in more court cases. The year before, John Filson's excerpt on Daniel Boone was added to a book published earlier on in England and Ireland. In its second edition, the book was called *Topographical Description of the Western Territory of North America*. The writer was Daniel's old land nemesis, Gilbert Imlay.

Kentucky's petition for statehood was granted on February 4, 1792, by George Washington, president of the United States. So on June 1, Kentucky became the 15th state.

Within the next six years, the Boone family lived in several more locations. The moves, of economic necessity, were brought about by the land claims and debts against Daniel. He had reached the point of not even caring to contest the claims. While still at Point Pleasant, a failed trading post accumulated so much debt that Daniel could not meet the supply demands of a militia contract.

Any damages to his reputation seemed to always hurt Boone the most. He fell back to his old love of hunting in these years, despite the rheumatism that had set

in. Many of his family members even went along on the hunting trips, including Rebecca.

By 1798, Boone was living in his last cabin in Kentucky — off the Little Sandy River, another tributary of the Ohio. The state had formed into more counties and with more regulations. To pay back taxes to the state, sheriffs in Clark and Mason counties were forced to sell 10,000 acres of his remaining land holdings.

Boone was soon drawn to the land of Missouri; initially this came about through son Daniel Morgan, who had gone there to look into its possibilities. It was under Spanish rule at that time, but Spain welcomed emigration (and the main demand that emigrants become Catholics was even given leeway). Missouri's lieutenant governor, Zenon Trudeau, invited Daniel to move there and promised him a grant of 850 acres of land. Others who went along would also receive acreage.

So in September 1799, a large group of Boones, Bryans, Callaways, and others left Kentucky for Missouri further west. Some made the journey up the Ohio and Mississippi rivers by dugout (with one built by Daniel and his son Nathan over 50 feet long), while others (like Daniel) took to the trails beside the rivers. But Daniel Boone led them all.

They arrived at St. Louis in October. Trudeau was there to greet them with a new lieutenant governor, Don Charles Delassus. For the only time in his life, Daniel was given military honors, complete with marching soldiers and beating drums.

The Missouri River then took the emigrants to the Femme Osage Valley, where they picked out their land and built their homes. But daughter Susannah died from fever before she and husband Will Hays found their land. Daniel selected his between the river and Daniel Morgan's, yet he and Rebecca lived with their son in his new cabin.

On June 11, 1800, Daniel Boone was made syndic (judge, jury and sheriff) of the Femme Osage. One of his most disturbing duties occurred four years later with his involvement in a murder trial; son-in-law Hays was shot and killed in an argument with James Davis (his own son-in-law and a hunting companion of Daniel's).

Boone had Davis indicted for murder. But then he testified for him at the trial in St. Charles; it was revealed that the act was in self-defense (since Hays pulled a gun initially and threatened to use it).

A lot of hunting was done by Daniel in his later years, which also saw the deaths of daughters Levina (of an undisclosed cause) in 1803, and Rebecca (of consumption) in 1805. His favorite hunting companion (for wife Rebecca never let him go alone when he was old) was Derry Coburn, a slave owned by Daniel Morgan.

But on a winter hunting trip in 1802-03, Daniel and Derry were robbed of their goods by Osage Indians. Injuries and illnesses also happened to Daniel on his hunting adventures.

On that same winter trip with Coburn, Boone caught his hand in a steel beaver trap; and two years later he fell through the frozen Missouri River, returning from another hunt with Daniel Morgan and Nathan.

Daniel's rheumatism flared up from time to time. Out hunting with Derry in 1808, he became so sick and depressed that he was ready to die; Daniel even had a grave picked out before he recovered.

Yet Daniel Boone just kept on hunting. He was part of a large party of men in 1810 (which included Derry, Flanders Callaway, and grandson Will Hays Jr.). They spent six months hunting and exploring the western country beyond Missouri; grandson Hays claimed they went as far as the Yellowstone in Wyoming.

Earlier on, in May 1804, another group of men was led by Meriwether Lewis and William Clark (younger brother of Daniel's Kentucky militia commander, George Rogers Clark) on a journey westward. They started at St. Louis and followed the Missouri River (past the Femme Osage where Boone was living), and into the vast territory of the Northwest. Along other waterways they went, and, by November 1805, this famous expedition reached Oregon and the Pacific Ocean.

The Louisiana Purchase of 1803 covered an area of 828,000 square miles (including Missouri and much of the territory explored by Lewis and Clark). The $11,250,000 sale to the United States by France (having been ceded the land by Spain just the year before) was made with the help of President Thomas Jefferson's envoys in Paris, Robert Livingston and James Monroe.

With Missouri no longer under Spanish sovereignty, Congress passed a law in 1805 (under the Jefferson administration) that for any of the prior emigration lands to be honored, they had to be cultivated and lived on. This Boone had not done; apparently he was given more land in 1800 for bringing the 100 or so emigrants with him. By 1809, this property of thousands of acres, as well as the 850 acres he was first given, was taken away.

On March 18, 1813, Rebecca Boone passed away after taking sick a few days earlier. She and Daniel were married for 56 years. For the last seven years, they were living in a cabin of their own on Nathan's land. Rebecca was buried on her cousin David Bryan's land, however, on Tuque Creek near the Missouri River.

The War of 1812 broke out between England and the United States over shipping practices (including the British blockading of American ports). Daniel Boone was among the first to volunteer his services, but he was told that he was too old.

Yet the Missouri governor, Benjamin

Howard, secured the services of Daniel Morgan and Nathan Boone as captains to lead local military units. Daniel's grandson (and Flanders and Jemima's son), James Callaway, was captain of another.

The Sauk Indians were among the allies of the British. In the spring of 1814, and allied with the Shawnee, Capt. Callaway was shot down by a Sauk brave. Later, in December, the treaty ending the conflict (with the Americans the victors) was signed in Europe; yet fighting continued until word of it reached the United States in early 1815.

Earlier on, Boone had petitioned to Congress for his Missouri land back. A special law was passed and signed by President James Monroe in 1814, which returned to Daniel the original 850 acres given to him. But he soon had to sell most of it to pay old Kentucky debts.

A portrait of Daniel Boone two years before his death.

To pay back any remaining debts, Boone went back to Kentucky in 1817. The money used came from his hunting. He supposedly had only 50 cents left when he returned to Missouri; and in 1819, Daniel sold off the remaining acreage there for $5,000.

Daniel spent his last remaining years in Missouri, living with different members of his family. He made powder horns for his grandchildren.

In the summer of 1820, while staying with Jemima, Daniel became ill. The resulting fever abated enough within several weeks for him to visit Nathan.

However, Boone seemed to know that this would be his last illness. Family and friends came to see him when he arrived, on September 21, at Nathan's grand stone home. Daniel then enjoyed a meal (which included one of his favorites, sweet potatoes), and he played with some of his grandchildren too.

The next day, Daniel complained of still feeling full; he was feverish and was bedridden for a few more days in the little room set aside for him. Daniel was talking to Jemima and Nathan, who were at his bedside each holding a hand, when he quietly died. It was on September 26, 1820, and he was 85 years old.

The death of Daniel Boone is reflected in at least two films. Both are previously mentioned — the animated *Daniel Boone* (in 1981), and the silent *Life of Daniel Boone* (in 1912).

Two other entries in the filmography are simply Westerns. They are 1941's *The Return of Daniel Boone* (Columbia), about a grandson only; and 1935's *The Miracle Rider* (Mascot), a 15-chapter serial. The character of Daniel Boone is only briefly seen in the serial (as was also the case four years earlier with the aforementioned *The Great Meadow*).

Just a few weeks after his father's death, Jesse Boone (who was serving in the

Missouri legislature) died. Daniel and Rebecca, buried side by side, were disinterred 25 years later, in 1845, to Frankfort, Kentucky (at the request of the Kentucky legislature). To honor Daniel, in 1860 a monument was erected at the final burial site.

By 1830, Boonesborough was no longer a fort or a community. But in 1963, the site was turned into a park (when 57 acres of land were sold to the Kentucky Department of Parks). A replica of the original fort was built there in 1974.

Between Disney's *Daniel Boone* and the famous series of the same name (and both already mentioned), is another television entry. It is a two-parter from 1964's show *The Great Adventure* (CBS).

The final entry in the Daniel Boone filmography is 2000's *Boonesborough: The Story of a Settlement* (Touchstone Energy). This video, which includes depictions of Jemima Boone's kidnapping and the fort's siege, is also the only entry made exclusively for Fort Boonesborough State Park.

Daniel Boone Filmography

1 *Attack on Fort Boonesboro*   1906
2 *Daniel Boone: or Pioneer Days in America*   1907
3 *Daniel Boone's Bravery*   1911
4 *The Chief's Daughter*   1911
5 *Life of Daniel Boone*   1912
6 *In the Days of Daniel Boone*   1923
7 *Daniel Boone*   1923
8 *Daniel Boone Thru the Wilderness* 1926
9 *The Great Meadow*   1931
10 *The Miracle Rider*   1935

11 *Daniel Boone*   1936
12 *The Return of Daniel Boone*   1941
13 *Young Daniel Boone*   1950
14 *Daniel Boone, Trail Blazer*   1956
15 *Daniel Boone*   1960-61
16 *The Great Adventure*   1964
17 *Daniel Boone*   1964–70
18 *Young Dan'l Boone*   1977
19 *Daniel Boone*   1981
20 *Boonesborough: The Story of a Settlement*   2000

1 *Attack on Fort Boonesboro*

American Mutoscope and Biograph Company / 1906 / 152 ft. / Silent / Black and White

CREDIT: G.W. Bitzer (camera).

SYNOPSIS: A battle is taking place at Fort Boonesborough between American frontiersmen and Indians.

NOTES: On June 23, 1906, *Attack on Fort Boonesboro* was released. It was filmed by G.W. Bitzer for the American Mutoscope and Biograph Company, just eight days earlier on June 15 and on location in Louisville, Kentucky.

A 152-ft. print exists in Washington,

D.C., at the Library of Congress. This accounts for only a moment or so of viewing time. Originally a 345-ft. version was shot which still accounts for only a few moments of footage.

Bitzer had his camera set above his reconstructed set, looking down at the 100 people used to stage the battle. Yet instead of a fierce fight, these participants seemed to be involved in more of a casual gathering. And Boonesborough is misspelled in the title.

The American Mutoscope and Biograph Company was founded 11 years earlier in 1895. George William Bitzer came aboard the following year, and by 1900 he was their top cameraman.

Two years after *Attack on Fort Boonesboro* was made, Bitzer began a successful collaboration with an actor turned director named D.W. Griffith. Although they would leave the Biograph company in five years to make silent films elsewhere, their union lasted with highs and lows until 1929. One of their joint efforts was 1915's *The Birth of a Nation*.

2 *Daniel Boone: or Pioneer Days in America*

The Edison Manufacturing Company / 1907 / 1,000 ft. / Silent / Black and White

CREDITS: Wallace McCutcheon (director); Edwin S. Porter (camera).

CAST: William Craven (Daniel Boone), Florence Lawrence (Boone's daughter). Also Lotta Lawrence, Susanne Willis, and Mrs. William Craven.

SYNOPSIS: Indians attack a cabin and kidnap Daniel Boone's two daughters. Following their trail, Boone is captured by the Indians. Their chief has him tied to a stake and then tortured.

But with the help of an Indian girl, Daniel escapes. He kills the chief and rescues his daughters.

NOTES: The Edison Manufacturing Company began production in New York City on *Daniel Boone: or Pioneer Days in America* during December 1906. Interiors were filmed at the Edison Studio, while exteriors were shot in the Bronx Park.

Extras were hired for this 12-minute silent who were then appearing in a live Wild West show at the Hippodrome Theater. Ironically it was called *Pioneer Days*.

Principal players came to a casting call. Included were Mr. and Mrs. William Craven (yet some sources say Carver), and mother and daughter Lotta and Florence Lawrence. William was cast as Boone and Florence as one of his daughters (although

it wasn't specified if it was Jemima Boone or another daughter).

If the year of her birth was correct at 1886 (with 1889 also cited by sources), Florence was 20 when she appeared in *Daniel Boone*. It was her first film.

Florence joined the Biograph Company two years later, becoming not only a member of D.W. Griffith's stock company but a leading lady. As Biograph did not list its cast members, she soon became known famously as the Biograph Girl. Florence Lawrence was considered the very first movie star.

Edwin S. Porter was sometimes regarded as the first director of American films. In 1903, he made *The Great Train Robbery*, which was often regarded as the first Western with a story line.

A collaboration began in 1905 between Porter and Wallace McCutcheon. For both were directors and cameramen with the Thomas Edison manufacturing company (regarded as the first to make American silent films).

McCutcheon was credited as the director of *Daniel Boone*, and Porter the film's cameraman. But Wallace actually worked under Edwin's supervision.

Daniel Boone: or Pioneer Days in America was received well enough after it was released on April 6, 1907. Still, in a June review, *Variety* felt that some of the scenes were "a confused series of adventures." A print of the film exists in New York City's Museum of Modern Art.

3 *Daniel Boone's Bravery*

Kalem Company / 1911 / 1,000 ft. / Silent / Black and White

NOTES: In 1907, when *Daniel Boone: or Pioneer Days in America* came out, the Kalem Company was started. *Daniel Boone's Bravery* was made four years later.

Like the earlier Boone adventure, it was a 12-minute silent film. Also highlighted was Boone's capture by Indians and subsequent escape. In this version, he uses a campfire to burn away the ropes binding his hands.

4 *The Chief's Daughter*

Selig Polyscope Company / 1911 / Silent / Black and White

CREDIT: Hobart Bosworth (director and screenplay).

CAST: Jane Keckley, Hobart Bosworth, Viola Barry, Adele Worth, Jack Conway, Bessie Eyton, and J. Barney Sherry.

SYNOPSIS: An Indian chief's daughter is taken captive by the son of Daniel Boone. But Daniel's daughters help to secure her freedom.

The daughters of Boone then become Indian captives, along with other settlers. The chief's daughter helps them all in return.

NOTES: Along with the Edison and Biograph companies, the Selig Polyscope Company began producing silent films in the 1890s. One of the filmmakers they later employed was Hobart Bosworth. He directed, wrote the script, and played in 1911's *The Chief's Daughter*.

Born in 1867, Bosworth began making films in 1907 when he reached middle age (having honed his thespian skills earlier in the theater). His rugged build and maturity made him an apparently suitable choice to fit the mold of a frontiersman. For Selig, he had the title role in 1910's *Davy Crockett* and again in 1911's *Kit Carson's Wooing*.

5 *Life of Daniel Boone*

Republic / 1912 / Two Reels / Silent / Black and White

NOTES: This silent, like *Daniel Boone's Bravery* and *The Chief's Daughter* before it, is a lost film and not listed with the AFI (American Film Institute). Republic is alleged to have made *Life of Daniel Boone* in 1912.

It remains unclear just which Republic company was responsible for producing the film. The Republic Distributing Corporation was not formed until 1919, and Republic Pictures not until 1935.

Also known as *Life and Battles of Daniel Boone*, the film was supposed to be a two-reeler. As a reel was approximately 1,000 ft. (or 12 minutes), this accounted for some 24 minutes of footage.

Some of the sequences were to have been about Boonesborough's conflicts with the Indians. And the death of Daniel Boone, with his family all around him, was also to have taken place.

6 *In the Days of Daniel Boone*

Universal Pictures / 1923 / 15-Chapter Serial / Two reels each (#1 3 Reels) / Silent / Black and White

CREDITS: William Craft, Jay Marchant, Frank Messenger (directors); Jefferson Moffitt (screenplay). From a story by Paul M. Bryan and Jefferson Moffitt.

CAST: Jack Mower (Jack Gordon), Eileen Sedgwick (Susan Boone), Duke R. Lee (George Washington/Simon Girty), and Charles Brinley (Daniel Boone).

CHAPTERS:
 1 "His Country's Need"
 2 "At Sword's Point"
 3 "Liberty or Death"
 4 "Foiling the Regulators"
 5 "Perilous Paths"
 6 "Trapped"
 7 "In the Hands of the Enemy"
 8 "Over the Cliff"
 9 "The Flaming Forest"
10 "Running the Gauntlet"
11 "The Wilderness Trail"
12 "The Fort in the Forest"
13 "The Boiling Springs"
14 "Chief Blackfish Attacks"
15 "Boone's Triumph"

NOTES: Universal Pictures, founded

back in 1912, made this lost 15-chapter serial in 1923. The first chapter of *In the Days of Daniel Boone*, released on June 25, was three reels; with the remaining chapters all two reels long.

Some sources credited Frank Messenger as either directing (with William James Craft and Jay Marchant) or cameraman. The scenario written by Jefferson Moffitt was adapted from his own story with Paul M. Bryan.

The serial supposedly began with the French and Indian War and the defeat of Gen. Edward Braddock in 1755. Then featured were the struggles of Daniel Boone and other settlers to settle Kentucky and Boonesborough.

While some sources also credited Jack Mower as Boone, Charles Brinley actually had the role. Both actors played in many silent Westerns — Brinley often in support as the skinny old-timer, and Mower, in his heyday, as the big, heroic lead. Mower did play a famous frontiersman two years later in the silent *Kit Carson Over the Great Divide*.

7 Daniel Boone

Yale University Press / 1923 / Two Reels / Silent / Black and White

CREDITS: Claude H. Mitchell (director); Esther Willard Bates (screenplay). Based on Constance Lindsay Skinner's book, *The Pioneers of the Old Southwest.*

CAST: Elmer Grandin and Virginia Powell.

NOTES: The silent two-reeler *Daniel Boone* was brought out by Yale University Press in December 1923. Claude H. Mitchell directed the script by Esther Willard Bates. It was adapted from the book written in 1919 by Constance Lindsay Skinner.

Yale University Press began a series of films in 1923 called *The Chronicles of America. Daniel Boone* was one of 14 actually made showcasing the history of the country (although 30 were planned). The series proved to be unsuccessful and was discontinued in 1925.

But all of the films still exist. They were lost for years until an assistant film curator at Yale, Fred Guida, found them stored away.

Daniel Boone included sequences on the siege against Boonesborough in 1778. Featured was the attempt by the Indians to dig a tunnel to get inside the fort.

8 Daniel Boone Thru the Wilderness

Sunset Productions / 1926 / Six Reels / Silent / Black and White

CREDITS: Robert North Bradbury, Frank S. Mattison (directors); Anthony J. Xydias (producer); J.S. Brown (photography); Della M. King (editor); Ben Allah (titles); and Rosa Rio, organist (music score).

CAST: Roy Stewart (Daniel Boone), Kathleen Collins (Rebecca Bryan), Frank Rice (Hank Vaughan), Jay Morley (Simon Girty), Tom Lingham (Otis Bryan), Bob Bradbury Jr. (Jim Bryan), James O'Neil (Chief Grey Eagle), and Edward Hearn (Will Bryan).

SYNOPSIS: In North Carolina, Daniel Boone and Hank Vaughan are attacked by renegade Simon Girty and a band of Indians. Girty is instead captured by Boone, who then frees him.

Girty later leads an Indian attack against Otis Bryan and his family. When Bryan's daughter Rebecca is captured, Daniel saves her.

Daniel falls in love with Rebecca. But when he sees her embrace another man, Boone feels rejected and goes to Kentucky with his friend Hank.

The Bryans, having been taken with Daniel's earlier stories about Kentucky, travel there as well. Soon Daniel learns that the man Rebecca was embracing was her older brother, Will, who had been away.

Now Simon Girty is in Kentucky, staying with the Cherokee Indians. While away from their village, Girty kills Chief Grey Eagle's son, who is protecting his sister Nanna from the renegade's advances.

Lying to the chief that the settlers did the killing, the Indians then attack them. Both Daniel and Rebecca are captured. She is saved by Jim, a younger brother, but Daniel is to be burned at the stake.

Nanna comes to Boone's aid and reveals that it was Girty who killed her brother. Girty is burned at the stake instead. Rebecca and Daniel are reunited.

NOTES: During the American Revolution, Simon Girty, like Daniel Boone, had fought with George Rogers Clark against the Shawnee Indians. But in 1778, Girty turned against the American cause. He felt the Indians were being mistreated and also remained loyal to the British. Thus, Girty soon was branded a renegade by the Americans when he began leading Indian attacks against them.

The events in *Daniel Boone Thru the Wilderness* have Girty and the Indians attacking when Boone first meets Rebecca Bryan. This was not accurate for Daniel married Rebecca over 20 years before, and Simon's attacks never occurred in North Carolina. Also Girty was not burned at the stake. In 1818, just two years before Boone's death, Girty died an old man in Canada.

In 1917, Roy Stewart took over the reins for silent cowboy star William S. Hart at the Triangle film company. Working for other outfits, including Sunset Productions, Stewart became a cowboy star in his own right.

For producer Anthony J. Xydias at Sunset, Roy appeared in four historical films; he had the title roles in two of them in 1926. They were *Buffalo Bill on the U.P. Trail* and *Daniel Boone Thru the Wilderness* (with the latter silent released on May 1).

Burly and stalwart, Stewart gave what is considered the best portrayal of Boone in the silent era. The film included the passage, like some of the earlier films, in which an Indian maiden saves Boone; it was also the last silent about the frontier hero.

Jay Morley played Simon Girty, and Kathleen Collins was Rebecca Bryan. Bob Bradbury Jr., who played young Jim Bryan, became a cowboy star during the sound era. His name was changed to Bob Steele.

The American Film Institute listed this Boone saga as six reels, and mentioned that sources credited either Robert North Bradbury (Steele's father) or Frank S. Mattison as director. Initially one exhibitor called it a "dandy good picture." Also known as *With Daniel Boone Thru the Wilderness*, an 81-minute version was put on video.

9 *The Great Meadow*

Metro-Goldwyn-Mayer Pictures / 1931 / 80 minutes / Black and White

CREDITS: Charles Brabin (director); Ben Taggert (assistant director); Edith Ellis, Charles Brabin (screenplay); William Daniels, Clyde DeVinna (photography); George Hively, Anne Bauchens (editors); Cedric Gibbons (art director); Rene Hubert (wardrobe); Douglas Shearer (recording director); Chief Whitespear (technical advisor). Based on the novel *The Great Meadow* by Elizabeth Madox Roberts.

CAST: John Mack Brown (Berk Jarvis), Eleanor Boardman (Diony Hall), Lucille LaVerne (Elvira Jarvis), Anita Louise (Betty Hall), Gavin Gordon (Evan Muir), Guinn Williams (Reuben Hall), Russell Simpson (Thomas Hall), Sarah Padden (Molly Hall), Helen Jerome Eddy (Sally Tolliver), James Marcus (James Harrod), Gardner James (Joe Tandy), and John Miljan (Daniel Boone).

SYNOPSIS: Daniel Boone, in 1777, enthralls a group of Virginians with his tales of Kentucky. So impressed is Berk Jarvis with Boone, his idol, that he leads other settlers there.

John Miljan as Daniel in *The Great Meadow.*

Among those accompanying Berk are his mother Elvira, brother Jack, and new wife Diony. After a journey of six months, in which Jack is killed by Indians, the settlers reach Fort Harrod.

While outside the fort gathering corn, Elvira and Diony are attacked by Shawnee Indian Black Fox. Protecting Diony, Elvira is killed and scalped.

When Berk is away collecting salt for the fort, Diony gives birth to their son, Tommy. Berk returns only to leave again to avenge his mother's death. In his absence, Diony's former beau, Evan Muir, takes care of Tommy and her.

Captured by the Indians, Berk is sold to the British and put in prison for a year. Freed, he does kill Black Fox only to be taken captive by the Shawnee for another year.

Finally, Berk escapes and returns home. He discovers that Diony believed he was dead and so remarried. At first Diony wishes to stay with Evan, her new husband, until she realizes that Berk is her true love.

NOTES: The character of Daniel Boone started out the sound era in small roles. They were in *The Great Meadow* and *The Miracle Rider*, in 1931 and 1935 respectively.

Briefly seen in the first film as Boone was John Miljan, undoubtedly conveying the charm to entice settlers to Kentucky (which Daniel assuredly was capable of), and which served the actor well in villainous roles also. A character actor from the silents to television, Miljan played another famous historical character, George Armstrong Custer, in 1936's *The Plainsman.*

John Mack Brown and Eleanor Boardman were the stars of Metro-Goldwyn-

Mayer's *The Great Meadow*. They too made the transition from silents to talkies. The romantic allure they brought to their pioneer couple was touching. And the concept of the hero being away from the heroine for two years in the wilderness was very much a part of Daniel Boone's own life.

While Eleanor soon retired from films, John Mack, who had scored a year earlier with the title role in MGM's *Billy the Kid* (a tale of the famous outlaw), went on to make many "B" Westerns for other studios. In 1933, he had the title role in the serial *Fighting with Kit Carson*.

The Great Meadow was based on Elizabeth Madox Roberts' 1930 novel of the same title, which combined elements of fact and fiction. Edith Ellis and the film's director, Charles Brabin, wrote the screenplay.

With its March release, the film received mixed reviews. "Dialog stumbles along like the characters," wrote *Variety*, "with the direction as poor as the rest of it." "It is a faithful and moving version of the story of the Virginia Long Knives," the *New York Times* wrote, however, "who plunged into the wilderness of Kentucky—called by the Indians the Great Meadow."

10 *The Miracle Rider*

Mascot Pictures / 1935 / 15-Chapter Serial / Black and White

CREDITS: B. Reeves Eason, Armand Schaefer (directors); Nat Levine (producer); John Rathmell (screenplay). From a story by Barney Sarecky, Wellyn Totman, and Gerald Geraghty.

CAST: Tom Mix (Tom Morgan), Jean Gale (Ruth), Charles Middleton (Zaroff), Jason Robards Sr. (Carlton), Edward Hearn (Janes), Pat O'Malley (Sam Morgan), Robert Frazer (Chief Black Wing), Ernie Adams (Stelter), Wally Wales (Burnett), Bob Kortman (Longboat), Black Hawk (Chief Two Hawks), Chief Standing Bear (Chief Last Elk), and Buffalo Bill Jr. (Daniel Boone).

CHAPTERS:
1 "The Vanishing Indian"
2 "The Firebird Strikes"
3 "The Flying Knife"
4 "A Race with Death"
5 "Double-Barreled Doom"
6 "Thundering Hoofs"
7 "The Dragnet"
8 "Guerrilla Warfare"
9 "The Silver Band"
10 "Signal Fires"
11 "A Traitor Dies"
12 "Danger Rides with Death"
13 "The Secret of X-94"
14 "Between Two Fires"
15 "Justice Rides the Plains"

SYNOPSIS: Captain of the Texas Rangers, Tom Morgan is also a blood brother of the Ravenhead Indians. The Indian reservation is beset by bad men, who want the explosive X-94 found there.

Zaroff, representing shady oil interests, and Longboat, a deceitful half-breed among the Indians, use an invisible ray to frighten the tribe. Trying to stop Tom from interfering, Zaroff's henchmen kill Chief Black Wing.

The chief's daughter, Ruth, is in love with Tom. With her help, Tom Morgan is finally able to stop the bad men and restore justice.

NOTES: *The Miracle Rider*, a 15-chapter serial, was produced by Nat Levine for Mascot Pictures in 1935. It marked the last film appearance of one of the most popular cowboy stars of all time, Tom Mix.

He began his film career with Selig Polyscope in 1910, during the silent era. Eight years later, Mix joined the Fox studios; and his Westerns there overshadowed everyone else's in the industry for their showmanship. Mix was with Universal for his first talking motion picture, *Destry Rides Again*, in 1932.

In his prime, Tom Mix did many of his own stunts for he was also a performer in various Wild West shows. Jay Wilsey performed too in a Wild West show. In the 1920s, he began making silent Westerns for Artclass Pictures. Although never reaching the popularity that Mix enjoyed, Wilsey became a cowboy star and even changed his name to Buffalo Bill Jr.

As Daniel Boone, Wilsey was seen briefly in *The Miracle Rider* (as was Bud Geary as Davy Crockett). Directed by Armand Schaefer and B. Reeves Eason, the serial's script (from a story by Gerald Geraghty, Wellyn Totman, and Barney Sarecky) was written by John Rathmell.

Although the serial was deemed thin, its Western theme (set in modern times) still proved popular. Unlike the previous entry, *The Great Meadow*, it can be found on video.

11 *Daniel Boone*

RKO Radio Pictures / 1936 / 77 minutes / Black and White

CREDITS: David Howard (director); George Sherman, William O'Connor (assistant directors); George A. Hirliman (producer); Leonard Goldstein (associate producer); Daniel Jarrett (screenplay); Frank Good (photography); Ralph Dixon, Joseph H. Lewis (editors); Frank Sylos (art director); Max Factor (makeup); and Hugo Riesenfeld, Arthur Kaye (music directors). From an original story by Edgecumb Pinchon. Songs: "In the Garden," words by Grace Hamilton, music by Jack Stern; and "Make Way," words and music by Stern.

CAST: George O'Brien (Daniel Boone), Heather Angel (Virginia Randolph), John Carradine (Simon Girty), Ralph Forbes (Stephen Marlowe), George Regas (Black Eagle), Dickie Jones (Jerry), Clarence Muse (Pompey), Huntley Gordon (Sir John Randolph), Harry Cording (Joe Burch), Aggie Herring (Mrs. Burch), Crawford Kent (Attorney General), and Keith Kenneth (Commissioner).

SYNOPSIS: Before leading settlers from North Carolina to Kentucky in 1775, Daniel Boone and his Indian companion, Black Eagle, capture renegade Simon Girty. With a band of marauding Indians, Girty has been attacking the settlers.

But because of a newly signed treaty with the Indians, Girty cannot be convicted. Boone and his fellow settlers are forced to set him free.

Among those joining Daniel on the journey to Kentucky are people with aristocratic bearings. Included are Stephen Marlowe and a woman the aristocrat is in love with, Virginia, the daughter of Sir John Randolph. In time, a romance blossoms between Virginia and Daniel.

For now, Boone has Marlowe go on ahead to warn an advance party herding cattle to return. Marlowe doesn't, and Girty with his Indians attack and kill the cattle herders.

Marlowe is part of a group of politicians, back in Virginia, who enforce a law which takes away any settler's land claim if legal title is not met by a fixed time. Once the new settlement of Boonesborough is fortified, Daniel Boone rides back to Virginia but fails to get the law changed.

Returning to Kentucky, Daniel is taken captive by Girty and the Indians. He is tied to a stake, but Black Eagle saves Boone from a fiery death.

Girty has united five Indian tribes and they attack the settlers at Boonesborough. For nine days there is fighting; with the fort on fire, a heavy rain helps to defeat the Indians.

Refusing to surrender, Simon Girty kills Boone's little friend, Jerry. Then Daniel fights the renegade, killing him. Daniel Boone now leads the settlers, including his beloved Virginia, further west to find new land.

NOTES: When Richard Henderson

George Regas (left), George O'Brien (as Daniel) and Heather Angel in 1936's *Daniel Boone*.

bought land in Kentucky from the Cherokee in 1775, it was meant to be for a 14th colony called Transylvania. Within a month of the purchase, the American Revolution had begun—Kentucky was made one of Virginia's counties—and Henderson's dream did not last a year.

Boonesborough, which was founded in the interim, was supposed to have been a capitol city and major port under the British crown. Yet at its peak, only 30 or so buildings stood within the stockade walls. After the Revolution, its population declined as it was no longer needed as a point of defense. It was true, as revealed in RKO Radio's 1936 film *Daniel Boone*, that some of the fort's settlers left because of invalid land claims.

Again, as with *Daniel Boone Thru the Wilderness* a decade earlier, Simon Girty's actions with the Indians were given a free rein. Girty, as pointed out in that previous entry, did not begin ravaging the Kentucky countryside until three years after the events depicted in both films. And he was not involved with the siege of Boonesborough. With the Indians during the siege was a Captain deQuindre, commanding the militia unit sent from Detroit by the British.

While similarities certainly existed between the 1926 and 1936 films, the most noticeable difference was that the heroine in the latter was a fictitious character named Virginia Randolph, and not Rebecca Bryan (whom Boone was married to at the time). Daniel Jarrett's script was derived, at least in this regard, from an original story by Edgecumb Pinchon.

Daniel Boone was a George A. Hirliman production. The director was David Howard. Emphasized, rather than just historical fact, was the action with its very capable star, George O'Brien.

After its October 17 release, the film followed the trend of a successful series of Westerns with O'Brien starring, first at Fox and then RKO. He was introduced to the film business in the 1920s by Tom Mix, and then director John Ford made O'Brien a star as the hero in the 1924 silent Western *The Iron Horse*.

O'Brien holds the distinction of being the finest portrayer of Boone in talking motion pictures (with Fess Parker the best on television). Close to the actual frontiersman's height of a few inches under six feet, O'Brien was perhaps more muscular than Daniel Boone.

A *New York Times* review nicely judged the actor. "For all his physical prowess," the newspaper wrote, "George O'Brien manages to project Daniel Boone as a shy, unassuming adventurer, which is presumably what the man was."

If O'Brien is the best Boone in the movies, then the same holds true for John Carradine as Simon Girty. Although not physically looking like Girty (who was short and burly, rather than tall and thin like the actor), Carradine's performance was splendidly villainous. A similar role was given to him in 1939's *Drums Along the Mohawk*.

Heather Angel, who played the heroine, was in another frontier adventure in 1936, *The Last of the Mohicans*. The fictitious yet famed frontiersman in that saga was called Hawkeye. Originally patterned after Boone in the James Fenimore Cooper book of the same title in 1826, the character's full name was Natty Bumppo. Actually five books were written by Cooper on this one subject and they were called the Leatherstocking Tales. The other stories were *The Deerslayer*, *The Pathfinder*, *The Pioneers*, and *The Prairie*.

12 *The Return of Daniel Boone*

Columbia Pictures / 1941 / 60 minutes / Black and White

CREDITS: Lambert Hillyer (director); Milton Carter (assistant director); Leon Barsha (producer); Paul Franklin, Joseph Hoffman (screenplay); Philip Tannura (photography); Mel Thorsen (editor). From a story by Paul Franklin. Songs: "Hitchin' Time in the Chapel," "The Sheep in Wolf's Clothing," and "A Cowboy's the Man for Me," words and music by Milton Drake.

CAST: Bill Elliott (Dan Boone), Betty Miles (Ellen Brandon), Dub Taylor (Cannonball), Ray Bennett (Leach Kilgrain), Walter Soderling (Mayor Elwell), Carl Stockdale (Jeb Brandon), Bud Osborne (Red), Francis Walker (Bowers), Lee Powell (Tax Collector Fuller), Tom Carter (Wagner), Edmund Cobb (Henderson), and the Rodik Twins (Melinda and Matilda).

SYNOPSIS: Dan Boone is the grandson of the famous frontiersman. Near a small town, en route to Tucson, Dan's horse is switched at gunpoint by Ellen Brandon, a rancher's daughter.

It seems Ellen is riding away after the accidental death of Fuller, a tax collector she was fighting with. Mayor Elwell and hotel owner Leach Kilgrain want the ranchers to have such high taxes that payments cannot be made on their ranches and foreclosure results.

When questioned by Kilgrain's cronies about Ellen's horse, Dan puts them in their place. Dan is then given the job as new tax collector by Kilgrain. Following Ellen to where the ranchers are meeting, Dan warns them to obey the law.

Dan sends for his friend Cannonball to help bring the problem to a head. Cannonball seems to have his hands full as well with twins Melinda and Matilda. And Dan has his own difficulties with Ellen, until she realizes he is trying to help the ranchers.

Simon Girty (John Carradine, left) and Daniel Boone (George O'Brien) fight to the death in 1936's *Daniel Boone.*

Both the mayor and Kilgrain are finally rounded up, as the law prevails. But Cannonball's problems with the twins are another matter.

NOTES: With a title like *The Return of Daniel Boone*, it sure sounded like George O'Brien was coming back for further adventures. But such was not the case with this little "B" Western produced by Leon Barsha in 1941 for Columbia Pictures.

"Here is one of the weaker westerns," according to the *New York Times*, "whose situations have by now become so standard as to be recognized by even the most puerile intellects."

Lambert Hillyer's direction was from Paul Franklin and Joseph Hoffman's screenplay (from a story by Franklin). Although

utilized were the fictional adventures of a Daniel Boone namesake, any character's name could have been used. The film's title in Great Britain was *The Mayor's Nest.*

The best thing about *The Return of Daniel Boone* was its rugged star, Wild Bill Elliott. Conveyed effectively as Dan Boone was the actor's bad guy/good guy screen persona. Less effective were the comic interludes with the hero's sidekick (although a regular commodity in many "B" Westerns), and in this case played by Dub Taylor.

Elliott became a Western star with Columbia only three years earlier in the serial, *The Great Adventures of Wild Bill Hickok* (and where he acquired the nickname "Wild Bill" for his film career). In

Bill Elliott (right), as the grandson of Daniel Boone, sharing some hijinks with Dub Taylor in *The Return of Daniel Boone.*

1939, he played the title role in another serial, Overland with Kit Carson.

13 *Young Daniel Boone*

Monogram Pictures / 1950 / 71 minutes / Cinecolor

CREDITS: Reginald LeBorg (director); William Calihan (assistant director); James S. Burkett (producer); Clint Johnston, Reginald LeBorg (screenplay); G. Warrenton (photography); Charles Craft, Otho Lovering (editors); Raymond Boltz Jr. (set dresser); T. Larsen (makeup); Nipo T. Strongheart (technical advisor); and Edward J. Kay (music director). From a story by Clint Johnston.

CAST: David Bruce (Daniel Boone), Kristine Miller (Rebecca Bryan), Damian

O'Flynn (Capt. Richard Fraser), Don Beddoe (Charlie Bryan), Mary Treen (Helen Bryan), John Mylong (Lt. Col. Kurt von Arnheim), William Roy (Little Hawk), Stanley Logan (Col. Benson), Herbert Naish (Pvt. Haslet), Nipo T. Strongheart (Chief Walking Eagle), Richard Foote (Lt. Perkins), Stephen S. Harrison (Sentry), and Chief Yowlachie (Indian Guide).

SYNOPSIS: After the massacre of British forces, by French-incited Iroquois Indians in 1755, there are survivors. One, Lt. Col. Kurt von Arnheim, is a Hessian serving with the British. Von Arnheim tries to help rescue merchant Charlie Bryan's daughters, Helen and Rebecca, captured by the Indians.

Scouting for the British, Daniel Boone and his Indian friend, Little Hawk, soon

Young Daniel Boone with David Bruce (left) and Joe Molino.

come to the aid of Bryan and von Arnheim. They use gunpowder charges to make the Indians believe a bigger force is on hand. The ploy works as the enemy is driven off and the sisters are rescued.

Boone and the others then take refuge in an abandoned fort. Capt. Richard Fraser, a French spy pretending to be British, follows them but is planning to use his Indian allies to capture von Arnheim.

While Boone and von Arnheim are away from the fort, Fraser takes the others captive. Yet when Shawnee Indians attack, who are enemies of both the French and British, Boone and Fraser form a truce to stop the menace. Meanwhile, Rebecca and Daniel become better acquainted.

The Shawnee finally retreat and Fraser is taken prisoner by von Arnheim. An Indian ally frees Fraser, who then gets the upper hand again. All except Boone are taken captive as he escapes.

Leaving the fort with the captives, Fraser and his Indians make camp. During the night, Daniel sneaks into their campsite and replaces the bullets in their guns with blanks.

Daniel walks into the camp in the morning and is fired at to no ill effect. The Indians, believing he has some magical power, run away.

But Boone is attacked by Fraser. In the fight that follows, Fraser is accidentally killed. With the others in their party now safe, Daniel and Rebecca decide to settle down together.

NOTES: *Young Daniel Boone* took place during the French and Indian War, when the frontiersman was a wagoner for the British and not a scout. Although Daniel knew of Rebecca Bryan as early as 1753, when he hunted with her brothers, their courtship did not begin for another three years and he had already returned from the war.

Both the March 5, 1950, release from Monogram Pictures and the silent *Daniel Boone Thru the Wilderness* showcased the hero's fictitious saving of Rebecca from Indian captivity. And both films had her father's name wrong — Otis in the earlier one, and Charlie in this one — when his real name was Joseph Bryan.

Director Reginald LeBorg cowrote the screenplay with Clint Johnston (from the latter's own story). Seemingly borrowed were the romantic attributes from Fenimore Cooper's *The Last of the Mohicans*. How appropriate, for Cooper had borrowed from Daniel Boone's life.

Certainly the tale of kidnapped sisters rescued by a noble frontier hero in this film can be traced back to Cooper's book, and before that to Daniel's rescue of daughter Jemima and the Callaway sisters. The incident was first used in films with 1907's *Daniel Boone: or Pioneer Days in America*.

David Bruce and Kristine Miller were just fine as the hero and heroine, although *Young Daniel Boone*'s merits favored its action over its acting. Bruce began his film career 10 years before at Warner Brothers, and in support of Errol Flynn in *The Sea Hawk* and *Santa Fe Trail*.

This 1950 entry was the first about Boone made in color. *Variety*'s review was particularly favorable when it said the film "benefits considerably from the color dressing it gets from the camera of G. Warrenton. His work is above average and hues sharpen production values supplied by James S. Burkett."

Neither *Young Daniel Boone* or the previous entry, *The Return of Daniel Boone*, are available on video.

14 *Daniel Boone, Trail Blazer*

Republic Pictures / 1956 / 76 minutes / Trucolor

CREDITS: Albert C. Gannaway, Ismael Rodriguez (directors); Jaime L. Contreras, Robert G. Vreeland (assistant directors); Albert C. Gannaway (producer); Ben Constanten, C.J. Ver Halen (executive producers); Tom Hubbard, Jack Patrick (screenplay); Jack Draper (photography); Leon Barsha, Fernando A. Martinez (editors); Charles Heard, Billy Coontz, and Tex Lambert (technical advisors); and Raul Lavista (music score). Songs: "Long Green Valley," "Stand Firm in the Faith," and "Dan'l Boone," music by Albert C. Gannaway and lyrics by Hal Levy.

CAST: Bruce Bennett (Daniel Boone), Lon Chaney Jr. (Blackfish), Faron Young (Faron Callaway), Kem Dibbs (Simon Girty), Damian O'Flynn (Andy Callaway), Jacqueline Evans (Rebecca Boone), Nancy Rodman (Susannah Boone), Freddy Fernandez (Israel Boone), Carol Kelly (Jemima Boone), Eduardo Noriega (Squire Boone), Fred Kohler Jr. (Kenton), Gordon Mills (John Holder), Claude Brook (James Boone), Joe Ainley (General Hamilton), and Lee Morgan (Smitty).

SYNOPSIS: Daniel Boone leads settlers, including his wife and children, from North Carolina to Kentucky in 1775. Their new home is at Boonesborough.

Behind Daniel, with a second group, is his son James. While camped, this party is attacked by Shawnee Indians and James is killed.

At war with the American colonists, the British are inciting the Indians to attack. A General Hamilton offers the Indians rifles in exchange for scalps. Also with the British and Indians is Simon Girty.

When Boone brings his son's body back to the fort at Boonesborough, colonist

Israel Boone (Freddy Fernandez) and his father, Daniel Boone (Bruce Bennett), in *Daniel Boone, Trail Blazer.*

Andy Callaway wants to leave. But Daniel refuses, feeling the settlement is the opening to the West. Daniel's daughter, Susannah, is in love with Callaway's son, Faron.

Boone and Chief Blackfish are blood brothers. Yet the chief, now in Girty's company, warns the settlers to leave. Soon Daniel's brother, Squire, and a group of children are waylaid by the Indians.

But Daniel goes to the rescue. He is later forced by Blackfish to run a gauntlet against his warriors' tomahawk blows. Still, Daniel believes the settlers and the Indians can live in peace.

Blackfish does send two of his sons to a distant waterfall to talk peace. Yet Girty has them secretly shot down.

One of the chief's sons is still alive. Boone, now knowing Girty was responsible, takes the badly wounded Indian to the fort.

As other Indians try to come into the fort, Andy Callaway shoots at them despite Boone's orders not to. Before long, Blackfish attacks Boonesborough with his warriors.

The settlers are overwhelmed, and Blackfish's son dies from his prior injury. Callaway is killed in a futile attempt to surrender.

Entering the fort, Blackfish sees Boone holding up the dead body of his son. Daniel feigns that the fallen Indian is still alive and pointing at Girty.

Daniel Boone, Trail Blazer with Bruce Bennett in the title role.

Girty tries to run away but is cut down by the chief. Peace is apparently restored between Blackfish's Indians and Daniel Boone's settlers.

NOTES: Unlike the events brought forth in Republic Pictures' release of *Daniel Boone, Trail Blazer*, on September 14, 1956, again Simon Girty was not yet opposing the American colonists. Daniel's son, James Boone, was killed trying to settle in Kentucky with his family, but two years earlier. At that time the Boones turned around to live in Tennessee until their second emigration together in 1775.

There were no settlers named Faron or Andy Callaway. Susannah and Jemima Boone, Daniel's daughters, were married to Will Hays and Flanders Callaway respectively. The film's inspiration for Andy was Flanders' uncle, Richard Callaway. Although Richard was killed by Indians, it wasn't until 1780.

Chief Blackfish and Daniel Boone were never blood brothers. Yet the chief adopted Daniel into the tribal family during his captivity with the Shawnee in 1778. Boone ran the gauntlet, and he was taken by Blackfish to the British outpost in Detroit commanded by Henry Hamilton (who was called the "Hair Buyer," because he paid the Indians for scalps).

Although a low-budgeted film made in Mexico for Gannaway–Ver Halen productions, the acting and action in *Daniel Boone, Trail Blazer* were quite good. Albert C. Gannaway was the producer, while C.J. Ver Halen was an executive producer with Ben Costanten.

Gannaway codirected the picture with Ismael Rodriguez (and also wrote the music for the songs). Tom Hubbard and Jack Patrick collaborated on the screenplay.

As with the prior Boone entry, the color photography was appreciated. "The Trucolor camera work by Jack Draper is clear and on the plus side," wrote *Variety*, "with the other technical credits also good."

Bruce Bennett was very heroic and stalwart, displaying Boone's physical prowess and cunning. Lon Chaney Jr. lent excellent support as Blackfish. Both actors were complemented by a fine cast which included Kem Dibbs as Simon Girty, Jacqueline Evans as Rebecca Boone, and Damian O'Flynn as Andy Callaway.

O'Flynn played Fraser, the French spy, in *Young Daniel Boone*. A popular country singer at the time, Faron Young, was on hand as the younger Callaway. The singer and the songs were a bit out of kilter with the film as a whole.

Around this time, Lon Chaney was involved portraying another Indian (and quite well). As Chingachgook, he was seen in *Hawkeye and the Last of the Mohicans*, a television series derived from the James Fenimore Cooper characters.

A couple of popular serials were earlier made with an actor named Herman Brix. They were *The New Adventures of Tarzan* in 1935, and *The Lone Ranger* in 1938. Brix, whose name was changed to Bruce Bennett in 1940, played the jungle man in the first, and for the second was one of five masked riders of the plains.

15 *Daniel Boone*

Walt Disney Presents/ABC Television / 1960-61 / Four Episodes / Each 48 minutes / Technicolor

CREDITS: Lewis R. Foster (director); Joseph McEveety (assistant director); Bill Anderson (producer); David Victor, Lewis R. Foster (teleplay); Ray Rennahan, Edward Colman (photography); Robert Stafford, Basil Wrangell, Cotton Warburton (editors); Marvin Aubrey Davis (art director);

Emile Kuri, William L. Stevens (set decoration); Peter Ellenshaw, Albert Whitlock, Jim Fetherolf (matte artists); Chuck Keehne (costumer); Pat McNalley (makeup); and Oliver Wallace, Buddy Baker, Frank J. Worth (music score). Song by George Bruns and David Victor. Based on the book *Daniel Boone: Master of the Wilderness* by John Bakeless.

CAST: Dewey Martin (Daniel Boone), Mala Powers (Rebecca Boone), Richard Banke (Squire Boone), Eddy Waller (John Finley), Anthony Caruso (Blackfish), Dean Fredericks (Crowfeather), Don Dorrell (John Stuart), Alex Gerry (Judge Henderson), Kevin Corcoran (James Boone), George Wallace (Mordecai), Brian Corcoran (Israel Boone), Kerry Corcoran (Jemima Boone), Whit Bissell (Governor Tryon), Ron Hayes (Cecil Calvert), Diane Jergens (Maybelle Yancey), William Herrin (Buddy Yancey), Slim Pickens (Captain Gass), Wally Brown (Cyrus Whittey), Stan Jones (Doc Slocum), and Jean Inness (Sarah Watkins).

EPISODE 1: "The Warrior's Path" (Aired 12/4/60)

SYNOPSIS: Daniel Boone and his family live on a farm in North Carolina. Hearing stories about Kentucky from John Finley, a wandering trader, Daniel yearns to move the family there one day.

With a scouting party, Boone searches for and finds the trail which leads through the Cumberland Gap and to Kentucky. But Shawnee Indians, especially Crowfeather, do not want any settlers there and cause problems.

EPISODE 2: "And Chase the Buffalo" (Aired 12/11/60)

SYNOPSIS: Back in North Carolina, Daniel Boone dreams of returning to Kentucky. Along with the other settlers, he is having problems with the British rule when taxes are raised.

Soon Daniel has no choice but to sell the farm to pay the taxes. He prepares for the journey back to Kentucky to find a new home for his family. At first, wife Rebecca resists, but later she joins him with their children.

EPISODE 3: "The Wilderness Road" (Aired 3/12/61)

SYNOPSIS: Bound for Kentucky, Daniel Boone leads other settlers in a wagon train. Again, hostile Shawnee Indians must be confronted.

When one of Daniel's sons is kidnapped by the Indians, he comes to the rescue. Crowfeather wants to kill Boone, having lost to him in an encounter.

EPISODE 4: "The Promised Land" (Aired 3/19/61)

SYNOPSIS: The settlers with Daniel Boone struggle to get their wagons over the mountains. When Boone forces them to lighten the loads, some of the party are upset.

With the Indians continuing their attacks, one of the settlers is killed by an arrow. But Daniel and the settlers are equally determined to make Kentucky their new home.

NOTES: During the 1959-60 television season, the weekly show called *Disneyland* became *Walt Disney Presents* on the American Broadcasting Company network. With the majority of programs on all the networks being Westerns, it was no surprise that the Disney/ABC show followed the same path with stories centered around frontier figures, the Swamp Fox, Elfego Baca, and Texas John Slaughter.

The latter character proved the most durable since *Disneyland's Davy Crockett* episodes several years earlier. Between the two, Disney had ran a separate popular show on another hero, Zorro. For the 1960-61 season, Zorro was brought back for a few episodes on *Walt Disney Presents*; as were John Slaughter and a frontiersman Disney was tinkering with back in the Crockett years, Daniel Boone.

"The Warrior's Path" followed by "And Chase the Buffalo" were the opening episodes of *Daniel Boone* in December 1960. The final segments, "The Wilderness Road" and "The Promised Land," were seen in March 1961.

The televised episodes were introduced by Walt Disney, who felt the Indians were selfish for not wanting to share with the settlers the vast bounties of Kentucky.

Although an exciting, well-produced miniseries, *Daniel Boone* did not catch on the way the *Davy Crockett* series had. No further segments were made. In fact, this was the last season for frontier heroes being so exclusive on the Disney television show.

Bill Anderson produced and Lewis R. Foster directed the four episodes. Foster also wrote the last two teleplays (and David Victor the first ones), which were based on the book written in 1939 about Boone by John Bakeless.

Dewey Martin portrayed Daniel in a nice, likeable way, and he was perhaps more the actual pioneer's size than anyone else. In the 1952 Western film *The Big Sky*, Martin played another frontiersman called Boone (although not our hero). For Walt Disney, the actor also appeared in 1963's Western *Savage Sam*, the sequel to *Old Yeller*.

Portraying Rebecca Boone in the miniseries was Mala Powers. And actual siblings— Kevin, Brian, and Kerry Corcoran — played the Boone children. Anthony Caruso was Chief Blackfish, while Dean Fredericks had the pivotal yet fictional role of Crowfeather.

Daniel Boone was brought out on video, but all the episodes may be hard to find. This applies to a lesser extent to the 1936 and 1956 film versions as well. And, of course, any film can turn up on video (and/or DVD) when for years it was unavailable.

16 *The Great Adventure*

CBS Television / 1963-64 / 26 Episodes / Each 60 minutes / Black and White

EPISODE 23: "Kentucky's Bloody Ground" (Aired 4/3/64)

EPISODE 24: "The Siege of Boonesborough" (Aired 4/10/64)

CAST: Peter Graves (Daniel Boone), Andrew Duggan (Colonel Callaway), David McCallum (Captain Hanning), Peggy McCay (Mrs. Callaway), Judee Morton (Jemima Boone), Arthur Hunnicutt (Simon Kenton), Richard Lupino (Lieutenant Brown), Stuart Cooper (Flanders Callaway), Laurie Mock (Frances Callaway), and Teddy Eccles (James Boone).

NOTES: John Houseman was asked to produce a new television series in 1963 by Hubbell Robinson, who was in charge of special productions with the Columbia Broadcasting System (CBS). Their collaboration resulted in *The Great Adventure*, an anthology series on the air in the 1963-64 season.

While only five shows were actually produced by Houseman, 26 were made and each ran an hour. Van Heflin narrated half the shows and Russell Johnson the other half.

Each week an episode about American history was touched upon on the show. The episodes about Daniel Boone, written by Calvin Clements, were seen in April 1964 (and they were numbers 23 and 24 in the series).

The first Boone episode was "Kentucky's Bloody Ground." It dealt with Daniel and other settlers struggling to build a new settlement in the wilderness.

"The Siege of Boonesborough" was the other Boone segment; it focused on the Indians killing Daniel's son, James, and the kidnapping of his daughter, Jemima. Daniel then had to negotiate with the Indians for her release and to protect the settlement from attack.

Peter Graves, a stalwart hero in other television shows, played Daniel Boone. Graves was the rancher in *Fury* (1955–60) and the team leader in *Mission: Impossible* (1967–73). He is also the younger brother of James Arness.

Earlier episodes of *The Great Adventure* were on incidents in the lives of Sam Houston and Kit Carson (and both are included in their filmographies). However noble the series seemed with the interesting interpretations, it apparently was too expensive to produce and was not a success for CBS-TV.

17 *Daniel Boone*

20th Century-Fox Television/NBC Television / 1964–70 / 165 Episodes / Each 52 Minutes / Black and White (1st Season) / DeLuxe Color

CREDITS: William Wiard, Nathan Juran, George Sherman, George Marshall, John Florea, Gerd Oswald, Earl Bellamy, John English, Fess Parker, Thomas Carr, Harry Harris, William Witney, Paul Landres, John Newland, Bud Springsteen, James B. Clark, Maurice Geraghty, Alex Nicol, Byron Paul, Barry Shear, David Butler, Bruce Humberstone, Harmon Jones, Tony Leader, Joseph H. Lewis, Ida Lupino, Arthur Nadel, Chris Nyby, Joel Oliansky, Lee Philips, Joseph Sargent, Lesley Selander, Robert Totten, and Robert Webb (directors); Barney Rosenzweig, George Sherman, Vincent M. Fennely, Paul King, Aaron Rosenberg, and Jules Schermer (producers); D.D. Beauchamp, David Duncan, Melvin Levy, Raphael Hayes, Jack Guss, Judith Barrows, Merwin Gerard, Paul King, Irv Tunick, Carey Wilber, Martha Wilkerson, Dan Ballock, Walter Black, Tom Blackburn, James Byrnes, Herman Groves, Rich Husky, Lee Karson, Stephen Lord, Harold Medford, Joel Oliansky, Robert Guy Barrows, Harry Basch, Robert Bloomfield, Frank Chase, William Driskill, Sid Harris, John Hawkins, Nathan Juran, Herman Miller, Dick Nelson, Paul Playdon, Lionel E. Siegel, Clyde Ware, Stanley Adams, Theodore Apstein, Albert Beich, Virginia Brooks, Arthur Browne Jr., Borden Chase, Richard Collins, Willard S. Davis Jr., Patricia Falkenhagen, M. Finley, N. Bernard Fox, Clair Huffaker, Don Ingalls, Rita Lakin, Thomas P. Levy, Lee Loeb, Helen McAvity, David Humphreys Miller, Frank Moss, Charles O'Neal, Ken Pettus, William Putman, Al Ramrus, Paul Savage, John Shaner, George F. Slavin, Jack Sowards, William L. Stuart, Barry Trivers, W.J. Voorhees, John Williams, Ward Williams, William Wright, and Preston Wood (writers); Lionel Newman, Alexander Courage, Irving Getz, Leigh Harline, Joseph Mullendore, Lyn Murray, Herman Stein, Fred Steiner, Leith Stevens, and Harry Sukman (music).

SONG: "Daniel Boone," performed by the Imperials Quartet.

CAST: Fess Parker (Daniel Boone), Patricia Blair (Rebecca Boone), Darby Hinton (Israel Boone), Dallas McKennon (Cincinnatus), Ed Ames (Mingo, 1964–68), Veronica Cartwright (Jemima Boone, 1964–66), Don Pedro Colley (Gideon, 1968-69), Jimmy Dean (Josh Clements, 1968–70), Roosevelt Grier (Gabe Cooper, 1969-70), Robert Logan (Jericho Jones, 1965-66), and Albert Salmi (Yadkin, 1964-65).

EPISODES/AIR DATES:

Season 1 (1964-65)
1 "Ken-Tuck-E" (9/24/64)
2 "Tekawitha McLeod" (10/1/64)
3 "My Brother's Keeper" (10/8/64)
4 "The Family Fluellen" (10/15/64)
5 "The Choosing" (10/29/64)
6 "Lac Duquesne" (11/5/64)
7 "The Sound of Wings" (11/12/64)
8 "A Short Walk to Salem" (11/19/64)
9 "The Sisters O'Hannrahan" (12/3/64)
10 "Pompey" (12/10/64)
11 "Mountain of the Dead" (12/17/64)

12 "Not in Our Stars" (12/31/64)
13 "The Hostages" (1/7/65)
14 "The Returning" (1/14/65)
15 "The Prophet" (1/21/65)
16 "The First Stone" (1/28/65)
17 "A Place of 1,000 Spirits" (2/4/65)
18 "The Sound of Fear" (2/11/65)
19 "The Price of Friendship" (2/18/65)
20 "The Quietists" (2/25/65)
21 "The Devil's Four" (3/4/65)
22 "The Reunion" (3/11/65)
23 "The Ben Franklin Encounter" (3/18/65)
24 "Four-Leaf Clover" (3/25/65)
25 "Cain's Birthday Part 1" (4/1/65)
26 "Cain's Birthday Part 2" (4/8/65)
27 "Daughter of the Devil" (4/15/65)
28 "Doll of Sorrow" (4/22/65)
29 "The Courtship of Jericho Jones" (4/29/65)

Season 2 (1965-66)
30 "Empire of the Lost" (9/16/65)
31 "The Tortoise and the Hare" (9/23/65)
32 "The Mound Builders" (9/30/65)
33 "My Name is Rawls" (10/7/65)
34 "The Old Man and the Cave" (10/14/65)
35 "The Trek" (10/21/65)
36 "The Aaron Burr Story" (10/28/65)
37 "The Cry of Gold" (11/4/65)
38 "The Peace Treaty" (11/11/65)
39 "The Thanksgiving Story" (11/25/65)
40 "A Rope for Mingo" (12/2/65)
41 "The First Beau" (12/9/65)
42 "Perilous Journey" (12/16/65)
43 "The Christmas Story" (12/23/65)
44 "The Tamarack Massacre Affair" (12/30/65)
45 "Gabriel" (1/6/66)
46 "Seminole Territory" (1/13/66)
47 "The Deserter" (1/20/66)
48 "Crisis of Fire" (1/27/66)
49 "The Gun" (2/3/66)
50 "The Prisoners" (2/10/66)
51 "The Fifth Man" (2/17/66)
52 "Gun-Barrel Highway" (2/24/66)
53 "The Search" (3/3/66)
54 "Forty Rifles" (3/10/66)

55 "The Scalp Hunter" (3/17/66)
56 "The Accused" (3/24/66)
57 "Cibola" (3/31/66)
58 "The High Cumberland Part 1" (4/14/66)
59 "The High Cumberland Part 2" (4/21/66)

Season 3 (1966-67)
60 "Dan'l Boone Shot a B'ar" (9/15/66)
61 "The Allegiances" (9/22/66)
62 "Goliath" (9/29/66)
63 "Grizzly" (10/6/66)
64 "First in War, First in Peace" (10/13/66)
65 "Run a Crooked Mile" (10/20/66)
66 "The Matchmaker" (10/27/66)
67 "Onatha" (11/3/66)
68 "The Losers' Race" (11/10/66)
69 "The Enchanted Gun" (11/17/66)
70 "Requiem for Craw Green" (12/1/66)
71 "The Lost Colony" (12/8/66)
72 "River Passage" (12/15/66)
73 "When a King Is a Pawn" (12/22/66)
74 "The Symbol" (12/29/66)
75 "The Williamsburg Cannon Part 1: (1/12/67)
76 "The Williamsburg Cannon Part 2" (1/19/67)
77 "The Wolf Man" (1/26/67)
78 "The Jasper Ledbedder Story" (2/2/67)
79 "When I Became a Man, I Put Away Childish Things" (2/9/67)
80 "The Long Way Home" (2/16/67)
81 "The Young Ones" (2/23/67)
82 "Delo Jones" (3/2/67)
83 "The Necklace" (3/9/67)
84 "Fort West Point" (3/23/67)
85 "Bitter Mission" 3/30/67)
86 "Take the Southbound Stage" (4/6/67)
87 "The Fallow Land" (4/13/67)

Season 4 (1967-68)
88 "The Ballad of Sidewinder and Cherokee" (9/14/67)
89 "The Ordeal of Israel Boone" (9/21/67)
90 "The Renegade" (9/28/67)
91 "Tanner" (10/5/67)
92 "Beaumarchais" (10/12/67)

93 "The King's Shilling" (10/19/67)
94 "The Inheritance" (10/26/67)
95 "The Traitor" (11/2/67)
96 "The Value of a King" (11/9/67)
97 "The Desperate Raid" (11/16/67)
98 "The Spanish Horse" (11/23/67)
99 "Chief Mingo" (12/7/67)
100 "The Secret Code" (12/14/67)
101 "A Matter of Blood" (12/28/67)
102 "The Scrimshaw Ivory Chart" (1/4/68)
103 "The Imposter" (1/18/68)
104 "The Witness" (1/25/68)
105 "The Flaming Rocks" (2/1/68)
106 "Then Who Will They Hang from the Yardarm If Willy Gets Away?" (2/8/68)
107 "Fort New Madrid" (2/15/68)
108 "Hero's Welcome" (2/22/68)
109 "Orlando, the Prophet" (2/29/68)
110 "The Far Side of Fury" (3/7/68)
111 "Nightmare" (3/14/68)
112 "Thirty Pieces of Silver" (3/28/68)
113 "Faith's Way" (4/4/68)

Season 5 (1968-69)
114 "Be Thankful for the Fickleness of Women" (9/19/68)
115 "The Blackbirder" (10/3/68)
116 "The Dandy" (10/10/68)
117 "The Fleeing Nuns" (10/24/68)
118 "The Plague That Came to Ford's Run" (10/31/68)
119 "The Bait" (11/7/68)
120 "Big, Black and Out There" (11/14/68)
121 "A Flag of Truce" (11/21/68)
122 "The Valley of the Sun" (11/28/68)
123 "The Patriot" (12/5/68)
124 "The Return of Sidewinder" (12/12/68)
125 "Minnow for a Shark" (1/2/69)
126 "To Slay a Giant" (1/9/69)
127 "A Tall Tale of Prater Beasely" (1/16/69)
128 "Copperhead Izzy" (1/30/69)
129 "Three Score and Ten" (2/6/69)
130 "Jonah" (2/13/69)
131 "Bickford's Bridge" (2/20/69)
132 "A Touch of Charity" (2/27/69)

133 "For Want of a Hero" (3/6/69)
134 "Love and Equity" (3/13/69)
135 "The Allies" (3/27/69)
136 "A Man Before His Time" (4/3/69)
137 "For a Few Rifles" (4/10/69)
138 "Sweet Molly Malone" (4/17/69)
139 "A Pinch of Salt" (5/1/69)

Season 6 (1969-70)
140 "A Very Small Rifle" (9/18/69)
141 "The Road to Freedom" (10/2/69)
142 "Benvenuto … Who?" (10/9/69)
143 "The Man" (10/16/69)
144 "The Printing Press" (10/23/69)
145 "The Traitor" (10/30/69)
146 "The Grand Alliance" (11/13/69)
147 "Target Boone" (11/20/69)
148 "A Bearskin for Jamie Blue" (11/27/69)
149 "The Cache" (12/4/69)
150 "The Terrible Tarbots" (12/11/69)
151 "Hannah Comes Home" (12/25/69)

152 "An Angel Cried" (1/8/70)
153 "Perilous Passage" (1/15/70)
154 "The Sunshine Patriots" (1/22/70)
155 "Mama Cooper" (2/5/70)
156 "Before the Tall Man" (2/12/70)
157 "Run for the Money" (2/19/70)
158 "A Matter of Vengeance" (2/26/70)
159 "The Landlords" (3/5/70)
160 "Readin', Ritin', and Revolt" (3/12/70)
161 "Noblesse Oblige" (3/26/70)
162 "The Homecoming" (4/9/70)
163 "Bringing Up Josh" (4/16/70)
164 "How to Become a Goddess" (4/30/70)
165 "Israel and Love" (5/7/70)

NOTES: Fess Parker starred in the comedy series, *Mr. Smith Goes to Washington*, in the 1962-63 television season. It was not a success, despite the actor's trademark homespun wisdom and sincerity very much in evidence. These ingredients assuredly helped to make him a star in the *Davy Crockett* series he did for Walt Disney during the 1950s. But then Mr. Smith did not have the same legendary proportions of Davy Crockett.

Certainly Daniel Boone did, and Parker was hopeful for another successful series. Initially he wanted to do another one about Crockett, but apparently Disney was not interested. Fess found others who were — Aaron Rosenberg and Aaron Spelling — and so for Arcola-Fespar Productions, in collaboration with 20th Century-Fox Television and the National Broadcasting Company, a new series was born.

A big financial stake was held in *Daniel Boone* by Parker and its executive producers, Spelling and Rosenberg. It paid off most handsomely, for the series ran six years and for 165 episodes.

Aired September 24, 1964, the first episode was called "Ken-Tuck-E" (and is available on video). It dealt with Boone being sent to the wilderness of Kentucky by George Washington to choose a site for a new fort and settlement. Boonesborough

Fess Parker in the title role of the television series *Daniel Boone.*

was then founded, where Daniel lived with wife Rebecca and their children, Jemima and Israel.

The last episode, aired May 7, 1970, was called "Israel and Love." And Daniel's young son was smitten with Brae, a woodcarver's daughter.

The stories, set during the time of the American Revolution, focused on the many characters in and out of Boonesborough. Included were settlers, the British and assorted tribes of Indians. Elements of fact were freely mixed to make Daniel Boone even more of a legendary figure. Never was there a more physically imposing and romanticized portrayal of the frontiersman than Fess Parker's. And none more likeable and enjoyable.

Episode 5: "The Choosing," had Indians kidnapping Jemima. Younger brother Israel (actually he was older than his sister) was kidnapped in several episodes; including #65: "Run a Crooked Mile," by renegades. Even Rebecca was a kidnap victim, by Indians, in Episode 13: "The Hostages."

Patricia Blair as Rebecca, Darby Hinton as Israel, and Dallas McKennon as tavern keeper Cincinnatus, were the only ones besides Parker who were part of the show's entire run. Veronica Cartwright was seen as Jemima for two seasons. There were others who were regular companions of Daniel's during its course. And the guest stars were legion.

Boone's sidekicks in adventure began with Ed Ames as Mingo, an Oxford-educated Cherokee, on the series for five years. Albert Salmi was traveler Yadkin in the first season. Robert Logan was settler Jericho Jones in the second; Don Pedro Colley was black Indian Gideon in the fifth;

Fess Parker surrounded by his television family in *Daniel Boone.* **With him are Veronica Cartwright (left) as Jemima, Darby Hinton as Israel, and Patricia Blair as Rebecca.**

and Roosevelt Grier was former slave Gabe Cooper in the last season. For the show's final two years, Jimmy Dean played trapper Josh Clements.

Before his regular stint as Josh, Dean guest starred in earlier episodes as other backwoodsmen, Delo Jones and Jeremiah. Often guest stars appeared in different roles. A young Kurt Russell was seen in five episodes as various characters during the run of the series. Still others reprised their guest starring roles, such as Forrest Tucker and Burl Ives as pirate Joe Snag and storyteller Prater Beasely respectively.

While these colorful supporting characters were fictitious, others were derived from fact. Robert F. Simon was Chief Blackfish and Simon Courtleigh was George Washington in the premier episode. In Episode 8, "A Short Walk to Salem," James Waterfield was Simon Girty. Walter Pidgeon was Lord Dunsmore in the first season (Episode 12: "Not in Our Stars"), and Roger Miller was Johnny Appleseed in the last year (Episode 140: "A Very Small Rifle").

There were a few two-part shows. Episodes 25 and 26, "Cain's Birthday," involved Daniel and other settlers surrendering to Indians at a salt making camp, and the women and children were left to defend the fort.

"The High Cumberland," episodes 58 and 59, told of an earlier time before Boonesborough where Daniel and Rebecca met for the first time. It was on a wagon train to Kentucky later besieged by renegades.

Episodes 75 and 76, "The Williamsburg Cannon," had Daniel and Mingo recruiting others to help take a cannon over enemy territory. The weapon was to help the Americans fight the British.

Numerous writers and directors were on hand. William Wiard and Nathan Juran directed the most episodes; and Fess Parker directed several, beginning with episode 106 in 1968, "Then Who Will They Hang from the Yardarm If Willy Gets Away?"

The most stories were written by D.D. Beauchamp, David Duncan, and Melvin Levy. However, the first show was written by Borden Chase and directed by George Marshall. Producing the most shows in the series were Barney Rosenzweig and George Sherman.

"Fess Parker, the coonskin cap, the narrative ballad and other reminiscences of Walt Disney's *Davy Crockett*," wrote *Variety* in an initial review, "only serve to emphasize what a throwback to an earlier TV era is NBC-TV's new *Daniel Boone* series."

Viewers were apparently enchanted with its old-fashioned adventures, which combined drama and humor with plenty of action. The picturesque scenery included location filming at Duck Creek Village in Utah; at the Fox studios in California, a forest and Boonesborough set were constructed. While the ratings were never spectacular, *Daniel Boone* reached No. 21 on the list of top 25 shows in the fifth season, and was No. 25 in its third year.

18 *Young Dan'l Boone*

20th Century-Fox Television/CBS Television / 1977 / Four Episodes / Each 52 minutes / Color

CREDITS: Earl Bellamy, Ernest Pintoff, Don McDougall, and Arthur Marks (directors); Jimmy Sangster (producer); Ernie Frankel (executive producer); and David P. Harmon (writer).

CAST: Rick Moses (Daniel Boone), Devon Ericson (Rebecca Bryan), Ji-Tu Cumbuka (Hawk), John Joseph Thomas (Peter Dawes), Eloy Phil Casados (Tsiskwa), and Jeremy Brett and Len Birman (Boone's Adversaries).

EPISODES:
1 "The Trail Blazer" (Aired 9/12/77)
2 "The Pirate" (Aired 9/19/77)
3 "The Salt Licks" (Aired 9/26/77)
4 "The Game" (Aired 10/10/77)

NOTES: Seven years after the long television run of *Daniel Boone*, an attempt was made to bring the frontier hero's exploits back on the air. Again by 20th Century-Fox Television, albeit a younger version, appropriately titled *Young Dan'l Boone*, and before he reached Kentucky. This time around it was in collaboration with Fox, CBS-TV, and Frankel Films.

Only four episodes were produced for the 1977-78 TV season. One of the writers from the previous series, Earl Bellamy, was on hand to direct the first new episode, "The Trail Blazer." It was written by David

P. Harmon and produced by Jimmy Sangster.

Reflected upon was Boone's trying to find a trail from Tennessee through the Cumberland Gap to Kentucky. A parcel of land was his prize and also the love of his sweetheart, Rebecca Bryan. Joining the frontiersman in his quest were the fictitious Tsiskwa, a Cherokee; Peter Dawes, a teenager; and runaway slave Hawk.

Rick Moses as Daniel and Devon Ericson as Rebecca gave satisfactory performances, although our hero never appeared more handsome and stylish. The main attraction of the brief series was the beautiful scenery shot in Tennessee at the Cumberland Gap.

Apparently the failure of *Young Dan'l Boone* was attributed to difficulties in production, and to its early America theme not then being popular. Yet this did not keep another series about pioneers, *Little House on the Prairie*, also on the air at the time, from enjoying a good run.

Rick Moses in the title role on television's *Young Dan'l Boone.*

19 *Daniel Boone*

Hanna-Barbera/CBS Television / 1981 / 60 minutes / Animated / Color

CREDITS: Geoff Collins (director); William Hanna, Joseph Barbera (executive producers); Doug Paterson, Chris Cuddington (associate producers); Kimmer Ringwald (writer); and Australian Screen Music (music).

CAST/VOICE TALENTS: Richard Crenna (Daniel Boone), Janet Waldo (Rebecca), Bill Callaway (Daniel Boone, age 14/Running Fox), Mike Bell (Henry Miller/1st Settler/Mr. Harding), John Stephenson (Stearns/Assemblyman/Squire Boone), Joan Gerber (Sarah/James/Quiet Dove), Joe Baker (Washington/Col. Morgan/2nd Settler), Vic Perrin (White Top/Painter/Floor Leader), Barney Phillips (Blackfish/Business Man/Indian Dragging Canoe), and Michael Rye (Girty/Oconostata/Finley).

SYNOPSIS: In 1820, Daniel Boone is an old man and recalls his life in flashback to a writer, Mr. Harding. And Daniel admits to never wearing a coonskin hat.

His recollections take him back to his father's farm in North Carolina, where he was a mischievous teenager. As a young man, Daniel recalls meeting George Washington and marrying his beloved Rebecca.

Daniel remembers exploring Kentucky. There he killed a bear and fought with the Indian called White Top. The founding of

Boonesborough is recalled; and a son was lost during the conflicts with the British and Indians. Boone's captivity with the Shawnee is remembered and his adoption into the tribe.

When a new Congress was formed, Daniel became one of the assemblymen. Upon completing his story, Daniel Boone begins his journey to heaven to be with his Indian father.

NOTES: On November 27, 1981, CBS Television aired *Daniel Boone* as part of its *Famous Classic Tales* series. The animated film was made by the famous team of William Hanna and Joseph Barbera, who brought such wonderful characters to life as Yogi Bear, Huckleberry Hound, and the Flintstones.

Richard Crenna lent his considerable acting skills to the voice of Boone, and Janet Waldo did the same for his wife, Rebecca. A teenaged Daniel was voiced by Bill Callaway, who, along with other cast members, acted more than one part.

Directed by Geoff Collins and written by Kimmer Ringwald, *Daniel Boone*, despite being only a cartoon, was both a fanciful and thoughtful interpretation of the frontiersman's life. It can be found on video.

20 *Boonesborough: The Story of a Settlement*

Kentucky's Touchstone Energy Cooperatives / 2000 / 16 minutes / Color

CREDITS: Jerry McDonald, Don Simandl (directors and writers); Troy House (producer); Roy Palk, Jerry McDonald, Phil Gray (executive producers); Jarboe (photography); Mike Priddy (editor); Randy Bucknam (art director); Bill Farmer (production designer); April Prager (makeup); and Mark Noderer (music).

CAST: Scott New (Daniel Boone), Jeff Havert (Blackfish), Bob Jump (Narrator), and a large cast of reenactors.

SYNOPSIS: The story begins with the purchase of Kentucky land by Richard Henderson from the Cherokee. Indian Dragging Canoe predicts trouble for the new settlers.

The settlement of Boonesborough is built. Daniel Boone's daughter, Jemima, is kidnapped by Indians along with the Callaway sisters. Boone and other settlers go to their rescue.

When the settlers, including Daniel, are away from the settlement making salt, they are captured by the Shawnee. Boone is a captive of Chief Blackfish for six months.

Daniel escapes back to Boonesborough. Blackfish and the Indians feign a treaty signing to try to capture the settlers there, but a long siege on their fort takes place. Torches are thrown by the enemy at the fort and a heavy rain extinguishes the flames. The Indians then depart much to the relief of Daniel Boone and the other defenders.

NOTES: In 2000, Kentucky's Touchstone Energy Cooperatives presented this 16-minute video for Fort Boonesborough and the Kentucky Department of Parks. The exciting and informative film was called *Boonesborough: The Story of a Settlement.*

Roy Palk, Jerry McDonald, and Phil Gray were the executive producers. McDonald also wrote and directed the film with Don Simandl. Location filming was done at several sites, including Fort Boonesborough State Park.

Scott New did fine work in his brief depiction of Daniel Boone, conveying the man's dignity and bravery. The actor's long hair and costumes were similar to Daniel Day Lewis' appearance as Hawkeye in the 1992 film version of *The Last of the Mohicans.*

Two

DAVY CROCKETT

Biography and Overview

David Crockett and his wife were killed during an Indian raid in 1778. This was not the same Davy Crockett who later died at the Alamo but his grandfather. Leading the raid of Cherokee and Creek Indians against the North Carolina settlers was Dragging Canoe, who had earlier on predicted bloodshed against settlers when Richard Henderson purchased part of Kentucky from the Cherokee nation. One of Davy's uncles, James, was captured in the raid and held captive for nearly 18 years; another uncle, Joseph, was wounded.

In 1780, John Crockett, brother of Joseph and James as well as Davy's father, was living in North Carolina with his wife Rebecca (nee Hawkins). He fought with the local militia in the Revolutionary War, defeating the British at King's Mountain. On August 17, 1786, when Davy was born, John and Rebecca had a small log cabin in Greene County on the banks of Big Limestone Creek and near the Nolichucky River (then the temporary state of Franklin; it again became part of North Carolina in 1789 and finally Tennessee in 1796). Davy was the fifth child of nine Crockett offspring of Scottish descent.

The Crocketts endured financial hardship in the years ahead and moved to other nearby locations. John and a business partner, Thomas Galbreath, lost a gristmill to a flood in 1794 at Cove Creek. The following year John Crockett had 300 acres of property near the Main Holston Road auctioned off to help pay a $400 debt. But the family ran a tavern beside the road, which was the thoroughfare between Knoxville, Tennessee, and Abington, Virginia.

When Davy was 12, his father, needing the money, hired him out to help a cattle drover named Jacob Siler. Young Crockett was reluctant to leave his family to make the 225-mile trip north to the area of Natural Bridge in Virginia. Yet Siler treated him well and paid Davy several dollars more than had been given his father. Siler even convinced the boy to stay on at his home for an extra month or so to help out.

Davy Crockett yearned to go home,

however, and snuck off one night during a snowstorm to join a group of teamsters bound for Tennessee. After going with the group for about 30 miles, Davy became impatient with the slow moving wagons and went ahead on foot. Soon a man leading some horses came along and offered him a ride. When he parted from the man, after traveling together for a few days, Davy was able to walk the rest of the way home.

This first adventure away from home occurred in late 1798. The following fall found Crockett, now 13, attending school for the first time. He was just learning to grasp the alphabet from the schoolmaster, Benjamin Kitchen, when Davy waylaid the class bully on the way home after the fourth day.

Afraid to return to school and face a possible whipping from the schoolmaster, Davy played hooky for awhile. But Kitchen sent a note home inquiring about his absence. John Crockett was drinking and went after his son with a hickory stick. Davy ran away and didn't come home again for nearly three years.

With another cattle drover, Jesse Cheek, Davy went back to Virginia, this time to Front Royal some 375 miles from home. After the drive was completed, the boy was heading home when he met Adam Myers, a wagoner, and traveled with him further north in Virginia.

Davy stayed with a farmer named John Gray near Winchester until the spring. Again with Myers, he went with the wagoner all the way to Baltimore, Maryland.

Never having seen a big city before, Crockett was especially impressed with the docks of Fells Point. He even managed to get a job as cabin boy aboard a ship bound for London.

Yet when Adam Myers heard of these plans, he threatened to whip Davy and forced him to return on his wagon to Virginia. The youngster had $7.00 to his name and this was in Myers' safekeeping.

Finally running off, Davy was unable to get his money back. Another wagoner, Henry Myers (but no relation to Adam), tried in vain to get the money for him. Henry was able to raise a few dollars from other wagoners for Davy at an inn they stopped at.

The money lasted Davy until he was a bit more than halfway home. Feeling a trade would be useful, he bound himself as an indentured servant to a Virginia hatter named Elijah Griffith. Going bankrupt after 18 months, Griffith left Crockett without any money.

But Davy found some odd jobs to earn enough to make his way back to Tennessee. He almost drowned while stubbornly trying to cross the New River during a storm.

Fifty miles from home, Davy stayed for a spell with his uncle, Joseph Crockett, before finding his way back to the family tavern. Not letting anyone know he was there, the 16-year-old had grown so considerably that no one recognized him; at least not until oldest sister Betsy yelled out that her lost brother had come home.

The entire family, including his father, were glad at his homecoming. But John made it clear that Davy had to obey his wishes. In debt for $36 to Abraham Wilson, John had his son work six months to pay it off; and this was to free Davy of any further obligation to his father.

Soon a Quaker farmer, John Kennedy, gave Davy work. Yet his father was also in debt to Kennedy for $40. Davy took it upon himself to work the next six months to pay this one off as well. It was a surprise gift to his father, who was very moved by the gesture.

A mature young man now, David Crockett was still less so with women. He lost his heart first to a niece of the Quaker, but she was engaged to one of Kennedy's sons. Crockett felt his lack of education made him a less attractive figure. So for six months he worked for and was taught by another of the Quaker's sons, who was a schoolmaster, the rudiments of reading, writing, arithmetic and other aspects of book learning.

A marriage license was taken out by Crockett to marry a lass named Margaret Elder, but she decided to marry someone else. Davy was heartbroken until months later and he met Mary Finley, whom everyone called Polly. She was two years younger than Davy and they fell in love. Their marriage took place the following year, on August 16, 1806, the day before his 20th birthday.

The couple were given two cows and two calves as a dowry by Polly's folks, and they lived on a farm in Jefferson County, Tennessee, on Bay Mountain. Davy was trying to make a living as a hunter with Polly helping as a seamstress. Two sons were born to them there, John Wesley in 1807 and William in 1809.

Within a few years, the family moved a couple of times. In Lincoln County, near the Elk River and the border of Alabama, they lived in a cabin on five acres of land. It was here that Davy was able to improve his hunting skills, for he had a natural aptitude with the long rifle. Still, this land and another 15-acre tract were lost to taxes.

In 1812, a daughter, Margaret, was born (but also called Polly). The Crocketts, the following year, were living in another cabin near the Alabama line, but in Tennessee's Franklin County at Bean's Creek. Apparently thinking about Daniel Boone (who was around 78 years old at the time), Davy Crockett called the new home "Kentuck."

While the character and memory of Davy Crockett is part of 38 entries in the filmography about him, wife Polly is at least featured in the most famous one of all. This is the 1955 film *Davy Crockett, King of the Wild Frontier* (Walt Disney). She does have an episode named after her

in the *Davy Crockett* television miniseries of 1988-89 (also Disney).

Daughter Polly is the star of the 1956 film *Frontier Woman* (Top Pictures). A nephew named after Davy is the headliner in 1950's feature *Davy Crockett, Indian Scout* (Reliance/United Artists). And a son, of course, is the star of another film, 1941's *The Son of Davy Crockett* (Columbia).

Americans were at war with the British in 1813. Knowing the enemy had Indian allies, settlers attacked a group of Creek Indians in Alabama at Burnt Corn Creek. The Indians struck back at the Alabama stockade of Fort Mims on August 30, 1813.

A man who was part Indian, William Weatherford (whose Creek name was Red Eagle), led the assault. Almost 500 people were killed — settlers, including women and children, and Mississippi militiamen.

When news of the attack reached Crockett, he joined the local militia despite Polly's protests. At Winchester, he was the 18th man to become part of the Tennessee Volunteer Mounted Riflemen in the Creek (or Red Stick) War. The date was September 24, and the enlistment period was for 90 days.

This cavalry division of some 1,300 Tennessee volunteers were commanded by Col. John Coffee (later a brigadier general). Gen. Andrew Jackson (later a major general), and Coffee's superior officer, was organizing the infantry division at Nashville.

Private Crockett went with Coffee's volunteers to Beaty's Spring, Alabama, to wait for Jackson to arrive with his troops. In the meantime, he was deployed by Maj. John H. Gibson to take part in a scouting mission. Davy chose George Russell, the young son of another militia officer, Maj. William Russell, to go along.

In the Disney film and miniseries already mentioned (and including the original three episodes of the 1954-55 television series from which the feature film was derived), a Georgie Russell (or initially

Russel with one l)is a prominent figure and sidekick to Crockett. The Creek War is featured in the first episode of the original series, the follow-up film, and the later miniseries.

At Ditto's Landing in Alabama, a 13-man scouting party crossed the Tennessee River where they picked up a guide. Going deeper into enemy territory, they separated; Maj. Gibson led one group and Crockett, because of his skills as a backwoodsman, another.

Crockett and his group were the first to report back to Coffee about an intended Indian strike against Jackson's advancing army. Only when Gibson returned later with the same news was it acted upon and Jackson alerted, much to Davy's concern that his initial report was ignored.

The news from both groups, however, proved to be incorrect, but Gen. Jackson had already brought his army in with a forced march. Coffee's militia force then advanced further into Alabama and erected an outpost called Fort Strother.

On November 3, 1813, John Coffee took 900 militiamen and attacked the Creek Indian town of Tallusahatchee. In this assault, 46 warriors were burned in a wooden lodge; 186 Indian men, women and children were allegedly killed. Even Crockett, who was there, was caught up in the violence against the Indians in retaliation for the earlier attack on Fort Mims.

Six days later, Jackson and Coffee had their militia forces surround the outpost of Fort Talladega, which was being besieged by Indians. Attempting to escape, the Creek suffered over 500 casualties and over 300 proved fatal. Again Crockett was a participant.

Facing starvation and the winter, the militiamen wanted to return home to replenish their supplies. A two-week furlough was given to some of them on November 22. Davy Crockett was among their number. He returned home to Polly and the children on Bean's Creek.

Meanwhile, back in Alabama, general unrest with the troops resulted in mutinying although it was repelled by Andrew Jackson. As Davy and others were rejoining the militia on December 8, they passed soldiers returning home because their enlistments were up.

Despite Jackson and Coffee wanting Crockett and the others to reenlist, he was among those who refused. On December 24, 1813, Pvt. David Crockett was honorably discharged. Payment for his services was $65.59.

So Davy was not with the generals the following spring of 1814; the Indians were defeated at Horseshoe Bend, and to all purposes this ended the Creek War. But another soldier was there by the name of Sam Houston.

Davy might have harbored some feelings of guilt over the Creek War because he feigned that his enlistment was longer at six months. Nonetheless, on September 28, 1814, he volunteered for further military service. Once more against Polly's wishes, this time it was for a six-month enlistment and Crockett was to help drive the British out of Pensacola, Florida.

Under Maj. William Russell, Crockett was made a third sergeant in a company of scouts of the Tennessee Mounted Gunmen. A British force was trying to use the then Spanish town to plan assaults against other towns like New Orleans.

By the time Russell, Sergeant Crockett, and company arrived in Pensacola on November 8, the British had been driven out by Gen. Andrew Jackson only the day before. Davy could only watch as the British ships in the harbor evacuated their soldiers.

The company of scouts moved back into Alabama for a few weeks. Then skirmishes were made back and forth against those Creek Indians who had resisted signing the treaty after the fight at Horseshoe Bend.

Yet the real fight for the men now was against hunger. This despite any skill on Crockett's part as a hunter. At Fort Strother, there were abundant food supplies; still, as it was February 1815, colder weather was also a problem.

Not knowing that Jackson had defeated the British in New Orleans (on January 8 with the help of pirate Jean Lafitte and 4,500 Kentucky and Tennessee sharpshooters), and that the War of 1812 was already over, Crockett took a furlough and went home to his family. He only had a month or so left on his enlistment.

Home briefly, Davy received word to return to his company. Instead he hired a surrogate to finish his term (for this was allowed). Although he was discharged honorably on March 27, 1815, Crockett found himself demoted to fourth sergeant. However, on May 22, the militia of Franklin County elected him a lieutenant.

During the summer of 1815, Polly Crockett suffered an undisclosed illness, perhaps malaria or typhoid, and died. She was 27 years old, and Davy buried her close to their cabin. Her death was the hardest thing yet that he had to face.

Feeling the need for female companionship and a mother for his children, Davy married again. It was to Elizabeth Patton in the summertime of 1816. Around Polly's age and with two small children, George and Margaret Ann, Elizabeth was a widow who had lost her husband, James Patton, in the Creek War.

Crockett had an itch to move again despite the big farm Elizabeth had in Tennessee. So in the fall, he and a few friends searched for fertile land in Alabama. Unfortunately, Davy contracted malaria and it was weeks before he recovered enough to return home. Elizabeth thought he had died.

The new Crockett family did move in 1817, to an area of Tennessee near the town of Lawrenceburg; it was on 160 acres of land called Shoal Creek. The purchase of so much acreage was undoubtedly due to the respective sales of Davy and his wife's prior homesteads, and to possibly the $800 Elizabeth had when they married. Davy and Elizabeth had four children of their own between 1816 and 1821—a son, Robert, and daughters Elizabeth Jane, Rebeckah, and Matilda.

Tennessee had been a state since Davy was about 10 years old. The Crockett homestead at Shoal Creek became part of the state's new Lawrence County. Local folks there included Crockett's name as a nominee for justice of the peace. On November 25, 1817, he was elected to the first public office of his political career.

While Davy really knew little about the law, he learned and had a step up in the frontier community in that he could read and write. His duties as a justice included handling damage suits, debtors, and even the sale of slaves. His frankness labeled him as a simple and honest man.

In 1818, a fellow by the name of Matthews was running for the title of lieutenant colonel in the Lawrence County militia. He urged Davy to run for major in the same militia. Well, when Crockett found out it was just a scheme to get him to run against Matthews' son, the frontiersman ran against Matthews instead. Davy won the title of lieutenant colonel on March 27 and held it for just over a year. But the colonel end of it stuck with him right into the Alamo in 1836.

Early in 1821, he gave up his position as justice. Like Daniel Boone, Crockett always fancied hunting and starting a new enterprise. He combined both that year in a bid as an assemblyman from Lawrence County in the legislature.

By besting his political opponent in a squirrel hunt, Davy also managed to rally the voters. It was true that he either avoided or didn't know some of the issues of the day; yet Davy Crockett was a dandy storyteller and folks just took to his homespun ways. In August he won the election, and Davy was soon off to the state capital, then in Murfreesboro.

As an assemblyman, Crockett wasted no time in showing he leaned toward helping the simple frontier folks of which he was one. He voted to help those unfortunates who had to pay stiff penalties for delinquent property taxes.

But Davy was only in office 12 days when on September 29 he was forced to take a brief leave of his duties. A gristmill, powder mill and distillery he had with Elizabeth on their Shoal Creek land were destroyed by a flood.

Following this disaster, Elizabeth Crockett thought the only thing left to do was to pay their debts by trying to sell the remaining property. This included the sale of slaves they owned. And in 1822, the court actually seized the Crockett property to settle the debts from lawsuits.

Even before the court's involvement, Davy and his eldest son, John Wesley, searched for another place to live. This was just after the 1st session of the 14th General Assembly had adjourned in November 1821 (in which Crockett was a novice assemblyman).

Traveling 150 miles further west in Tennessee, Davy had staked out around 25 acres of land off the Obion River; called Rutherford's Fork, the property was then in a part of Carroll County. This western land was a virtual hunter's paradise.

Davy soon had the opportunity to prove that the hunting was good and with a new Kentucky rifle. It was a gift given to him by some of his political supporters in Nashville on May 5, 1822. This was the famous "Old Betsy" he used in the years ahead.

A special session of the legislature was called that summer. When it was over, Davy moved with his family to the new homestead where two log cabins were joined by an 8-foot passageway. Davy planted corn and supplied the family with meat from his hunting.

During the winter of 1823, he was gone so long hunting for one spell that his wife again gave him up for dead. His hunting, which brought in deer, bear, even wolf hides, was at that time the family's only source of income.

In his earlier tenure as an assemblyman, Crockett had been referred to as "the gentleman from the cane" by an affluent member, James Mitchell. Although Mitchell didn't mean to belittle him, or so he claimed, the sobriquet stuck thanks in no small part to Davy himself. He actually used it to further his image as a goodhearted backwoodsman of the common folk, despite some initial opposition to the reference.

Living in another new county and having his name announced (supposedly without his knowledge) as a candidate, again for the legislature, Crockett appeared to be annoyed only long enough to decide to run for office. His opponent in this instance was none other than a nephew of Andrew Jackson's, Dr. William E. Butler.

Davy's annoyances at the tactics of others only served to booster his own sense of tomfoolery, which seemed thus far to do well for him in the game of politics. Crockett was full of vim and vinegar. The pranks he pulled against Butler were directed right at the man's affluence amongst the poorer voters. When the opening session of the new assembly met in September 1823, it was Davy Crockett who made the ride again to the state capital.

In the 15th General Assembly, he was for the resolution that the Bank of Tennessee have branches in each county to provide loans for poor farmers and struggling businesses. A bill that Crockett personally introduced was for financial aid to widows.

By the time his second term as an assemblyman ended in October 1824, Crockett proved that he was unquestionably a man of the people. He took his legislative responsibilities seriously. Yet sometimes the actions he favored seemed self-serving, until it was remembered that Davy too lived like many of his own constituents.

Davy Crockett also had an independent streak that begged to differ from his fellow politicians. He favored Andrew Jackson for the presidency in 1824 (which he lost). But in 1823, when Jackson opposed incumbent John Williams in the Senate race (yet declined the win), Crockett believed Williams was actually the best man for the job.

The Crockett homestead at Rutherford's Fork was part of another new district, Gibson County, when Davy returned home from his political duties. Once more it was his hunting that provided the money coming in, along with the produce the Crocketts grew on their land.

In 1824, Crockett was urged by friends to run for Congress in the following year's election. This idea probably came to him before his friends did. But Crockett lacked the funds sorely needed to run a bigger campaign. There was also criticism against him for his independent streak and with other issues.

One particular issue concerned another bill he had introduced during the previous assembly. Crockett tried to change the county court's meeting days in West Tennessee. Apparently it was without considering how it affected the constituents who may have already gone to great lengths to arrange their initially set court dates.

Anyway, David Crockett lost his bid to a first Congress seat in 1825 to Adam Alexander. As a rich planter with influential friends, Alexander assuredly had the financial support that Crockett did not. Not handling the loss well, Davy even feigned that his opponent won by only two votes instead of 267.

Afterwards, Davy's sense of humor served him in good standing about the whole thing. He liked to tell a story of how, during the campaign, he didn't even have the money to buy drinks for his prospective voters. Davy claimed to have traded a raccoon fur at a tavern run by Job Snelling for drinks.

When Snelling then tossed the fur behind the bar, Crockett saw the tail poking out. He secretly pulled it free and traded it for another round of drinks. According to Davy, he pulled this stunt 10 times in a row.

Perhaps to minimize the damage to his wounded pride over the congressional defeat, Crockett turned his fury on the bears in his neck of the woods. Between the fall of 1825 and the spring of 1826, he claimed to have hunted down 105 black bears for their meat and skins.

During that period he was hunting, Crockett was involved in another enterprise to make money. He had a group of men cut wooden staves and build two flatboats to haul them to market in New Orleans.

Davy was then aboard one of the boats when they floated along the Obion River and onto the mighty Mississippi. None of the crew, including Crockett, were experienced boatmen. The boats, overloaded with some 30,000 staves, were tied together against the river's strong currents.

So forceful was the river that the crew could not control and stop the boats. During the very first night out from that day's departure, the flatboats hit a sawyer (which was a snag of uprooted trees that had swept along and formed a barrier in the river).

Below deck, Crockett was trapped as water gushed through the hatch and down on him. After great effort, he was pulled free from a small opening in the boat's side.

Stuck on the snag, Crockett and his crew were rescued and taken to nearby Memphis where they were fed and given fresh clothes. The boats were lost in the ordeal; the one Davy was on broke up, and he later learned that the other was seen drifting further downriver past Natchez.

Something amazing happened out of this misfortune. In Memphis, Davy was known there because of his previous campaign for Congress. He was an underdog that the folks treated almost like a hero. One resident in particular, a dry goods merchant named Marcus B. Winchester, offered him financial support to run again for Congress in 1827.

The political career of Davy Crockett

A portrait of David Crockett in the frontier garb for which he was famously known — note that the hat is not a coonskin cap.

is part of the filmography, as are some river adventures. He is seen initially as a defeated congressman in the last silent film entry, 1926's *Davy Crockett at the Fall of the Alamo* (Sunset Productions). Part of 1955's *Davy Crockett, King of the Wild Frontier* reflects on his politics (as did the second episode of the three-part Disney television show which preceded the feature film).

Legendary exploits about Davy on the Ohio River are seen in Walt Disney's follow-up film in 1956, *Davy Crockett and the River Pirates* (which was originally derived from a two-part television show). Also, Hanna-Barbera made an animated television film in 1976, *Davy Crockett on the Mississippi.*

A newfound confidence settled over David Crockett knowing he had Winchester's backing and clearly the people's approval. Voters seemed tickled that he used their exaggerated vernacular. It was nothing for Crockett to boldly boast that he was "half horse and half alligator," and could "whip his weight in wildcats."

The summer election of 1827 drew three strong candidates — Crockett, William Arnold, and incumbent Adam Alexander. But he whipped them both with 5,868 votes. Alexander, the runner-up, lagged behind Davy by 2,221 votes.

Before Congressman Crockett started out that fall for Washington City (which was what the nation's capital was called back then), he bought more Tennessee land. Although right next to his Gibson County property, the new 225 acres were part of Weakley County.

While traveling to Washington City, Crockett developed a fever (possibly from a malaria attack or

Biography and Overview

51

even pleurisy). Confined to bed for a few
weeks at the Tennessee farm of his father-
in-law, Robert Patton, he managed to
make it in time for the opening of the
20th Congress on December 3. A few more
days were lost that month when Davy re-
lapsed.

In Washington City, Davy stayed at
the boardinghouse of Mrs. Ball on Pennsylvania Avenue. His behavior as a fresh-
man in Congress in the next year and more
was somewhat questionable, undoubtedly
influenced by a new social whirligig of
fancy parties and even gambling.

Shortly before Andrew Jackson's March
1829 presidential inauguration, Crockett
had to borrow money from fellow Congressman Robert McHatton. The sum of
$700 was apparently to cover expenses
against losses at the gaming tables. It was
rumored that at one party, Davy even drank
from the finger bowls; to his credit, he had
a letter printed in various newspapers to
disclaim any embarrassing conduct in the
latter instance.

Congress (or the House of Representatives) was certainly different for David
Crockett than the Tennessee assembly had
been. The speeches by his peers seemed so
endless and boring that sometimes he didn't
even show up for work.

Yet Crockett could be diligent when
he wanted to be, especially on a vacant land
bill issue already approved by the legislature in Tennessee though not by Congress.
It was to help raise education funds by letting the United States turn over unoccupied Tennessee land in the public domain
to the state to be sold.

Just before the first session of Congress adjourned in May 1828, the land bill
was tabled (or put on hold). Davy did not
return home right away but waited until
summer due to his recurring illness. Then
it was to face the fact that he was in debt
on the Weakley County property where another mill was built and where the Crock-

etts now lived. They sold the home in Gibson County.

The second session of Congress began,
again on December 3, and Davy was five
days late. Debate on the land bill started
anew during January 1829. Crockett brought
forth an earlier proposal, an amendment
that eliminated the need to sell any land.
Instead the land would be given to squatters (160 acres per man) who already were
living on it and making improvements. He
supposedly was concerned that if the land
was sold, the money would go to build
universities for the rich and not common
schools for the poor.

James K. Polk, the Tennessee congressman who initiated the land bill proposal earlier in 1825, opposed Crockett's
amendment to it. Both men, however, were
part of the Democratic Party that came
about in the Jackson presidency. Polk was
among the Democrats who were staunch
supporters of Andrew Jackson. While Davy
had supported Jackson again in the 1828
presidential election, the independent
thinking he continued to show in political
matters bothered these Jacksonians.

The Democratic-Republican Party
was created in 1792 by Thomas Jefferson.
It split in 1828 due to the rivalry between
incumbent John Quincy Adams and Jackson to be the new president of the United
States. Not only was there a new Democratic Party born from it, but in 1834 the
opposing Whig Party. When a faction of
the opposition endorsed the Crockett
amendment, this created more animosity
against Davy from the Jackson men. On
January 14, 1829, the House of Representatives once again tabled the land bill along
with the amendment.

Home again in the spring of 1829, following his tenure in Congress, Crockett
wasted little time in gathering his political
resources for the next election. And this
was despite Polk and the other Jacksonians
continuing to be against him.

Adam Alexander, who ran against Davy in the previous two elections, was once more his main opponent. In that summer's election, Crockett won his second congressional seat with 6,773 votes as compared to 3,641 for his adversary. Polk was also reelected in his district.

After the 21st Congress met in December 1829, Crockett commenced his fight over the land bill. He even became chairman of a special committee that offered further revisions. Among the changes were that squatters could buy their acreage at 12½ cents per acre, and that money raised from sold land would go to help with the common schools.

When the new revised bill was defeated in early May 1830, Davy did manage to have the decision brought up for reconsideration. Although the bill then was not lost in defeat, it was still tabled.

On May 24, 1830, David Crockett voted against the Indian Removal Bill. It had passed by only five votes (102 to 97), but Crockett's stand not only alienated him from the president and his supporters in Congress but also from many of the folks back in Tennessee.

President Jackson personally championed the Indian Removal Bill. It was done to relocate several of the Eastern tribes, like the Chickasaw and the Creek, west of the Mississippi River. Crockett felt the Indians were mistreated, made to leave their homes for the expansion of settlers.

There were other politicians besides Crockett who were breaking away from the politics of Jackson and his supporters. They were leaning now toward the politics of the anti–Jackson forces led by Henry Clay.

While Crockett spoke openly of his own dissatisfaction with the president, during a February 24, 1831, session of Congress, Clay was far more outspoken an adversary always. Clay even ran unsuccessfully against Jackson for the presidency in 1832.

His second tenure as a congressman completed that spring of 1831, Davy Crockett was perhaps only too glad to return home and face the problems there in realization to what he left behind. At home there was debt and a troubled marriage with Elizabeth. In Congress there was, of course, a stalled land bill, and a feeling that Davy had no influence whatsoever. Despite his constituents, colleagues and president turning against him, perhaps Davy found some solace in that he did what he believed was right.

Before Crockett had even arrived home, Jackson wrote a letter to friends in Tennessee expressing his feelings that the voters not return him to Congress. The Jacksonians pushed one of their own, William Fitzgerald, to run against Davy in the 1831 summer election. And Crockett lost, if only by 586 votes.

Following the election, Davy had a petition filed for him asserting, among other things, that the ballots were tampered with. There might have been some irregularities in the voting, but it came to naught and Fitzgerald remained the new congressman.

Heavily in debt, Crockett couldn't repay a loan made with the Bank of the United States for his prior campaign funding. The payment note against him was actually dropped, although Davy had planned to honor the loan. To ease some of the debts as well, George Patton, Elizabeth's brother, purchased 25 acres of Crockett property in Weakley County. Patton later bought a slave girl owned by the family.

Crockett managed to acquire a lease from a friend on 20 new acres of land on the Obion River in Tennessee. Here he spent 18 months or so building a cabin and clearing the land for farming. But Elizabeth and the children were not with him, and instead were living with her side of the family in Gibson County.

Sometime in 1832, Davy returned for

a visit to Washington and also went to Philadelphia. He was determined to run again for Congress the following year. In preparation for another struggle with the Jacksonians, Crockett was trying to secure the support needed from those who were followers of the Whigs and their forthcoming party. This included Nicholas Biddle, president of the Bank of the United States.

The support of the bank for the Whigs only hastened Jackson's resolve to see it closed. The president actually withdrew government deposits from it to weaken the bank's structure. By late 1834, the bank was forced to close.

While not financially, additional help for Davy Crockett's return to Congress was triggered by a pair of successful literary sources which boosted his fame and popularity. The first, a play called *The Lion of the West*, debuted in 1831. Written by James Kirke Paulding and starring James Hackett, it was a parody on a fictional Kentucky congressman named Nimrod Wildfire. The character was patterned after Crockett.

The other source was a book written about him in 1833. It was titled *Life and Adventures of Colonel David Crockett of West Tennessee* (and with a follow-up edition, the first part of the title was changed to *Sketches and Eccentricities*). Although no author was listed, the book's writer was believed to be Matthew St. Clair Clarke.

The Jacksonians did not let Crockett's popularity or fame stop them from another attempt to keep him out of Congress using incumbent William Fitzgerald. While Tennessee's Madison County had been so important in helping to defeat Crockett last time at the polls in his district, it was now scheduled for redistricting. However, Fitzgerald and his colleagues were instrumental in having the county attached to the smaller 12th District, where he and Crockett were then running.

The plan almost worked against Davy. Yet when the votes were tallied in the 1833 congressional race, they were in Davy Crockett's favor 3,985 to 3,812. The margin of victory was just 173 votes.

In 1833, during President Jackson's second term, Vice President John C. Calhoun resigned from his office. Apparently Calhoun had disagreed with Jackson on a number of issues, including a government tariff put on his home state of South Carolina. Anyway, Martin Van Buren succeeded Calhoun and was also groomed by the Democrats to run in 1836 for the presidency.

By the time the Whig Party was given official recognition in 1834, the Whigs had thought of Crockett as a possibility to be a presidential candidate in 1836. Crockett certainly had good cause to be elated by the turn of events in his favor; enough so that upon entering the House of Representatives for a third term, he began writing his own life story.

In his autobiography, Crockett wrote of the hardships of his youth and the Creek War. He still felt some shortcomings on his role in the latter for he embellished his adventures, such as having taken part in Indian fighting at Entotachopco Creek and Emuckfau Creek. But he reveled in his long hunts. Although Davy never mentioned the names of all his family in the book (including his wives), and only touched upon his performances in Congress, he did write more extensively about Jackson and having stood up to him and his supporters.

A congressman from Kentucky, Thomas Chilton, helped Davy write the book and received half of the royalties from the Philadelphia publisher Carey and Hart after it came out in March 1834. Also included in the book's adventures were the backwoods humor and rise from poverty Crockett wanted to convey. While Davy never made a fortune from it, the book nonetheless was a best seller. Its title was *A*

Narrative of the Life of David Crockett of the State of Tennessee.

To help promote the book and his own presidential aspirations, Crockett accepted invitations from the Whigs to tour several cities in the Northeast. On April 25, 1834, Davy took a short leave from his Washington duties claiming he needed a rest. He went first to Baltimore, then Philadelphia and New York, and on to Boston. Everywhere he went on this tour Crockett was paraded to great fanfare. Nearly three weeks later, around May 13, he returned to Washington.

Just before Congress recessed that summer, Crockett went back to Philadelphia to pick up a gift now ready from his prior trip — a new custom-made rifle which he called "Pretty Betsy." From Philadelphia, he went to Pittsburgh and down the Ohio River and home to Tennessee.

No sooner was he there than Crockett was set upon by Democratic discords in the press for neglecting his duties as a congressman (and yet being paid his $8 per day). It was over his taking time to tour in the Northeast when Congress was still in session, and for even departing just before the recess.

Davy's debts continued to plague him despite his book's success; so when he returned to Congress after the recess, he began collaborating on another. This time it was with Pennsylvania representative William Clark and it was about Crockett's tour.

Carey and Hart was again the publisher. In March 1835, the book was brought out as a compilation of newspaper clippings and both serious and amusing commentaries. However, *An Account of Col. Crockett's Tour to the North and Down East, in the Year of Our Lord One Thousand Eight Hundred and Thirty-four* was not the resounding success expected. The book never even sold out its first printing.

By this time, David Crockett had fallen out of favor with the Whigs. There was apparently concern over his loans adding to his debts, and his verbal attacks against both Jackson and Van Buren had simply worn thin. Surmising that no Whig candidate could beat Van Buren anyway, Crockett found himself in December 1834 endorsing Senator Hugh Lawson White, a Tennessee Democrat, for president.

In the spring of 1835, Crockett was involved in a third book with his publisher. But Carey and Hart feared a libel suit since it was a negative work about the vice president and his baldness. It was called *The Life of Martin Van Buren: Hair-Apparent to the Government and the Appointed Successor of General Andrew Jackson.*

Although Crockett's name was on the book, he only contributed portions to it on his dislike and ridicule of Van Buren. For the most part it was written by former Georgia judge Augustin S. Clayton. And Carey and Hart need not have feared any libel action for the book was not a success when it was published that June.

Home from Congress, Crockett ran again during the summer of 1835. His opponent was a Jackson man named Adam Huntsman, who felt he could beat Davy since his land bill still hadn't been passed. Huntsman even brought out that Crockett did not accomplish much that he set out to do in all three of his terms.

When the votes came in, the final tally was 4,652 to 4,400 in Huntsman's favor. Davy lost by 252 votes and accused his opponent's side of buying votes for $25 each. To make matter worse, earlier in May, Van Buren did get the Democratic nod for president; Hugh Lawson White hadn't even seriously challenged him yet planned to later as a Whig.

Crockett then told his constituents who didn't vote for him for Congress that they could go to hell, as he was going to Texas. And so he did, departing from his estranged wife and his family on November 1, 1835. Accompanying him were a nephew, William Patton, and neighbors Abner Burgin and Lindsay Tinkle.

They rode on horseback to Memphis and crossed the Mississippi by ferry boat. Riding through Arkansas, Crockett was short on funds; he sold an expensive pocket watch for a cheaper watch and some cash. His fame followed him as others were eager to ride along for various distances.

In Texas, Davy Crockett boasted of wanting to participate in the revolution with the influx of Anglo-Americans who wanted the vast land as their own, and against the Mexican government actually ruling it. On January 12, 1836, in Nacogdoches, Crockett and his nephew joined others and took an oath of allegiance to the provisional government of Texas of which Sam Houston was the commander in chief.

Each man who promised to fight for the freedom of Texas for six months was to be compensated with over 4,600 acres of land. Crockett had added to the oath the stipulation that the fighting was for a republican government. Despite his past rivalry with President Andrew Jackson, Crockett shared his plan of Manifest Destiny for the expansion of the United States of America.

As had his predecessor John Quincy Adams, Jackson tried to buy Texas from Mexico (initially in 1829). The offer was rejected, and the following year the Mexican government passed a law to block any further American colonization. Thousands of colonists were already settled in Texas and more kept coming.

Both Crockett and Jackson felt that Texas belonged to the United States through the earlier Louisiana Purchase; although the province was ceded in 1819 to Spain by then President James Monroe. As Spain did with Daniel Boone in Missouri, it welcomed emigration in Texas. The first American colonization of 300 families was granted in 1821 to Moses Austin and then his son Stephen. That same year, Mexico declared its independence from Spain and recognized Texas as one of its own provinces.

In 1835, the tension was so great between Mexico and the Anglo-Americans in Texas (along with their Mexican allies in the province, called Tejanos) that it resulted in a revolution. Not only was Mexico's attempt to prevent emigration an issue, but a ban on slavery and higher taxes and tariffs were also.

Stephen Austin, released from a Mexican prison after eight months for trying to peacefully present a separate constitution for the Anglo-American settlers, now supported the fighting that had already commenced to achieve independence. He even led a command of 500 rebels to San Antonio de Bexar.

Although Austin left Texas to elicit further support in the United States, Bexar was captured by his followers on December 10, 1835, after five days of fighting. Gen. Edward Burleson had command of the rebels, and one, Ben Milam, rallied at least 300 against the Mexican force under Gen. Martin Perfecto de Cos.

While Milam was shot and killed, the town was taken along with a dilapidated mission used as a fortress by the enemy during the struggle. It was called the Alamo.

The struggle was not only against the enemy. Internal disagreements within the Anglo-Texan provisional government and the General Council created a lack of resolution. The government under Gov. Henry Smith wanted complete independence, while the council under Lt. Gov. James W. Robinson wanted to restore the Mexican Constitution of 1824.

As a result, Sam Houston's position as commander in chief was denigrated. And it would be until early March 1836 when a convention met and voted for a declaration of independence. His last command until that convention was to order Col. James Bowie to blow up the Alamo.

When Bowie went there in January, the fortress was under the command of Col. James C. Neill. Instead of blowing it up, they agreed to fortify the Alamo with the 80 men or so still there along with Bowie's 30 volunteers. William Barret Travis arrived in early February with 30 more men, all army regulars.

On February 8, 1836, Davy Crockett rode into Bexar with about 12 other men. They called themselves the Tennessee Mounted Volunteers. That night all the men threw a fandango for Davy. Neill left the Alamo the next day due to an illness in his family. His command was turned over to Col. Travis.

Most of the entries in the Crockett filmography are about the Alamo, beginning with four silent films. They are 1911's *The Immortal Alamo* (Star Film Company); 1914's *The Siege and Fall of the Alamo* (State of Texas); 1915's *The Martyrs of the Alamo* (Fine Arts/Triangle); and the aforementioned *Davy Crockett at the Fall of the Alamo* in 1926.

A portrait of David Crockett with his own famous motto: "I leave this rule, for others when I am dead. Be always sure you are right, then go ahead."

The first sound film depicting the battle was 1937's *Heroes of the Alamo* (Sunset/Columbia), followed in 1938 by *The Fall of the Alamo* (National Pictures). Walt Disney's *Davy Crockett, King of the Wild Frontier* in 1955 (and its preceding third television show), along with 1960's *The Alamo* (Batjac/United Artists), are the most famous.

Nineteen fifty-five's movie *The Last Command* (Republic) and 1987's *The Alamo, 13 Days to Glory* (NBC) star Jim Bowie above Crockett. In 1988, the film *Alamo … The Price of Freedom* (IMAX) was presented for daily viewing near the actual site in San Antonio.

Crockett plays a smaller role in several films about Sam Houston and the Texas Revolution. The initial movies are *Man of Conquest* (Republic) in 1939, and *The First Texan* (Allied Artists) in 1956. The others for television are *Houston: The Legend of Texas* (CBS) in 1986, and *James A. Michener's Texas* (ABC) in 1995. Another movie with Davy Crockett in a supporting role is 1953's *The Man from the Alamo* (Universal-International).

Various television shows reflect on the Alamo. They include the series *You Are There* (CBS) in 1953 and 1971; *The Time Tunnel* (ABC) in 1966; and *Amazing Stories* (NBC) in 1985. There are also a couple of special presentations from 1982 — *Texas and Tennessee, A Musical Affair* (Syndicated), and *Seguin* (PBS).

There was rivalry between Bowie and Travis over command at the Alamo. They actually shared it until Jim Bowie became seriously ill from what was attributed to perhaps pneumonia or typhoid fever.

Crockett did not impose his old militia rank of colonel on Travis (although he was sometimes called by it), and was content to simply being regarded as a high private. He and his men who followed Travis' command were more than willing to defend the south palisade, which was regarded as the Alamo's most vulnerable area.

On February 23, Santa Anna, president of Mexico and generalissimo of its military forces, arrived in Bexar. He was determined to crush the rebel forces throughout Texas, beginning at the Alamo where his brother-in-law, Gen. Cos, was defeated not long before.

For 12 days, the defenders of the Alamo withstood the shell and cannon fire of Santa Anna, whose forces were said to be between 2,400 and 4,000 men. Pleas of help were sent by Travis for his own 150 or so men; and a group of men from Gonzales were able to break through the enemy lines and make it into the Alamo. This brought the total to 189 defenders.

During the siege, Col. Travis had nothing but praise for Davy Crockett, who seemed to be everywhere encouraging the men. Legend said that Crockett killed the first enemy soldier from the Alamo, with a rifle shot of over 200 yards.

In the early morning of the 13th day of the siege, March 6, 1836, Santa Anna attacked the Alamo with around 1,800 men. The defenders repulsed the enemy twice, but on the third charge the Mexican soldiers swarmed over the walls. Travis was among the first killed when a bullet struck him in the forehead. Bowie was cut down as he laid on his cot suffering from his illness.

Stories abound on how Crockett perished. Some say he went down fighting using his broken rifle as a club, the bodies of the enemy soldiers he had killed all around him. Another story related how, overwhelmed by the Mexicans, he was among some 80 men who tried to escape over the palisade only to be stopped by the lancers.

Still another story about Crockett's death was that he was among seven survivors brought exhausted and bloodied before Santa Anna, by one of his generals,

Manuel Fernandez Castrillon, who sought clemency for them. But a furious Santa Anna had the survivors tortured and killed.

Before he died at the Alamo, at age 49, Crockett had written to his family asking them not to worry about him and that he was with his friends. He had hoped to find a place in the political convention which met just a few days before the final battle; and to be reconciled with his family in Texas to build a new home and life.

In December 1836, Martin Van Buren was elected president of the United States. Davy's son, John, became a Tennessee congressman in the year ahead, and in 1841 helped to finally pass a land bill for squatters. In 1854, Davy's wife, Elizabeth, was awarded his compensation of land as a soldier fighting for Texas (1,280 acres). She made the move there with other members of the family and died in Texas in 1860.

Col. Crockett's Exploits and Adventures in Texas, Written by Himself was a popular book published by Carey and Hart (using the imprint of T.K. and P.G. Collins) shortly after Davy's death. Really written by Richard Penn Smith, it pretended to be from the frontiersman and exaggerated and fictionalized his exploits right through the Alamo and into folklore.

Of course, the Davy Crockett almanacs, originating with a Nashville imprint from publisher Snag and Sawyer, did much to boost the folklore as well with their wild yet amusing tall tales. They actually began in 1835 and lasted until 1856.

After the American Civil War, Crockett started being written about in a more romantic, if still fictitious, vein. There was a particularly successful play called *Davy Crockett; Or Be Sure You're Right, Then Go Ahead*. Written by Frank Murdock, it was performed by Frank Mayo from 1872 to 1896.

This play served as the basis of four silent movies about Crockett beginning in 1909. The first was *Davy Crockett — In Hearts United* (Bison/New York). The others were 1910's *Davy Crockett* (Selig Polyscope); 1915's *Davy Crockett Up to Date* (Superba); and 1916's *Davy Crockett* (Morosco Photoplay). All are included in the filmography.

Also included are a couple more entries pertaining to his myth or folklore. They are from 1987's television show *Shelley Duvall's Tall Tales and Legends* (Showtime), and 1992's animated video *Rabbit Ears — Davy Crockett* (Movies Unlimited/ Rabbit Ears).

The entries left in the Crockett filmography are a few small roles and a big one. The smaller roles are a serial, *The Painted Stallion* (Republic), in 1937; a television episode of *The Adventures of Jim Bowie* (ABC) in 1958; a comedy film, *Alias Jesse James* (United Artists) in 1959; and a television special in 2000, *Dear America: A Line in the Sand* (HBO). The big role is in the 2004 film, *The Alamo* (Touchstone/ Imagine).

Davy Crockett Filmography

1 *Davy Crockett — In Hearts United* 1909
2 *Davy Crockett*   1910
3 *The Immortal Alamo*   1911
4 *The Siege and Fall of the Alamo* 1914
5 *The Martyrs of the Alamo*   1915
6 *Davy Crockett Up to Date*   1915
7 *Davy Crockett*   1916
8 *Davy Crockett at the Fall of the Alamo* 1926
9 *The Painted Stallion*   1937
10 *Heroes of the Alamo*   1937
11 *The Fall of the Alamo*   1938
12 *Man of Conquest*   1939
13 *The Son of Davy Crockett*   1941
14 *Davy Crockett, Indian Scout*   1950
15 *You Are There*   1953 and 1971
16 *The Man from the Alamo*   1953
17 *Davy Crockett, King of the Wild Frontier*   1955
18 *The Last Command*   1955
19 *The First Texan*   1956

20 *Davy Crockett and the River Pirates* 1956
21 *Frontier Woman*   1956
22 *The Adventures of Jim Bowie*   1958
23 *Alias Jesse James*   1959
24 *The Alamo*   1960
25 *The Time Tunnel*   1966
26 *Davy Crockett on the Mississippi*   1976
27 *Seguin*   1982
28 *Texas and Tennessee, A Musical Affair* 1982
29 *Amazing Stories*   1985
30 *Houston: The Legend of Texas*   1986
31 *The Alamo, 13 Days to Glory*   1987
32 *Shelley Duvall's Tall Tales and Legends* 1987
33 *Alamo … The Price of Freedom*   1988
34 *Davy Crockett*   1988-89
35 *Rabbit Ears — Davy Crockett*   1992
36 *James A. Michener's Texas*   1995
37 *Dear America: A Line in the Sand* 2000
38 *The Alamo*   2004

1 *Davy Crockett—In Hearts United*

Bison Films/New York Motion Picture Company / 1909 / 836 feet / Silent / Black and White

CREDITS: Fred J. Balshofer (director); Adam Kessel Jr., Charles Bauman (producers); Charles K. French (screenplay).

CAST: Charles K. French (Davy Crockett), Evelyn Graham (The Girl), Charles Bauman (The father), and Charles W. Travis.

SYNOPSIS: Davy Crockett and a girl, Anna, meet when he fixes a saddle girth for her. While waiting, she reads aloud Sir Walter Scott's romantic poem about the brave and noble Lochinvar.

Alas, Davy is just a simple country fellow although he is taken with Anna. He learns that she is planning on a city man named Blake to be her husband. Realizing he does have the qualities of a Lochinvar, Davy rescues Anna from marrying the wrong man.

NOTES: *Davy Crockett — In Hearts United* was the first film made about the legendary frontiersman. It was also the first based on Frank Murdock's play, *Davy Crockett; Or Be Sure You're Right, Then Go Ahead.*

Premiering on September 23, 1872, the play starred Frank Mayo. Over 2,000 performances were given in the United States and England until June 6, 1896. The story was about Crockett the backwoodsman gallantly rescuing his love, the cultured Eleanor, from an unscrupulous marriage arrangement.

The New York Motion Picture Company was created in 1909 by Adam Kessel Jr. and Charles Bauman. When their production outfit began making films in California, it was as Bison Motion Pictures (or Bison Films). *Hearts United* (the alternate title for the Crockett film) was made in New Jersey, including in Fort Lee.

After its release on June 6, *Hearts United* was considered a success. Charles K. French, who also wrote the script, starred by most accounts as the heroic Davy Crockett (yet one source cited Kessel doing the part). Evelyn Graham played the heroine.

This short silent, around 10 minutes, no longer exists to prove or disprove matters. But a purported highlight of the film, directed by Fred J. Balshofer, was the climactic part of the play where the hero and heroine were trapped by wolves in a cabin.

2 *Davy Crockett*

Selig Polyscope / 1910 / 3,000 feet / Silent / Black and White

CREDIT: Frank Boggs (director).

CAST: Hobart Bosworth (Davy Crockett), Betty Harte (Mary), and Tom Santschi.

SYNOPSIS: Although her mother has promised her to another in marriage, Mary is still in love with Davy Crockett.

Able finally to rescue his beloved, Davy and Mary then ride off together.

NOTES: Selig Polyscope released the silent *Davy Crockett* on April 21, 1910. Hobart Bosworth had the starring role. The following year he was seen in the Daniel Boone adventure for Selig, *The Chief's Daughter.*

Frank Boggs directed this Davy Crockett adventure which was also derived from the play by Frank Murdock. Betty Harte portrayed the heroine this time.

Supposedly used as well was the scene with the wolves attacking. Davy, with only his arm, barred the cabin door to keep them out. But there are no existing prints either of *Davy Crockett.*

3 *The Immortal Alamo*

Star Film Company / 1911 / 1,000 feet / Silent / Black and White

CREDITS: William F. Haddock (director); Gaston Méliès (producer); William Paley (cinematographer); Horace Young (scenic artist).

CAST: Francis Ford (Navarre), William Carroll (Lieutenant Dickenson), Edith Storey (Lucy Dickenson), William Clifford (Travis), Donald Peacock (Baby), and Gaston Melies (Padre).

NOTES: Released on May 25, 1911, *The Immortal Alamo* was produced by Gaston

Méliès. He was the brother of Georges Méliès, the pioneering French filmmaker, whose techniques with special effects were quite innovative during the early 1900s.

By 1910, however, the films were losing their popularity. Gaston then was able to move his brother's Star Films to San Antonio, Texas, to make Westerns. Filming on this particular one, directed by William F. Haddock, intended to use the real Alamo site. But a painted backdrop of the chapel was built instead at a nearby sulphur springs resort.

Another nearby location, the Mission San Jose, was also utilized. An unidentified actor playing Davy Crockett was filmed fighting Mexican soldiers here supposedly, but it may have been for the next film listed.

Other sources are seemingly inaccurate in casting Francis Ford as Crockett. Supposedly Ford played the fictitious Navarre, the Mexican spy who lusts after Lieutenant Dickenson's wife, Lucy, until he is stopped at swordpoint.

Ford was the older brother of John Ford, the legendary filmmaker. As he grew old, Francis appeared in many of his brother's films, including *Stagecoach* in 1939.

Edith Storey and William Carroll portrayed the Dickensons, whose relationship was the focal point of this lost film. Producer Melies also played a padre in Santa Anna's camp.

Almeron Dickenson was the artillery lieutenant in the Alamo. Susannah was actually his wife's name and she and their baby daughter were among the survivors. While Almeron was killed during the Alamo's last stand, in *The Immortal Alamo* he is not there but with Sam Houston. A romantic liberty so he could be reunited with his wife.

Additional notes are in the Jim Bowie and Sam Houston filmographies.

4 *The Siege and Fall of the Alamo*

State of Texas / 1914 / Silent / Black and White

CAST: Ray Myers (Davy Crockett).

NOTES: *The Siege and Fall of the Alamo* was produced by the State of Texas in 1914. An alternate title was *The Fall of the Alamo*.

For years, Ray Myers went uncredited as to the role he had in this lost silent film. Stills which existed with the actor were erroneously credited to Francis Ford as Davy Crockett in *The Immortal Alamo*.

Regarded as a handsome actor in his day, Myers had previously appeared in other silent pictures with Ford. Included were 1912's *The Law of the West* and *War on the Plains* (and for the latter, Myers also wrote the script).

Additional notes are in the Bowie and Houston filmographies.

5 *The Martyrs of the Alamo*

Fine Arts Company/Triangle Film Corporation / 1915 / Five Reels / Silent / Black and White

CREDITS: William Christy Cabanne (director); D.W. Griffith (supervisor); William Christy Cabanne, Theodosia Harris (screenplay); William E. Fildew (photography); Joseph Carl Briel (music arrangement). Based on *Martyrs of the Alamo*, the novel by Theodosia Harris.

CAST: Sam DeGrasse (Silent Smith), Walter Long (Santa Anna), A.D. Sears (David Crockett), Alfred Paget (James Bowie), Fred Burns (Almeron Dickinson), John Dillon (William B. Travis), Tom Wilson (Sam Houston), Juanita Hansen (Old Soldier's Daughter), Ora Carew (Mrs. Dickinson), and Augustus Carney (Old Revolutionary War Soldier).

SYNOPSIS: In San Antonio, Susannah Dickinson is disturbed by her treatment by a Mexican officer. Almeron, her husband, kills the officer and is jailed.

This incident acts as the rallying cry

for the Americans living there who are opposed to the Mexican rule. David Crockett, James Bowie and William B. Travis are among the men who decide to fight the enemy forces led by Santa Anna, president of Mexico.

Silent Smith is a scout for the Texas fight for freedom. He is in love with the daughter of an old soldier from the American Revolution.

When Travis and Bowie disagree over their joint command at the Alamo, which is under constant enemy attack, Crockett reminds them they are both fighting for Texas. During the siege, Col. Travis draws a line in the dirt asking those defenders who want to stay to cross.

One defender crosses right away. The others hesitate until Crockett crosses over. All follow him but one. Bowie is the last man to cross as he suffers from consumption.

In the final assault by the Mexicans, the defenders are killed as are women and children. Bowie is stabbed to death with bayonets on his cot. Crockett falls near the Alamo chapel surrounded by the enemies he has slain.

Trying to get help for the Alamo, Silent Smith later joins Gen. Sam Houston to defeat the Mexicans at San Jacinto and take Santa Anna prisoner. Smith is reunited with the woman he loves as Texas does become free.

NOTES: Adam Kessel Jr. and Charles Bauman, who were responsible for the first Davy Crockett film, were also involved in the 1915 silent *The Martyrs of the Alamo*. They and the departing head of Mutual Films, Harvey Aitken, set up the Triangle Film Corporation. Ironically the new company wasn't named after them but for their three foremost directors—Thomas Ince, Mack Sennett and D.W. Griffith.

The Fine Arts Company was that part of Triangle under Griffith, who supervised the Alamo film directed by William Christy Cabanne. Cabanne also assisted in the screenplay with Theodosia Harris; a novel was credited as the script's source.

After *The Martyrs of the Alamo* was released on November 21, it received the subtitle of *The Birth of Texas*. This was an apparent reference to the successful release in 1915 of Griffith's *The Birth of a Nation*.

Both films had themes with racist overtones. The Alamo film depicted the Mexicans accosting American women, and even killing them and children. This was not historically accurate by most accounts. Antonio Lopez de Santa Anna (played by Walter Long) was depicted as a drug addict. This, however, was apparently accurate.

As played by Alfred Paget, Jim Bowie displayed the more aristocratic bearing attributed to Col. Travis in history. John Dillon's Travis wore the frontier garb usually given to Bowie and Davy Crockett. In fact, like A.D. Sears' Crockett, Travis had on a coonskin cap. The real Travis never dressed like a frontiersman who wore buckskin, at least not in the Alamo.

Both Paget and Sears did well by their roles. Sears may have been the more engaging simply because his Davy was the more amiable character. He was extremely winning when he smiled and crossed Travis' line knowing that death in battle was inevitable. The camaraderie the other men felt when they followed the frontiersman added up to a touching moment.

Sam DeGrasse was the actual star of the film as scout Silent Smith. While a fictional character, the role was derived from his real-life counterpart, Deaf Smith, who had allied himself with Sam Houston. Houston was played by Tom Wilson.

Filming took place at the Fine Arts Studio in Hollywood. The sets constructed included a handsome version of the Alamo chapel (although it was far too new looking to be an authentic replica of the more weathered chapel).

The Martyrs of the Alamo was the first and only film to suggest that a tunnel was used to get in and out at times. And a group of defenders were brought before Santa Anna during the film's Alamo battle and then killed (but Davy Crockett was not one of them).

Not the blazing success of D.W. Griffith's earlier epic on the Civil War and its aftermath, it was still successful. A favorable review even compared the films. Stated *Variety*, "Some of the battle scenes excel those in Griffith's immortal *The Birth of a Nation*."

Additional notes are in the Bowie and Houston filmographies.

6 *Davy Crockett Up to Date*

Superba Company / 1915 / Silent / Black and White

CAST: W.E. Browning (Davy Crockett), and Rolinda Bainbridge.

NOTES: The Superba Company was part of the United Film Service, which was started just the year before the release of *Davy Crockett Up to Date*.

Specializing in one-reel comedies, Superba's take on the frontier legend was alleged to be a parody of the Frank Murdock play.

No prints of this silent film exist.

7 *Davy Crockett*

Oliver Morosco Photoplay Co./Pallas (Paramount) Pictures / 1916 / Five Reels / Silent / Black and White

CREDITS: William Desmond Taylor (director); Frank Mayo, Elliot Clawson (screenplay); Homer Scott (cameraman).

CAST: Dustin Farnum (Davy Crockett), Winifred Kingston (Eleanor Vaughn), Harry de Vere (James Vaughn), Herbert Standing (Col. Hector Royston), Howard Davies (Oscar Crompton), and Page Peters (Neil Crompton).

SYNOPSIS: Backwoodsman Davy Crock-ett walks in the forest with wealthy Eleanor Vaughn. She reads to him the poem about Lochinvar, who rides to the rescue of his lady fair.

After two years in England, Eleanor returns but becomes engaged to foppish Neil Crompton. Davy saves their lives from wolves during a winter storm.

Eleanor discovers that the engagement was arranged with her guardian to pay off the gambling debts made by Neil's father. Davy and Eleanor realize they are in love. Like Lochinvar, he rides to her rescue.

NOTES: This fourth film from the Frank Murdock play was scripted by Frank Mayo, grandson of the play's star, and Elliott Clawson. William Desmond Taylor directed. *Davy Crockett* was made by the Oliver Morosco Photoplay Company, for release by Pallas (Paramount) on July 13, 1916.

While the Murdock tale of Crockett saving his true love was fictional, its popularity sustained the play's run for 24 years and into the silent film era. Yet the theme of the backwoodsman, rising from his lowly station in life to find a higher one, was very real (if not the romantic allusions in the play and films).

Dustin Farnum, handsome and muscular, probably gave the best account of Davy Crockett as Sir Walter Scott's Lochinvar. Winifred Kingston was his leading lady. Included in the film was the famous scene with Davy blocking the door to the cabin with his arm, to keep the wolves from getting him, Eleanor and her betrothed.

Just two years earlier, Farnum had made his leading-man debut in Cecil B. DeMille's first silent film, *The Squaw Man*. Farnum also starred in 1914 in the first version of *The Virginian*.

"The scenic surroundings were well worth looking at and were it not for the drawn out and padded story, this *Davy Crockett* could have been a corker." This was from a *Variety* review in August 1916, no doubt referring to the 10 to 12 minutes of each of its five reels.

Sadly, it is another lost film.

8 *Davy Crockett at the Fall of the Alamo*

Sunset Productions / 1926 / Six Reels / Silent / Black and White

CREDITS: Robert North Bradbury (director); Anthony J. Xydias (producer); Ben Allah Newman (screen adaptation); J.S. Brown, Elvert M. McManigal (photography); Della M. King (editor); Clover Roscoe (titles); Wilson Silsby, Paul Cosgrove (art directors).

CAST: Cullen Landis (Davy Crockett), Kathryn McGuire (Alice Blake), Joe Rickson (Colonel Travis), Bob Fleming (Colonel Bowie), Ralph McCullough (Colonel Bonham), Fletcher Norton (Gen. Santa Anna), Anne Berryman (Kate Kennedy), Jay Morley (Zachary Kennedy), Thomas Lingham (Dandy Dick Heston), Frank Rice (Lige Beardsley), Betty Brown (Myra Winkler), Bob Bradbury Jr. (Pinky Smith), Steve Clemento (Mose), and Edward Hearn (Fred Warren).

SYNOPSIS: A little boy is being read a story by his grandfather about Davy Crockett. It is from *William F. Cody's Story of the Wild West and Camp-Fire Chats.*

In 1835, Davy is defeated for reelection to Congress. Saddened, he returns home to his cabin. Yet his spirits perk up when he decides to go and fight for Texas' independence.

Crockett is accompanied to Texas by his friends. Included are Lige Beardsley and the Bee-Hunter. They join the colonels Travis and Bowie in the Alamo with their men.

Mexican leader Santa Anna is besieging the Alamo with his overwhelming army. A courier, Pinky Smith, arrives with the news that there will not be any reinforcements.

Travis then makes a line in the ground with his heel, wanting those men to cross it who will stay and fight. Both Crockett and Travis help a sick Bowie across.

The night before the final attack from the enemy, Travis is killed. When the Mexicans swarm the walls on March 6, 1836, Crockett and 60 others are driven from their defense at the palisade and back to the chapel.

As he proudly waves a flag, courier Smith is shot down. Lige and the Bee-Hunter are killed. It takes 10 soldiers to take down Davy Crockett with bayonets.

The grandfather has finished his story. Captivated by it all, the child realizes all the brave defenders in the Alamo, including the ailing Jim Bowie, wouldn't give up until they perished.

NOTES: *Davy Crockett at the Fall of the Alamo* was released on August 1, 1926, three months after *Daniel Boone Thru the Wilderness.* Both silent films, directed by Robert North Bradbury, were produced as well by Anthony J. Xydias for his Sunset Productions.

Cullen Landis, who would go on to star in the first all-talking film (1928's *Lights of New York*), portrayed Crockett. Although short in stature, and not having Roy Stewart's more rugged appearance as Boone, Landis' frontiersman still had plenty of vigor. His Davy even fights bare-chested at the Alamo, and the enemy soldiers pile on top of him to bring him down.

However, the humor that was generally part of the real Crockett was lacking. A.D. Sears in his earlier portrayal from *The Martyrs of the Alamo* conveyed better (albeit in a smaller role) the combined prowess and wit. Only when he is dying, does Landis share a bit of the humor; it is when his Davy grins at his victors with defiance.

An alternate title was *With Davy Crockett at the Fall of the Alamo.* Colonel Bowie was played by Bob Fleming and Travis by Joe Rickson in heroic fashion.

Fletcher Norton was the villainous Santa Anna. As with the earlier Daniel Boone adventure, Bob Bradbury Jr. (who became famous later as Bob Steele) was on hand again, this time as another of the Alamo's heroes.

While the production was somewhat shoddy, sets constructed included a palisade and chapel. This Alamo chapel had a pointed top instead of the more customary rounded one seen in film and television.

Ben Allah Newman (known also as Ben Ali Newman, or simply Ben Allah for his work on Sunset's Boone film) wrote the Crockett screenplay. Clearly with its opening and closing scenes, with the grandfather telling the story to the child, the whole thing was intended as a juvenile adventure. This despite the rather intense brawling that characterized the fighting between the Alamo defenders and their adversaries.

Copies of *Davy Crockett at the Fall of the Alamo* and *The Martyrs of the Alamo* still exist. Both the Library of Congress and Museum of Modern Art have a partial print of the 1926 film and an entire print of the 1915 film.

Additional notes are in the Jim Bowie filmography.

9 *The Painted Stallion*

Republic Pictures / 1937 / 12-Chapter Serial / Black and White

NOTES: Main information is in the Kit Carson filmography. Additional notes are in the Jim Bowie filmography.

After Bud Geary in 1935's *The Miracle Rider* (in the Daniel Boone filmography), the second actor to play Davy Crockett in sound films was Jack Perrin in *The Painted Stallion*. The title was in reference to the horse ridden by the mysterious rider, played by Julia Thayer.

Perrin's Crockett was part of the highly fabricated story in New Mexico (a place the real Davy never went). The role was a secondary one, as were those for legendary figures Kit Carson (Sammy McKim) and Jim Bowie (Hal Taliaferro).

A longtime Western stalwart, Perrin began his film career in the silent era. In 1937, the same year Republic released the serial *The Painted Stallion*, he was in the epic *Wells Fargo*.

10 *Heroes of the Alamo*

Sunset Productions/Columbia Pictures / 1937 / 75 minutes / Black and White

CREDITS: Harry Fraser (director); Anthony J. Xydias (producer); Jack Corrick (assistant director); Roby Wentz (screen adaptation); Robert Cline (photography); Arthur A. Brooks (editor); Clarence Bricker (art director); Harold Clandening (costuming). Song: "The Yellow Rose of Texas," owned by Mary Daggett Lake and William J. Marsh.

CAST: Bruce Warren (Almerian Dickinson), Ruth Findlay (Anne Dickinson), Lane Chandler (Davy Crockett), Rex Lease (William Travis), Roger Williams (James Bowie), Julian Rivero (Santa Anna), Lee Valianos (James Bonham), Earl Hodgins (Stephen Austin), Jack Smith (William H. Wharton), Edward Peil (Sam Houston), Willy Costello (General Cos), Paul Ellis (General Castrillon), Jim Corey (Hank Hunter), Steve Clark (Frank Hunter), and Marilyn Haslett (Angelina Dickinson).

SYNOPSIS: The Texas border is closed to further emigration from the United States, in 1833, by orders of Mexican President Santa Anna. Already in Texas, newlyweds Almerian and Anne Dickinson still plan a future there together.

Attending a convention to debate independence from Mexico, Al Dickinson persuades the others, including Stephen Austin, William Travis and James Bowie, to negotiate for their freedom. Austin, acting as their representative, is later imprisoned by Santa Anna.

After Austin is freed and Texas declared a republic, Santa Anna leads his large army to dispose of the Texans. To seek more support for the fight, Austin returns to the United States.

At Dickinson's urging, Bowie, Travis and a small band of Texas defenders fortify the Alamo against the encroaching enemy troops. Davy Crockett soon joins the brave men in the Alamo.

On February 23, 1836, the siege by the Mexicans begins. Anne Dickinson joins her husband in the Alamo with Angelina, their newborn daughter.

As they run out of ammunition after 13 days, the defenders cannot withstand the Mexican surge and are killed. Dickinson, Crockett, Travis and Bowie are shot.

Davy, crawling along the ground from his wound, is seen by Santa Anna. An enemy soldier is ordered to club the frontiersman to death. Al dies in his wife's arms. Then with her child, Anne is allowed to leave the Alamo and tell Sam Houston the tragic story.

NOTES: *Heroes of the Alamo* was the first talking motion picture about the 13-day siege. Producer Anthony J. Xydias wanted to remake his earlier historical silents into sound films (including *Daniel Boone Thru the Wilderness*) for his Sunset Productions. But he was only able to get around to the Alamo saga, which proved to be his last film.

Extensive battle footage was actually incorporated into the film from the producer's previous *Davy Crockett at the Fall of the Alamo*. The production costs were also so tight that only the lower portion of the Alamo chapel was built on a sound stage, with full shots of the earlier film's chapel used.

This combination of sound and silent film footage gave *Heroes of the Alamo* quite an amateurish look. It hardly helped its box office appeal after the initial release from Astor Films on September 24, 1937,

and again the following year from Columbia Pictures. The film, however, was shortened and used as an educational tool in some schools around 10 years later; the title then was *Remember the Alamo*.

Director Harry Fraser and screenwriter Roby Wentz centered the movie around the Dickinsons (Bruce Warren and Ruth Findlay), with Crockett, Bowie and the others then revolving around them and the struggle for independence from Santa Anna. This story had the defenders' ammunition running out (which was not the case in the actual Alamo).

Lane Chandler, another durable Western stalwart, played Davy Crockett. His was an easygoing persona that was comparable to Fess Parker's later image. But Chandler's frontiersman was not given, nor were Rex Lease's William Travis and Roger Williams' Jim Bowie, the big death scene usually reserved for each character.

The three heroes are simply shot down. Crockett is especially degraded afterward; utterly defenseless, he is finished off with a gun butt to the head by the orders of Julian Rivero's Santa Anna.

This version of the Alamo story can be found on video.

Additional notes are in the Bowie and Houston filmographies.

11 *The Fall of the Alamo*

National Pictures / 1938 / Two Reels / Partial Silent / Black and White

CREDITS: Stuart Paton (director, editor); H.W. Kier (producer); Harry Forbes (photography); T. Ralph Willis (music). Based on Lenoir Hunt's book *Bluebonnets and Blood*.

CAST: Coates Gwynne (Travis), Sterling Waters (Crockett), J.R. Klumpp (Bowie), Clarence Risien (Dickenson), Florence Griffith (Mrs. Dickenson), and Paul Willett (Santa Anna).

NOTES: *The Fall of the Alamo* was

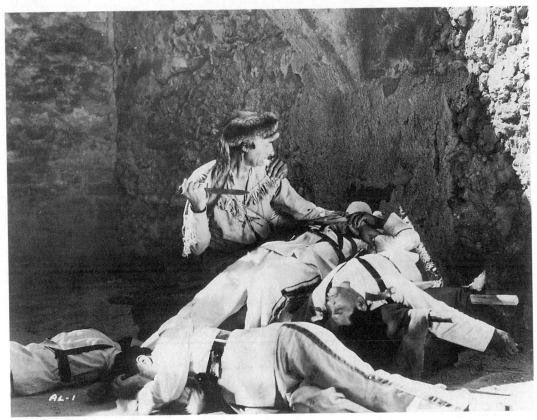

Sterling Waters (center) as Davy Crockett fighting the Mexican soldiers in *The Fall of the Alamo* (retitled on video as *Alamo: Shrine of Texas Liberty*).

made in San Antonio during June 1938 (although one source cited the year it was produced as 1935). Shooting took place at the Mission San Jose, where a part of *The Immortal Alamo* was filmed.

The producer was a local Texan, H.W. Kier. The film's director was Stuart Paton, who initially started out in the silent era. Paton also edited the picture.

Other local Texans performed in it, including a young man named Sterling Waters. His mother made the frontier outfit and coonskin cap he wore as Davy Crockett.

Although there were sound effects and recorded music in *The Fall of the Alamo*, the acting was done all in pantomime. And despite the film's intent to be another educational source, like the previous entry, it may or may not have been initially released by the producer's National Pictures.

Long considered a lost film, it resurfaced in 1999 as a 45-minute educational video. And it had a new title, *Alamo: Shrine of Texas Liberty*. Alamo historian and author Frank Thompson prepared the video release and produced a documentary that was added to it. Thompson is also credited with preparing other early Alamo films for video—included are the silents *The Martyrs of the Alamo* and *Davy Crockett at the Fall of the Alamo*.

Additional notes are in the Jim Bowie filmography.

12 *Man of Conquest*

Republic Pictures / 1939 / 97 minutes / Black and White

NOTES: Main information is in the Sam Houston filmography. Additional notes are in the Jim Bowie filmography.

Republic's *Man of Conquest* in 1939 was a rousing biography of Sam Houston. Richard Dix portrayed the Texas leader, who in this depiction is seen riding to the defense of the Alamo.

A fine replica of an exterior portion of the famed fortress was constructed in California's San Joaquin Valley. The chapel's interior was shot at Republic Studios.

The Alamo segment of the film was not even five minutes long but very well done. With his comrades having fallen, Davy Crockett is shot down by an enemy pistol. His slow fall to the ground signifies the end of the battle.

The Crockett from *Heroes of the Alamo*, Lane Chandler, played gallant defender James Bonham. Robert Barrat did well by the frontiersman, and he was the sole buckskin-clad figure in the film.

Barrat's lengthy film career included other frontier adventures. In the 1936 version of *The Last of the Mohicans*, he played Chingachgook. And he supported George Montgomery in the forthcoming *Davy Crockett, Indian Scout*.

13 *The Son of Davy Crockett*

Columbia Pictures / 1941 / 59 minutes / Black and White

Credits: Lambert Hillyer (director, screenplay); Leon Barsha (producer); Milton Carter (assistant director); Irving Briskin (executive producer); Benjamin Kline (photography); Mel Thorsen (editor).

Cast: Bill Elliott (Dave Crockett), Iris Meredith (Doris Mathews), Dub Taylor (Cannonball), Kenneth MacDonald (King Canfield), Richard Fiske (Jesse Gordon), Eddy Waller (Gerald Mathews), Don Curtis (Jack Ringe), Paul Scardon (Zeke), Edmund Cobb (Lance), Steve Clark (Curly), Harrison Greene (President Grant), and Lloyd Bridges (Sammy).

Bill Elliott in *The Son of Davy Crockett.*

Synopsis: Dave Crockett is the son of the legendary frontiersman. With his friend Cannonball, he attempts to find the three men responsible for the poisoning deaths of several others.

Finding two of the killers in a small town, Dave gets into a gunfight and has to shoot them down. But the town's corrupt marshal accuses Dave of murder.

Fleeing, Dave and Cannonball are captured by Union soldiers. Taken to President Grant, Dave is offered a pardon if he helps Gerald Mathews and other ranchers in the Yucca Valley Strip.

The strip is not yet part of the Union and is being controlled by King Canfield and his gang. Dave meets Mathews and his granddaughter, Doris.

When Dave protects Canfield from a lynching, the ranchers think that they are in cahoots. Jack Ringe is actually in league with Canfield (and also the third man behind the earlier poisoning deaths in the strip).

Davy Crockett, Indian Scout with (left to right) George Montgomery, Noah Beery Jr., and Philip Reed.

Ringe and Canfield try to stop the election which will decide the Union issue. In the ensuing struggles that take place between them and Dave Crockett, both Canfield and Ringe are killed. The Yucca Valley Strip then becomes a part of the United States.

NOTES: *The Son of Davy Crockett* was released in July 1941, just two months after *The Return of Daniel Boone.* Lambert Hillyer directed and Leon Barsha produced both "B" Westerns for Columbia Pictures.

The films also starred Bill Elliott and Dub Taylor as the rugged hero and his comic sidekick. Some 10 Westerns were made together by the duo. They were even cast as Wild Bill Elliott and Cannonball in an unsold television pilot in 1950, *The Marshal of Trail City.*

Director Hillyer wrote the script too for this Crockett entry. The dialogue seemed to be stressed more than the action in this totally fabricated story. The real Davy never had a son named after him either.

14 *Davy Crockett, Indian Scout*

Reliance Pictures/United Artists / 1950 / 71 minutes / Black and White

CREDITS: Lew Landers (director); Edward Small (producer); Harold Knox (assistant director); Grant Whytock, Bernard Small (associate producers); Richard Schayer (screenplay); George Diskant, John Mescall (photography); Stuart Frye, Kenneth Crane (editors); Rudolph Sternad, Martin Obzina (art directors); C.I. Steenson, Howard Bristol (set decorators);

Edward Lambert, Elmer Ellsworth (wardrobe); Don Cash (makeup); Paul Sawtell (music). Based on a story by Ford Beebe.

CAST: George Montgomery (Davy Crockett), Ellen Drew (Frances Oatman), Philip Reed (Red Hawk), Noah Beery Jr. (Tex), Paul Guilfoyle (Ben), Addison Richards (Captain Weightman), Robert Barrat (Lone Eagle), Erik Rolf (Mr. Simms), William Wilkerson (High Tree), John Hamilton (Colonel Pollard), Vera Marshe (Mrs. Simms), Jimmy Moss (Jimmy Simms), Chief Thundercloud (Sleeping Fox), Kenneth Duncan (Sergeant Gordon), and Ray Teal (Captain McHale).

SYNOPSIS: A wagon train escorted by the cavalry is attacked, in 1848, by Indians. Army scout Davy Crockett (whose uncle was the famous frontiersman) aids his Indian partner, Red Hawk, when he is accused of being a spy.

Crockett tells the story of the wagon train's journey west. Both Davy and Red Hawk suspect an impending Indian attack. The army's captain, Weightman, is warned; however, Lone Eagle, his Indian agent, assures him there is little risk.

Red Hawk suspects too that the spy is Frances Oatman, a passenger on the wagon train. It turns out that Frances is the daughter of Lone Eagle, who is a chief planning an attack on the wagons.

When Frances realizes her father is also going to kill the women and children, she warns Davy. But at first he doesn't believe her.

As the cavalry escorts the wagons through a mountain pass, the attacking Indians use explosives. An avalanche separates the wagon train from the soldiers.

With a wagon of explosives, Davy blows a hole in the rocks to free the soldiers. Davy Crockett and the cavalry then rescue the wagon train.

NOTES: *Davy Crockett, Indian Scout* was made by Reliance Pictures in collaboration with Edward Small Productions. In fact, Reliance was initially set up in 1932 by producer Small and Harry M. Goetz. United Artists released the Western on January 6, 1950.

This standard yarn, about a stalwart hero and soldiers and Indians clashing, was written by Richard Schayer from a story by Ford Beebe. Director Lew Landers made particularly good use of the action scenes and a fine cast.

George Montgomery starred as the nephew of Davy Crockett (although some sources cited cousin). *Variety* said, "Performances are competently handled, with Montgomery registering nicely in the top role."

A strong, handsome Western star, one of Montgomery's first roles was as one of the masked rangers in *The Lone Ranger* serial a dozen years earlier. He portrayed heroic frontiersmen in other films, including again for Edward Small in the same year's *The Iroquois Trail*, and in Columbia's 1953 version of *The Pathfinder*. The heroes from both these films were based on James Fenimore Cooper's Hawkeye.

When the Davy Crockett film was shown on television, the title was simply *Indian Scout*. Robert Barrat, who played Crockett briefly in *Man of Conquest*, had another key supporting role in this piece albeit as the villain.

Neither *Davy Crockett, Indian Scout* nor *The Son of Davy Crockett* have been placed on video.

15 *You Are There*

CBS Television / 1953 and 1971 / Each 30 minutes / Black & White and Color

NOTES: *CBS Is There* was a 1947 radio show (changed to *You Are There* after a year), and it was hosted by John Daly. The imaginative premise took modern correspondents back in time to report actual historical events as they happened.

On February 1, 1953, *You Are There*

premiered on CBS television. Walter Cronkite hosted the television show, which ran until October 1957. Charles Russell and James D. Fonda were credited as producers. The black and white episode "The Defense of the Alamo" aired on May 24, 1953.

You Are There returned as a weekly series in September 1971, and it ran until May 13, 1973. Once more Cronkite was the host, with Vern Diamond producing. The color episode "The Siege of the Alamo" aired on October 9, 1971. Fred Gwynne (of television's *Car 54, Where Are You?* and *The Munsters*) played Davy Crockett in this later episode.

Additional notes are in the Jim Bowie filmography.

16 *The Man from the Alamo*

Universal-International Pictures / 1953 / 79 minutes / Technicolor

CREDITS: Budd Boetticher (director); Aaron Rosenberg (producer); Tom Shaw (assistant director); Steve Fisher, D.D. Beauchamp (screenplay); Russell Metty (photography); Virgil Vogel (editor); Alexander Golitzen, Emrich Nicholson (art directors); Russell A. Gausman, Ruby R. Levitt (set decorators); Bill Thomas (costumes); Bud Westmore (makeup); Frank Skinner (music). From a story by Niven Busch and Oliver Crawford.

CAST: Glenn Ford (John Stroud), Julia Adams (Beth Anders), Chill Wills (John Gage), Hugh O'Brian (Lt. Tom Lamar), Victor Jory (Jesse Wade), Neville Brand (Dawes), John Day (Cavish), Myra Marsh (Ma Anders), Jeanne Cooper (Kate Lamar), Mark Cavell (Carlos), Edward Norris (Mapes), Guy Williams (Sergeant), Dennis Weaver (Reb), Trevor Bardette (Davy Crockett), Howard Negley (Sam Houston), Stuart Randall (Jim Bowie), and Arthur Space (Bill Travis).

SYNOPSIS: In the Alamo, Lt. Col. Bill Travis is besieged by Mexican troops under the rule of Santa Anna. Among those in Travis' command are Davy Crockett, Jim Bowie and John Stroud.

When word reaches the Alamo that the nearby town of Ox Bow is in danger, its Alamo defenders hold a drawing to determine who will go back to help. Stroud is chosen; he leaves the Alamo and faces some criticism of being a coward.

In Ox Bow, John finds a massacre has taken place. Among the dead are his own wife and child. He soon realizes it was done by white men posing as Mexicans.

By this time, the Alamo has fallen. Recognized as the man who left from there, John is almost lynched by an angry mob of Alamo sympathizers.

Put in a jail cell to protect him, Stroud is sharing it with Dawes, a member of the outlaw gang responsible for the massacre. When the gang's leader, Jess Wade, breaks Dawes out, John goes along to infiltrate the gang.

As the outlaws try to rob a wagon train, Stroud gives warning and is then shot and wounded by Wade. Beth Anders, recently evacuated from her Texas home, nurses John until he recovers.

Now leader of the wagon train, Stroud and his party defeat the outlaws in a gunfight. After killing Wade, John Stroud rides off to join Sam Houston in the fight against Santa Anna.

NOTES: *The Man from the Alamo* is the first film in color as part of the Crockett filmography. Even though the Alamo scenes were brief, they conveyed the gravity of the men under duress and fire. The Alamo set was constructed on a soundstage at Hollywood's Universal Studios.

Universal-International released the Western in August 1953. Aaron Rosenberg produced and Budd Boetticher directed it all capably (with the emphasis on the intrigue and action).

The script by D.D. Beauchamp and

Glenn Ford stands behind the line of men in *The Man from the Alamo* (the fifth face visible from the left). In that line are Stuart Randall's Bowie (center, in pale clothing, with his arm around a compatriot's shoulder) and Trevor Bardette's Crockett (in the coonskin hat next to that compatriot).

Steve Fisher was derived from a story by Niven Busch and Oliver Crawford. Elements of history were added to the fabricated story line, although a man did actually leave the Alamo.

It was not, however, Glenn Ford's John Stroud but a man named Lewis (or Moses) Rose. The real Col. Travis gave the men the chance to leave and Rose did.

There was some initial concern from the custodians of the Alamo (the Daughters of the Republic of Texas) that Rose would be the subject of the film. Although he wasn't, Rose's character was explored in at least two television shows— on an episode of *Frontier* ("The Texicans" in 1956), and on an episode of *Wagon Train* ("The Jose Morales Story" in 1960).

Longtime Western star Ford headlined *The Man From the Alamo*, with his customary stalwart screen persona. Trevor Bardette had the small role of Davy Crockett.

Just a year earlier, Bardette lent fine support as well in another film about Texas, *Lone Star*. And in the 1939 serial, *Overland with Kit Carson*, he was the villain up against Bill Elliott.

Additional notes are in the Jim Bowie and Sam Houston filmographies.

17 Davy Crockett, King of the Wild Frontier

Walt Disney Productions/Buena Vista / 1955 / 93 minutes / Technicolor

CREDITS: Norman Foster (director); Bill Walsh (producer); James Judson Cox (assistant director); Tom Blackburn (screen-play); Charles P. Boyle, Bert Glennon (photography); Chester Schaeffer (editor); Marvin Aubrey Davis (art director); Emile Kuri, Pat Delaney (set decorators); Norman Martien (costumes); Lou Phillipi, Dave Newell (makeup); Peter Ellenshaw (matte artist); George Bruns (music). Songs: "Fare-well," by Davy Crockett, George Bruns; and "The Ballad of Davy Crockett," by Tom Blackburn, George Bruns.

CAST: Fess Parker (Davy Crockett), Buddy Ebsen (George Russel), Basil Ruys-dael (Andrew Jackson), Hans Conried (Thimblerig), William Bakewell (Tobias Norton), Kenneth Tobey (Col. Jim Bowie), Pat Hogan (Chief Red Stick), Helene Stan-ley (Polly Crockett), Nick Cravat (Busted-luck), Don Megowan (Col. Billy Travis), Mike Mazurki (Bigfoot Mason), Jeff

Congressman Crockett (Fess Parker) in *Davy Crockett, King of the Wild Frontier.*

Thompson (Charlie Two Shirts), Henry Joyner (Swaney), Benjamin Hornbuckle (Henderson), Hal Youngblood (Political Speaker), Eugene Brindel (Billy), Ray Whitetree (Johnny), Campbell Brown (Bruno), and Jim Maddux and Robert Booth (Congressmen).

SYNOPSIS: Davy Crockett's journal opens with the Creek War in Alabama. Gen. Andrew Jackson wants the frontiers-man posthaste, as he is the best volunteer scout in the conflict with the Indians. Crockett is found fighting with a bear.

With friend Georgie Russel, Davy is sent by Jackson to lead Maj. Tobias Nor-ton and his soldiers on a scouting mission. The major thinks he can do better without the scouts, but is soon trapped by Chief Red Stick's warriors. Crockett and Russel, however, come to the rescue; by pretend-ing to be an entire regiment, the scouts drive the Indians off.

During a later battle against the Indi-ans, Crockett saves Russel's life. Yet Georgie returns the favor after Davy is stunned by a tomahawk blow from Red Stick.

Following a brief leave back home to Tennessee, to supply wife Polly and their two boys with provisions, Davy returns with Georgie to the Creek War. When Rus-sel is captured by the Indians, Crockett challenges Red Stick to a fight. Beating the chief, Davy Crockett promises that the In-dians can keep their land to secure the peace.

Searching for new Tennessee land for their families, Davy and Georgie come to an area being ridden roughshod over by Bigfoot Mason. First besting Mason in a shooting match, Crockett whips him in a fist fight for stealing an Indian's land. For Davy is the new magistrate.

As he is urged to run for the state leg-islature, Davy receives word that Polly has died from a fever. His sons are taken care of by his sister-in-law. Davy does win the election and is later persuaded by Andrew

Jackson to run for Congress. He becomes a congressman in Washington and Jackson becomes president of the United States.

Sent by Tobias Norton on a speaking tour of several cities to supposedly help his own future chances for president, Davy is presented with the rifle "Old Betsy" in Philadelphia. Georgie Russel informs Davy that Norton really wanted him away from Washington, so as not to interfere with Jackson's Indian bill which will take away their land. Rushing back, Davy Crockett makes an impassioned speech against the bill and then leaves his political career behind him.

To help in the fight for liberty against Santa Anna, Crockett and Russel set out for Texas. En route to the Alamo, they are joined by riverboat gambler Thimblerig and a Comanche Indian they call Bustedluck.

Chased right into the Alamo with his party by Santa Anna's Mexican soldiers, Crockett meets Col. Billy Travis and his commander, Col. Jim Bowie. Injured from an earlier fall, Bowie reveals to Crockett that they are low on food and ammunition and need reinforcements.

Risking his life to race through the enemy lines for help, Russel returns with the news that there will be none. Travis then draws a line with his sword asking the Alamo's defenders to cross it if they choose to stay and fight. Georgie and Davy cross together first and the others follow. Bowie is helped across on his cot.

In the final assault, the Mexican army pours over the fort's walls. Bustedluck is killed, then Travis and Thimblerig. Jim Bowie is slain in his quarters. Russel, mortally wounded, dies at Davy's side. As the enemy soldiers rush at him, Davy Crockett furiously uses "Old Betsy" as a club against them.

NOTES: Legend has it that Walt Disney wanted to do a Davy Crockett film as early as 1946. But other film projects were given priority for one reason or another. It wasn't until 1954 that Disney and Crockett first teamed up.

The television series *Disneyland* premiered in October '54 on the ABC network. Originally the series was made up of four separate segments (one each week)—*Adventureland*, *Fantasyland*, *Frontierland*, and *Tomorrowland*.

A three-part show that was featured on *Frontierland* began on December 15, 1954. It was called "Davy Crockett, Indian Fighter." Following it, on January 26, 1955, was "Davy Crockett Goes to Congress," and, on February 23, 1955, came "Davy Crockett at the Alamo."

The Crockett episodes, produced by Bill Walsh and directed by Norman Foster, were such an overwhelming success that they were edited into a feature film by Walt Disney Productions. Released on May 25, 1955, by the company's own distributing outfit, Buena Vista, the collective adventures became *Davy Crockett, King of the Wild Frontier*. It too was a rousing success. Youngsters all over the world took Davy to their hearts.

The commercial tie-ins with the television episodes and subsequent film were even more phenomenal. Some 10 million coonskin caps were sold to resemble what Davy wore (but like Daniel Boone, the real frontiersman may never have worn one). Tom Blackburn, who wrote the fanciful script, also collaborated with George Bruns on the equally fanciful song "The Ballad of Davy Crockett."

That song was No. 1 on the *Hit Parade* list of popular songs for 13 weeks. It sold supposedly 18 million copies. Over 20 versions of the ballad were recorded by various artists, including none other than the film's star, Fess Parker.

While Fess didn't sing the ballad in the film, he did sing another song called "Farewell" (on the night before the fall of the Alamo). It was written by George Bruns and supposedly the real Davy Crockett (based on an 1835 poem he was given some credit for writing, which was called "Farewell to the Mountains" or "His Parting Blessing").

When Walt Disney was searching for the right actor to play Davy Crockett, he was asked to take a look at James Arness playing in the 1954 sci-fi film, *Them!* Disney, however, felt Parker, in a much smaller role, was the better choice.

Both Arness, at 6 feet 7, and Parker, at 6 feet 5, were tall men with heroic-looking countenances (and they were much taller than the real Crockett at about 5 feet 10). But Disney was particularly swayed by the sincerity and charm Fess projected, and which the actor used to help make Davy so popular.

Ironically, Disney had no idea just how popular Davy Crockett would become and voiced some concern for killing him off in the initial third television episode. The way the death scene was first filmed (but never shown), Crockett was among the others who lay dead.

But Crockett's last stand at the Alamo was filmed over, this time with him swinging his rifle into immortality. This single image of Davy Crockett is perhaps the one most remembered so as to enrich both the man and the myth.

Buddy Ebsen was also considered to play Davy, but played his sidekick Georgie Russel instead. The scenes shared between Ebsen and Parker further enriched the facts and legends about the frontiersman.

It is Buddy's equally endearing Russel who sings and tells stories about Davy throughout (with the off-screen chorus also singing the ballad). Their fellowship was not the way it actually happened, yet it is the way it should have been.

In its review for the first television episode, *Variety* commented, "Parker is perfectly typed to the part with all the backwoodsy flavor and in Buddy Ebsen has a running mate who meets all the requirements for the lighter moments."

While the original television episodes were aired in black and white, they were filmed in Technicolor and thus shown in all their glory when turned into a motion picture. Location filming included sites in North Carolina and Tennessee, with magnificent vistas of the Great Smoky Mountains. Footage from some of the Disney nature films was incorporated, such as when Davy tangles with a gator.

Fess Parker promoting Disney's Crockett for *Davy Crockett, King of the Wild Frontier,* at New York's La Guardia Airport.

Arthur Hunnicutt's Davy Crockett (center) entertains his admirers in *The Last Command*. Included are Richard Carlson's Travis (dark uniform with epaulet, left) and Sterling Hayden's Bowie (tall with buckskin, near right).

The Alamo battle was done on a soundstage, like *The Man from the Alamo* before it. In fact, Disney incorporated a shot from that film into his own. And both films are available on video.

Conveyed most magnificently in *Davy Crockett, King of the Wild Frontier* is the rough and tumble frontiersman of the legends and the great spirit of the man. The sincerity, ideals, courage and humor are all part of the film's chosen path that follows the real Crockett's motto, "Be Always Sure You Are Right — Then Go Ahead."

Additional notes are in the Jim Bowie filmography.

18 *The Last Command*

Republic Pictures / 1955 / 110 minutes / Trucolor

NOTES: Main information is in the Jim Bowie filmography. Additional notes are in the Sam Houston filmography.

Released less than three months after *Davy Crockett, King of the Wild Frontier*, Republic's *The Last Command* was about the battle of the Alamo. But Jim Bowie (Sterling Hayden) was the star of this adventure, with Davy Crockett (Arthur Hunnicutt) in support. This was the reverse concept of the Disney film where Bowie (Ken Tobey) supported Fess Parker's Crockett.

Despite having a beard and looking grizzled, Hunnicutt's buckskin-clad Crockett was a mite closer in size to the real frontiersman. Yet his appearance and especially his humor were priceless and he seemed to capture the qualities of a true backwoodsman. Some writers have even given him credit with the best interpretation of Davy Crockett, although Hunnicutt was overshadowed by both Parker and later John Wayne.

Ironically, Wayne was all geared up to make an Alamo picture with Republic Pictures until he had a falling out with studio head Herbert Yates. Several similarities thus exist between 1955's *The Last Command* and 1960's *The Alamo*. Not the least are the death scenes for Crockett in each as he torches the powder magazine.

No slouch when it came to portraying frontiersmen, Arthur Hunnicutt received an Academy Award nomination (as best supporting actor) for his Crockett lookalike, Zeb, in 1952's *The Big Sky*. In 1963, he was Simon Kenton (who saved Daniel Boone's life in history) in the Boone television episodes that made up *The Great Adventure*.

19 *The First Texan*

Allied Artists Pictures / 1956 / 82 minutes / Technicolor / CinemaScope

NOTES: Main information is in the Sam Houston filmography. Additional notes are in the Jim Bowie filmography.

As with 1939's *Man of Conquest*, 1956's *The First Texan* was a biography about Sam Houston. This Allied Artists release starred Joel McCrea.

James Griffith played Davy Crockett. The role was brief, but Griffith did a commendable job making a speech.

Just the year before, Griffith had played another historical figure, Doc Holliday, in the film *Masterson of Kansas*. In 1959, he joined John Bromfield on the television show *U.S. Marshal* (formerly *The Sheriff of Cochise* from 1956 to 1958).

20 *Davy Crockett and the River Pirates*

Walt Disney Productions/Buena Vista / 1956 / 81 minutes / Technicolor

CREDITS: Norman Foster (director); Bill Walsh (producer); Ivan Volkman (assistant director); Tom Blackburn, Norman Foster (screenplay); Bert Glennon (photography); Stanley Johnson (editor); Feild Gray (art director); Emile Kuri, Bertram Granger (set decorators); Carl Walker (costumes); David Newell, Phil Sheer (makeup); Peter Ellenshaw (matte artist); George Bruns (music). Songs: "Yaller, Yaller Gold," "King of the River," and "The Ballad of Davy Crockett," by George Bruns and Tom Blackburn.

CAST: Fess Parker (Davy Crockett), Buddy Ebsen (George Russel), Jeff York (Mike Fink), Kenneth Tobey (Jocko), Clem Bevans (Cap'n Cobb), Irvin Ashkenazy (Moose), Mort Mills (Sam Mason), Paul Newlan (Big Harpe), Frank Richards (Little Harpe), Walter Catlett (Colonel Plug), Douglass Dumbrille (Saloon Owner), and George Lewis (Black Eagle).

SYNOPSIS: Following an 1810 fur-trapping expedition, Davy Crockett and Georgie Russel reach a Kentucky port on the Ohio River. They meet Mike Fink, the self-proclaimed "King of the River," and decide to take their furs to market down in New Orleans.

Fink offers to take them on his keelboat, the *Gullywhumper*, for an outrageous fee. Declining, Davy and Georgie arrange terms with Cap'n Cobb on his *Bertha Mae*.

When Georgie gets drunk, he accepts a challenge from Mike to see which keelboat can get to New Orleans first. The stakes are the furs and the "King of the River" title. Although annoyed, Davy honors the challenge.

During the river race, Mike and his crew cheat by removing a warning of rapids ahead; nonetheless, the *Bertha Mae* makes it through by Davy and his crewmembers. Despite this, Crockett helps the *Gullywhumper* to drive off Sam Mason and his river pirates.

Still cheating, Fink sabotages the

Fess Parker (left) and Buddy Ebsen in *Davy Crockett and the River Pirates.*

Bertha Mae's rudder. Georgie wants to cheat by switching rudders, but Davy stalls for time instead with Mike in a tavern until the rudder is repaired.

The *Bertha Mae* loses its lead now in the race by helping a stranded old man and his animals. To repay Davy for this kindness, he tells him of a shortcut.

Sure enough, it works and the *Bertha Mae* just wins the race. But Mike Fink is humbled and then moved by Davy Crockett's gesture that he keep his furs and Mike keep his title. The two legends become friends.

Returning upriver with Mike, Davy and Georgie are captured by Chief Red Horn's Chickasaw Indians. There is an apparent conflict going on between settlers and the Indians over riverboat attacks. Davy feels the attacks were made by the river pi-rates disguised as Indians and promises the chief to stop them.

Crockett and Russel use Mike Fink's help to flush out the culprits. Posing as a rich man, Mike takes aboard his boat a passenger named Colonel Plug.

In cahoots with Sam Mason, Plug uses a song to signal the river pirates. Davy is wise to it and has Plug bound and gagged.

In the melee that follows, the pirates (in their Indian disguises) are beaten by Crockett, Fink and their men. Going after Mason to his cave lair, Crockett defeats him in a savage fight. With Mike Fink's help, Davy Crockett has brought peace again between the Indians and settlers.

NOTES: Walt Disney knew he had a good thing in Davy Crockett and brought him back again on television and with another film.

This scene from *Davy Crockett and the River Pirates* shows (left to right) Walter Catlett, Fess Parker, Jeff York, Buddy Ebsen, and an unidentified player.

How the frontiersman was resurrected after the Alamo was easy; he just wasn't dead after all. For the new stories were not sequels but prequels, taking Davy and Georgie Russel back some three years before the Creek War setting that opened *Davy Crockett, King of the Wild Frontier.*

The two new tales, part of the *Disneyland* television program, ran under the banner title of "The Legends of Davy Crockett." They were "Davy Crockett's Keelboat Race," which aired on November 16, 1955; and "Davy Crockett and the River Pirates," which aired on December 14, 1955.

Bill Walsh again produced, and Norman Foster again directed and received a writing credit with Tom Blackburn this time. Blackburn collaborated once more with George Bruns on the songs, including

new stanzas for "The Ballad of Davy Crockett" to reflect on that other legendary figure now part of the stories, Mike Fink.

Although not as big a legend as Crockett, Mike was a real man too who became a popular folk hero. Jeff York played the "King of the River" with rascally comic splendor. Both Fess Parker and Buddy Ebsen were back as Davy and Georgie, filling their roles with broader humor than their original portrayals.

These heroes and their adventures were assuredly presented here as tall tales. While not as successful as the original episodes and their follow-up film, they were equally delightful. "Davy Crockett and the River Pirates" was even nominated in '55 for a television Emmy Award as best single program of the year (although it lost).

By the time these two episodes were edited together and released as a feature film by the Disney company's Buena Vista arm, on July 18, 1956, the Davy Crockett craze was winding down. Thus, the feature called *Davy Crockett and the River Pirates* was not as successful as the one that came before it. It can be found on video and as a DVD duo together.

But Parker and York went on to other Disney features with frontier themes in the next several years, including 1957's *Old Yeller*. The last one for Fess was in 1958, *The Light in the Forest*.

While Disney's Crockett was geared for youngsters, there were indeed quite a few realistic fighting scenes. In *Davy Crockett, King of the Wild Frontier*, the warfare against the Creek Indians and Mexican soldiers was fast and furious, with Davy clubbing them and using his knife on them. In *Davy Crockett and the River Pirates*, the frontiersman fights for his life against both a chain and torch with the pirate leader.

Yet underneath all the blazing action was Disney's simple message that Crockett's fortitude, his bravery, revolved around his attempts to treat others as he would be treated. Walt Disney was loyal to the legend of Davy Crockett as both a man of his word and a scrapper who was as rough and tumble as he had to be. The basic key to the success of the Crockett reflected here was when he was born on that mountain top in Tennessee, it was as a genuine hero.

21 *Frontier Woman*

Top Pictures / 1956 / 80 minutes / Eastman Color

CREDITS: Ron Ormond (director); Lloyd Royal, Tom Garraway (producers); Paul Piel (screenplay); Ted Allen (photography); Hugh Winn (editor); Walter Greene (music director).

CAST: Cindy Carson (Polly), Lance Fuller (Catawampus Jones), Ann Kelly (Rosebud), James Clayton (Neshoba), and Rance Howard (Prewitt).

SYNOPSIS: Polly is the daughter of the late Davy Crockett of Tennessee. She has been raised by an Indian woman whose son, Neshoba, is in love with her. An Indian girl named Rosebud loves Neshoba and is jealous of Polly, who only has feelings for him like a sister.

A trader, Prewitt, uses Rosebud's jealousy to try to steal land away from settlers. He convinces her to lead Indian attacks against them.

In the ensuing conflicts, both Neshoba and his mother are killed. Another trader, Catawampus Jones, tries to help Polly and the settlers.

Forced to fight Rosebud, Polly wins but spares her life. Rosebud then saves Catawampus from Prewitt by stopping him with one of her arrows. In love, Polly and Catawampus plan a life together.

NOTES: *Frontier Woman* (subtitled *Daughter of Davy Crockett*) was released by Top Pictures in July 1956. Producers Tom Garraway and Lloyd Royal made it in Mississippi on the Chunky River.

Ron Ormond directed Paul Piel's script on the fictional adventures of Polly Crockett, Davy's actual daughter. Cindy Carson played Polly.

This little Western film was set after Davy Crockett's death. All but forgotten, it cannot be found on video.

Margaret "Polly" Crockett was raised by her father's second wife, Elizabeth, after her own mother died from a fever-related illness when Polly was a baby. When Polly married in 1830, Davy was unable to attend the wedding.

22 *The Adventures of Jim Bowie*

ABC Television/Desilu Productions / 1956–58 / 76 Episodes / Each 30 minutes / Black and White

NOTES: Main information is in the Bowie filmography. Additional notes are in the Sam Houston filmography.

The Adventures of Jim Bowie, made by Desilu Productions, ran for two seasons on the ABC network. Scott Forbes had the title role in the television series.

The episode "A Night in Tennessee" aired on 4/25/58. Written by Tom Reed and directed by Anton M. Leader, it was a fictitious account of the first encounter between Bowie and Davy Crockett (played by George Dunn).

Set in Tennessee and before the Alamo (which was where the legends actually met), the story has Jim angry at Davy for bad-mouthing Andrew Jackson. A trio of crooks manipulate Bowie's anger in a scheme to keep Crockett from challenging Old Hickory for president of the United States.

Among Dunn's film and television appearances was a recurring role during 1958 and 1959 in another Western series, *Cimarron City* (starring George Montgomery).

23　*Alias Jesse James*

Hope Enterprises/United Artists / 1959 / 92 minutes / DeLuxe Color

CREDITS: Norman McLeod (director); Jack Hope (producer); Bob Hope (executive producer); William Bowers, Daniel D. Beauchamp (screenplay); Lionel Lindon (photography); Marvin Coil, Jack Bachum (editors); Hal Pereira, Roland Anderson (art directors); Sam Comer, Bertram Granger (set decorators); Edith Head (costumes); Joseph J. Lilley (music director). From a story by Robert St. Aubrey and Bert Lawrence.

CAST: Bob Hope (Milford Farnsworth), Rhonda Fleming (The Duchess), Wendell Corey (Jesse James), Jim Davis (Frank James), Gloria Talbott (Indian Maiden), Will Wright (Titus Queasley), Mary Young (Ma James), Sid Melton (Fight Fan), George E. Stone (Gibson Girl Fan), James Burke (Charlie), and Joe Vitale (Sam Hiawatha).

Guest Stars (unbilled): Hugh O'Brian (Wyatt Earp), Ward Bond (Maj. Seth Adams), James Arness (Matt Dillon), Roy Rogers (Himself), Fess Parker (Davy Crockett), Gail Davis (Annie Oakley), James Garner (Bret Maverick), Gene Autry (Himself), Jay Silverheels (Tonto), Bing Crosby (Himself), and Gary Cooper (Himself).

SYNOPSIS: Milford Farnsworth, a life insurance salesman, unknowingly sells a policy worth $100,000 to notorious outlaw Jesse James. The Duchess, Jesse's mistress, is the beneficiary.

To correct his blunder, Milford tries to protect the outlaw until he can get the policy back. He has no choice but to join the James Gang. Soon enough, Jesse has Milford pretend to be him so the salesman can be bumped off and then the outlaw can collect on his own policy.

But Milford avoids being killed by wearing a bulletproof vest. Switching her love to Milford, the Duchess helps him in the ensuing gun battle against Jesse and his gang. Much-needed reinforcements come to their rescue.

NOTES: Bob Hope's own production outfit, Hope Enterprises, made this mildly amusing comedy Western called *Alias Jesse James*. It was released by United Artists in the spring of 1959. Not only its executive producer, Hope was also its star.

Jesse James was broadly played by Wendell Corey, but not as much as Bob's beleaguered hero. The script was by Daniel D. Beauchamp and William Bowers, and the direction by Norman McLeod. The results were more of a half riot than a laugh riot.

But the film's highlight with its parade of guest stars, showing off their marksmanship in Bob's defense, was a real nice surprise. The cameos were a who's who of Western film and television personalities.

Included in this circle were Gary Cooper (an Oscar winner for *High Noon*), James Arness (Marshal Dillon from television's *Gunsmoke*), and none other than Fess Parker (yup, as Davy Crockett). And Hope's old pal from their *Road* pictures, Bing Crosby, even lent a helping hand.

Alias Jesse James is available on video.

24 *The Alamo*

Batjac Productions/United Artists / 1960 / 202 minutes / Technicolor / Todd-AO

CREDITS: John Wayne (director, producer); Robert E. Relyea, Robert Saunders (assistant directors); James Edward Grant (associate producer, screenplay); William H. Clothier (photography); Stuart Gilmore (editor); Alfred Ybarra (art director); Victor Gangelin (set decorator); Ann Peck, Frank Beetson (costumes); Web Overlander (makeup); Lee Zavitz (special effects); Dimitri Tiomkin (music); Paul Francis Webster (lyrics). Songs: "Here's to the Ladies," "Tennessee Babe," and "The Green Leaves of Summer."

CAST: John Wayne (David Crockett), Richard Widmark (James Bowie), Laurence Harvey (William Barret Travis), Richard Boone (Sam Houston), Frankie Avalon (Smitty), Patrick Wayne (James Bonham), Linda Cristal (Flaca), Joan O'Brien (Sue Dickinson), Chill Wills (Beekeeper), Joseph Calleia (Juan Seguin), Ken Curtis (Captain Dickinson), Carlos Arruza (Lieutenant Reyes), Jester Hairston (Jethro), Veda Ann Borg (Blind Nell), John Dierkes (Jocko Robertson), Denver Pyle (Thimblerig), Aissa Wayne (Lisa Dickinson), Hank Worden (Parson), Bill Henry (Dr. Sutherland), Bill Daniel (Colonel Neill), Wesley Lau (Emil), Guinn Williams (Lieutenant Finn), Olive Carey (Mrs. Dennison), Jack Pennick (Lightfoot), and Ruben Padilla (Santa Anna).

SYNOPSIS: Mexican General Santa Anna, in 1836, is marching north into Texas with his army and committing acts of oppression. Trying to raise his own army against the dictator, Gen. Sam Houston orders Col. William Travis to hold back the advancing enemy forces for as long as possible.

Travis decides to fortify the Alamo in San Antonio with his 27 soldiers and Col. Jim Bowie's 100 volunteers. The antagonism between the two men is furthered when Bowie protests this battle plan and Travis' dismissal of Alcalde Juan Seguin's scouting reports on Santa Anna's position.

With 23 Tennesseans, Col. Davy Crockett arrives and acknowledges to Travis the desire of Texas to fight against its Mexican rule and declare a republic. Davy later gets into a quarrel with a merchant, Emil, over a woman named Flaca. And Bowie helps Crockett defeat the thugs the merchant sends against him.

Flaca informs Davy that Emil has hidden munitions in the church. With his comrades Smitty, Beekeeper and the Parson joining him and Jim to retrieve the munitions, Davy is forced to kill Emil.

After taking the munitions to the Alamo, Crockett is urged by Travis to lie to his men about the reinforcements pending from Goliad as larger than anticipated. Crockett, with Flaca's help, has written a letter pretending it is from Santa Anna and threatening his men. Although Davy admits the letter was a ruse to get them to fight, the Tennesseans want to join up with Travis.

Having fallen in love with Flaca, Davy sends her away to safety. Soon the Mexican soldiers begin entering the town, demanding the Alamo's surrender. Travis answers with a cannon blast.

Capt. James Bonham brings news that the reinforcements are on their way, although he, following Travis' orders, lies about the additional number which will face the 7,000 Mexican troops. When the enemy threatens the Alamo with a huge cannon, it blows up Beekeeper's prized whiskey barrel.

Before the weapon inflicts serious

Richard Widmark (left) as Bowie, Laurence Harvey as Travis, and John Wayne as Crockett appear in 1960's *The Alamo*.

damage on the Alamo, Bowie sneaks off with Crockett and others to destroy it. While the mission is successful, Captain Dickinson, Travis' aide, has to go to their rescue. Young Smitty saves Jim's life.

Furious at Bowie's insubordination at risking the lives of the men, Travis threatens him with arrest. Bowie threatens to take his volunteers and leave. Crockett tries to mediate between them.

Juan Seguin arrives with 32 more volunteers from Gonzales. Bowie later receives word that his wife has been struck down by cholera. Another strike against the enemy is sanctioned by Travis with a raid for cattle. Smitty is sent to find Sam Houston.

Arriving with his main force, Santa Anna allows the Alamo to evacuate its women and children. Dickinson's wife, Sue, decides to stay with their daughter and a servant boy.

In the initial attack, the Alamo holds off the enemy. But 28 of its defenders are killed, including the Parson. Bowie receives a serious leg injury.

The report from Bonham that the reinforcements were ambushed and killed causes Davy Crockett and Jim Bowie to prepare to take their men out. However, Bowie's decision to make a last stand with Col. Travis is the catalyst for Crockett and the others to do the same.

Making it to General Houston, Smitty then heads back to the Alamo. Houston hopes Texas remembers the brave men in the Alamo and their sacrifice.

Santa Anna's army hits the Alamo from all sides and breaches the walls. William

Travis is shot, then Captain Dickinson. Both Capt. Bonham and Beekeeper are run through with swords.

Col. Crockett, mortally wounded with a lance, blows up the gunpowder with a torch. Col. Bowie had earlier freed his slave, Jethro, who now fights with him. Jethro tries to protect him but both men are bayonetted to death.

All the combatants in the Alamo are killed. Only Sue Dickinson and the two children survive and are allowed to leave. Approaching from a distant ridge, Smitty waits for them to join him.

NOTES: On September 9, 1959, Father Peter Rogers, of San Antonio's St. Mary's Catholic Church, gave a special blessing. His words were, "O, Almighty God, we ask thee that the film *The Alamo* will not only be the world's outstanding production, but will also be a tribute to the spirit of the men who first built it, who lived in it, who died in it."

This blessing was given the day filming began on John Wayne's *The Alamo*, which he produced, directed and starred for his own Batjac Productions. Wayne had hoped to make the film years earlier for Republic Pictures, but had left there over disagreements concerning production costs and other matters all relating to the film.

United Artists agreed to release *The Alamo* only if Wayne did star, instead of doing the intended guest star turn as Sam Houston (played by Richard Boone). Duke Wayne wanted Burt Lancaster to play Jim Bowie, but Richard Widmark was actually signed; as was Laurence Harvey to play William Travis rather than Charlton Heston.

When *The Alamo* was released on October 24, 1960, it was not a box office success, simply because its initial earnings of nearly $8 million would have made it a hit if not for costing $12 million to make. A 1967 rerelease and other future marketing, including on television and video, did make the film successful.

Duke Wayne and his dream film received criticism for its excessiveness, mainly in regards to its patriotic stance and speechifying. The script was by his old crony, James Edward Grant. Even so, *The Alamo* is a treasure. Wayne's heart and soul are in the film; and, while as a cohesive whole it may falter, so many magnificent images are there that will live forever. The *New York Times* reflected, "It cannot help but have certain moments and even long image crowded passages by which the audience is piercingly affected and visually overwhelmed."

The Alamo and town of San Antonio de Bexar of 1836 were stunningly reconstructed in Brackettville, Texas. Still standing on Happy Shahan's property and today a tourist attraction called the Alamo Village, they were used in other films, including 1987's *The Alamo, 13 Days to Glory* and 1988's *Alamo ... The Price of Freedom*.

Chill Wills' Beekeeper and Denver Pyle's Thimblerig were fictional characters derived from the 1836 book by Richard Penn Smith, *Col. Crockett's Exploits and Adventures in Texas* (and Hans Conried was Thimblerig in the Disney film). The boisterousness and stockiness of the Wills character may have been more in keeping with the actual Davy Crockett.

An Oscar nomination for best supporting actor was given to Wills. The film received six other nominations, including for best picture. But it won for just best sound (Gordon E. Sawyer, Fred Hynes).

While Wayne's frontiersman is full of humor and heroism perhaps more in keeping with his own larger-than-life screen persona, he is unforgettable. John Wayne stands right next to Fess Parker as the most memorable Davy Crockett.

Perhaps the most impressive thing about Wayne's interpretation is the vulnerability laid bare. Three scenes in this regard are especially captivating.

The first scene occurs after the Parson

Davy Crockett and his Tennesseans arrive at the Alamo in 1960's *The Alamo*: (left to right) Hank Worden, Frankie Avalon, John Wayne, Chill Wills, and Denver Pyle.

dies and Davy shares a tearful prayer with all his Tennesseans. The second is the night before the final battle and Wayne's Crockett is sitting in the shadows alone "just remembering." And the third is his last stand when, torch in hand, he can only fall back before the weight of the enemy and then be impaled by a lance.

The full director's cut of *The Alamo* is available on MGM/UA video. Both the film and *Davy Crockett, King of the Wild Frontier* are also in the Library of Congress.

Additional information on the film can be found not only in the Bowie and Houston filmographies, but also in the author's first book with McFarland, *The Golden Corral*.

25 *The Time Tunnel*

ABC Television / 1966-67 / 30 episodes / Each 60 minutes / Color

NOTES: *The Time Tunnel* was a science fiction television series created and produced by Irwin Allen. Although only 30 episodes were made for its one season (1966-67) on the ABC network, several of the episodes were compiled into longer versions.

The fantastic premise of the series revolved around a tunnel for time traveling built in an underground facility in the Arizona desert. Scientists Dr. Tony Newman (James Darren) and Dr. Doug Phillips (Robert Colbert) are trapped in the time tunnel, traveling both to the past and the future at crucial moments in history.

Episode 13 was called "The Alamo." Aired on 12/9/66, it was directed by Sobey Martin and written by Bob and Wanda Duncan.

In the story, Newman and Phillips land in the Alamo on March 6, shortly before its fall. They meet both Colonel Travis (Rhodes Reason) and Jim Bowie (Jim Davis), but are told that Davy Crockett was killed the day before.

The scientists try to warn Travis of the consequences to the wounded unless he evacuates them. Only when he is mistakenly brought back briefly to the tunnel's control center does Travis comprehend the severity of the situation. After he is sent back, Tony and Doug are rescued only to land in another time period.

Additional notes are in the Jim Bowie filmography.

26 *Davy Crockett on the Mississippi*

CBS Television/Hanna-Barbera Productions / 1976 / 60 minutes / Color

CREDITS: Charles A. Nichols (director); Iwao Takamoto (producer); William Hanna, Joseph Barbera (executive producers); Sid Morse (writer); Gairden Cooke, Hoyt Curtin (music).

CAST/VOICE TALENTS: Ned Wilson (Davy Crockett), Randy Gray (Matt Henry), Mike Bell (Honeysuckle/Pete/The Settler), Ron Feinberg (Mike Fink/Flatboat Sailor), Kip Niven (Running Wolf/Jake), Pat Parris (Settler's Wife/Amanda/Susie), and John Stephenson (Sloan/Andrew Jackson/Blacksmith).

SYNOPSIS: On a peace mission to the Indians for President Andrew Jackson, Davy Crockett travels with his pet bear, Honeysuckle. They are soon joined by Matt Henry, an orphan boy searching for his uncle.

Davy meets Mike Fink on a keelboat going down river. Later, Davy and Matt help Mike to recover his boat from river pirate Sloan and his two sons. Shawnee Running Wolf also helps.

Leaving Matt with Mike to take to his uncle in New Orleans, Davy Crockett departs with Running Wolf to continue his peace mission.

NOTES: Like 1981's *Daniel Boone*, the animated *Davy Crockett on the Mississippi* was made by Hanna-Barbera for CBS television and can be found on video. Initially aired on November 20, 1976, it too was part of the *Famous Classic Tales* series for children.

Ned Wilson was the voice for Crockett and Ron Feinberg for Mike Fink. Charles A. Nichols directed and Sid Morse wrote the yarn.

A tall tale and reminiscent of Disney's *Davy Crockett and the River Pirates*, the frontiersman even has a talking bear for a companion. In the many tall tales written about him, Davy did have a pet bear which he called Death Hug.

27 *Seguin*

PBS Television / 1982 / 90 minutes / Color

NOTES: The Public Broadcasting Service (PBS) made *Seguin* as part of its *American Playhouse* series. Televised on January 26, 1982, it was directed and written by Jesus Salvador Trevino.

The sensitive story told of Juan Nepomuenco Seguin (A. Martinez), a Mexican born in San Antonio who opposed Santa Anna during the Texas Revolution. His father, Don Erasmo Seguin (Henry Darrow), had invited Stephen Austin (Robert Viharo) to begin Texas colonization. Juan was a courier at the Alamo.

Explored in the film was the Tejano point of view of conflicting cultures for Juan Seguin, who later fought in the Mexican War in 1846 with Santa Anna (Edward James Olmos). *Seguin* is especially noteworthy for its awareness of the Hispanic contributions in the early struggles for Texas.

Joseph Calleia played Seguin in a smaller but still dignified role in John Wayne's *The Alamo*. And *Seguin* had a short sequence on the Alamo siege (made in Brackettville on the same site as the Wayne film).

Included in *Seguin*'s Alamo passage is the execution of several prisoners by the Mexican soldiers. There is the implication that the one with the coonskin hat might be Davy Crockett.

The National Latino Communications Center (NLCC) has made *Seguin* available on video.

Additional notes are in the Jim Bowie filmography.

28 Texas and Tennessee, A Musical Affair

Syndicated Television/Multimedia Program Distribution / 1982 / 120 minutes / Color

NOTES: *Texas and Tennessee, A Musical Affair* was a syndicated television special produced by Billy Galvin and Jim Owens. It was aired in various markets on different dates during April 1982. Lee Bernhardi directed and the writing chores were shared by Pat and Billy Galvin with Bill Oakey.

Jerry Reed hosted the show's festivities, which were a mite overdone in their tribute to Texas musical artists who made their mark in Nashville, Tennessee. Many performers were on hand to lend their talents with Reed, including Kris Kristofferson, Tanya Tucker and Jimmy Dean.

A 15-minute dramatic entry about the Alamo siege (filmed in Brackettville) featured Dean as Travis and Reed as Davy Crockett. Dean, of course, was part of the earlier *Daniel Boone* television series.

Additional notes are in the Jim Bowie filmography.

29 Amazing Stories

NBC Television / 1985–87 / 45 episodes / Each 60 minutes / Color

NOTES: *Amazing Stories* was an anthology series of unusual tales in the *Twilight Zone* mode. Steven Spielberg was the show's producer for the two seasons (1985–

87) it ran on NBC television. The 45 episodes attracted a fine selection of directors and performers.

"Alamo Jobe" was the title of the third episode which aired on 10/20/85. Michael Moore directed while John Falsey and Joshua Brand were the writers.

The story opens in 1836 and Jobe, a young Tennessean, is a messenger riding for help for Travis in the Alamo. As he leaves, Jobe sees contemporary tourists around the Alamo grounds. He soon finds himself in the San Antonio of 1986. But Jobe is determined to find his way back and deliver the message.

Kelly Reno played Jobe. Credited as Davy Crockett was Richard Young.

30 Houston: The Legend of Texas

CBS Television/J.D. Feigelson Productions/Taft Entertainment / 1986 / 180 minutes / Color

NOTES: Main information is in the Sam Houston filmography. Additional notes are in the Jim Bowie filmography.

Sam Elliott starred in *Houston: The Legend of Texas*. Televised by CBS in 1986, the film featured a short Alamo sequence which was shot in Brackettville, Texas.

The aftermath of the famous battle is seen. Davy Crockett is among the slain being taken away by the Mexican soldiers to be burned. And six Alamo survivors are executed.

31 The Alamo, 13 Days to Glory

NBC Television/Briggle-Hennessy-Carrothers Productions/The Finnegan Company/Fries Entertainment / 1987 / 180 minutes / Color

NOTES: Main information is in the Bowie filmography. Additional notes are in the Houston filmography.

The Alamo, 13 Days to Glory was televised by NBC in 1987; and the film was made on the same site as John Wayne's 1960 epic. James Arness topped the cast as

Brian Keith's Davy Crockett is bayonetted in *The Alamo, 13 Days to Glory.*

Jim Bowie, followed by Brian Keith as Davy Crockett.

It was Wayne's youngest son, Ethan, who wore the only coonskin cap, however, in this later version (as Alamo defender Edward Taylor). While Keith was much too old for his role, he did wear a buckskin jacket and conveyed the frontiersman's actual stocky look and winning humor.

In a number of scenes Keith is an engaging Davy, like when he tries to pick off Santa Anna with his rifle and then jokes about it. His storytelling just might be his strongest point though, like when he tells about Bowie's earlier heroism in fighting an adversary in a dark room.

Yet Keith's Davy Crockett is abundantly heroic as well, like when he leads the raid to sabotage the enemy cannons. During the siege, he fights frantically with his gun and knife before he is killed by a Mexican soldier's bayonet.

Brian Keith had a long and productive film and television career. He starred in the 1963 Disney sequel to *Old Yeller*, *Savage Sam*, and in the popular 1966–71 situation comedy *Family Affair*.

32 *Shelley Duvall's Tall Tales and Legends*

Showtime Cable Television / 1985–87 / Nine episodes / Each 60 minutes / Color

NOTES: *Shelley Duvall's Tall Tales and Legends* ran on the Showtime cable channel between 1985 and 1987. The nine episodes were about characters, both real and fictional, that became part of American folklore.

Not only did Duvall create and host the series (which was a follow-up to her *Faerie Tale Theatre* series), but she was its executive producer. She even starred in an episode, "Darlin' Clementine."

Episode 8, "Davy Crockett," was televised on 9/21/87. It starred a likeable and charming Mac Davis. David Grossman directed the episode, and Susan Denim, Lisa A. Bannick and Jack Carrerow were its writers.

Available on video, it is a fantasy about a boy, Ben, who uses a magical book to journey back in time to share the frontiersman's adventures and simple virtues. Davy grins a bear down, catches the tail of a comet, and rides off to Texas. Ben (Adam Carl) even helps Davy not to lose heart against President Andrew Jackson (McLean Stevenson) over the bill which will take the land away from the Indians.

33 Alamo ... The Price of Freedom

IMAX/Rivertheatre Associates/Texas Cavalcade Corporation / 1988 / 48 minutes / Color

CREDITS: Keith Merrill (director, producer); George A. McAlister (executive producer); Ray Herbeck Jr. (associate producer); Keith Merrill, George A. McAlister (script); Reed Smoot, David Douglas (photography); Ben Burtt (editing, sound design); Roger Ragland (art director); Ray Giron (set decorator); Michael Boyd (wardrobe); Greg Moon, Roland Barajax (makeup); Rick Josephsen (special effects); Merrill Jenson (music). From the book, Alamo ... The Price of Freedom, by George A. McAlister.

CAST: Casey Biggs (William B. Travis), Enrique Sandino (Antonio Lopez de Santa Anna), Merrill Connally (David Crockett), Steve Sandor (James Bowie), Derek Caballero (Juan Seguin); Don Swayze (James Bonham), Martin Cuellar (Toribio Losoya), Charley Sloan (James Allen), David Pitman (Galba Fuqua), Lee Connally (Almaron Dickenson), Clara Peacock (Susannah Dickenson), Allie Smoot (Angelina Dickenson), Alex Solis (Francisco Esparza), Eddi Solis (Gregorio Esparza), Michael Boyd (Baugh), Hans Kirsch (Gaston), Kevin

Young (Kimball), Mark Turrletta (Jimenes), Stanley Moore (Martin), Gordon Frye (Williamson), Ray Giron (Blazeby), Roger Ragland (Jameson), David Cotton (Pollard), Andrew Garcia (Torres), Pepe Arteaga (Urizza), Sergio Mireles (Cos), Elroy Barrera (Castrillon), Carlos Valdez (Amat), James F. Neill (Rose), Steve Abolt (Evans), Rudy Rodriquez (Almonte), Luis Munoz (Sesma), and Richard Reed (Sutherland).

NOTES: On March 6, 1988, the 152-year anniversary of the Alamo's fall, 75 people held a protest in San Antonio, Texas. Led by City Councilman Walter Martinez, the protest was against the opening of the film called Alamo ... The Price of Freedom.

The dissension was apparently caused over the purported lack and distortion of Hispanics in the "docudrama," which was a 48-minute version of the immortal siege. The film's story revolved around William B. Travis (Casey Biggs). While a scene had been eliminated showing an Alamo defender and a Hispanic woman flirting with each other, no additional footage was added to appease the protesters.

According to the film, nine Tejanos did give their lives in defense of the Alamo; and Juan Seguin (Derek Cabellero) is one of its famous couriers. Ray Herbeck Jr., the associate producer, defended the film and said, "There was more battle coverage of the Tejanos than there was of (Davy) Crockett."

Cast as Crockett was Merrill Connally, brother of former Texas governor John Connally. He is also the father of Lee Connally, who played Almaron Dickenson.

Convincingly conveyed by Merrill was the frontiersman's wit and political zest. Some 500 reenactors played both Mexican soldiers and Alamo defenders. One reenactor, Dave Kanawah, doubled for Connally in Crockett's final fight scenes, when the actor collapsed on the renovated Alamo Village set in Brackettville. Connally, however, recovered by the following day from the arduous task to duplicate the intense fighting.

Although *Alamo … The Price of Freedom* attested to being an authentic depiction, still certain liberties were taken with history. This included the Hollywood type of heroic death for Davy Crockett. He goes down fighting, using his rifle to keep the enemy at bay, until his head is cut with a sword and he is killed by Mexican bayonets.

Keith Merrill directed and produced the Rivertheatre Associates Presentation for Texas Cavalcade Corporation Productions. The writing of the script was shared by Merrill with George A. McAlister, from whose book the film was based. McAlister was also credited as executive producer of the film.

It was filmed in the "image maximization" process (IMAX), which utilizes a massive six-story high screen and a six-track sound system. *Alamo … The Price of Freedom* is shown daily in the Alamo IMAX Theatre in Rivertheatre Mall, just 200 steps from the historic site.

Additional notes are in the Jim Bowie filmography.

34 *Davy Crockett*

Walt Disney Television/Echo Cove Productions / 1988-89 / 5 episodes / Color

EPISODE 1: "Davy Crockett: Rainbow in the Thunder" 2 hours (Aired 11/20/88)

CREDITS: David Hemmings (director); Frank Fischer (producer); William Blinn (executive producer, script); Isidore Mankofsky (photography); Andrew Cohen (editor); Ian Thomas (art director); Chris August (set decorator); Tom Bronson (costumes); Jayne Dancose (makeup); Joel McNeely (music).

CAST: Tim Dunigan (Davy Crockett), Gary Grubbs (George Russell), Cheryl L. Arutt (Young Ory/Delia O'Connor), Richard Tyson (Lute Newhouser), Matt Salinger

(Young Andrew Jackson), Samantha Eggar (Ory Palmer), David Hemmings (President Andrew Jackson), and Johnny Cash (Elder Davy Crockett).

SYNOPSIS: On his way to Texas, Davy Crockett visits with President Andrew Jackson at the White House. They reminisce about their days in the Creek War.

In that earlier campaign of 1813, Davy was among the Tennessee volunteers with then General Jackson. Also in Jackson's army was George Russell.

Out on a scouting mission, Crockett and Russell rescued settler Ory Palmer from Indians. When the army later attacked a Creek village, volunteer Lute Newhouser, upset over the carnage caused, kidnapped Ory as a peace offering to the Indians.

Again at the White House, it is revealed that Ory is now the president's housekeeper. The older Davy tells her he lost his wife Polly some years earlier.

After the younger Ory was taken by Lute, Davy found them being besieged by the Creek Indians in a cabin. Although Lute was killed, Ory was saved by the young Davy Crockett.

NOTES: Fess Parker was asked by Walt Disney Television to reprise his role of Davy Crockett, but he turned the offer down. This was for part of a five-episode miniseries in collaboration with Echo Cove Productions and NBC television for the 1988-89 season of *The Magical World of Disney* series.

Instead of Parker, Johnny Cash took the role in the opening episode. Like Mac Davis in the earlier *Tall Tales and Legends*, Cash was a popular country singer as well as a film and television personality.

Actually, Cash played the elder Davy Crockett rendezvousing with President Andrew Jackson on his way to immortality at the Alamo. Seen in flashbacks here and in the subsequent four episodes circa the Creek Indian War is a younger Davy played by Tim Dunigan. Sidekick Georgie

Russell, played by Gary Grubbs, is also back to share in the adventures.

Davy Crockett (and also known as *The New Adventures of Davy Crockett*) bowed in November 1988. The initial episode was called "Rainbow in the Thunder."

The executive producer of the miniseries, William Blinn, developed the concept and wrote the first script. David Hemmings, who played President Jackson, directed this episode.

EPISODE 2: "Davy Crockett: A Natural Man" 1 hour (Aired 12/18/88)

CREDITS: Charles Braverman (director); Frank Fischer (producer); William Blinn (executive producer); Steven Baum, Neil Alan Levy (script); Isidore Mankofsky (photography); Andrew Cohen (editor); Ian Thomas (art director); Chris August (set decorator); Tom Bronson (costumes); Joanne Smith (makeup); Joel McNeely (music).

CAST: Tim Dunigan (Davy Crockett), Gary Grubbs (George Russell), Barry Corbin (Jimmy Crockett), Molly Hagan (Mary Ann Gibbons), Jeff Irvine (Lieutenant North), Rodger Gibson (Eyes Like Sky), Charles Andre (Zale), Stephen Dimopoulos (Hawkins), Don S. Davis (Will), and Frank C. Turner (Morton).

SYNOPSIS: While in the Creek War, Davy Crockett saves Georgie Russell's life from a grizzly bear. They find Davy's uncle, Jimmy Crockett, who had vanished 20 years earlier in an Indian raid and is now living with the Creek.

Back in the army camp, the other men are curious about Jimmy's Indian life. Believing the Creek Indians have gold hidden, a group of soldiers try to find it and are ambushed.

One of the Indians in the ambush is Logan, Jimmy's son from an Indian marriage. Other soldiers attack the Creek village for revenge. Although Georgie captures Logan, Davy lets him go free.

NOTES: "A Natural Man" was the second episode of the Disney miniseries *Davy Crockett*, and was televised in December 1988. It was directed by Charles Braverman. Neil Alan Levy and Steven Baum were the writers.

In the story, the adventures of Davy Crockett and Georgie Russell (Tim Dunigan, Gary Grubbs) in the Creek War include finding the frontiersman's missing uncle (Barry Corbin), who has been living with the Indians for years.

Crockett's Uncle James' actual 18-year Indian captivity was ended when his brothers, William and John (Davy's father), successfully negotiated for his ransom. Davy was just a boy when his uncle, a deaf mute, was freed.

EPISODE 3: "Davy Crockett: Guardian Spirit" 1 hour (Aired 1/13/89)

CREDITS: Harry Falk (director); Frank Fischer (producer); William Blinn (executive producer); Robert Sonntag, Deborah Gilliland (script); Isidore Mankofsky (photography); Edward Salier (editor); Ian Thomas (art director); Chris August (set decorator); Tom Bronson (costumes); Joanne Smith (makeup); Joel McNeely (music).

CAST: Tim Dunigan (Davy Crockett), Gary Grubbs (George Russell), Garry Chalk (Major Benteen), Jeff Irvine (Lieutenant North), Henry Kingi (Indian Chief), Evan Adams (Indian Boy), Craig Brunanski (Guard No. 1), Bill Croft (Guard No. 2), David Longworth (Rider), and Charlie Sam Jr. (Indian Warrior).

SYNOPSIS: When a large number of Creek Indians gather, the soldiers in the army camp expect an attack. According to Davy Crockett, the Indians are simply uniting for a yearly ceremony.

Sent by Major Benteen to scout out the situation, Davy and Georgie Russell come upon an Indian boy in the midst of a ritual into manhood. Initially not interfering, Davy must later save the boy from a wolf.

Afterward, Crockett takes the young Indian back to camp much to Benteen's animosity. Imprisoned, the Indian is allowed to escape by Crockett.

Soldiers then chase after the boy and run into an Indian ambush. Davy is wounded and feigns blindness so as to be able to return the Indian boy safely to his village.

NOTES: "Guardian Spirit" was the third title of the *Davy Crockett* miniseries. Although still part of *The Magical World of Disney* television show, this episode ran as a special in January 1989 on a different day than its normal time slot.

Tim Dunigan and Gary Grubbs' continuing escapades, as the noble hero and his trusty sidekick, were directed by Harry Falk. Deborah Gilliland and Robert Sonntag wrote the tale.

EPISODE 4: "Davy Crockett" A Letter to Polly" 1 hour (Aired 6/11/89)

CREDITS: Harry Falk (director); Frank Fischer (producer); William Blinn (executive producer); Paul Savage (script); Isidore Mankofsky (photography); Edward Salier (editor); Ian Thomas (art director); Chris August (set decorator); Tom Bronson (costumes); Joanne Smith (makeup); Joel Mc-Neely (music).

CAST: Tim Dunigan (Davy Crockett), Gary Grubbs (George Russell), Aeryk Egan (Aaron), Garry Chalk (Major Benteen), Jeff Irvine (Lieutenant North), Jerry Wasserman (Soldier No. 1), Ian Black (Soldier No. 2), Robin Mossley (Settler Father), Sheelah Megill (Settler Mother), Lalainia Lindberg (Settler Daughter), and Eric Bryant Wells (Volunteer).

SYNOPSIS: Scouting for the army, Davy Crockett and Georgie Russell are attacked by Creek Indians. Distracted by thoughts of wife Polly and their children, Davy's life is in jeopardy. But Georgie saves the day.

Davy tries without success to obtain leave to see his family from Major Benteen. The Creek have allied themselves with an-

other tribe, and the major needs Crockett in a planned strike against the Indians in just a few days.

In the interim, Davy volunteers to secure supplies at a nearby fort. He also hopes to get a letter for Polly to a peddler who will be traveling by the Crockett homestead.

The obstacles that confront Davy in this task include helping both an Indian woman deliver her baby and a settler repair a wagon. While he fails to send his letter, Davy Crockett makes it back in time to join the Indian strike.

NOTES: In June 1989, the fourth *Davy Crockett* episode for the Disney miniseries was televised. It was called "A Letter to Polly."

The script, by Paul Savage, touched upon the pangs felt by Davy as he missed his family while fighting in the Creek War. Harry Falk directed for the second time in a row.

In this excursion, Tim Dunigan's frontiersman faces possible court-martial charges if he fails to return in time from his quest to send his dear Polly Crockett a letter. In reality, Davy did take leave to return home to his loved ones.

EPISODE 5: "Warrior's Farewell" 1 hour (Aired 6/18/89)

CREDITS: James J. Quinn (director); Frank Fischer (producer); William Blinn (executive producer, script); Isidore Mankofsky (photography); Andrew Cohen (editor); Ian Thomas (art director); Chris August (set decorator); Tom Bronson (costumes); Joanne Smith (makeup); Joel McNeely (music).

CAST: Tim Dunigan (Davy Crockett), Gary Grubbs (George Russell), Ken Swofford (Callahan), Garry Chalk (Major Benteen), Jeff Irvine (Lieutenant North), Sherri Stoner (Amy), Prudence Wright Holmes (Mrs. Pickering), Lloyd Berry (Willard), and Clem Fox (Medicine Man).

SYNOPSIS: An Indian medicine man,

chanting on a hill above the army camp, is blamed for causing an earthquake.

In the camp, Davy Crockett works with a man named Callahan on a new weapon. It is a Ferguson Rifle to be used against the Creek.

Planning to shoot the medicine man, Callahan is kept from doing it by Crockett. In the Indian village, Davy destroys the rifle. Moved by Davy Crockett's good will, the Indians now seek peace.

NOTES: The fifth and last title of the *Davy Crockett* miniseries was "Warrior's Farewell." Like the previous episode, it too was televised in June 1989.

Executive producer William Blinn, who scripted the first episode, likewise wrote the final one. The director was James J. Quinn. All five episodes for *The Magical World of Disney* were produced by Frank Fischer in British Columbia in Canada.

While NBC gave the miniseries a strong promotion, *Davy Crockett* failed to excite the public the way the Walt Disney properties had over 30 years earlier. The newer shows still had plenty of excitement, even sentiment, yet the frontiersman may have been turned into too sensitive of a Good Samaritan for his own good.

Tim Dunigan's earlier television work included the 1983 pilot for *The A-Team*. In its review for the initial *Davy Crockett* episode, *Variety* gave the actor a compliment by saying, "Dunigan looks like he might just grow into the earthy path Fess Parker once set his boots in."

Perhaps it was just too tall of an order.

35 *Rabbit Ears—Davy Crockett*

Movies Unlimited/Rabbit Ears Productions / 1992 / 30 minutes / Color

NOTES: The animated video film, *Rabbit Ears—Davy Crockett*, was distributed in 1992 by Movies Unlimited. Just prior to its video release, it was one of 13 weekly television shows made by Rabbit Ears Pro-

ductions for Showtime. The series ran under the banner title of *American Heroes and Legends*.

Each one of the films utilized around 200 illustrations of an artist and the voice talents of a celebrity. *Davy Crockett* featured the artwork of Steve Brodner. Narrating the exploits of the frontiersman was Nicholas Cage.

36 *James A. Michener's Texas*

ABC Television/Spelling Television / 1995 / Two parts / 360 minutes / Color

NOTES: Main information is in the Sam Houston filmography. Additional notes are in the Jim Bowie filmography.

James A. Michener's Texas, ironically, was a video in 1994 before it became a television miniseries the following year. Charlton Heston narrated.

The saga's main historical characters were Sam Houston (Stacy Keach) and Stephen Austin (Patrick Duffy). The Alamo sequence was filmed in Brackettville, Texas.

John Schneider, who first rose to prominence in 1979 with television's *The Dukes of Hazzard* series, briefly portrayed Davy Crockett. While his very long hair in the role seemed a bit of a distraction, the actor nonetheless cast a handsome profile much like Fess Parker's.

The frontiersman is introduced at the end of the first part. He is one of the last Alamo defenders in line who crosses over to join William Travis (Grant Show), when the commander makes his famous line in the sand with a sword.

The line in the sand, like many of Crockett's exploits, is based on legend. Schneider's Davy shares a lively bit of banter with Jim Bowie (David Keith) when they trade quips over their legendary prowess wrestling bears and alligators.

Unfortunately, *Texas*, for as big a story as it is, doesn't allow for any fighting to the death scenes for Travis, Bowie or

Crockett. Only visualized is the horrible aftermath. An unforgettable image does have their bodies lying together, and waiting to be cremated by the Mexican soldiers on a funeral pyre.

37 *Dear America: A Line in the Sand*

HBO Television/Scholastic Productions / 2000 / 26 minutes / Color

CREDITS: William Fruet (director); Sherry Garland (script); David B. Thompson (editing); Ian Brock (production design); Dawn H. Fisher (art department apprentice). Based on Sherry Garland's book, *A Line in the Sand*.

CAST: Amy Stewart (Lucinda Lawrence), Adrian Hough (Papa Lawrence), Tamsin Kelsey (Mama Lawrence), Steven McCarthy (Willis Lawrence), Kristin Adams (Mittie Roe), and Scott Wickware (Davy Crockett).

NOTES: *Dear America: A Line in the Sand* was made by Scholastic Productions and shown on HBO television on April 10, 2000. Derived from a group of children's stories published by Scholastic Books, it was part of a series of *Dear America* specials.

Each of the specials revolved around the troubles faced by a fictitious young woman in a historical setting. This one was written by Sherry Garland (from her book) and directed by William Fruet.

Lucinda Lawrence (Amy Stewart) is a farm girl in the Texas town of Gonzales whose life is forever changed by the Texas Revolution in 1836. While the Alamo battle is the show's centerpiece, the final siege is never shown.

As played by actor Scott Wickware, Davy Crockett shares a short passage with Lucinda. A review in *Tulsa World* commented, "a mythic figure in his own time, Crockett can't be underplayed effectively; but it's the only moment that doesn't work

in this lovely little drama that's worth 30 minutes of any family's time."

38 *The Alamo*

Touchstone Pictures/Imagine Entertainment / 2004 / 137 minutes / Technicolor

NOTES: Main information is in the Sam Houston filmography. Additional notes are in the Jim Bowie filmography.

Probably until the end of time, comparisons will be made between *The Alamo* films of 1960 and 2004 (especially with their easy access on both video and DVD). While expansive, epic qualities are shared by both, the earlier film may have the edge as far as panoramic vistas and larger than life heroics are concerned. There is a far more realistic and intimate regard to history in the later film. Despite the criticism leveled at them, both have many inspiring and touching moments.

In the wake of the John Wayne classic, the Alamo entries which followed borrowed freely from the impressive sets built in Brackettville, Texas, under the supervision of art director Alfred Ybarra. But production designer Michael Corenblith's fabulous newer sets, constructed on a ranch some 30 miles west of Austin, Texas, conveyed with more authenticity the true Alamo and supposedly the town of San Antonio de Bexar in 1836.

John Lee Hancock's direction and screenplay (the latter shared with Leslie Bohem and Stephen Gaghan) was undoubtedly influenced by history and historians. While the film is a politically correct version, at the same time it seems richer in reflecting real men with flaws as they coexist with their legendary personas.

Initially, Ron Howard was slated to direct this April 9 release for Touchstone and Imagine Entertainment. Instead he opted to produce only with Mark Johnson and Brian Grazer.

The interpretation of Davy Crockett

(Left to right) William Travis (Patrick Wilson), Davy Crockett (Billy Bob Thornton), and James Bowie (Jason Patric) in 2004's *The Alamo*.

may well be the most pivotal role in *The Alamo*. "So compelling is the Crockett character," said the *Baltimore Sun*, "that audiences may wish the film was about his entire life, rather than this concluding chapter in it."

Billy Bob Thornton seems to capture the essence of Crockett's soul. While both Fess Parker and Duke Wayne's frontiersmen will never be tarnished, Thornton's portrayal just might be the most defining in presenting David the man and Davy the legend.

A delightful surprise in the film are those scenes showcasing Davy's fiddle playing. For he is at his charismatic best, whether lighting up a crowded room with joyful glee or bringing about a lull in the cannonading by the enemy with a haunting tenderness.

To remain faithful to his legend and the historians, Crockett's death is handled just right. He is among the last few men as they stand side by side to confront the enemy soldiers. Touchstone Pictures is a part of the Disney organization, and Davy is seen swinging his rifle (in a scene reflective of Parker's last stand in the earlier Disney film). Surviving the fighting, Crockett is brought before Santa Anna to beg for his life. Instead he tells the Mexican leader to surrender; then he is executed at Santa Anna's orders.

Hence, the legend of Davy Crockett is only further enriched in *The Alamo*. Although it has gone beyond the mere boundaries of king of the wild frontier. But sadly, the film's blend of myth and history was poorly received at the box office.

Three

JIM BOWIE

Biography and Overview

Like David Crockett, James Bowie was named after a grandfather of Scottish ancestry. Instead of settling in North Carolina, however, as had Davy's grandfather, Jim's settled in 1760 in South Carolina before moving on to Georgia as a farmer. Among the offspring, twin sons were born to grandfather James and his wife two years later. Their names were Rezin and Rhesa Bowie.

During the American Revolution, in 1779, Rezin was 17 and fought with Col. Francis Marion. For his daring strikes against the British, Marion was famously known as the "Swamp Fox."

Rezin received a serious cut to his hand from a British saber in the attack against the enemy in Savannah, Georgia. But his wound healed with the care of a volunteer nurse, whom he fell in love with, named Elve Ap-Catesby Jones.

By 1784, Elve and Rezin were married and had their own farm on his war service land grant of 287.5 acres in Georgia's Washington County. Twelve years later, and having moved to an area of North Carolina which became Tennessee land, and then to Kentucky, son James was born, perhaps on April 10, 1796. It was on then Terrapin Creek in Kentucky's Logan County.

Although twin girls, the couple's first-born, died as infants, a total of 10 children were born over the years. Jim Bowie was the eighth (possibly ninth) sibling. The year of birth of his brother, David, remains a mystery as to whether he was actually younger or older. When he was 17 years old, David was said to have drowned in the Mississippi River.

The exact day of Jim's birth is even considered a mystery. As would be many of his later knife fights and duels, and, like Crockett, his death at the Alamo.

The Bowies were well-off by frontier standards. By the time Jim was born, they had 200 acres of Kentucky land (and it would grow to 400). On their farm were small herds of cattle and horses. They also owned a mill and had eight slaves to help with the workload.

Like Daniel Boone in 1799, Rezin Bowie was part of the restless tide of emigration that found Kentucky too crowded and ventured into then Spanish-held Missouri. Jim was only three in February 1800 when the family, including a sister of his father's and their three brothers, traveled to Missouri staying briefly in Livingston.

Soon the Bowie family all went by flatboat on the Ohio River to live in Missouri's Twappity Bottom. It was near where the Ohio and Mississippi rivers met.

Two cabins were built and 50 acres cleared on their land concession. And, like Boone, Rezin was able to avoid the Spanish requirement for Catholic conversion in the two years or so the Bowies lived in Missouri.

Elve Bowie taught her children at home her own Christian religious beliefs and those of her husband. Barely literate when she first married, Elve taught herself to read and became the teacher for the Bowie children with their book learning as they grew. Rezin naturally taught all five of his sons the practical ways of the wilderness and how to use firearms, ropes and knives.

Jim's knowledge of things really began after the family had pulled up stakes again and moved on to Louisiana. The Bowies started making a new living there in 1803, when Jim was seven and when President Jefferson acquired the territory from the French as part of the Louisiana Purchase.

First settling on a land grant on Bushley Bayou in the county or parish of Rapides, Louisiana (30 miles from Natchez), the Bowies operated a whiskey distillery. Around six years later, they moved to the Bayou Teche in St. Landry Parish (formerly Opelousas Parish, and near the town of Opelousas). The means of livelihood there also included growing cotton and cutting timber. In 1812, a claim was made in Attakapas Parish's Bayou Vermilion (not far from Opelousas), where the prosperous timber business was continued.

The Bowies also continued to own slaves on the plantation in which they now lived. But Jim and his brothers in these years did their share of the work as well. Jim Bowie grew to be a strong 6-footer capable of any task he set his mind to, although he still preferred exploring the bayou country in his dugout canoe or fishing and hunting.

Especially close to his brother, Rezin Jr. (who was three years older), Jim early on was showing that reckless daring which helped make him famous. More than once he roped an alligator by the snout in the Bayou Teche, and then jumped on its back for a wild ride.

When bears raided the corn, Jim came up with a method to stop them. He placed honey into a hollow cypress knee and then drove spikes down into it. Putting its head in it to get the honey, any bear became stuck on the spikes trying to pull free and was an easy mark for a rifle.

In the beginning of 1815, Rezin Jr. was already married and Jim was 18 years old when they enlisted to fight the British in the War of 1812. Actually, that conflict had ended when the Treaty of Ghent was signed overseas on December 24, 1814; but the news had not yet reached American shores when militia troops were mustered to help Andrew Jackson stop the enemy advancement on New Orleans earlier in the month.

The Bowie brothers were privates in the company of Capt. Coleman A. Martin, before various militia units were merged under the command of Josiah S. Johnston. The entire group was called the Consolidated Louisiana Militia Regiment. Upon reaching New Orleans on January 24, the regiment discovered that General Jackson had already forced the British from the city on the eighth of the month. This was the very day of Jim and Rezin's enlistment.

Made part of the Second Brigade of Louisiana Militia, the Bowie brothers bivouacked upriver for two weeks and then returned and spent a month in New Orleans. Discharged on March 31, they were each paid $21.93 for their brief military service.

Sometime during 1815, Jim Bowie left home and squatted on unoccupied land in Avoyelles Parish's Bayou Boeuf. He built a cabin and supported himself by using a whipsaw to cut timber into planks, which he transported down the Bayou Boeuf to Opelousas.

In April 1817, with $300 which he saved, Bowie purchased the land he was on. He also wrote out promissory notes to purchase slaves from his father and additional timberland from various bayous.

Jim's first move into the land speculation business was in October 1818. With a partner, John Stafford, Bowie obtained more Bayou Boeuf land for a note of $1,000, planning to subdivide it for sale. Ambitious and adventurous, Bowie knew that cultivating friendships and business associations could be profitable, both financially and socially.

Nearly two years before father and son, Moses and Stephen Austin, began their 1821 colonization in Texas and before Mexico overthrew the Spanish rule there, a treaty was made between Spain and the United States that affected Texas. It would lead to an Anglo-American attempt to win an earlier Texas independence. James Bowie was part of that venture.

On February 22, 1819, the United States and Spain signed the Adams-Onis Treaty. This relinquished to Spain any prior claims the U.S. had for Texas (by the earlier Louisiana Purchase), and in turn ceded West Florida to the U.S. by Spain.

Upset over this, Dr. James Long left his home in Natchez, Mississippi, that June. He led an expedition with the intent of taking Texas back. Bowie, undoubtedly intrigued by both the adventure and Long's promise to sell Texas land for $1 an acre,

was with the expedition in Texas over the summer.

By early October, however, Jim was already back in Louisiana. So he was not with Long when Long was driven out of Nacogdoches, Texas, on the 28th of the month.

Dr. Long was behind another expedition in late 1820 to wrest Texas away from Spain. At La Bahia (and also called Goliad), he was captured by 500 Spanish troops. Taken to Mexico City, Long was still waiting for his trial in 1821 when he was assassinated.

So instead of buying land in Texas at $1 an acre, Jim Bowie was involved with slave smuggling on Galveston Island in Texas at $1 a pound. It was with the privateer Jean Lafitte and Bowie's own brothers, John (the eldest) and Rezin.

Before the American Civil War, slavery was legal in the United States, although the foreign importation of slaves had been illegal since January 1, 1808. Over 650 black slaves, taken from the Spanish by Lafitte, were kept in a barracks surrounded by high walls on Galveston Island. It was in the village of Campeachy, where Lafitte had built himself a fortress of sorts called Maison Rouge.

Jim and Rezin made their initial visit to Lafitte's base of operations in either 1818 or 1819. In 1820, the Bowies gave up slave smuggling and Lafitte shortly thereafter did the same thing.

In the interim, several smuggling trips were made by Jim to buy slaves and bring them back to the United States. John Bowie handled the business end of it in Louisiana, perhaps Alabama, with Rezin doing the same in Mississippi. Jim ended up selling everything he owned, including the Bayou Boeuf property on which he lived to his youngest brother, Stephen, to get his share of the investment money to pay Jean Lafitte.

Forty slaves at a time were brought

out and turned over to the U.S. customs officers. Bribery may have taken place to keep any suspicious officials quiet; one official, in Mississippi, may have been the brother-in-law of the Bowies' sister, Martha. Having turned the slaves over to the proper authorities, the Bowie brothers were eligible to receive half of any sales when the slaves were publicly auctioned off.

The Bowies then bought back at the auction their own smuggled slaves at a low price. Able to sell them now legally, and at a higher price, they also reaped their percentage from the previous auction sale. The profits from the "blackbirding," as the whole venture was called, were $65,000 and which the brothers split three ways.

The dangers that were faced by Jim Bowie in the previous decade, such as riding alligators, trying to usurp the Spanish law in Texas, and slave smuggling, paled before the violent contests that awaited him in the last 16 years of his life. His adventures in the 1820s and early 1830s, prior to the Texas Revolution, are part of four entries in the 26 that make up the Bowie filmography.

Perhaps 1952's *The Iron Mistress* (Warner Brothers) is the best reflection of his early life and the myths which surround it. Yet 1950's *Comanche Territory* (Universal-International) likewise reveals the legendary, even fictitious, exploits of the adventurer, as does a 1995 television miniseries, *James A. Michener's Texas* (ABC), during its first part.

The Adventures of Jim Bowie, the 1956–58 television series (ABC), was another fictional account, interspersed with facts, of his pre–Alamo days. Both the series and *The Iron Mistress* are the only entries which showcase Bowie's exploits in Louisiana, at the time he actually lived there, and his mark upon the Creole city of New Orleans.

After James Bowie sold his Louisiana property to his brother, he still lived there with Stephen and his wife. Jim made his winter quarters, however, in New Orleans where he lived lavishly off his smuggling proceeds. When that money ran out, he took out loans from friends.

When Bowie made that earlier purchase of land in 1818 with John Stafford for speculation purposes, it was later found to be a faulty property. Before they discovered this, John D. Reeves, who had sold them the property, tried to take them to court when their promissory note for the purchase came due.

What Reeves did to lure in buyers was a common enough practice among speculators. Fortunately, in Bowie and Stafford's case, they lost nothing for no money was put forth, only their note. But Bowie would learn from it and practice the same tactic during the 1820s as he tried to become a dominant force in land speculation.

Creating his grants and deeds of sale for what was first Spanish land, and the names of grantees and even witnesses, Jim Bowie proposed to claim ownership to 65,000 acres of Louisiana land. This was done with the help of squatters acting as witnesses and associates, like Robert Martin and William Wilson, who were paid by Bowie to register certain grants and pass the deeds over to him. A state since 1812, Louisiana honored all Spanish claims if filed by the end of 1820.

And Bowie did just that, forging the names of past Spanish governors for authorization. The filing of the claims was done with the registers in the district land offices. Bowie knew enough of the Spanish language to forge the needed documents, although no attempt was made to change the handwriting.

The handwriting first became suspect with register Samuel Harper in the New Orleans office. A letter of concern was sent by Harper to the secretary of the Treasury in Washington, D.C., but it was lost. Before he could survey the claims, Bowie still had to wait for approval from Congress.

By March 1823, the approval came to Bowie to begin his surveying. The first of different surveyors hired by Bowie over the years was Milo Johnson, who worked out of the Washington, Mississippi, land office. It took nearly a year for these initial surveys to be completed and returned to the land office. While fraud was suspected then, nothing was done until George Davis became the supervising surveyor of the area.

The suspicions of Davis grew as he looked more closely at the Bowie documents and conducted his investigations. Among other things found, the questionable claims covered the best areas and other residents had not even heard of the names Bowie reported as grantees.

Although he had not received any patents on the surveyed land, Jim Bowie was still able to initiate the sale of 6,431 acres with his personal bond. Anxious for the patents, Bowie went to Davis. Other discrepancies were pointed out to him, and Bowie managed to remove all his original papers from the Mississippi land office. He also removed any incriminating documents from other offices as time went on.

Having lived with brother Stephen for a few years, Jim moved to Alexandria in October 1824. The city, in Rapides, Louisiana, was closer to where most of his claims were located in the bayous above the Red River.

The General Land Office, which was the headquarters for all its office branches, was in Washington, D.C. Commissioner George Graham was in charge. Kept abreast of Bowie's activities in Louisiana, Graham believed, by the end of 1824, that Bowie was connected to perhaps nine faulty claims.

By the fall of 1825, Bowie managed to register over 8,000 more acres of faulty claims. They were with the Opelousas, Louisiana, land office.

With his surveys this time not being approved, and still none of his patents, Jim Bowie actually went to Washington to see what could be done. Bowie met with Graham in February 1826, but nothing was rectified; the approvals were being stalled through the commissioner's office.

Bowie's Washington trip wasn't a total loss for he did cultivate a friendship there with Congressman William Brent, representing western Louisiana. Back in Alexandria that spring, Jim did the same thing with an attorney named Samuel L. Wells, who had political aspirations.

Perhaps to help further his friendship with Wells, Jim may have had a romance with Samuel's cousin, Cecilia Wells. Jim was 30 years old at the time and Cecilia was 21.

Other women were linked romantically with Bowie in his past, including a bayou girl named Sibil Cade (rumored to be his first love), and Catherine Villars. A former quadroon mistress of none other than Jean Lafitte, Catherine even had a baby in 1818 with the notorious privateer.

Friends of Jim Bowie weren't the only ones involving themselves in the politics of the day. His own brothers were both elected state legislators in 1826 for their respective counties—Rezin in Avoyelles, and John for a second term in Catahoula. Sometime between 1825 and 1826, John Bowie even joined Jim in creating faulty land claims in Arkansas, perhaps as much as 60,000 acres.

While land fraud was certainly practiced by others, it just wasn't quite on the large scale of the Bowies. Nonetheless, it didn't seem to hinder Jim's own chances in the political arena. He had proven his loyalty and trust at least to his friends to warrant consideration as a possible successor to William Brent in the 1828 congressional race.

Before Bowie made the trip to look into the Arkansas land, he campaigned in Alexandria for Samuel Wells running for sheriff. Wells won the election in January 1827 against incumbent Norris Wright.

Jim's verbal attacks on Wright during the campaign brought Wright to bash Bowie, particularly on his land speculating, while he was still away in Arkansas.

In mid–December of 1826, Jim had returned to his Alexandria residence at Bailey's Hotel. Confronting Wright over his previous remarks, Jim was soon staring down at a pistol pointed at him. As Bowie tried to hit him with a chair, Wright fired the weapon.

Although struck in the left side of his chest, the powder charge wasn't strong enough for the bullet to penetrate Bowie's skin (and the shot might have been deflected by a coin in his pocket). But Jim was badly bruised and possibly had a fractured rib; even so, he knocked Wright down and began beating him with his fists and biting him. He was that mad.

Attempting to open a clasp knife with his teeth to use on Wright, Bowie realized that it gave time for his adversary's friends to pull him off and save Wright's life. Taken to his hotel room by his own friends, Jim recovered after resting for several days.

Jim Bowie made a promise to himself after that incident. For the rest of his life he would carry, in a leather scabbard on his belt, a hunting knife he could pull out in an instant.

Such a weapon was given to him by brother Rezin. There was a story that the knife had been made sometime earlier for Rezin by a Louisiana blacksmith named Jesse Cliffe. According to Rezin, however, he made the knife himself from an iron file. The blade was 1½ inches wide and 9¼ inches long; a protective crosspiece was between the blade and handle.

In the spring of 1827, Jim Bowie inadvertently allowed his surveys to go through for 17,600 acres filed in the New Orleans land office. Yet Commissioner Graham felt that Bowie may have forged a letter which prompted surveyor George Davis to give him title to the land. Graham even threatened to have the surveys rendered void with an order from the president of the United States, John Quincy Adams.

The encroaching success of Bowie with his land speculating, and Samuel Wells becoming sheriff, played a part in the culminating tension and resulting feuds that arose with their allies and Norris Wright and his allies. Petty hatreds and jealousies would escalate into a final horrendous encounter on September 19, 1827.

Near Natchez, on a sandbar along the Mississippi River, 12 men gathered for a duel between Samuel Wells and Thomas Maddox. Wells' second was George McWhorter, and his physician was Dr. Richard Cuny. Further support for Wells came from Thomas J. Wells, Samuel Cuny, and James Bowie. Maddox was joined by his second, Robert Crain, and physician, Dr. James Denny. Also supporting Maddox were Alfred and Carey Blanchard, and Norris Wright.

Wells and Maddox exchanged pistol shots twice, but neither was hit. Deciding that their honor was satisfied, they shook hands. However, Samuel Cuny remarked to Crain that they settle their own differences. Cuny and Crain drew pistols as did Bowie. Firing at each other, Bowie and Crain missed; Crain then fired another pistol, hitting Cuny in the thigh (where an artery was severed and he soon died). Bowie also fired another pistol at Crain, but again missed his mark.

With his knife now in his hand, Bowie went after Crain, who threw his empty gun hard at Bowie's head. Maddox tried to hold Bowie down and was pushed aside. McWhorter than gave Bowie a pistol; and Bowie and Wright fired upon each other but missed. As Wright fired at Bowie with another gun, McWhorter did the same thing against Wright and inflicted a superficial wound to his side. But Wright's shot hit Bowie in the chest and exited his body through a lung. Dr. Denny, who was in the way, lost a finger.

The Blanchards also opened fire, one of their shots going through Bowie's leg. Wright and Alfred Blanchard attacked Bowie with drawn sword canes and stabbed him in the hand and breastbone. Holding onto Norris Wright for support, Jim Bowie then sank his knife into Wright's chest and killed him instantly. As Bowie laid under Wright's dead body, he then cut Blanchard with his knife; Blanchard continued to stab at Bowie until Thomas Wells shot Blanchard in the arm.

The fighting was over. It only lasted 90 seconds or so but two men were killed, and Bowie was believed by all to be dead soon enough. Ironically, Robert Crain came to his side with water and helped to take him back across the river to Vidalia where Bowie's wounds were treated. Bowie didn't die, but it was nearly two months before he was well enough to leave the area. His injuries plagued him the rest of his life.

The infamous sandbar fight made the regional newspapers. It even spread to Philadelphia and New York. In January 1828, a grand jury met in Mississippi over the incident. There were no indictments. Despite the killings, frontier violence often went beyond the boundaries of the law.

While many of the entries in the Jim Bowie filmography display his legendary knife-fighting prowess, the previously mentioned *Iron Mistress* of 1952 includes the sandbar fight. It is also alluded to in 1960's *The Alamo* (Batjac/United Artists), and the 2004 film of the same title.

In November 1827, Jim moved to New Orleans. For money to live on, he was able to sell $1,200 worth of land claims. By spring of 1828, Bowie made over $33,000 in various Louisiana land sales; none of them were from his vast claims registered above the Red River with Daniel J. Sutton.

Not only were Louisiana claims selling for Jim, but the Arkansas land claims with brother John were being confirmed by the superior court, as they had to be until that territory became a state in 1836. But as Jim did in Louisiana with William Wilson and Robert Martin, he used front men and transferred titles over to them with the understanding that they would buy the land from the Bowies for special rates. Well over 50,000 acres of Arkansas land received confirmation by the end of 1827.

Although Bowie's faulty claims in both Louisiana and Arkansas were proving to be successful ventures, his support for an 1828 seat in Congress was not. Samuel Wells had died from fever, and incumbent William Brent decided to run again (but lost). Jim felt somewhat betrayed by those whom he considered his friends.

Six months or so into 1828, Bowie traveled through Texas to have a look-see at the enormous land possibilities there. Briefly stopping in a few towns, Jim ended up in San Antonio de Bexar. When Texas was still under the rule of Spain, Bexar became the capital in 1773. Yet after Mexico's takeover in 1821 and the Constitution of 1824, that ended when it became part of the Mexican state of Coahuila-Texas.

In Bexar, Jim met its one-time alcalde and perhaps still most prominent resident, Juan Martin de Veramendi. And Jim was also introduced to his lovely daughter, Ursula, who was only 16 years old. But Bowie was back in Louisiana by sometime in August, undoubtedly thinking of many things about Texas; perhaps again of the vast lands and of Ursula de Veramendi.

John and James Bowie began seeing the sales for the Arkansas land that October. In 1828 as well, Rezin Bowie Jr. bought for Jim 220 acres of Louisiana land in Bayou Lafourche. They used this land to start a sugar plantation.

By January 1829, 800 more acres had been added to the plantation. Over 70 black slaves worked on it. Equipment to run it came from selling nearly all of Jim's remaining claims that were earlier registered through Samuel Harper; now the land had earned Bowie over $50,000.

But when Bowie tried to push through his claims above the Red River that winter, he was stymied by James Turner, the official sent by Commissioner Graham to enforce more stringent regulations. These claims would then have to be taken to court by Bowie to prove their legality. Turner was even showing interest in the Harper-registered claims.

Jim Bowie returned to San Antonio in 1829. Two future possibilities were brought up with Juan Veramendi—the building of a cotton mill in Texas, and marrying Ursula (although Jim again might have had a romantic attachment to Cecilia Wells, who died that year from fever). Other matters also interested Jim on this Texas trip, including learning about the silver mine of Los Almagres in the remote San Saba region.

Searching with others for the mine, 120 miles from Bexar and in Comanche Indian country, Bowie found nothing. Los Almagres was actually further away and the mine not even operational.

When Bowie learned that James Turner could prove forgery on an original document mistakenly left behind in one of the land offices, he went to Washington, D.C., over the summer. Bowie attempted to have George Graham removed as commissioner, but it prove futile.

Not only was Turner uncovering more substantial evidence against Bowie on the Louisiana land forgeries, but Graham had another official, Isaac T. Preston, doing the same thing in Arkansas. Original claim documents found there, and somehow not removed by the Bowies, were also being proven as forgeries.

Andrew Jackson, who was now president, became aware of Preston's findings by November 1829. Arkansas was a territory of the United States, and Jackson believed that there could be legal recourse against the Bowies, whose faulty claims had grown over the years to cover over 73,000 acres (and 80,000 for Jim in Louisiana).

Meanwhile, even the sugar plantation was turning sour for Bowie. Over two dozen slaves there had died from smallpox during 1829. Creditors took Jim to court for debts over $30,000 concerning the original bayou land sold by Jean Maronges to Rezin Jr. (and given to Jim). In September, the land was sold at auction and Stephen Bowie was able to buy it back for around $600.

But Jim Bowie realized it was time to try to get away from the land speculating in both Louisiana and Arkansas before he was prosecuted for the forgeries on the land.

In January 1830, Bowie managed to

A portrait of James Bowie.

transfer what land he still had on the plantation to brothers Stephen and Rezin. However, most of the $42,000 that came from the transaction went to pay past debts; the $10,000 left was to be sent to Jim at Saltillo, the capital of Coahuila-Texas (but it never was).

Accompanied by a friend, Caiaphas Ham, Jim went back to Texas to make it his new home. As a possible colonist, under the Mexican law he had to have a reference, which he acquired from Texas merchant Thomas F. McKinney.

Bowie met Stephen F. Austin that March. Living in San Felipe, Austin provided the passports needed to later go to Saltillo. While much of Austin's control over his settlement in Texas was now under an elected council, he was still encouraging emigration.

However, the Mexican president, Anastasio Bustamente, closed the borders of Texas to further emigration from the United States on April 6, 1830. The apparent reason was the concern over the vast tide of emigrants taking over Texas and wanting it to be part of the U.S.

Bowie and Ham traveled with others into San Antonio. There Jim was welcomed once more by Ursula and her father. When Bowie spoke of the cotton mill venture again, he received a letter of recommendation from Juan Veramendi to present in Saltillo.

Received well by the members of the Mexican Congress in Saltillo, and by its prominent businessmen, Bowie was there several months cultivating friendships and furthering his goals, although some found him to be a braggart.

Two requirements were necessary before the proposal for a cotton and woolen mill was approved by the Mexican Congress—one was that Jim Bowie had to be baptized into the Catholic faith (and he was on June 26, 1828, during that initial visit to San Antonio), and the other was that he had to become a Mexican citizen (which he did on September 30, 1830, in Saltillo).

Bowie had not rated as a colonist for the grant initially of a Texas league or so of land when he came there earlier in 1830 (because of President Bustamente's edict against further emigration from the U.S.). However, Jim was free to buy land. Perhaps as much as 16 grants of land were legally committed to Bowie, of a million acres, for future use.

The Veramendi family had come to Saltillo, for Juan was to be the new lieutenant governor for Coahuila-Texas and was there to take his oath of office. Returning with the family to San Antonio that fall, Jim proposed to Ursula. While she accepted, her father wanted a statement of Jim's assets and part of it to go for his daughter's security.

Going back to Louisiana to raise as much money as possible, Bowie learned that George Graham had died. Still, Graham made sure that the new commissioner would not intentionally confirm Bowie's faulty claims. The failing sugar plantation was sold by the Bowies for around $90,000 to businessmen Robert J. Walker and James C. Wilkins; and Jim received a share from it of $16,000.

And the sale of the rest of the Samuel Harper-registered claims, and at least 24 of the Daniel Sutton-registered claims were finagled by Jim as well to Walker, Wilkins and their associates. Everything, including the plantation land, was around 70,000 acres. Jim's cash settlement of the total sales was perhaps $20,000, the rest of his share being promissory notes. The new buyers weren't about to simply give all their cash away realizing all too well the enormous risks taken.

When Bowie went back to Veramendi in Texas, assets of over $160,000 were claimed instead of the actual cash received and notes worth about $65,000. His Texas grants were excluded.

But it was enough for James Bowie and Ursula de Veramendi to be married. It happened on April 25, 1831, in Bexar's San Fernando Parish Church. The bride was 19, and the groom was 35 years old.

Ursula and James lived briefly in rented homes in Bexar, and on land given to them by her father. Yet by 1832, the couple had moved in with Juan and the rest of Ursula's family in the large one-story home on Soledad Street.

In November 1831, Juan financed a trip back to the San Saba country again looking for silver. Joining Jim were brother Rezin, Caiaphas Ham and nine others—Thomas McCashlin, Robert Armstrong, David Buchanan, James Coryell, Mateo Dias, Matthew Doyle, Jesse Wallace, and servants named Gonzales and Charles.

Journeying on horseback 100 or so miles northwest of San Antonio de Bexar, the 12 men encountered two Comanche with a Mexican captive. The Indians were friendly, and Jim Bowie informed them that it was safe to take stolen horses recovered back to Bexar.

The following day, on November 20, the Mexican captive was sent to warn Bowie's party that some 124 hostile Indians–mostly Tawakoni–were stalking them for their own horses and supplies. Not able to reach an abandoned fort near the San Saba River before nightfall, Bowie and his men camped in a dense grove of oak trees and thicket. Surrounding the area were a stream, hills and prairie.

The marauders attacked early the next morning. A dozen Indian shots opened up and Buchanan was hit in the leg just outside the campsite; and Rezin managed to carry him back. Although Buchanan was wounded twice more, none of his injuries proved life threatening. Arrows were used as well by the Indians. The defenders fought back gamely.

In the conflict, both Ham and Jim shot down chiefs. But the attackers also wounded Doyle and killed McCashlin. So far the fighting had only lasted for 20 minutes.

Later that morning, the Indians set fire to the brush and grass trying to burn the men out; the flames fortunately died out short of their mark. Yet late in the afternoon, another fire did reach the trees where Bowie and his comrades were holding off the attackers and building a breastwork of wood, dirt and stones.

The fire was put out, but it left the defenders partially exposed; Coryell had also been wounded, and Jim and the others still able to fight surrounded their injured comrades. With their backs to each other, the men were prepared to make a last stand.

Instead of attacking, the Indians only cleared their dead (21 were seen to fall by Jim) and wounded. The Tawakoni departed the next day, and eight more days were spent in camp as Bowie's party tended to the injured.

When the men did set out then for home, no other mishaps occurred, although they had to redirect their route when they came across signs of the Tawakoni. By the time they reached Bexar on December 6, Jim, Rezin and the others had been given up for dead. Stephen Bowie was among those waiting with Ursula.

In December 1831, the Bowie brothers journeyed to Louisiana. Jim's intent was to procure an installment payment from the notes due him for the previous Walker-Wilkins land sales. According to a blacksmith named James Black, Jim stopped at his shop in Washington, Arkansas, with a design for a new knife with a longer and wider blade. Supposedly having lost the knife Rezin gave him, Jim had Black make him another.

Back in Texas, Bowie assembled a company of 27 men and in late January they began searching for the Tawakoni as well as for lost silver mines. The expedition, which lasted 10 weeks, was all in vain.

Also in January, Mexican Gen. Antonio Lopez de Santa Anna started an uprising against the government under President Bustamente. Stephen Austin at the time was a member of the state legislature for Coahuila-Texas.

Santa Anna was promising a liberal government as compared to Bustamente's centralist one. There was even support for the general in Austin's own community of San Felipe. Yet Austin was wary of the political power struggle between Santa Anna and Bustamente, for he didn't want to damage any chances to repeal the president's 1830 edict stopping U.S. emigration.

Knowing of Jim Bowie's leadership in the San Saba fight and of his Texas land interests, Austin sent him to Nacogdoches that summer to help quell the political turmoil there. Bowie found in the town some 300 supporters for Santa Anna had forced the evacuation of Bustamente troops commanded by Col. Jose de la Piedras. Caught up in the furor, Bowie and 20 men with him chased after the soldiers, killed one, and ended up capturing the rest. This happened after Piedras turned over command to Capt. Francisco Medina, who then surrendered to Bowie.

This action could only inadvertently help Santa Anna, as did an earlier encounter in the spring of 1832 at Anahuac. A lawyer from Alabama, William Barret Travis, was arrested by Bustamente supporter, Col. Juan Bradburn, over a number of actions; that possibly began when Travis tried to raise a militia and go after marauding Indians (just as Bowie did earlier that year and which was against the law).

Texans or Texians (Anglo-Americans living in the Mexican state of Coahuila-Texas) rallied and finally forced Travis' release as well as that of other political prisoners. And it was the same Colonel Piedras, who then removed Bradburn from his command, whom Jim Bowie would find himself running up against in Nacogdoches.

In the fall of 1832, Juan Veramendi became governor when Jose Maria Letona, his predecessor, died. Veramendi was all too aware of the crumbling Bustamente government and worked with Bowie to have the state capital moved from Saltillo to Monclova, where the interests of Texans could be better served. One of their concerns was to separate Texas from Coahuila.

While trying to muster support in these matters, Jim met Sam Houston in San Felipe during late December. A host of reasons brought Houston to Texas, not the least was the apparent nod by President Andrew Jackson to look into the possible future annexation of Texas by the United States.

When Santa Anna fully took power on April 1, 1833, he had already expressed his loyalty to the Mexican Constitution of 1824. Abolished in part by the Bustamente regime, that document bore similarities with the U.S. Constitution of 1787 following the American Revolution.

Bowie's excursions in 1833 included another trip to Louisiana over the summer to look into his business ventures. Veramendi had sent $10,000 there perhaps to allow Jim to start buying the equipment for the anticipated cotton-woolen mill yet to be built (and which never would be). An earlier January ruling from the U.S. Supreme Court, concerning an Arkansas land deal, now ended all of James and John Bowie's faulty claims there, and also the Walker-Wilkins land sales in Louisiana.

The respective Supreme Court case that changed everything was called *Sampeyrac and Stewart v. the United States*. While Bernard Sampeyrac had been a real person, the Bowie brothers' land title using his name and sold to an unsuspecting Joseph Stewart was certainly forged. As the title was therefore invalid, Stewart lost his property rights.

In Natchez, Bowie convinced friends Samuel Gustine and William Richardson to loan him $8,000 for investing in land speculation in Texas. Before Jim could return there, however, he contracted malaria that October. Close to death, Jim even made out a will–while Ursula was included, so were the children of his now deceased brother Stephen.

Jim's beloved Ursula was with her parents in Monclova the month before when a cholera epidemic struck. Juan, along with his wife, Josefa Navarro, and daughter were among those who died. Taking the loss of his wife extremely hard, Jim turned to drinking heavily.

Jim never mentioned having any children of his own in his will. But good friend Caiaphas Ham would claim that Ursula gave birth to two children who died young.

By March 1834, Jim Bowie was back in San Antonio. His energies were again directed toward his Texas land dealings. The 15 or 16 grants (11 leagues of land per grant), obtained in 1830, were actually leased with an associate, Isaac Donoho. Although Bowie was able to sell one of the grants in 1833, Samuel Williams, an assistant to Stephen Austin, hadn't yet made the locations known for the selling of the remaining grants.

A year or so later, Bowie was appointed a land commissioner by the Monclova legislature to oversee several hundred leagues of land belonging to another entrepreneur, John Thompson Mason. As payment, Jim was to receive his own 95 leagues of land. But Santa Anna had the legislation annulled.

Having become president of all Mexico, Santa Anna was now showing his true colors as a dictator. Instead of ceding to each of the states their rights, under the Constitution of 1824, to run their respective governments (for better or worse), he, like Bustamente before him, was bent on a centralist government.

Men like Mason and Bowie were so intent in carrying out their ambitious land schemes that they defied Santa Anna. The Mexican president, aware that the Monclova legislature and the movements of the speculators were tied together, sent troops to thwart the massive speculation.

Bowie was with the Monclova militia in April 1835 and confronted the troops led by Martin Perfecto de Cos. Although no actual fighting broke out, Bowie was among those arrested the next month and sent to Matamoros. But he soon escaped.

On July 13, Jim Bowie was elected a colonel by the militia in Nacogdoches. Bowie and the militia then broke into the armory and stole weapons to arm themselves. But any expectant rebuttal from Mexican troops did not come. Less than a month before, William Travis led a volunteer force and attacked the Mexican garrison at Anahuac; the action was a violent protest against the unfair tariff and shipping duties imposed on them.

The same day that Bowie became a colonel, Stephen Austin was released from his imprisonment in Mexico City at the hands of Santa Anna. Daring to propose changes including a Texas separate from Coahuila, Austin's motives, which saw him jailed, were originally intended for a peaceful resolution. Yet after his incarceration, Austin recommended the kind of actions Bowie and Travis were demonstrating and more.

Despite the previous encounters with the Mexican forces, the first battle of the Texas Revolution was fought on October 2, 1835. Some 150 Texans defeated an equal number of enemy troops in the town of Gonzales. It was over a cannon the Mexicans wanted back; the Texans refused and used the weapon to make the enemy withdraw.

Santa Anna's General Cos marched unopposed with 500 troops into San Antonio and made his headquarters in the Alamo mission. Chosen the initial commander of the volunteer Texas forces,

Stephen Austin wanted to then make his own headquarters as close as possible to San Antonio.

As an aide-de-camp to Austin, Jim Bowie was sent to reconnoiter the area. Accompanied by Capt. James Fannin and 92 men, Jim bivouacked, instead of returning to Austin, not far from San Antonio—it was along a bend of the San Antonio River and just a few hundred yards from the mission Concepcion.

The next morning, on October 28, Bowie, Fannin and their men were soon trading gunfire with Mexican soldiers. When the prevailing fog lifted, the Texans saw they were nearly surrounded by a larger enemy force. The Mexicans had even managed to cross down river with a cannon and were facing the Texans along the bend of the river.

Using the river banks and the trees for protection, the Texans were rallied by Jim to keep cool heads and make their shots count. Repeatedly downing the artillerymen by the cannon, the Texans not only drove off their adversaries but also captured the cannon; they lost only one man, while Bowie erred in reporting that 67 Mexican soldiers were killed.

Bowie was upset with Austin for not giving him more than 92 men in the first place; perhaps if he had, according to Jim, the Texans might have been able to follow the retreating Mexicans right into San Antonio. While Austin was deemed overly cautious in his performance as general, he did allow a vote on the matter by his men, and it was decided to lay siege rather than attack the town. The rebel forces had grown to possibly 1,000 men, but General Cos' forces may have grown to around 1,400 with reinforcements. In San Antonio and the Alamo, the Mexicans also had a considerable number of cannons.

Tejano friends of Jim Bowie in town tried to help the rebels with as much information as possible about what was happening there. One of the Tejanos, Juan Seguin, was a captain in the Texas army.

When Sam Houston became the supreme commander of the Texas forces in November 1835, Austin became one of three commissioners sent to the United States to seek help for the Texas cause. Bowie was then under the immediate command of Edward Burleson in the San Antonio area.

On November 27, Burleson had Jim lead a raid of 40 men against a convoy of Mexican soldiers and pack animals approaching San Antonio. It was believed the convoy was even carrying silver and gold to pay Cos' soldiers. When Cos sent out reinforcements against Bowie, Burleson reciprocated with 100 more men commanded by William Jack. The Texans then sent the Mexicans back in defeat.

Yet there was no money found in the convoy, only grass for Cos' cavalry horses. In the "Grass Fight," as it was called, as many as 50 enemy soldiers were perhaps killed and one Texan wounded.

It is not entirely clear what Jim Bowie's role was when San Antonio and the Alamo were taken by the rebels that December. But he may have gone later in the month to San Felipe, and supposedly argued for and won a formal commission as colonel in the Texas army.

The 1,000 or so men laying siege against San Antonio had dwindled down to little more than half that number. This was due to general unrest among the troops and simply going home to care for their families.

Texan Ben Milam's rallying cry was the catalyst that enabled a few hundred of the men to attack Bexar and defeat Cos and his troops. During the fighting in town, Milam, struck in the head by an enemy bullet, died in the courtyard of the Veramendi home. After their victory, the Texans agreed to free Cos after his promise not to return to Texas (a promise he would never keep).

With the coming of 1836, the conflicts of interest had escalated between the two factions of the Texas leadership opposing Santa Anna–the provisional government and its General Council. James Robinson's council didn't want to break from the 1824 Mexican Constitution in the revolution, but Sam Houston and Jim Bowie supported Henry Smith's governorship for a full declaration of independence.

Smith, Bowie and Houston's official capacities were then encroached upon by Lieutenant Governor Robinson and his supporters. Particularly at issue was a planned expedition that January to wrest Mexican control from the port at Matamoros.

Earlier in December, Bowie received an order from Houston to raise volunteers and lead the Matamoros expedition. However, the General Council ignored Houston and elected to send instead Dr. James Grant and Col. Frank Johnson.

By January 17, Johnson and Grant nearly stripped the Alamo of supplies and men, leaving around 80 or so men there under the command of James Neill. Then, changing his mind about sending Bowie to Matamoros, Houston ordered him to San Antonio to help take the artillery and manpower on to the better defenses at Goliad. Another stipulation of Houston's was for Bowie to destroy the Alamo.

Perhaps Jim was spared an earlier death by not going to Matamoros, if only by a few days. The Grant-Johnson expedition never did achieve its goal either. Instead, Dr. Grant and 41 of his followers were killed by Mexican troops under the command of Santa Anna's general, Jose Urrea. This was on March 2, 1836, the day Texas declared its independence from Mexico and four days before Bowie's death at the Alamo.

When he first arrived with his volunteers at the Alamo on the 19th of January, Jim Bowie supported Colonel Neill. Their goal was not to destroy the mission but to build up its fortifications. Among the other men there with Bowie and Neill were James Butler Bonham and Almeron Dickenson.

On February 2, Bowie dispatched a letter to Governor Smith on the change of Houston's orders. Apparently agreeing, Smith had already dispatched Lieutenant Col. William Travis from San Felipe to go to the Alamo. Travis arrived there the day following Bowie's dispatch, and his own men a couple of days later.

Davy Crockett and his volunteers came into the Alamo just five days after Travis. When Neill then left to tend to a family emergency, he put Travis in charge. But the volunteers disagreed with this action. A vote was cast on February 12 and Jim Bowie was chosen to command.

Yet Bowie's drunken behavior to celebrate included wildly riding through Bexar and releasing prisoners. This conduct did not hold well with Travis. After he sobered up, Jim and Travis agreed to a joint command of the Alamo garrison.

Upon the arrival of the overwhelming Mexican forces beginning on the 23rd of February–and of Santa Anna–William Travis began sending his urgent dispatches throughout Texas calling for help for the much smaller band of men inside the Alamo. But the only additional confirmed help came on March 1 with 32 more men from Gonzales.

By this time, Bowie was desperately ill; his sister-in-law, Juana Navarro Alsbury, who was in the Alamo and caring for him, believed it was typhoid fever. Other women, even children, were still in the Alamo including Almeron Dickenson's wife, Susannah, and their daughter, Angelina.

Wary of his contagious condition, Bowie was placed alone in a small room near the main gate and along the south wall. It was here that he laid near death from his sickness when Santa Anna's troops came over the walls that 6th day of March and killed the Alamo's defenders. It took but 90 minutes.

James Bowie's death, like David Crockett's, is steeped in legend. Perhaps Bowie did have sufficient strength remaining in his debilitated state to fire off two pistols and wield his fabled knife one last time as the enemy came into his room. Yet it is more likely that he was so delirious that he was unaware of the shot to his head which killed him and the onslaught of bayonets which followed.

Three funeral pyres were built by the Mexican soldiers in the aftermath and the defenders of the Alamo were cremated. The fires burned throughout the rest of the day and long into the night.

Most of the titles in the Bowie filmography are included in the Davy Crockett filmography. The exceptions are again the movies *Comanche Territory* and *The Iron Mistress* along with the TNT-TV film *Two for Texas* in 1998.

In the latter, Jim Bowie supports Sam Houston as he does in other television entries–the aforementioned *James Michener's Texas*, and the CBS film *Houston: The Legend of Texas* in 1986. Republic's *Man of Conquest* in 1939, and Allied Artists' *The First Texan* in 1956 are movies that also have Jim playing a supporting role to Houston.

Bowie lends support to others in the totally fictitious Republic serial *The Painted Stallion* in 1937, and the Universal-International movie *The Man From the Alamo*

in 1953. He is also part of the fantasy of the 1966 episode of ABC-TV's *The Time Tunnel*.

The 1982 television specials, PBS' *Seguin* and the syndicated *Texas and Tennessee, A Musical Affair*, are included in the filmography because they have segments which focus on the Alamo; as well as footage from the Jim Bowie film adventure *The Last Command*. Also included are episodes of the CBS-TV series *You Are There* from 1953 and 1971 which focus on the Alamo.

Beginning with Star Film's silent *The Immortal Alamo* in 1911, Bowie has only a supporting role in the Alamo films right up to the 1955 film for Walt Disney, *Davy Crockett, King of the Wild Frontier*. Between these two entries are other silent pictures–State of Texas' *The Siege and Fall of the Alamo* in 1914, Fine Arts/Triangle's *The Martyrs of the Alamo* in 1915, and Sunset's *Davy Crockett at the Fall of the Alamo* in 1926–and in the sound era, Sunset/Columbia's *Heroes of the Alamo* in 1937, and National's *The Fall of the Alamo* in 1938.

Following Republic's *The Last Command* in 1955, however, Bowie had more starring roles. Not only did he star in his own television series, *The Adventures of Jim Bowie*, in 1956–58, but was featured more prominently in all the remaining Alamo films. Along with *The Alamo* of 1960, they are NBC-TV's *The Alamo, 13 Days to Glory* in 1987, IMAX's *Alamo … The Price of Freedom* in 1988; and Touchstone/Imagine's *The Alamo* in 2004.

Jim Bowie Filmography

1 *The Immortal Alamo*   1911
2 *The Siege and Fall of the Alamo*   1914
3 *The Martyrs of the Alamo*   1915
4 *Davy Crockett at the Fall of the Alamo*
   1926

5 *The Painted Stallion*   1937
6 *Heroes of the Alamo*   1937
7 *The Fall of the Alamo*   1938
8 *Man of Conquest*   1939
9 *Comanche Territory*   1950

1 *The Immortal Alamo*

Star Film Company / 1911 / 1,000 feet / Silent / Black and White

NOTES: Main information is in the Davy Crockett filmography. Additional notes are in the Sam Houston filmography.

As *The Immortal Alamo* remains a lost film, a thorough cast listing is unavailable. However, a small number of stills apparently have withstood the test of time.

One still, also credited as being from 1914's equally lost *The Siege and Fall of the Alamo*, depicts a fallen Crockett and another man (possibly Bowie) on a cot as the Mexicans attack.

While both the actors portraying Crockett and Jim Bowie remain a mystery, William Clifford portrayed William Travis in *The Immortal Alamo*.

2 *The Siege and Fall of the Alamo*

State of Texas / 1914 / Silent / Black and White

NOTES: Additional notes are in both the Crockett and Houston filmographies.

Like *The Immortal Alamo*, *The Siege and Fall of the Alamo*, made three years later in 1914, is a lost silent film. No complete credits exist and only one cast member is known.

A synopsis does exist under this title, but it may very well be a different lost film. It begins with Mexican troops entering San Antonio in 1836. Colonel Travis rushes to have James Bonham, Davy Crockett and Jim Bowie bring their separate details of rebels into the Alamo garrison.

The enemy is at first repulsed by the men inside the Alamo. But under Santa Anna's command, the Mexicans come over the walls and the garrison is wiped out. Crockett meets his death fighting in the stockade. Shooting down a few of the Mexican soldiers from his cot, Bowie is then shot and killed.

3 *The Martyrs of the Alamo*

Fine Arts Company/Triangle Film Corporation / 1915 / 5 Reels / Silent / Black and White

NOTES: Main information is in the Crockett filmography. Additional notes are in the Houston filmography.

Legendary filmmaker D.W. Griffith was credited as supervisor of *The Martyrs of the Alamo* in 1915. Yet he was actually more occupied making the film *Intolerance*, for release the following year.

A.D. Sears, who played Davy Crockett in the Alamo film, was in that year's Griffith classic, *The Birth of a Nation*. Alfred Paget, who was James Bowie, worked on *Intolerance* and other later films for Griffith.

During their time together at the Alamo, Paget's Bowie and Sear's Crockett share an engaging argument over their respective choice of weapons. In the fatal battle, Crockett is seen fighting to the death against the Mexican soldiers. Bowie, stricken with consumption to his cot, dies with two bayonets in his chest. Before he goes, Bowie kills a soldier with his knife.

Prints of this silent film do still exist.

4 *Davy Crockett at the Fall of the Alamo*

Sunset Productions / 1926 / 6 Reels / Silent / Black and White

NOTES: Main information is in the Davy Crockett filmography.

Bob Fleming portrayed Colonel Bowie in 1926's *Davy Crockett at the Fall of the Alamo*. It was the last film during the silent era about Bowie and Crockett.

A real cowboy, Fleming's Western film appearances included a few talkies. One of them was in 1930, *The Lone Star Ranger*, where he lent support to George O'Brien (who some six years later starred in RKO's *Daniel Boone*).

Initially thought a lost film, parts of the silent about the Alamo and its heroes exist. After Travis (Joseph Rickson) makes his legendary line in the sand for the defenders to cross over to his side, he and Crockett (Cullen Landis) help the ailing Bowie to walk over.

Around 68 years later, Crockett and Travis aid him in a similar way to cross the line in *James A. Michener's Texas*. In the previous silent entry, *The Martyrs of the Alamo*, Jim Bowie staggers over on his own to join his comrades.

5 *The Painted Stallion*

Republic Pictures / 1937 / 12-Chapter Serial / Black and White

NOTES: Main information is in the Kit Carson filmography. Addition notes are in the Davy Crockett filmography.

This serial from 1937, *The Painted Stallion*, was the first film entry in the sound era with Jim Bowie. However, the tale was completely fictitious.

Jim and Kit Carson are part of a wagon train bound for the American Southwest and being protected by a mystery rider. In on the ensuing action as well is Davy Crockett.

Playing Jim was Hal Taliaferro, whose sturdy support in a heap of Westerns was remarkable. Formerly known as Wally Wales, the actor's work included roles in 1935's *The Miracle Rider* (with Tom Mix), and 1948's *Red River* (with John Wayne).

6 *Heroes of the Alamo*

Sunset Productions/Columbia Pictures / 1937 / 75 minutes / Black and White

NOTES: Main information is in the Davy Crockett filmography. Additional notes are in the Sam Houston filmography.

As did the first Alamo silent back in 1911, this initial Alamo talkie of 1937 focused more on the actual Dickenson family. The deaths of James Bowie, David Crockett and William Travis are rather low-keyed in *Heroes of the Alamo*.

Embodied by Roger Williams, Bowie is a reserved and withdrawn man. Yet even he cannot fail to be moved the night before the Alamo's last stand, when his comrades sing "The Yellow Rose of Texas." Although not actually composed at the time of the 1836 siege and battle, the song served to reflect on the camaraderie shared by the defenders.

When Travis (Rex Lease) draws his line on the ground, he uses the musket of James Bonham (Lee Valianos). Helpless on his cot, Bowie calls for assistance and is carried over by four others.

This is the only Alamo film in which the Mexican soldiers realize the danger of getting too close to Jim Bowie's knife. They merely stand in the doorway to his room and he is then shot down.

Williams, like Hal Taliaferro before him, had supporting roles in many Western films. His own work included parts in

J. R. Klumpp (on horse) as Jim Bowie in *The Fall of the Alamo* (retitled on video as *Alamo: Shrine of Texas Liberty*).

the serials *Zorro Rides Again* in 1937 and *The Lone Ranger Rides Again* in 1939.

Sadly, the merits of *Heroes of the Alamo* were overshadowed by its faults. The story and acting seemed to suffer more because of the poor production values.

Scenes from the movie were nonetheless also used in the Cecil B. DeMille-supervised production, *Land of Liberty*. A pictorial account of America, this latter film was made in 1939 for both the San Francisco Exposition and the New York World's Fair.

7 *The Fall of the Alamo*

National Pictures / 1938 / 2 Reels / Partial Silent / Black and White

NOTES: Main information is in the Davy Crockett filmography.

1938's *The Fall of the Alamo* was filmed in San Antonio, Texas. And local talent was recruited for the cast.

One J.R. Klumpp played Bowie. Sterling Waters, who was Crockett, had to remind both the producer and director, during the filming of the line drawn by Travis (Coates Gwynne), that Jim Bowie was carried over on his cot.

As the film remained lost for years, Waters couldn't remember whether any death scenes were even made for Crockett or Bowie.

8 *Man of Conquest*

Republic Pictures / 1939 / 97 minutes / Black and White

NOTES: Main information is in the Houston filmography. Additional notes are in the Crockett filmography.

While the Alamo segment was indeed short in this Sam Houston film, it nonetheless was quite effective. Its depiction of the defenders was simply as citizens who have united.

Travis, Bonham, Crockett and Bowie are all together inside the Alamo when they receive word to blow it up. After Travis (Victor Jory) makes a suggestion to hold it instead against the enemy forces, all the other men come together in unison to defend the Alamo.

Robert Armstrong's Jim Bowie is already sick at this point. Although his death is not actually seen in the film, Bowie dies with Travis and Crockett inside the chapel.

Especially memorable was Armstrong as Carl Denham in 1933's *King Kong* and *Son of Kong*–and as Max O'Hara in 1949's *Mighty Joe Young*.

9 *Comanche Territory*

Universal-International Pictures / 1950 / 76 minutes / Technicolor

CREDITS: George Sherman (director); Leonard Goldstein (producer); John F. Sherwood (assistant director); Oscar Brodney, Lewis Meltzer (screenplay); Maury Gertsman (photography); Frank Gross (editor); Bernard Herzbrun, Richard H. Riedel (art directors); Russell A. Gausman, Joseph Kish (set decorators); Yvonne Wood (costumes); Bud Westmore (makeup); Frank Skinner (music). From a story by Lewis Meltzer.

CAST: Maureen O'Hara (Katie Howard), MacDonald Carey (James Bowie), Will Geer (Daniel Seeger), Charles Drake (Stacey Howard), Pedro De Cordoba (Quisima), Ian MacDonald (Walsh), Rick Vallin (Pakaneh), Parley Baer (Boozer), James Best (Sam), Edmund Cobb (Ed), Glenn Strange (Big Joe), and Iron Eyes Cody (Indian).

SYNOPSIS: In Texas, during the 1820s, adventurer James Bowie is attacked by Comanche Indians. Helping Bowie, Daniel Seeger receives a bullet in the shoulder. Soon both men are taken captive.

Comanche chief Quisima then saves Dan and Jim from being killed by the Indians. After Jim shows the Indians how to make the Bowie knife, the chief agrees to a treaty renewal and allowing silver mining on their land.

Having actually come from Washington, D.C., with the government treaty, Dan admits it was stolen from him. While in the town of Crooked Tongue with Jim, Seeger also realizes it was businesswoman Katie Howard who shot him and not the Indians.

Katie and her brother, Stacey, want to monopolize the silver mining interests in the area. Pretending to be a buyer, Bowie is seduced by Katie to buy from them.

In the Comanche village, Bowie tries to maintain peace over the stolen treaty. Yet he is forced into a fight with Quisima's son, Pakaneh.

Jim is able to convince Katie that the treaty will bring prosperity to everyone. But Stacey has it and deceives the Comanche Indians into turning over their guns.

Both Jim and Dan go to warn the Indians that Stacey and his cohorts are planning to kill them for the silver. Unarmed and defenseless, the Indians are saved when Katie returns their weapons in a wagon.

In the ensuing fight with the Indians, Stacey's men are defeated. Stacey attempts to get away, but Jim Bowie chases and captures him.

NOTES: The first Jim Bowie film in color was *Comanche Territory*, released in April 1950. Veteran Western director George Sherman helmed the Universal-International picture, and Leonard Goldstein was the producer. *The Bowie Knife* was its working title during production.

Although Bowie actually had problems with Indians in Texas, the tale told here was all made up. Lewis Meltzer conceived

Comanche Territory features Will Geer (left), MacDonald Carey, and Maureen O'Hara.

the story idea and wrote the script along with Oscar Brodney. The *New York Times* felt the proceedings were "painfully transparent goings-on." Yet the newspaper also thought MacDonald Carey portrayed Bowie with "admirable restraint."

Carey made for a sophisticated and stalwart hero; and he even fights barechested with his knife against a Comanche brave. A real eyeful, however, was beautiful Maureen O'Hara as a wildcat of a lady. Complete with guns and buckskins, she was sort of like a female version of the real Jim Bowie.

No slouch to Westerns, Carey was effective too playing bad guys. The year before *Comanche Territory*, he made a strong showing as the bandit in *Streets of Laredo*. In 1951, he portrayed Jesse James in *the Great Missouri Raid*.

10 *The Iron Mistress*

Warner Brothers Pictures / 1952 / 110 minutes / Technicolor

CREDITS: Gordon Douglas (director); Henry Blanke (producer); Oren Haglund (assistant director); James R. Webb (screenplay); John Seitz (photography); Alan Crosland Jr. (editor); John Beckman (art director); George James Hopkins (set decorator); Marjorie Best (wardrobe); Gordon Bau (makeup); Max Steiner (music). Based on Paul I. Wellman's novel, *The Iron Mistress*.

CAST: Alan Ladd (Jim Bowie), Virginia Mayo (Judalon de Bornay), Joseph Calleia (Juan Moreno), Phyllis Kirk (Ursula de Veramendi), Alf Kjellin (Philippe de Cabanal), Douglas Dick (Narcisse de Bornay), Tony Caruso (Bloody Jack Sturdevant), Ned Young (Henri Contrecourt),

Opposite page: Poster art for the Jim Bowie adventure *Comanche Territory*.

George Voskovec (James Audubon), Richard Carlyle (Rezin Bowie), Robert Emhardt (General Cuny), Donald Beddoe (Dr. Cuny), Harold Gordon (Andrew Marschalk), Gordon Nelson (Dr. Maddox), Jay Novello (Judge Crain), Nick Dennis (Nez Coupe), Sarah Selby (Mrs. Bowie), Dick Paxton (John Bowie), George Lewis (Colonel Wells), Edward Colmans (Juan de Veramendi), David Wolfe (James Black), Stanley Fraser (Al Blanchard), and Roger Cole (Carey Blanchard).

SYNOPSIS: In 1825, Jim Bowie lives with his mother and brothers, Rezin and John. From their home in Bayou Sera, Louisiana, Jim travels to New Orleans to sell the family lumber.

In the city's French-oriented society, Jim meets artist James Audubon. An influential family, the de Bornays, take offense when the artist prefers to paint birds rather than the lovely Judalon de Bornay.

Going to Audubon's defense, Jim is then challenged to a duel by Narcisse, Judalon's brother. But Jim's choice of snowballs as weapons amuses Narcisse and they become friends.

Narcisse is concerned for Jim when he falls in love with his spoiled sister. Another suitor, Henri Contrecourt, challenges Bowie to a duel over Judalon's honor. Interceding in Jim's behalf, Narcisse is killed by Contrecourt.

Bowie then faces Contrecourt in a dark room armed only with a knife. Despite his adversary's skill with a sword, Jim is the victor and avenges Narcisse's death.

Selling the lumber business, Jim returns to his family and begins a cotton-growing enterprise. His rival is Juan Moreno, who soon loses a lot of money to Bowie betting on a horserace. Foreseeing trouble, Jim has a stronger knife made by blacksmith James Black.

Although she has married the weak Philippe de Cabanal, Judalon plans a divorce and will possibly marry Moreno. Yet Jim is still in love with her. Fighting breaks out with Bowie and his friends opposing Moreno and his supporters. Jim is wounded but kills Moreno with his new knife.

Judalon promises to leave her husband and join Jim in Texas, if he helps free Philippe from a gambling debt. Bowie succeeds by defeating gambler Bloody Jack Sturdevant in a knife fight when he cuts his arm. Afterwards, Judalon decides not to go with Jim.

Traveling to Texas, Jim Bowie is waylaid by Sturdevant's henchmen, whom he also defeats. Injured, Jim is forced to leave his knife behind when he is taken away and nursed by Ursula de Veramendi, the daughter of the vice governor of San Antonio.

Jim proposes to Ursula, who feels he is still smitten with Judalon. Planning to return to Ursula, Jim journeys by riverboat back to sell his Louisiana property; on board he runs into Judalon and her husband. Once again Bowie helps Philippe when he is cheated by gamblers.

When Judalon threatens to leave him for Jim, Philippe goes to Bowie's cabin to kill him. But Jack Sturdevant is there instead with Bowie's knife. Both men end up killing each other.

Leaving Judalon, Jim drops his knife into the river. He returns to Texas and marries Ursula.

NOTES: Although short in stature, Alan Ladd seemed the epitome of a romantic and dashing film hero. He was handsome, athletic and conveyed a reserve and melancholy aura that enhanced his mystique.

Certainly such was the case with his gunfighter in 1953's *Shane* and for his knife fighter in *The Iron Mistress*. Ladd's role as Jim Bowie in the latter film was his first in a contract with Warner Brothers, the studio which released the motion picture on November 19, 1952.

Produced by Henry Blanke and directed by Gordon Douglas as a conventional Western, the film especially set itself apart with its fierce action and an unforgettable score by Max Steiner. The romanticized scenario was written by James R. Webb from Paul I. Wellman's novel of the same name.

Wellman's book takes Bowie right to his death in the Alamo. The film, however, ends with his marriage to Ursula de Veramendi (Phyllis Kirk) in Texas.

The femme fatale seemingly behind every fight in the movie, Judalon de Bornay (Virginia Mayo), may or may not have existed. That family name apparently was not included in any census of the period. The same rule of thumb applies to the villainous Bloody Jack Sturdevant (Tony Caruso).

Legend has it that Jim Bowie went to the rescue of the son of the governor of Mississippi in 1829. The young man had been cheated out of his money playing cards by a John (or Jack) Sturdivant in a gambling den in Natchez. The money was won back by Bowie, who was then challenged by Sturdivant to a fight. Bowie and Sturdivant's left hands were tied together; with their free hands they fought with knives until Bowie disabled his opponent. A variation of this is in the film, as is a riverboat confrontation over gambling.

Among the other legends about Bowie is one set on the riverboat *Rob Roy* in 1835. Again he was aiding another being cheated in a card game. The gambler who challenged Bowie this time was none other than Jean Lafitte's son, John. A duel with pistols ensued and Lafitte was killed. One of the problems with this story was that Jean's son was named Pierre.

Alan Ladd's Jim Bowie in a terrific publicity pose for *The Iron Mistress.*

Perhaps the most memorable aspects of *The Iron Mistress* were its also mythicizing the creation of the Bowie knife and the sandbar fight. Here James Black (David Wolfe) forges the blade with its double-edged point from a piece of meteor. Ladd's Bowie has a sword protruding from his chest in the sandbar incident; and he kills, not Norris Wright, but an unsavory fellow named Juan Moreno (Joseph Calleia).

Well aware of the legends being played for all their worth was the *New York Times*. Part of the paper's review of the film included this passage: "The early career of Bowie is thoroughly fabled and carpentered into a biography of the sort of hero who is most conveniently played by Alan Ladd."

Jim Bowie (Alan Ladd, left) has just defeated Bloody Jack Sturdevant (Tony Caruso) in *The Iron Mistress.*

While the previous Bowie entry, *Co-manche Territory*, is available on video, sadly *The Iron Mistress* is not.

11 *You Are There*

CBS Television / 1953 and 1971 / Each 30 minutes / Black & White and Color

NOTES: Additional notes are in the Davy Crockett filmography.

"What sort of a day was it? A day like all days filled with those events that alter and illuminate our times ... and you were there."

These words were spoken by host Walter Cronkite at the end of each episode of the television series, *You Are There.* Its over-four-year run on Sunday evenings between 1953 and 1957 included the episodes "The Defense of the Alamo" in 1953

and "The Gunfight at the O.K. Corral" in 1955.

From 1971 to 1973, the series was revamped with new episodes on Saturday afternoons which were geared for children. The 1971 episode "The Siege of the Alamo" included the scene where William Travis draws the line for his comrades to cross. It was acted out in the small quarters of Jim Bowie.

12 *The Man from the Alamo*

Universal-International Pictures / 1953 / 79 minutes / Technicolor

NOTES: Main information is in the Davy Crockett filmography. Additional notes are in the Sam Houston filmography.

The Alamo siege was a short segment at the film's beginning. The rest of the film then went on to tell the tale of *The Man From the Alamo*.

Stuart Randall's Jim Bowie and Arthur Space's Bill Travis share a friendly banter with each other in the Alamo sequence, unlike some other films which reflect the intense rivalry between Travis and Bowie. The latter is also depicted here with a slave named Sam in the Alamo.

While there was a story in which Jim saved a slave years earlier from being whipped by an abusive owner, and then freed the black man, it was Travis who apparently had a slave with him during the actual battle. He was a young man named Joe; and he survived the ordeal along with Susannah Dickenson and other noncombatants.

Both Susannah and Joe later claimed that Bowie was killed as he laid so sick upon his bed that he couldn't even lift his head. While this may be so, by their own accounts they were not with him in his quarters when death came.

Supporting player Randall made appearances in many Westerns over the years, including in two films in which frontiersman Jim Bridger was a character. They were 1951's *Tomahawk* and 1953's *Pony Express*.

13 *Davy Crockett, King of the Wild Frontier*

Walt Disney Productions/Buena Vista / 1955 / 93 minutes / Technicolor

NOTES: Main information is in the Crockett filmography.

"Davy Crockett at the Alamo" was the final episode of the original *Disneyland* television trilogy and was aired in early 1955. That spring the three episodes were edited into the motion picture *Davy Crockett, King of the Wild Frontier*.

On Stage 1 of the Walt Disney Studios in California, a football field-sized replica of the Alamo, complete with walls and courtyard, was constructed. But the famed chapel seen in the film was actually a matte painting created by scenic artist Peter Ellenshaw.

When Fess Parker's Davy Crockett rides into the Alamo with his companions, he discovers from Col. Billy Travis (Don Megowan) that Col. Jim Bowie (Kenneth Tobey) is still in command. This despite his ailing from an earlier fall (not filmed). Bedridden, Jim touchingly reveals to Davy the demoralizing conditions in the Alamo and how having the legendary Crockett there can only bring encouragement to the other men.

In a moment that recalls *The Martyrs of the Alamo*, Crockett and Bowie share a bit of humor over their famous weapons. Of course, these would be "Old Betsy" the rifle and the Bowie knife, which is referred to by Davy as the Arkansas toothpick.

As with Crockett, Bowie dies a hero's death. When the Mexican soldiers break into his room, he fires two pistols from his bed and flails his knife.

Ken Tobey was also in Disney's *Davy Crockett and the River Pirates* the following year as Mike Fink's sidekick, Jocko. As frontier figure Bat Masterson, he was seen alongside Burt Lancaster's Wyatt Earp in 1957's *Gunfight at the O.K. Corral*.

14 *The Last Command*

Republic Pictures / 1955 / 110 minutes / Trucolor

CREDITS: Frank Lloyd (director, associate producer); Herb Mendelson (assistant director); Warren Duff (screenplay); Jack Marta (photography); Tony Martinelli (editor); Frank Arrigo (art director); John McCarthy Jr., George Milo (set decorators); Adele Palmer (costumes); Bob Mark, Ann Gilliam (makeup); Howard and Theodore Lydecker (special effects); Max Steiner (music). From a story by Sy Bartlett. Song: "Jim Bowie," music by Max

Steiner, lyrics by Sidney Clare and Sheila MacRae, and sung by Gordon MacRae.

CAST: Sterling Hayden (Jim Bowie), Anna Maria Alberghetti (Consuela), Richard Carlson (William B. Travis), Arthur Hunnicutt (Davy Crockett), Ernest Borgnine (Mike Radin), J. Carrol Naish (Santa Anna), Ben Cooper (Jeb Lacey), John Russell (Lieutenant Dickinson), Virginia Grey (Mrs. Dickinson), Jim Davis (Ben Evans), Eduard Franz (Lorenzo de Quesada), Otto Kruger (Stephen Austin), Russell Simpson (The Parson), Roy Roberts (Dr. Sutherland), Slim Pickens (Abe), Hugh Sanders (Sam Houston), Morris Ankrum (Juan Bradburn), Vincent Padula (General Cos), Don Kennedy (Bonham), Cheryl Callaway (Dickinson Child), Edward Colmans (Seguin), and Pepe Hern (Seguin's son).

SYNOPSIS: Texas is part of the Republic of Mexico in the 1830s when Jim Bowie arrives in Anahuac. He is informed by young Jeb Lacey of the oppression being forced upon the American settlers by President Santa Anna.

As a spokesman for the settlers, William Travis has been arrested by the Mexicans. But Bowie helps to get Travis released. Jim and Lorenzo de Quesada are both Mexican citizens. The latter cautions Travis and another, Mike Radin, on their militia activities against the Mexican government.

Quesada's teenage niece, Consuela, wonders why Jim didn't take a stand against Radin and Travis. Yet Bowie is forced into a knife fight with Radin and beats him. In doing so, Bowie earns Radin's respect.

Homeward bound, Bowie is taken by Mexican soldiers to Santa Anna who is his friend. Jim then learns the plague has killed his wife and children. While Santa Anna frees another political prisoner, Stephen Austin, he has General Cos and the Mexican troops secure the town of San Antonio. Austin, like Travis, wants to fight the Mexicans.

As the Texas militia confront Cos and his soldiers, Jim leads a small party of men against enemy reinforcements and defeats them. Still the question of whether Bowie's allegiance is fully to Texas' breaking with Mexico almost causes a fight with Travis.

With Santa Anna leading his troops against the Texas rebels, Jim is elected by the men to command. He chooses Travis to share it. Davy Crockett arrives with 29 more men and they all move into the Alamo.

Meeting with Santa Anna, Jim refuses to have the rebels give up their weapons and surrender. In the ensuing bombardment from Santa Anna against the Alamo, Bowie is among those injured and cared for by Consuela and other women. Although feeling she loves Jim, Consuela is actually loved by Jeb.

When it is realized that reinforcements are not coming to their aid against the larger enemy forces, Travis, now in sole command, has the men cross a line to declare who will stay and fight to the death. Bowie is able to walk across with his comrades. Dispatched with a letter for Sam Houston, general of the Texas forces, Jeb is also given a letter from Jim to continue trying to win Consuela's love.

The Mexican troops break through the Alamo's defenses. Both Radin and Travis are shot down. Crockett sets off an explosion killing several of the enemy but also himself. Another gallant defender killed is Lieutenant Dickinson, whose wife and child are in the Alamo. The injured Jim Bowie rises from his bed to fight and kills several more enemy soldiers before he is overpowered by their bayonets.

Jeb reaches General Houston, and so do the women of the Alamo. As Consuela cries, Jeb comforts her.

NOTES: Additional notes are in the Crockett and Houston filmographies.

In the early 1950s, John Wayne was the biggest star at Republic Pictures. Sterling Hayden was another of its big stars, and his Westerns for the studio included 1954's *Johnny Guitar* and 1955's *The Last Command.*

Wayne initially wanted to do a film about the Alamo at Republic and even had James Edward Grant work on a screenplay. But Wayne left the studio when he and its head man, Herbert Yates, couldn't agree on location filming and production costs. Still Yates, apparently holding some control over Grant's scenario, had Sy Bartlett do a story treatment and Warren Duff a screenplay.

Elements of the Grant script were thus retained when Yates made his own Alamo picture to spite Duke Wayne. This includes the antagonism between Jim Bowie (Hayden) and William Travis (Richard Carlson); and the courier Jeb Lacey (Ben Cooper) can be compared to Smitty (Frankie Avalon) in the later Wayne film with United Artists.

In the spring of 1955, Herb Yates began production on *The Last Command*; its events leading up to the final blazing battle all revolved around the main character of Bowie. Other working titles for the film included *The Texas Legionnaires* and *Men Who Dared.*

Near Brackettville, Texas, on the ranch of Louis Hobbs (and not far from where Wayne made *The Alamo*), a partial replica of the Alamo's walls and palisade was built. Back in Hollywood, a part of the chapel was also constructed; and as with *Davy Crockett, King of the Wild Frontier*, a matte painting was used to view the entire chapel.

After *The Last Command* premiered on August 5, 1955, the Disney Crockett merchandise craze was still going on. But it didn't help make audiences rush to see another Alamo rendering with a different Davy Crockett on hand. Republic spent some $2 million to create its own account of the heroic Texas stand.

The film was director Frank Lloyd's

Sterling Hayden's Jim Bowie in *The Last Command*. The knife was the same one used by Alan Ladd in *The Iron Mistress*.

last (and he was also its associate producer). Yet second unit director William Witney was largely responsible for staging the impressive Alamo battle, making do with around 400 extras.

Liberties were taken with the overall dramatic presentation of the film as a whole. Bowie never helped free Travis from jail in the town of Anahuac, nor was he a close friend of Santa Anna. J. Carrol Naish's portrayal of the dictator was the first to regard him with a bit of dignity rather than as a one-dimensional villain.

Some criticism was perhaps unfairly leveled against Sterling Hayden for what was deemed a stiff performance. *Variety*'s review said, " part of Bowie calls for a fearless, strong, shrewd type and Hayden fulfills these qualities admirably...."

Dying in his bed in previous pictures, Bowie here finds the resolve to stand and confront his enemies. It is an unforgettable moment as Hayden, even taller than the real Jim Bowie, dominates the scene with his presence.

The Last Command is available on video.

15 *The First Texan*

Allied Artists Pictures / 1956 / 82 minutes / Technicolor / CinemaScope

NOTES: Main information is in the Houston filmography. Additional notes are in the Davy Crockett filmography.

Jeff Morrow costarred as Jim Bowie in the Sam Houston film of 1956, *The First Texan*. Along with Morrow and James Griffith as Crockett, William Hopper played Travis and Dayton Lummis was Stephen Austin.

Morrow made his film debut in an earlier CinemaScope motion picture in 1953, *The Robe*. The actor was also a regular on the 1957-58 television series *Union Pacific*.

16 *The Adventures of Jim Bowie*

ABC Television/Desilu Productions / 1956–58 / 76 Episodes / Each 30 minutes / Black and White

CREDITS: Lewis Foster (director, producer, writer); Louis F. Edelman (executive producer); Ken Darby (music). Additional directors: George Archainbaud, Anton M. Leader, Hollingsworth Morse, and Christian Nyby. Additional writers: Albert Beich, Lee Berg, John Dunkel, Orville H. Hampton, Polly James, Tom Kilpatrick, Tom Reed, Arthur Ripley, Maurice Tombragel, and Don Ullman. Songs: "Jim Bowie" and "Natural Man, Jim Bowie," by Ken Darby.

CAST: Scott Forbes (Jim Bowie), Peter Hanson (Rezin Bowie), Minerva Urecal (Maw Bowie), and Robert Cornthwaite (John James Audubon).

EPISODES/AIRDATES:

Season 1 (1956-57)
1 "The Birth of the Blade" (9/7/56)
2 "The Squatter" (9/14/56)
3 "An Adventure with Audubon" (9/21/56)
4 "Deputy Sheriff" (9/28/56)
5 "Trapline" (10/5/56)
6 "Broomstick Wedding" (10/12/56)
7 "Natchez Trace" (10/19/56)
8 "Jim Bowie Comes Home" (10/26/56)
9 "The Ghost of Jean Battoo" (11/2/56)
10 "The Secessionist" (11/9/56)
11 "Land Jumpers" (11/16/56)
12 "The Select Females" (11/23/56)
13 "Jim Bowie and His Slave" (11/30/56)
14 "Outlaw Kingdom" (12/7/56)
15 "The Swordsman" (12/14/56)
16 "The Return of the Alciblade" (12/21/56)
17 "Monsieur Francois" (12/28/56)
18 "A Horse for Old Hickory" (1/4/57)
19 "The Beggar of New Orleans" (1/11/57)
20 "Osceola" (1/18/57)
21 "Master at Arms" (1/25/57)
22 "Convoy Gold" (2/1/57)
23 "Spanish Intrigue" (2/8/57)
24 "Bayou Tontine" (2/15/57)
25 "German George" (2/22/57)
26 "An Eye for an Eye" (3/1/57)
27 "The Captain's Chimp" (3/8/57)
28 "Jackson's Assassination" (3/15/57)
29 "Rezin Bowie, Gambler" (3/22/57)
30 "Thieves' Market" (3/29/57)
31 "The Pearl and the Crown" (4/5/57)
32 "The General's Disgrace" (4/12/57)
33 "The Lottery" (4/19/57)
34 "The Intruder" (4/26/57)
35 "Country Cousin" (5/3/57)
36 "The Bound Girl" (5/10/57)
37 "The Bounty Hunter" (5/17/57)
39 "Gone to Texas" (5/24/57)

Season 2 (1957-58)
39 "Epitaph for an Indian" (9/6/57)
40 "Flowers for McDonogh" (9/13/57)
41 "The Irishman" (9/20/57)
42 "Counterfeit Dixie" (9/27/57)
43 "Bullet Metal" (10/4/57)
44 "The Quarantine" (10/11/57)
45 "A Fortune for Madame" (10/18/57)
46 "House Divided" (10/25/57)

47 "The Whip" (11/1/57)
48 "The Pearls of Talimeco" (11/8/57)
49 "Charivari" (11/15/57)
50 "Hare and Tortoise" (11/22/57)
51 "The Bridegroom" (11/29/57)
52 "The Alligator" (12/6/57)
53 "Country Girl" (12/13/57)
54 "Mexican Adventure" (12/20/57)
55 "Silk Purse" (12/27/57)
56 "Choctaw Honor" (1/3/58)
57 "The Close Shave" (1/10/58)
58 "Pirate on Horseback" (1/17/58)
59 "Curfew Cannon" (1/24/58)
60 "Home Sweet Home" (1/31/58)
61 "Deaf Smith" (2/7/58)
62 "Ursula" (2/14/58)
63 "Apache Silver" (2/21/58)
64 "A Grave for Jim Bowie" (2/28/58)
65 "Up the Creek" (3/7/58)
66 "The Lion's Cub" (3/14/58)
67 "Horse Thief" (3/21/58)
68 "Jim Bowie, Apache" (3/28/58)
69 "The Brothers" (4/4/58)
70 "Patron of the Arts" (4/11/58)
71 "Bad Medicine" (4/18/58)
72 "A Night in Tennessee" (4/25/58)
73 "Bowie's Baby" (5/2/58)
74 "The Cave" (5/9/58)
75 "Man on the Street" (5/16/58)
76 "The Puma" (5/23/58)

Scott Forbes and an unidentified actress in *The Adventures of Jim Bowie.*

NOTES: Additional notes are in the Crockett and Houston filmographies.

Desi Arnaz and Lucille Ball's Desilu Productions made *The Adventures of Jim Bowie* for ABC-TV. The two seasons and 76 episodes the series aired were from September 7, 1956, to August 29, 1958.

Derived from a novel on Bowie by Monte Barrett, *The Tempered Blade*, the show's executive producer was Louis F. Edelman. The wishful thinking of both Edelman and its star, Scott Forbes, was to duplicate the success of the Disney Crockett television episodes earlier on. While the Bowie series had its merits, including a strong hero and equally strong themes to explore (even racism was dealt with), the legendary Jim Bowie never reached the same heady heights of popularity as did Davy Crockett.

Forbes, who had appeared with Errol Flynn in 1950's Western film, *Rocky Mountain*, initially believed that Edelman wanted someone else–like John Derek–to play Bowie. Winning the part, Scott boned up by reading other books about the frontiersman and played him with an exciting brashness. A sort of Western swashbuckler (which was also evident in the earlier *Iron Mistress*). Like other television Western shows, such as *The Adventures of Kit Carson*, Jim Bowie here was often seen too as the kind of selfless hero who helped those in distress.

The Adventures of Jim Bowie takes his life from Louisiana in the late 1820s to Texas in the early 1830s. He is a rich planter and

Scott Forbes with unidentified performers in *The Adventures of Jim Bowie.*

bold adventurer. Jim's brother Rezin was played by Peter Hanson, and Minerva Urecal was their mother. Robert Cornthwaite was Bowie's friend, the painter John James Audubon. Rezin, Mrs. Bowie and Audubon were also represented in *The Iron Mistress* (and played respectively by Richard Carlyle, Sarah Selby and George Voskovec).

Among the other recurring characters in Bowie's life seen in the series were Peter Mamakos as Jean Lafitte, Chuck Connors as Cephas (not Caiaphas) K. Ham, and Sidney Blackmer as Juan de Veramendi. Ursula de Veramendi was portrayed by Eugenia Paul.

Lewis Foster directed the entire first season of shows, and was also involved as a producer and writer. The unaired pilot, called "The Tempered Blade," was written and directed by Foster as well. It dealt with

Forbes' Bowie challenging a Frenchman (Maurice Marsac) to a duel for kidnaping his servants.

"The Birth of the Blade," the initial episode aired, was written by Dan Ullman from a story by Foster. Walter Sande guest starred as Samuel (not James) Black who comes out of retirement as a blacksmith to forge Bowie his knife. A number of the Bowie episodes are available on DVD or video, including the pilot and very first show and the aforementioned episode in the Crockett filmography.

Also on video are "Apache Silver" and "Jim Bowie, Apache." Written by Maurice Tombragel and directed by George Archainbaud (during the second season), these episodes deal with Bowie's quest for the San Saba silver mine.

One of the main differences between this television series and the others with their Western heroes, was that Jim Bowie carried a knife at his side and not a six-gun. The knife was originally used more during the action scenes until protests came in fearing kids would try to imitate his stunts. Thus Bowie's action with the blade was seriously (pardon the pun) cut back.

17 *The Alamo*

Batjac Productions/United Artists / 1960 / 202 minutes / Technicolor / Todd-AO

NOTES: Main information is in the Davy Crockett filmography. Additional notes are in the Sam Houston filmography.

John Wayne's *The Alamo* dealt with a number of plot devices, some good, some bad, but all of which culminated in its final battle footage. Both Wayne and second unit director Cliff Lyons must be commended for the awesome dynamics realized when the Alamo's defenders fight their way into immortality. The single most attractive attribute of the entire film is William H. Clothier's cinematography.

Perhaps the best recurring theme, prior to the battle, was the rivalry between Jim Bowie (Richard Widmark) and William Barret Travis (Laurence Harvey). Bowie wants to blow up the Alamo and use hit-and-run tactics against Santa Anna while Travis decides to fortify the Alamo. Ironically the two sequences which highlight guerrilla warfare–the mission to destroy a cannon and the raid for cattle–are both successful.

History reflects that both Travis and Bowie united to build up the Alamo's meager defenses; their differences were over who was to command. In *The Alamo*, it is Bowie who is the first to walk to Travis' side (although there is no drawn line to cross like in other films). That the two men, opposed bitterly to each other prior to this event, are now together makes for a moving scene.

Davy Crockett (John Wayne) and Jim Bowie (Richard Widmark) in 1960's *The Alamo.*

Widmark's "knife fighting adventurer," as he is referred to by Travis in the film, was the most angry depiction of Bowie at that point in 1960. But the real Jim Bowie was equipped with a raging temper when pushed to the edge.

While the performance by the actor is a powerful one, sometimes the histrionics tend to be a bit overwhelming. The death of Bowie's wife by cholera is depicted during the siege instead of actually earlier in time; likewise *The Last Command* has her dying during the time leading up to it.

Colonel Bowie's own death in the film (as he lies injured), has him expiring with his ex-slave Jethro (Jester Hairston). Not only does Bowie fight with pistols and knife, but with a shotgun that takes down several of the enemy at one time.

For 1961's Western *Two Rode Together* (with James Stewart), Richard Widmark returned to the Brackettville, Texas, location where *The Alamo* was filmed.

Highlights from the latter figured into a television special as well. Hosted by John Wayne, *The Spirit of the Alamo* was televised by ABC on November 14, 1960, to

The death of Jim Bowie (Richard Widmark) in 1960's *The Alamo*.

coincide with the film's release. In addition to scenes being utilized, showcased were musical and comedy tidbits involving the actual cast members.

18 *The Time Tunnel*

ABC Television / 1966-67 / 30 Episodes / Each 60 minutes / Color

NOTES: Additional notes are in the Davy Crockett filmography.

The scientists played by Robert Colbert and James Darren always seemed to just escape the worst possible fates as they journeyed in *The Time Tunnel*. The initial episode of the television series in 1966, "Rendezvous with Yesterday," was about the *Titanic*.

"The Alamo" episode, also from 1966, used footage from *The Last Command* for

the battle scenes. Jim Davis, who played Alamo defender Ben Evans in that earlier movie, was now Jim Bowie in the television show.

Davis is probably best remembered as patriarch Jock Ewing (between 1978 and 1981) on the television series *Dallas*.

19 *Seguin*

PBS Television / 1982 / 90 minutes / Color

20 *Texas and Tennessee, A Musical Affair*

Syndicated Television/Multimedia Program Distribution / 1982 / 120 minutes / Color

NOTES: Additional notes are in the Crockett filmography.

Both of these 1982 television presentations, *Seguin* and *Texas and Tennessee, A Musical Affair*, included segments on the historical aspects of the Alamo battle. Along with the filming which took place on Duke Wayne's original *The Alamo* site, footage was also used for both from the Jim Bowie film *The Last Command*.

21 *Houston: The Legend of Texas*

CBS Television/J.D. Feigelson Productions/Taft Entertainment / 1986 / 180 minutes / Color

NOTES: Main information is in the Houston filmography. Additional notes are in the Crockett filmography.

In the 1986 television movie *Houston: The Legend of Texas*, Jim Bowie (Michael Beck) first encounters Sam Houston (Sam Elliott) aboard a riverboat playing cards. Bowie is bound for Texas.

During the assault by the Texans to take San Antonio away from the Mexicans, Bowie is seen fighting with the men. A brief yet imposing segment after the Alamo battle includes Beck's Bowie lying dead and being dragged away by enemy soldiers.

After his appearance in this film, Beck became one of the *Houston Knights* in that series (during 1987 and 1988 and also for CBS-TV) about a couple of contemporary Texas cops.

22 *The Alamo, 13 Days to Glory*

NBC Television/Briggle-Hennessy-Carrothers Productions/The Finnegan Company/Fries Entertainment / 1987 / 180 minutes / Color

CREDITS: Burt Kennedy (director); Bill

Sam Houston (Sam Elliott, left) and Jim Bowie (Michael Beck) in *Houston: The Legend of Texas*.

Finnegan, Pat Finnegan, Sheldon Pinchuk (producers); Stockton Briggle, Richard Carrothers, Dennis D. Hennessy (executive producers); Clyde Ware, Norman McLeod Morrill (writers); John Elsenbach (photography); Michael N. Knue (editor); Ward Preston (production design); Eileen Kennedy (costumes); Byrd Holland, Rick Jones (makeup); Rick Josephson, Lynn Maugham (special effects); Peter Bernstein (music). Based on Lon Tinkle's book, *13 Days to Glory: The Siege of the Alamo*.

CAST: James Arness (Jim Bowie), Brian Keith (Davy Crockett), Alec Baldwin (William Travis), Raul Julia (Santa Anna), David Ogden Stiers (Colonel Black), Jim

Metzler (James Bonham), Tom Schanley (Daniel Cloud), Fernando Allende (Almonte), Kathleen York (Susannah Dickinson), Isela Vega (Senora Cos), Gene Evans (John McGregor), Michael Wren (Juan Seguin), Jon Lindstrom (Lieutenant Dickinson), Hinton Battle (Joe), David Sheiner (Louis Rose), Noble Willingham (Dr. Pollard), Eloy Casados (Gregorio), Tony Becker (George Taylor), Thomas Calloway (James Fannin), Ethan Wayne (Edward Taylor), Laura Martinez-Herring (Elena Musquiz), Tom Everett (Major Evans), Buck Taylor (Colorado Smith), and Lorne Greene (Sam Houston).

SYNOPSIS: During festivities in San Antonio, Col. William Travis rides in from the nearby Alamo. With Davy Crockett, Travis meets with co-commander Jim Bowie. Travis and Bowie disagree on the position of Santa Anna's opposing Mexican army of 4,000 men. Crockett clarifies that the American settlers invited into Mexico should fight for their rights. Yet only around 150 men are there to fight Santa Anna.

Just 10 miles away with most of his troops, General Santa Anna informs his officers that he will not go around San Antonio but will confront the rebels against him. One of the general's officers is an Englishman, Colonel Black.

When the enemy soldiers are sighted, young Daniel Cloud sounds the alarm. As the Alamo is being fortified by Travis, Crockett volunteers to defend its most vulnerable point at the picket fence. Lieutenant Dickinson brings Susannah, his wife, and their baby into the Alamo.

Maj. James Bonham arrives with word that Col. James Fannin will be coming to the Alamo's aid with reinforcements. As the commander in chief, Sam Houston, is nowhere to be found, Fannin has taken command. Travis dispatches Bonham to find Houston.

In the ongoing arguments that arise between Bowie and Travis, Crockett tries

to mediate. As Bowie is now in the Alamo, Santa Anna moves into his home in town. Cannon fire is exchanged between the opposing factions.

Susannah Dickinson gives to Travis a flag to fly, and a reminder to Santa Anna of the promise of the Mexican Constitution of 1824 allowing immigrant settlement in Texas. Santa Anna scolds Colonel Black for voicing his opinions.

Having taken a fancy to a local senorita, Santa Anna marries her as his soldiers make an assault on the Alamo. After the enemy is pushed back, Travis and Bowie blow up nearby ruins that are used by the Mexicans for cover.

Courier Juan Seguin brings a small number of reinforcements into the Alamo and goes for more help. But James Bonham fails to get help from Gen. Sam Houston. Houston doesn't have an army ready to come to the Alamo's defense.

Standing behind a recoiling cannon, Jim Bowie is knocked off a wall and badly injured. Realizing his need for the bedridden Bowie, Travis is given encouragement from Joe, a black servant whose life he once saved.

Waiting for his cowardly brother-in-law to arrive with the remaining forces, Santa Anna receives encouragement. It comes from his brother-in-law's wife, Santa Anna's own sister, Senora Cos.

Setting out for the Alamo, Colonel Fannin returns to Fort Defiance discouraged over disabled wagons and stubborn oxen. Bonham reminds Fannin of his word to help the Alamo but to no avail.

Travis reads to Bowie a letter he sends out as a call for help. Bowie is moved by the inspired words.

Davy Crockett leads a nighttime raid to sabotage the enemy cannons. When Santa Anna learns of it, he takes his frustration out on his officers.

Courier Colorado Smith returns with the last of the Alamo's reinforcements. Also word is brought that a Texas convention will vote for independence from Mexican rule.

After Bonham rides in with the news that neither Houston nor Fannin are coming, Colonel Travis draws a line in the sand desiring those who will fight to cross. All do except for Louis Rose. Bowie is carried over.

The Alamo's 181 defenders are surrounded by Santa Anna's forces. Twice the enemy is repulsed. But in the next assault, the Mexican soldiers break through and kill them all.

Dickinson and Bonham fall together. Crockett falls in the courtyard near the chapel. Travis dies brandishing both his sword and pistol. Rising from his bed, Bowie meets death protecting the women and children.

In the aftermath, Santa Anna rides into the Alamo and wishes to dip his fingers in the blood of Bowie, Crockett and Travis. Joe, Susannah and her daughter, and a few other women and children are allowed to leave and tell the story of the fall of the Alamo.

Crockett (Brian Keith, left) and Bowie (James Arness) in *The Alamo, 13 Days to Glory.*

NOTES: Additional notes are in the Crockett and Houston filmographies.

In the summer of 1986, the cast and crew of *The Alamo, 13 Days to Glory* began filming at the Alamo Village in Brackettville, Texas. Just wrapping up there was the company for *Houston: The Legend of Texas.*

Stockton Briggle, one of the executive producers (along with Richard Carrothers and Dennis D. Hennessy), seemed to be the guiding light for this Alamo film made for NBC-TV. The source for writers Clyde Ware and Norman McLeod Morrill was the book by Lon Tinkle, *13 Days to Glory: The Siege of the Alamo.*

Yet like all the other Alamo depictions before it, liberties were taken with the film. Both Jim Bowie (James Arness) and Davy Crockett (Brian Keith) are far too old here. The real Bowie and Crockett were 39 and 49 respectively at that moment in history. The death of William Travis (Alec Baldwin) comes late during the final battle instead of historically much earlier on.

But Keith's humor and Arness' overwhelming presence more than compensate for the age differences. As with *The Alamo*'s Richard Widmark, Bowie here is a drinker and there is a running antagonism with Travis.

Bowie's final scene is reminiscent of Sterling Hayden's in *The Last Command*— with the frontiersman getting to his feet to fight. "The horrible death of Bowie is played down," said *Variety*, —"in this version he's surrounded by Mexican soldiers like Roman Senators putting away Caesar."

An old hand at directing Westerns, Burt Kennedy made the most of the budget restrictions, which were apparent. While several shots are repeated, the last battle overall is captivating. An Emmy nomination went to John Elsenbach for his photography.

The Alamo, 13 Days to Glory is available on video. Unfortunately after the initial telecast on January 26, 1987, it came in 32nd in the ratings. Footage from *The Last Command* is included.

James Arness is to television Westerns what John Wayne is to cinema Westerns: they are giants who convey the fortitude and spirit of the American frontier. Ironically, Wayne had Arness under a film contract in the 1950s and introduced him for the opening episode in 1955 of *Gunsmoke*. So memorable an impression has Jim made in that 20-year television series it is easy to believe the character of Marshal Matt Dillon might really have lived.

Published by McFarland and written by the actor with James E. Wise Jr. is a book —*James Arness: An Autobiography*.

23 *Alamo ... The Price of Freedom*

IMAX/Rivertheatre Associates/Texas Cavalcade Corporation / 1988 / 48 minutes / Color

NOTES: Main information is in the Davy Crockett filmography.

The battle fought in 1988's IMAX presentation, *Alamo ... The Price of Freedom*, takes place just before dawn when it is still dark, just as it was in history on that fateful March morning in 1836. Both *The Alamo, 13 Days to Glory* and *Davy Crockett, King of the Wild Frontier* began the final

assault when it was dark but finished the battle in the daylight.

While reenactors did double duty as both Texas rebels and the Mexican army, professional actors were cast in the more prominent roles. Steve Sandor was Jim Bowie. And here Bowie is sick and drunk and played in a raspy, coarse manner.

When the enemy soldiers come into his room, Bowie fires only a single pistol before being cut down. He is then carried above them on their bayonets. This last act is not actually shown only the shadows thrown against the wall.

Sandor's acting career included appearances in a 1968 episode of television's *Gunsmoke* and the 1978 miniseries *Centennial*.

24 *James A. Michener's Texas*

ABC Television/Spelling Television / 1995 / 2 Parts / 360 minutes / Color

NOTES: Main information is in the Sam Houston filmography. Additional notes are in the Davy Crockett filmography.

David Keith is one of the most charismatic Jim Bowies in either the cinema or television. The boldness, charm and physical appearance all come together and capture fully the mythic proportions of the frontiersman.

He is first introduced chained to a log and dueling to the death with his knife against another man. It is a riveting scene as is a later fight against two men.

While Keith's Bowie was a larger part than John Schneider's Crockett, in 1995's miniseries of *James A. Michener's Texas*, it was still smaller than Patrick Duffy's Stephen Austin or Stacy Keach's Houston. Instead of any related tension over command at the Alamo with Travis, as in some other depictions, Jim Bowie is seen quarreling with Austin over the latter's early command of the Texans.

Along with Bowie's legendary knife

fighting, emphasized was the heavy drinking attributed to the man. Other than perhaps *The Iron Mistress*, the Bowie knife has never been better realized as a weapon of both deviltry and beauty.

Among the numerous acting performances from Keith was another memorable one, as Richard Gere's tragic comrade, in 1982's *An Officer and a Gentleman*.

25 Two for Texas

TNT Presentation/Bleecker Street Films Production / 1998 / 96 minutes / Color

NOTES: Main information is in the Houston filmography.

This concocted tale, set in 1836, focuses on a pair of escaped convicts (Kris Kristofferson, Scott Bairstow) bent on joining up with Sam Houston (Tom Skerritt). In Houston's camp just before he leaves for the Alamo is Jim Bowie (Peter Coyote). He is seen suffering from consumption.

Coyote's acting credits included the part of Keys, who befriends young Elliott and his mother in 1982's *E.T. The Extra-Terrestrial*. In 1998's cable film for TNT called *Two for Texas*, Coyote shares a jim-dandy of a scene with Kristofferson, whose character just happens to be an old friend of the knife fighter's.

In fact, the *New York Times* called it "the best scene in the movie," as Kristofferson and Coyote sit around a campfire and raucously entertain the crowd with tales about wrestling gators and playing poker with the pirate Jean Lafitte.

After the Alamo's fall (only the aftermath is seen), Jim Bowie's body is found in the infirmary. His knife is still in its scabbard.

26 The Alamo

Touchstone Pictures/Imagine Entertainment / 2004 / 137 minutes / Technicolor

NOTES: In *The Alamo*, Jason Patric's Jim Bowie and Patrick Wilson's William Travis agree the fort should not be destroyed and the cannons removed, unlike the 1960 film, where Richard Widmark's Bowie and Laurence Harvey's Travis were at odds over the matter. But contention for command is reflective in both films.

Bowie's prior fight on that Natchez sandbar is actually alluded to in both films as well. Whereas Widmark casually brushed it aside, Patric uses the violent content to make Billy Bob Thornton's Davy Crockett realize the horrible threat they face in the Alamo with the Mexican army.

Afemo Omilami played Bowie's slave, Sam, in the film (the slave was Jester Hairston's Jethro in the earlier film). Yet historians share the conclusion that Bowie may not have had a slave with him at that time.

Before succumbing to his consumption, in the 2004 film, Jim mischievously banters with Crockett over the latter's legendary status. There is a wild, dangerous aura to Patric's portrayal befitting the real man, which even goes beyond sharing a bad temper with Widmark.

A deeply spiritual interpretation is accorded Jim Bowie's illness in the Alamo. Lying delirious in his small room with its many lighted candles (and even a window shaped like a cross), he envisions the enchanting form of Safia Gray's Ursula, his dead wife, through Estephania LeBaron's Juana, his sister-in-law. It is an especially poignant moment, as is when Crockett quietly sets his pistols beside him and helps Bowie to cock them he is so weakened.

There is a powerful sense of vulnerability and tragedy throughout *The Alamo*, and never more personally realized than with the sickness and death of Bowie. Firing his weapons at the enemy from his bed, Jim reaches for his knife and takes hold instead of a cameo of his beloved wife before he is killed.

Main information is in the Sam Houston filmography. Additional notes are in the Crockett filmography.

Four

SAM HOUSTON

Biography and Overview

Two days before George Washington's second inauguration as president of the United States, Sam Houston was born on March 2, 1793. His mother and father were Elizabeth (nee Paxton) Houston and Samuel Houston. Four sons were already born to his parents, while another son and three daughters followed Sam.

The Houston family lived in Virginia's Rockbridge County, near Lexington, and owned a big farm. Their ancestors came to America from England during the 1730s.

Sam's father served with Washington in the American Revolution as a captain of Morgan's Rifle Brigade. By the year of Sam's birth, his father was a colonel in the Virginia militia and often traveled to inspect other militia units. When Sam was 12, his father died after becoming sick on an inspection trip.

In 1807, Elizabeth and the family sold the farm and moved in two covered wagons to Tennessee. With them were several slaves. As Elizabeth's older sons were young men, they built a new home and farm on 419 acres of land in Blount County's Maryville.

Young Sam was neither farmer nor hunter. But he was an admirer of classical literature, particularly *The Iliad*. And this with very little schooling as a boy in either Virginia or Tennessee.

Not having known his father very well because he was away so much on his inspections, Sam also found himself isolated due to personality conflicts from his mother and siblings. When he was 16 years old, Sam ran away from home and lived with the Cherokee Indians.

The brave warriors from *The Iliad*, Homer's story of the final year of the war between the Greeks and Trojans, enthralled young Houston. He compared them to the Indians he bonded with in friendship during that first year he was away from his family. The Cherokee were led by Oo-Loo-Te-Ka, whom Sam and others called John Jolly.

Between 1809 and 1812, Sam Houston was with the Indians learning their language and culture; and earning his first nickname, the Raven. John Jolly became like a father to him. Brief trips back to Maryville were made by Sam, which included working as a clerk in a store.

As the United States was getting ready to fight Great Britain in the War of 1812, Houston was a teacher in Maryville with 20 students. But in 1813, on the day before he turned 20, he became a private in the U.S. Army; this was after a short stint furthering his own schooling at the Porter Academy in Tennessee.

Sam became an ensign that July in the 39th Infantry under the command of Col. Thomas Hart Benton, future governor of Missouri. He made an imposing figure, having reached his full height of 6 feet 5 inches.

Gen. Andrew Jackson was already involved in the campaign fighting the Creek Indians, who were led by William Weatherford. The 39th Infantry, including Houston, was part of Jackson's army by early 1814. And Sam was now a third lieutenant.

The command of the 39th was turned over to Lt. Col. John Williams by Colonel Benton when the army followed Jackson to Horseshoe Bend in Alabama. As the army attacked the Creek there on March 27, Houston was hit by an Indian arrow on his left thigh near his groin.

When General Jackson called for volunteers to go against some 100 of the enemy positioned along a riverbed, Houston rose to the task and others soon followed. Yet Sam was hit again, this time by enemy musket fire in his right arm and shoulder. Jackson lost 70 soldiers and Indian allies that day, while over 900 of the Creek Indians were killed.

Although the defeat of the Indians at Horseshoe Bend ended the Creek War, Sam Houston was felt by the company surgeon to be near death from his wounds. The arrow in his thigh and musket ball in his arm were removed; however, the ball in his shoulder was not at the time.

Taken some 70 miles away to Fort Williams for further care, Sam later in 1815 had operations in both New Orleans and New York to remove ball fragments. For the rest of his life the thigh injury never fully healed, and for years bone chips bothered him in his shoulder.

Overwhelmed by Houston's bravery at Horseshoe Bend, Jackson would prove to be his mentor in the years ahead. Following his operations, Sam was actually assigned to the general's Tennessee home, the Hermitage. And Sam was promoted to first lieutenant despite an apparent dislike by his previous commander, Colonel Williams (who politically opposed Jackson).

During 1816, the Cherokee Indians in a Tennessee treaty ceded over 1 million acres of land back to the state in exchange for new lands in the Arkansas territory. Soon the Indians, including John Jolly, were having doubts about the treaty agreement.

Jackson had Houston apply for a temporary post as a subagent for the Indians to ensure they honored the treaty. The appointment for Sam came the following year, in October 1817, when he was on an army leave.

Intending to join the Cherokee delegation in Washington, Houston instead suffered a bout of malaria. In January 1818, John Jolly took his tribe of 341 Cherokee to live in Arkansas. Sam was able to provide them with supplies that included blankets, traps and muskets.

The following month, Sam had to face accusations that he smuggled slaves and sold whiskey to the Indians among other things. Houston believed Colonel Williams was behind this; yet once Secretary of War John C. Calhoun investigated, Sam Houston's name was cleared.

Nonetheless, Houston's pride was hurt and he resigned from the army on March 1. Apparently he also stopped being a subagent on behalf of the Indians.

With his back pay as a subagent, Houston studied law under Judge James Trimble. Sam then started a small law practice in Lebanon, Tennessee. With financial assistance from a merchant named Isaac Halladay, Sam was able to obtain an office and law books.

In early 1819, Jackson also helped Sam to get appointed to the state militia as adjutant general. While his duties were easy enough, Sam raised the furor of Calhoun by pressing for army back pay he felt entitled to. Calhoun believed otherwise but finally gave in to Sam's persistence and paid him $170.

When the Cherokee needed his help over land disputes with the Osage Indians, Sam initially had obtained another position as a subagent. But then Jackson and Gov. Joseph McMinn of Tennessee urged him to campaign as attorney general in Davidson County. Houston did and in October 1819 assumed that position.

Around this time, Sam Houston began dressing in rather an ornate style. He gave up being attorney general after only a year and opened up a law practice in Nashville. During the fall of 1821, Sam was elected to the Southern Militia of Tennessee as a major general.

Sometime in 1822, Houston purchased shares in a land speculating company called the Texas Association of Tennessee. He may have held onto these shares for the next five years. This seemed to be his first interest in the land of Texas.

Sam Houston ran unopposed in 1823 for the congressional seat in Tennessee's 9th District. This was when Andrew Jackson, planning soon to run for U.S. president, used a Senate seat win as a stepping stone. Jackson and Houston traveled together to Washington to begin their respective terms.

While Houston was in Tennessee, the Nashville Inn was the watering hole with his political peers; in Washington it was a place called O'Neale's. Sam became a heavy drinker.

In his initial speech before Congress in January 1824, Houston used comparisons with his beloved *Iliad*. He was also somewhat responsible for trying to convince Henry Clay, who was then a presidential contender, to swing his electoral votes to Jackson when that election showed no clear winner. But Clay gave his votes to John Quincy Adams, who thus became president in 1825.

Reelected to Congress in 1825, Houston was being groomed as the next governor of Tennessee. Being an avid Jackson Democrat at the time could only help his political career.

On September 22, 1826, Congressman Houston was involved in a duel. Having taken offense when President Adams nominated a non–Jackson supporter, John Erwin, as Nashville postmaster, Houston verbally attacked Erwin's character. Erwin responded by challenging Houston with a surrogate duelist named John Smith.

Initially refusing to the duel on the grounds that Smith wasn't a Tennessean, Sam agreed to fight another instead, a William A. White. As Sam was the one challenged, he chose pistols. After an exchange of gunfire on the Kentucky-Tennessee border, Houston was still standing unharmed and White was hit in the groin. Sam never acknowledged the legal recourse sought by Kentucky afterward.

In the summer of 1827, Houston ran in the gubernatorial race against Newt Cannon. The election was especially close, with Sam's opponent getting over 40 percent of the votes. In this same election season in Tennessee, Davy Crockett won his first congressional race.

In Nashville's First Baptist Church, on October 1, 1827, Sam Houston was inaugurated as Tennessee's governor. The following year, Jackson ran again for the presidency and won the election this time around.

Andrew Jackson's wife, Rachel, died in late 1828. Houston was the main pallbearer at her funeral. On January 22, 1829, Sam married; his bride was 20-year-old Eliza Allen. Like Jim Bowie, when he married Ursula de Veramendi, Houston was 35 at the time.

Eliza was the daughter of Sam's friend John Allen. The Allens were Tennessee horsebreeders, and Eliza was an accomplished rider. Houston may have first met her in 1824. The wedding took place in her father's mansion. The newlyweds lived above the Nashville Inn and Eliza did not care for either the place or for Sam's drinking there.

A great deal of mystery surrounds the separation of Sam and Eliza Houston, not quite three months into their marriage (and eventually they were divorced). Supposedly Eliza revealed that her husband was so suspicious and jealous with her that it made him crazy. Sam begged her forgiveness yet she refused to go back to him.

Scandal resulted from the failed marriage. Houston even resigned the governorship over it on April 16 and gave up any hopes for reelection.

Sam Houston's relationship with Eliza Allen is included among the 28 entries in the Houston filmography. It is first seen in the 1917 silent film *The Conqueror* (Fox), and then in the sound film era in 1939's *Man of Conquest* (Republic). And at the very least there are a couple of television entries (for CBS) regarding their relationship–an episode of the series *The Great Adventure* in 1964, and the film *Houston: The Legend of Texas* in 1986.

Following his separation and resignation, Houston returned to live with John Jolly and the Cherokee. The Indians were living near the small military outpost at Cantonment Gibson, Arkansas, which was around 100 miles from the Texas border.

While with the Cherokee during the summer of 1829, Sam suffered another attack of malaria. His drinking continued with the outpost's commander, Col. Matthew Arbuckle.

The Cherokee were involved in conflicts with the Osage and other Indian tribes. Sam also continued to be known by the Indians as the Raven as he tried to keep peace among the tribes. On October 21, Houston was given citizenship in the Cherokee Nation for his efforts.

Dressed in buckskins, Houston and three subchiefs arrived in Washington in January 1830. Their visit was to address the concern that the Cherokee were being cheated out of their Federal annuity payment by Indian agent Maj. E.W. Duval.

In Washington, Sam involved himself in a contract to buy around 10,000 acres of land on the Tennessee-Georgia border for gold speculating. But he never did find any gold. Another contract, which actually fell through, would have had Sam supplying meat and salt rations to the Cherokee.

Houston's inquiries into the Indians being cheated did bring about the removal of Duval and others held responsible. Duval then accused Sam of fraud attempting to get that rations contract.

Still in Washington, Houston was also accused by Dr. Robert Mayo of admitting to a planned takeover of Texas from Mexico using the Indians. While no such plot was actually uncovered, ex–President Adams believed that Andrew Jackson had intended for Houston to start a rebellion in Texas.

In an Indian ceremony in 1830 back in Arkansas, Sam married Tiana Rogers. She was the niece of John Jolly. The couple lived at Wigwam Neosho on the Texas Road where Sam also had a trading post.

Through the rest of the year and into 1831, Sam Houston lived with his second wife among the Cherokee. His drinking of whiskey became so bad that the Indians began calling him the Big Drunk. Due to the bad behavior which resulted from the drinking, Sam was defeated in a bid for a place on the Indian council.

Returning briefly to Tennessee in 1831, Sam found himself still under harsh criticism for his earlier marriage and treatment of his first wife. Yet when he was again with the Cherokee, Sam was able to join their delegation bound for Washington.

The Indian delegation arrived in the nation's capital in February 1832 and stayed five months. On March 31, Congressman William Stanbery of Ohio brought up in the House of Representatives that earlier rations contract and Sam's involvement. Houston sent a dispatch to Stanbery to be prepared to defend himself over the matter. Stanbery then began carrying pistols.

On April 13, 1832, Houston confronted Stanbery on a Washington street. As Stanbery tried to use a pistol against him, which only misfired, Houston beat him repeatedly with a hickory stick. The companions Sam was with had to pull him off his adversary.

Since Houston was a former member of Congress, the House voted to arrest him over the incident. Stanbery's injuries included a fractured hand and a concussion.

The House of Representatives tried Sam, who had as his counsel Francis Scott Key, writer of the "Star-Spangled Banner." Sam handled the summation himself the next month; his defense was deemed brilliant and he received only a slight reprimand.

Stanbery, not satisfied, had Houston tried for assault in civil court that June. While Sam received a $500 fine, President Jackson later had it remitted.

Failing in a bid as a land agent, in partnership with James Prentiss and the Galveston Bay and Texas Land Company, Houston decided to go to Texas as a free agent. An arrangement was made with Jackson for Sam to travel there for peace talks with the Comanche Indians, who were making raids against settlers.

The Anglo-American immigrants, who arrived in Texas before Houston and numbered around 15,000 at the time, were not lost to him or Jackson. Both men shared a vision for a future acquisition of Texas.

Journeying to Texas, Sam left Tiana behind (and they too divorced). Among the things he gave her were supposedly the trading post and Wigwam Neosho.

On December 10, 1832, Sam Houston crossed the Red River by ferry. He was then in Jonesborough, the first Anglo-American settlement in Texas.

Proceeding on horseback, Houston went to San Felipe planning to meet with Stephen Austin. His early pioneering efforts for emigration would lead Austin to become known as the "Father of Texas."

As Austin wasn't at San Felipe just then, Houston may have traveled in Jim Bowie's company to San Antonio de Bexar. And there Sam met Bowie's father-in-law, Juan de Veramendi.

Sam also met in Bexar with the Comanche of southern Texas. For not having met with the more fierce northern Comanche Indians, Houston found the U.S. War Department cut back the expense account he received as Jackson's Indian commissioner.

Better news awaited Sam when he went back to San Felipe at Christmastime. Austin welcomed him and accepted Houston's application for a land grant; a league in Texas (some 4,428 acres) was transferred over to him.

In April 1833, Sam was elected a delegate at the convention in San Felipe. With Jim Bowie and others, Houston conceived a memorandum for the Mexican government. Among its proposals were separation of Texas from Coahuila and the reopening of Anglo-American immigration.

Houston became a Catholic under the Mexican law during 1833, and also an attorney in Nacogdoches. For most of the following year, Sam was in the United States drumming up interest in Texas.

On April 21, 1835, the year before the Battle of San Jacinto, Sam Houston became a Mexican citizen. But Sam favored the war party in Texas opposing President Santa Anna's centralist government. Although Stephen Austin was the leader of the peace party, his imprisonment by Santa Anna (after carrying to him the earlier memorandum from the Convention of 1833) only made him favor the cause of revolution.

The war party, which was led by Thomas J. Rusk, appointed Houston to command the military forces in Nacogdoches in September 1835. The men of Gonzales elected Austin to command against the Mexican troops under General Cos in San Antonio.

An October meeting in the town of Columbia held that Houston was commander of all the Texas forces; a consultation the next month at San Felipe reinforced him as commander with the rank of major general.

During this consultation, the Texas provisional government and General Council were formed to decide the future course of the Texas Revolution. Houston opted for independence.

As with Austin, Houston was criticized for any caution shown in his military strategy; some volunteers even called Sam cowardly. And despite being accused of spending the last months of the year in drunken seclusion, Houston tried to build a regular army. Gov. Henry Smith authorized Sam to offer land and cash bonuses to those men who pledged themselves to Texas' military service.

Houston not only had the Mexicans to deal with, but undisciplined Texas volunteers and the General Council as well. Without informing Smith or Houston, the council took manpower away to organize its own commands and undermined their authority.

A portrait of Sam Houston at the time of the Texas Revolution.

The General Council chose Col. James Fannin to take Houston's command. Sam was ordered to negotiate with the Cherokee and other tribes. This was for their neutrality in the war with the Mexican forces of Santa Anna.

On February 23, 1836, Houston and Indian agent John Forbes met with the Indians. Promises of Texas land persuaded them to remain neutral.

While he was away negotiating with the Indians in northern Texas, Sam's detractors came down on him hard since this proved to be the direst of times. Santa Anna had surrounded William Travis and his small force of rebels in the Alamo.

Houston's arrival at Washington-on-the-Brazos, on the 28th of February, was when he learned of the danger at the Alamo.

A convention of delegates met there on the Brazos; on his 43rd birthday, a declaration of independence for Texas was proclaimed. David Burnet was chosen president by the new provisional government, with Lorenzo de Zavala his vice president. Chosen commander in chief of the armies of the Republic of Texas was Sam Houston.

At Gonzales on March 11, Houston was told of the fall of the Alamo as he was raising troops to go to its defense. Susannah Dickenson, her daughter, and Travis' slave, Joe, were among the survivors who had come to Houston. The tragic story was told to him by Susannah, who also claimed that Santa Anna was on the way to Gonzales with 5,000 troops.

The Texas retreat from the enemy was called the Runaway Scrape. Texas settlers fled in fear from Santa Anna. Houston and around 400 men, who were in Gonzales to join his army, were soon part of the exodus.

Survivors from the Alamo who came to Sam Houston are included in the filmography. They are part of the endings of 1937's film *Heroes of the Alamo* (Sunset/Columbia), and 1955's film *The Last Command* (Republic).

Scenes where Houston is told of the impending battle are included too. Such entries are the motion picture *The Alamo* (United Artists) from 1960, and the television movie *The Alamo, 13 Days to Glory* (NBC) from 1987.

On March 11, 1836, Houston sent a dispatch to Colonel Fannin at Fort Defiance in Goliad to pull out due to the threat of Santa Anna's army. He didn't in time; with his own army, Fannin was captured by the advancing forces of Gen. Jose Urrea on the 19th. Following Santa Anna's edict, just as at the Alamo for no mercy, Urrea ordered the prisoners executed. While Fannin was blindfolded and shot inside the fort on March 27, about 400 of his men were marched outside then shot and bayonetted.

Houston's own army grew to over 1,000 men as it went north in Texas. But there were problems with desertion and dissension. With his retreat, there were those who again accused Houston of cowardice. A petition was even made to remove him from command; only his supporters kept this from happening.

Down to 760 men, Houston's army was trying to locate the provisional government which had abandoned, due to the advancement of the Mexican army, its headquarters at Washington-on-the-Brazos and then Harrisburg. However, the enemy forces had separated into several units; when the Texans captured a Mexican courier, they discovered that Santa Anna was close with 900 men.

Houston decided then to become the pursuer instead of the pursued. On April 18, he encamped his army at San Jacinto within a short distance from Santa Anna's own camp. Both armies were aware of the other.

On the morning of the 21st, Santa Anna received 500 or so more reinforcements from General Cos. Houston then had scout Deaf Smith burn the bridge over Vince's Bayou, apparently to prevent the enemy from receiving further reinforcements. Late that afternoon, while some Mexican soldiers were building a breastworks, most of the enemy army was taking a siesta.

Sword in hand and astride his white stallion, Saracen, Sam Houston had his Texans form a 1,000-yard line. With a pair of six-pound cannons called the Twin Sisters, the Texans attacked Santa Anna's army. Houston's army was made up of Col. Sidney Sherman's 2nd Volunteers on the left (assisted by Juan Seguin's Tejanos), Col. Edward Burleson's 1st Volunteers in the center, and Lt. Col. Henry Millard's regulars on the right. Cavalry led by Mirabeau Lamar came in on the far right.

Breaking through the breastworks to sporadic enemy retaliation, the Texans shouted "Remember the Alamo." The battle was over in 18 minutes, but the killing went on for hours. Around 630 Mexican soldiers were killed; out of over 600 prisoners, 200 or more were wounded. Among the prisoners were Cos and, the following day, Santa Anna. Disguised and found hiding, Santa Anna was brought before a wounded Sam Houston.

During the battle, Houston's horse was struck down. Mounting another horse, it too was hit, as was Sam when an enemy shot shattered his leg just above his right ankle. But Houston climbed on still another horse. Six Texans were killed and 24 wounded in the fighting (although some later died from their wounds).

General Houston's victory at San Jacinto is featured in the majority of entries in the filmography. It begins with 1911's *The Immortal Alamo* (Star Film Company); and continues with such silent films as the 1914 *The Siege and Fall of the Alamo* (State of Texas), and 1915's *The Martyrs of the Alamo* (Fine Arts/Triangle).

The aforementioned *Man of Conquest* and *Houston: The Legend of Texas* both contain

The San Jacinto Monument stands 570 feet tall and overlooks the battleground where Sam Houston defeated Santa Anna.

sequences on the battle. Other entries do as well — the 1956 motion picture *The First Texan* (Allied Artists) and for television, 1995's miniseries *James A. Michener's Texas* (NBC), and 1998's film *Two for Texas* (TNT).

Houston and the Texas Revolution are also part of more entries: for television–a 1950 episode of the *Pulitzer Prize Playhouse* series (ABC), and a 1957 episode of the series *Telephone Time* (ABC); for motion

pictures–1953's *The Man from the Alamo* (Universal-International), and 2004's *The Alamo* (Touchstone/Imagine).

After the victory at San Jacinto, Gen. Sam Houston sent word back to an elated President Jackson. Along the Texas–United States border, Jackson actually had a military force waiting in case Santa Anna was victorious and continued his advance across the border.

Although army surgeon Alexander Ewing treated Houston's leg wound, removing bone chips, it became infected. Sam went to New Orleans for further treatment. Accompanying him to Galveston Bay aboard a steamer was Santa Anna. Willing to accept the independence of Texas, Santa Anna was imprisoned for a time at a plantation near Galveston until Mexico accepted it as well.

As Santa Anna signed the Treaty of Velasco on May 14, 1836, acknowledging the Republic of Texas, Houston proceeded to New Orleans. Doctors worked on Sam's wound at the home of William Christy where over 20 pieces of shattered bone were removed.

By August, Houston returned to Texas albeit with a limp that would continue to trouble him. An election took place the following month to choose the president of the Republic of Texas. When all the votes were counted, Sam Houston won with 5,199; Henry Smith followed with 743 and Stephen Austin with 587. The new vice president was Mirabeau Lamar. Both Smith and Austin served in Sam's cabinet respectively as treasurer and secretary of state.

At the new capital in Columbia, Houston took the oath of office on October 22, 1836. One of the things Sam did as president was to organize groups of men to protect the frontier. These men would become the Texas Rangers.

Included in the filmography are entries which relate to Sam and the rangers. They are the motion pictures *The Ranger and the Lady* (Republic) in 1940, and *Down Rio Grande Way* (Columbia) in 1942. The aforementioned *James Michener's Texas* contains a passage about the rangers (and also the death of Stephen Austin).

Two days after Christmas 1836, Austin passed away from illness. Sam had his memory honored throughout Texas with gun salutes.

Sam never really cared for Columbia

as the capital. By April 1837, 100 buildings and 1,500 people were part of the new town of Houston, Texas, where the capital was moved. In 1840, another new town, Austin, became the capital and remains so to this day.

Annexation of Texas to the United States was an ongoing struggle. On his last day of office in March 1837, President Jackson had recognized as an independent country the Lone Star Republic of Texas. An initial petition, however, that summer for annexation failed to go through; issues that weighed against it were the threat of war with Mexico and the emergence of Texas as another slave state.

The three previously mentioned entries in the filmography relate to annexation. As does the 1952 motion picture *Lone Star* (MGM.).

In 1838, Sam Houston contended with agents from Mexico stirring up the Indians. It wasn't hard for the Indians' land in Texas was wanted by the settlers just like it was in the United States. Houston's attempts to extend fair treatment to the Indians were resented even by his fellow Texans.

Mirabeau Lamar became president of Texas that December (with David Burnet his vice president). A short war broke out in Texas over land with the Cherokee in the summer of 1839; Chief Bowl (John Jolly's successor) died in the fighting. The Cherokee Indians were force to migrate.

While the conflicts with the Indians were going on (and hostilities went on for years with the Comanche), Sam went to the United States. In May 1839, in Mobile, Alabama, he met a young lady named Margaret Lea.

On May 9 the following year, Sam and Margaret were married in Alabama; he was 26 years older than his 21-year-old wife. Yet their marriage lasted the rest of his life and eight children were born between 1843 and 1860–Sam Jr., Nancy, Margaret, Mary, Antoinette, Andrew, William, and Temple.

The last-named son became the subject of a 1963-64 television series (for NBC). Included in the filmography, it is entitled simply *Temple Houston*.

Sam ran again for president of the Republic of Texas in September 1841. He beat David Burnet with a vote of 7,508 to 2,574. With Edward Burleson as his vice president, Houston took the oath of office on December 13.

With Texas struggling to become a financially solvent nation, Sam Houston tried to restore the good relations with the Indians that were damaged during Lamar's presidency. Sam felt that by forming trading posts with the Indians, it would help commerce as well. The Texas Congress felt otherwise and wouldn't allow Sam the $20,000 requested for an Indian fund.

Raids by the Mexicans into Texas, including San Antonio, during 1842 resulted in Congress passing a war bill. Although Sam had taken action already by blockading Mexican ports, he vetoed the bill. Houston's nonviolent stand didn't sit well with his detractors, whom were always quick to label him a coward for not rushing into warfare.

But that fall, Houston planned to utilize Gen. Alex Somerville and 1,000 troops against Mexico. When Somerville was unable to maintain control of the men, Col. William Fisher, supposedly without authority, led 300 men across the Rio Grande and attacked the Mexican town of Mier. Mexican troops retaliated and 176 Texans were marched as prisoners to Mexico City.

Santa Anna, who had seized power in 1841 and was once again president of Mexico, wanted to execute all the prisoners. Seventeen of the Texans were shot instead after Francisco Mexia, governor of Coahuila, intervened.

With financial interests in both Mexico and Texas, Great Britain helped to form a truce during 1843. And in September 1844, the U.S. envoy to Mexico, Waddy Thompson, arranged for the release of the remaining prisoners.

This episode was just one of many between Texas and Mexico before war actually broke out after the United States annexed the Lone Star Republic. Despite the question of slavery, the U.S. was more concerned that Great Britain would become a dominating force if Texas wasn't annexed.

For Sam Houston was using his wiles to muster support for annexation by threatening to expand Texas (with British cooccupation of the Oregon territory). Expansion would also include the then territories of California and Santa Fe (which would become New Mexico).

Before this could happen, Houston's second term as president ended in December 1844 (with Anson Jones chosen as his successor). And on February 28, 1845, by the slight margin of 27–25, the U.S. Senate voted for annexation of Texas. Acceptance by the House of Representatives followed.

Andrew Jackson died that June and didn't see Texas officially enter the Union on December 29. By April of the following year, Mexico declared war on the United States of America, and the U.S. soon reciprocated. However, just prior to the war, a new U.S. senator from Texas was elected on February 21, 1846. He was Sam Houston.

President James Polk sent Gen. Zachary Taylor with American troops to the U.S.-Mexican border on the Rio Grande. Houston supported Taylor and his army invading Mexico that May.

By September 1846, Santa Anna was the commanding general of the Mexican army (if no longer president of Mexico). But his 15,000 troops were defeated by Taylor's 4,800 men in February 1847 at the Battle of Buena Vista. This forced Santa Anna to return to Mexico City.

Moving toward Mexico City were

A daguerreotype of Sam Houston when he was governor of Texas.

American troops under Gen. Winfield Scott. After the breakdown of an armistice with Mexico, Scott's army marched victoriously into Mexico City in September. By the end of 1847, Houston, who only had a two-year Senate seat, won a full six-year term.

On February 2, 1848, the United States signed the Treaty of Guadalupe Hidalgo which ended the Mexican War. Texas was recognized by Mexico as belonging to the U.S.; and for a payment of $15 million to the Mexican government, over 500,000 square miles of land was ceded to the U.S., which included the future states of New Mexico and California.

Earlier on, in 1846, the contested issue with Great Britain over the future state of Oregon was resolved in favor of the United States. Houston was even prepared to fight the British in another war over the matter.

Mexican War hero Zachary Taylor was elected U.S. president in 1848. Controversy between the northern and southern states over slavery was expounded by proslavery Senator John Calhoun of South Carolina. Calhoun reflected the South's future role in secession.

Senator Houston felt the Union as a whole was more important than division over slavery. In 1849, Sam even proposed a resolution in the Senate which left each state the right to vote for slavery or not. He supported Senator Henry Clay's Compromise of 1850, however, which prohibited (among other things) slavery in California when it became a state that year.

Some of Houston's peers considered him as a candidate by 1851 for president of the United States. His life had even been written about in a popular work of the day, *Sam Houston and His Republic*, by Charles Edward Lester. Instead, Franklin Pierce received the Democratic nomination and was chosen president in 1852.

Sam may not have been president but he did win a third Senate seat in the fall of 1853. And in the year ahead he became part of a new political party. It was called the Know-Nothing (or American) Party. Writer Lester later rewrote his earlier biography on Houston to include the Know-Nothing Party. The new title was *Life of Sam Houston*.

In 1854, Sam Houston predicted a civil war over slavery with the passing of the Kansas-Nebraska Act in both the House and Senate. This bill made void the earlier Missouri Compromise of 1820, created to balance out the slave and nonslave states.

Having given up his excessive drinking in 1851 due in no small way to his wife's influence, Sam became a Baptist in 1854, which was Margaret's faith. Over the years, the Houstons had owned three homes in Texas—at Cedar Point, Independence, and at Huntsville.

White the Know-Nothing Party was rather short-lived, in 1856 Houston had some interest in running again as a presidential candidate on that ticket. Another former Democrat, Millard Fillmore, was instead the party's choice. The Democrats won the election anyway with their own candidate, James Buchanan.

Texas made it clear two years before his term as senator ended in 1859 that Houston would not be reelected. Although Texas was a slave state, Sam just didn't support the expansion of slavery.

Opposition against Sam for his beliefs also resulted in losing an initial bid as governor of Texas in 1857. Hardin Richard Runnels won; and Sam was even accused of being a bitter old man for his verbal attacks on him.

Yet Houston regained his popularity in the 1859 gubernatorial race in Texas. He won this election from incumbent Runnels with a vote tally of 36,257 to 27,500. When he took office on December 21, at age 66, Sam actually was with no political party. He was simply a man of the people.

Part of Sam's newfound popularity was due to his interest in the reclamation of Mexico for the United States. While a militia bill to raise volunteers was passed in 1860 by the Texas legislature, the government in Washington became leery of the whole thing.

Robert E. Lee, then commanding the U.S. Army in Texas, dismissed the companies of Texas Rangers waiting along the Rio Grande to invade Mexico. Feeling it too costly, President Buchanan even turned down Houston's request for weapons.

With little campaigning done by Sam in 1860, he nonetheless received some support from the Constitutional Union Party for another presidential bid. And once more someone else, ex–Senator John Bell, became the actual nominee.

Stephen Douglas was the Democratic nominee for president (with southern detractors nominating John C. Breckinridge). But the Republican nominee won the election of November 1860. He was Abraham Lincoln.

Dissension over slavery between the Democrats and Republicans would lead to the American Civil War. Many Democrats seemed to favor slavery, at least in the southern states, while many Republicans were opposed.

Prior to Lincoln's becoming president of the United States, Sam Houston believed the southern states would secede from the Union. In 1860, Texas had a population of over 430,000 white people, and more than 180,000 black people who were slaves.

A month after President Lincoln took office, South Carolina became the first state to secede. Ten more states followed during 1861.

The Secession Convention met in Texas in January 1861, and, despite Houston's objections, passed an ordinance to secede. Texas officially seceded on February 23. So desperate was Sam to avoid secession that he put forth an effort for Texas to again become an independent republic.

Although Houston made an appeal not to fight the Union, and with Texas Ranger companies under Edward Burleson Jr. supporting his concept of an independent Texas, another ordinance was passed that March. This one made Texas a part of the Confederate States of America. Jefferson Davis had already been chosen the president of the Confederacy.

On March 14, 1861, all state officials in Texas had to swear allegiance to the Confederacy at the capital in Austin. Sam Houston refused to answer when his name was called to take the oath; and thus on the 18th, he was removed as governor of Texas and replaced by Lt. Gov. Edward Clark.

At least two entries in the Houston filmography deal with his gubernatorial life in Texas. Both were for television–a 1964 episode of the series *Profiles in Courage* (NBC), and a 1975 special called *The Honorable Sam Houston* (ABC).

If not to the Confederacy, Houston declared his allegiance to Texas in May 1861; and so supported the will of the people for secession. Sam wanted Texas to keep its troops within the state when war broke out between the Union's northern states and the Confederacy's southern states.

War did break out once Fort Sumter, South Carolina, was fired on by Confederate soldiers on April 12, 1861. And it was only a matter of time before Texans were deployed wherever they were needed.

Sam Jr., Houston's oldest child, was 18 years old when he became a Confederate soldier in the 2nd Texas Infantry. In April 1862, young Sam was among the over 16,000 southern troops wounded during the Battle of Shiloh in Tennessee. Legend has it that a Bible given to him by his mother deflected the shot to his groin which might have been otherwise fatal.

Old Sam Houston's health quickly deteriorated during the Civil War. With his eyesight failing and his own army wounds still bothering him, Houston made out a last will and testament on April 2, 1863. Among its inclusions were for his loving wife, Margaret, to have nearly all of his personal possessions. Sam Jr. was left the sword his father carried years before at San Jacinto.

In the early evening of July 26, Sam was bedridden with pneumonia; he was in his room on the first floor of his Huntsville home (called the Steamboat House). Margaret was sitting at his side when he passed away. He was 70 years old. Legend has it too that he called out then for his wife and for Texas.

Twelve slaves were included in the inventory of Houston's estate after his death, although another legend had him freeing them shortly before. Houston apparently invested in over 34,000 acres of land over the years. While some of the ownership might have been questionable, Margaret was able to sell some of the land, although at lower prices due to the period of Reconstruction following the war.

A 1997 television miniseries, *True Women* (CBS), included Sam as it wove a tapestry from the Texas Revolution to the Civil War and beyond. It is part of the Sam Houston filmography, as is the 1942 motion picture *Men of Texas* (Universal), which is set after the Civil War and Houston is a ghost.

Still other entries are included. They are the television series *The Adventures of Jim Bowie* (ABC), in which Sam made some appearances during 1957; and a 1992 video, *Sam Houston: Man of Honor* (Grace Products), in which he is interviewed.

The Civil War ended when its greatest general, Robert E. Lee, surrendered the Confederate forces to Union Gen. Ulysses S. Grant. It was at Appomattox Court House in Virginia on April 8, 1865.

Margaret Houston was again living in Independence when she died during a yellow fever epidemic on December 3, 1867. Because of the severity of the epidemic, she had to be buried immediately instead of with her husband, who had been laid to rest in Huntsville. Her own mother's remains, however, were later interred with Margaret's.

For many years of their marriage, Margaret and Sam were apart due to the demands of his political career. Ironically, in death their physical remains were apart as well. Yet always their kindred spirits were together.

Sam Houston Filmography

1 *The Immortal Alamo*

Star Film Company / 1911 / 1,000 feet / Silent / Black and White

NOTES: Main information is in the Davy Crockett filmography. Additional notes are in the Jim Bowie filmography.

In 1911's *The Immortal Alamo*, both the fall of the Alamo and the aftermath at San Jacinto were depicted (at least according to one source), despite this lost film's length of just one reel.

While Almeron Dickenson was among the Alamo's fallen in history, he was part of Sam Houston's army at San Jacinto in the film. An existing still does reflect history as it shows a wounded Houston lying on a blanket beneath a tree with a captive Santa Anna standing beside him. Unlike history, Dickenson is in the still trying to keep his fellow Texans from attacking the Mexican leader.

Neither of the actors who portrayed Sam Houston or Santa Anna are identified.

2 *The Siege and Fall of the Alamo*

State of Texas / 1914 / Silent / Black and White

NOTES: Additional notes are in the Crockett and Bowie filmographies.

The Siege and Fall of the Alamo, with its alternate title *The Fall of the Alamo*, is listed on the Internet Movie Data Base (IMDb). No American Film Institute (AFI) listing exists for the film, however. It remains a lost silent.

Along with the Alamo's fall, the still-existing synopsis said the film also dealt with the San Jacinto battle that followed. It appears to be an accurate reflection of the events. Two of Gen. Sam Houston's men burn down Vince's Bridge in preparation of the ensuing fight. The general then marches his troops against Santa Anna's camped army.

While some Texans, according to the synopsis, do fall under enemy fire, the Mexicans are soon defeated. Many of the enemy soldiers flee. Found hiding in tall grass, Santa Anna is brought before a wounded Houston. Papers are signed and Texas is liberated.

On June 1, 1914, at the Royal Theater in San Antonio, a five-reel silent film called *The Siege and Fall of the Alamo* was initially shown. This makes the motion picture the first feature-length entry about both the Alamo and San Jacinto.

3 *The Martyrs of the Alamo*

Fine Arts Company/Triangle Film Corporation / 1915 / Five Reels / Silent / Black and White

NOTES: Main information is in the Davy Crockett filmography. Additional notes are in the Jim Bowie filmography.

Of the silent motion pictures which dealt with the Alamo and San Jacinto, 1915's *The Martyrs of the Alamo* is the most famous. This was due in no small way to the supervision (if limited) of film great D.W. Griffith.

While a short segment, the battle featured here between Tom Wilson's Sam Houston and Walter Long's Santa Anna was nonetheless the climactic highlight, just as was the final encounter between the two commanders in any earlier silent. The action sequences throughout *Martyrs* were given special distinction.

Wilson was in Griffith's *The Birth of a Nation* the same year and his *Intolerance* the next. In the years leading up to the sound era, the actor was also seen giving support to both Douglas Fairbanks Sr. and Tom Mix in a series of films.

4 *The Conqueror*

Fox Film Corporation/Standard Pictures / 1917 / Eight Reels / Silent / Black and White

CREDITS: Raoul Walsh (director, scenarist); Del Clawson (cameraman); George G. Grenier (set designer). From a story by Henry C. Warnack.

CAST: William Farnum (Sam Houston), Jewel Carmen (Eliza Allen), Charles Clary (Sidney Stokes), J.A. Marcus (Jumbo), Carrie Clarke Ward (Mammy), William Chisholm (Dr. Spencer), Robert Dunbar (Judge Allen), Owen Jones (James Houston), and William Eagle Shirt, Chief Birdhead, Little Bear (Chiefs).

NOTES: *The Conqueror* was released by the Fox Film Corporation on September 16, 1917. Its director, Raoul Walsh, was also credited as the scenarist (although sources also list Chester B. Clapp as writing the script). The initial story, by Henry C. Warnack, was supposedly called *A Man's Revenge*.

A *New York Times* review of this biography of a young Sam Houston called it "good movie entertainment and at least reasonably accurate history." It is believed a lost film.

While *The Conqueror* was historically correct in having Houston living with the Cherokee Indians, and marrying Eliza Allen when he was governor of Tennessee, many of the surrounding events were highly fanciful and romanticized. In the silent, Sam leaves her upon realizing she only wished to become first lady, and Eliza chases after him until there is an ultimate reconciliation.

William Farnum was the hero and Jewel Carmen the heroine, whom he saves, with the help of the Cherokee, from a lusting, murderous villain (Sidney Stokes) and marauders. Earlier on, Sam's father (Owen Jones) dies, leaving a great void in his son's life; the father is called James instead of Samuel, his real name.

The younger brother of Dustin Farnum (of 1916's silent, *Davy Crockett*), William followed him to Hollywood in 1914. He became famous that year for the big fight sequence (with co-star Tom Santschi) in the first film version of *The Spoilers*. But Raoul Walsh felt Farnum's stockiness made him wrong for the role of the very tall Sam Houston. At least one critic did call the performance "splendid."

Despite its influx of action and tragedy, *The Conqueror* displayed a good bit of comedy earlier on. One instance was even reflective of a page in the life of Davy Crockett. In 1825, Davy had tried to win voters over during his initial run for Congress by trading a raccoon skin repeatedly for drinks. Before he becomes governor in the film, Sam runs for constable using a similar device with a fox skin.

5 *Heroes of the Alamo*

Sunset Productions/Columbia Pictures / 1937 / 75 minutes / Black and White

NOTES: Main information is in the Davy Crockett filmography. Additional notes are in the Jim Bowie filmography.

1937's *Heroes of the Alamo* concludes before any revenge can be exacted by the Texans on the Mexican army. After the fall of the Alamo in the film, Anne (not Susannah) Dickinson survives with her baby daughter and is sent by Santa Anna to tell the story to Sam Houston.

Houston was played by Edward Peil (Sr.). A Western character player for over 30 years, Peil was in many silent and talking motion pictures. Among his films were John Ford's 1924 silent *The Iron Horse* and the first sound Western in 1929, Raoul Walsh's *In Old Arizona*.

6 *Man of Conquest*

Republic Pictures / 1939 / 97 minutes / Black and White

CREDITS: George Nicholls Jr. (director); Sol C. Siegel (associate producer); Kenneth Holmes (assistant director); Wells Root, E.E. Paramore Jr., Jan Fortune (screenplay); Joseph H. August (photography); Edward Mann (editing); John Victor Mackay (art director); Adele Palmer, Edith Head (costumes); Howard Lydecker (special effects); Victor Young (music). Based on a story by Wells Root and Harold Shumate.

CAST: Richard Dix (Sam Houston), Gail Patrick (Margaret Lea), Edward Ellis (Andrew Jackson), Joan Fontaine (Eliza Allen), Victor Jory (William B. Travis), Robert Barrat (Davy Crockett), George Hayes (Lannie Upchurch), Ralph Morgan (Stephen Austin), Robert Armstrong (James Bowie), C. Henry Gordon (Santa Anna), Janet Beecher (Mrs. Lea), Pedro de Cordoba (Oolooteka), Max Terhune (Deaf Smith), Kathleen Lockhart (Mrs. Allen),

Leon Ames (John Hoskins), Charles Stevens (Zavola), Sarah Padden (Mrs. Houston), and Lane Chandler (Bonham).

SYNOPSIS: Sam Houston is badly wounded at the Battle of Horseshoe Bend against the Creek Indians. But an enduring friendship begins with his commander, Gen. Andrew Jackson. Both men enter politics, and in time Houston becomes the Tennessee governor and Jackson the U.S. president.

Sam marries Eliza Allen, but she cannot cope with his political lifestyle and leaves him. Resigning the governorship over the resulting scandal, Sam lives with his Indian friends, the Cherokee.

As Indian ambassador in Washington, Houston is against the way the government mistreats the Indians. At a ball, he meets Margaret Lea; on a stagecoach together to Texas, they fall in love.

But his future with Margaret must wait when Sam becomes involved in making Texas an independent country from its Mexican ruler. Colonist Stephen Austin is opposed to Houston's desire to fight the Mexicans until their leader, Santa Anna, leads an army to crush any who stand in his way. President Jackson has hopes that Sam can help make Texas part of the United States.

As leader of the Texas army, Sam Houston tries to help the defenders of the Alamo against Santa Anna. But Sam is too late and the Alamo falls.

Yet at San Jacinto, Houston and his men strike back. Santa Anna is defeated in battle and Texas is freed.

A number of years pass. Although he is now dying, Andrew Jackson is overjoyed to see that Sam has played a part in making Texas a state in the Union.

NOTES: During production on *Man of Conquest* in early 1939, its working title was *Wagons Westward*. Republic Pictures put more money into the motion picture than any of its films up to that time, and

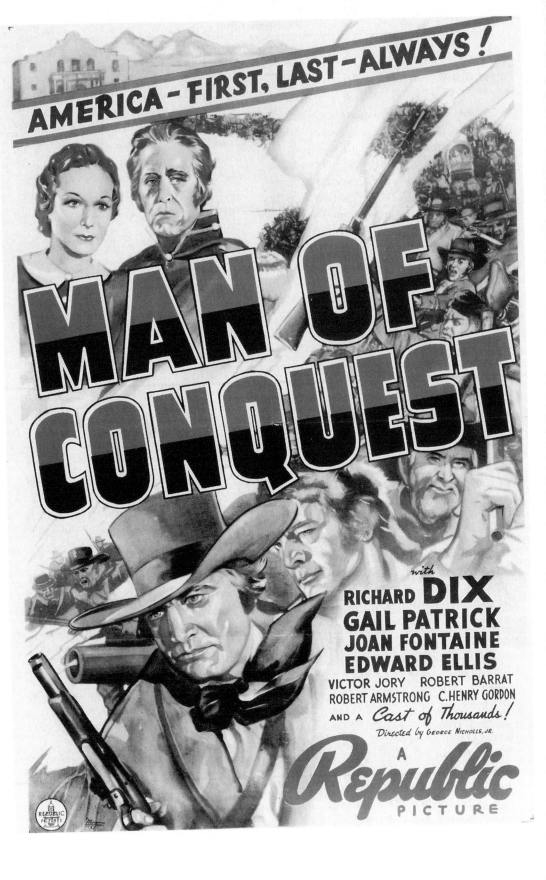

Richard Dix as Houston (as an Indian ambassador, left) and Edward Ellis in *Man of Conquest.*

this included the advertising for its release that same year on April 28.

Excellent production values were accorded the film from its director, George Nicholls Jr., and associate producer, Sol Siegel. Especially splendid were the action sequences under the guidance of second unit director Reeves Eason, stuntman Yakima Canutt and photographer Joseph August. Both the battles at the Alamo and San Jacinto were equally good.

"Houston, as Richard Dix has played him, is a full-bodied portrait, earthy, human and virile," boasted the *New York Times*. Many of the performances were first-rate.

A colorful portrait of Andrew Jackson was given by Edward Ellis. Ralph Morgan was Stephen Austin. Of the ladies in Sam Houston's life, Gail Patrick's Margaret Lea seemed to fare better than Joan Fontaine's Eliza Allen. C. Henry Gordon played Santa Anna; initially he had been set to play William Travis in the Alamo sequence until he fell ill.

A story by Wells Root and Harold Shumate was the inspiration for the screenplay done by Root, E.E. Paramore Jr. and Jan Fortune. Their work was very faithful to Houston's life with some romanticized incidents. Sam never actually met Margaret until after the Texas Revolution, and Andrew Jackson was already dead by the time Texas became the 28th state.

During this actual period in history, Houston was in love with a lady from

Opposite page: Poster art for *Man of Conquest.*

Nacogdoches, Anna Raguet. While the love was never returned, she did make the crimson sash and sword belt he wore in battle at San Jacinto.

Dix, who was a strapping 6-footer, gave one of the strongest performances of Houston seen over the years. Also appearing in the first Western to win a best picture Oscar–1931's *Cimarron*–the actor's other historical roles included Wild Bill Hickok in 1941's *Badlands of Dakota* and Wyatt Earp in 1942's *Tombstone, the Town Too Tough to Die.*

Man of Conquest apparently has not been placed on video. This is a little ironic since it was regarded as one of the finest biographies of Sam Houston.

Additional notes are in the Crockett and Bowie filmographies.

7 *The Ranger and the Lady*

Republic Pictures / 1940 / 59 minutes / Black and White

CREDITS: Joseph Kane (director, associate producer); William O'Connor (assistant director); Stuart Anthony, Gerald Geraghty (screenplay); Reggie Lanning (photography); Lester Orlebeck (editor); Cy Feuer (music director); Peter Tinturin (songs). From an original story by Bernard McConville.

CAST: Roy Rogers (Capt. Roy Colt), George "Gabby" Hayes (Sgt. Gabby Whittaker), Jacqueline Wells (Jane Tabor), Henry Brandon (Gen. Augustus LaRue), Harry Woods (Kincaid), Noble Johnson (El Lobo), Si Jenks (Hank Purdy), Ted Mapes (Kramer), Yakima Canutt (McNair), and Davison Clark (Sam Houston).

SYNOPSIS: Sam Houston, president of the Texas Republic, is in Washington attempting to secure statehood. While he is away, Gen. Augustus LaRue, chief of the Texas Rangers, forces an unjust toll tax on wagoners using the Santa Fe Trail to haul freight.

When Jane Tabor's wagons are taxed, she refuses to pay. LaRue orders Texas Ranger Capt. Roy Colt to arrest her, despite the captain's objections. And Colt is surprised when Jane then forms an alliance with LaRue which will benefit mainly her wagon train.

Colt and his partner, Sgt. Gabby Whittaker, quit the rangers and send word to President Houston. It is revealed that Jane only wanted to get in good with LaRue to exact revenge because he had her father killed.

Arrested by LaRue's crony, Kincaid, and sentenced to die, Colt is saved by Jane. Colt then joins Houston to stop an ambush by LaRue and save the day.

NOTES: *The Ranger and the Lady* was released by Republic Pictures in July 1940. Joseph Kane served as both the film's director and associate producer. The script was written by Gerald Geraghty and Stuart Anthony from Bernard McConville's story.

Richard Dix (right) spends a tense moment with an unidentified actor in *Man of Conquest.*

For the most part, the film was a vehicle for Roy Rogers, who was then the third biggest moneymaking Western star (right behind Gene Autry and William Boyd). In this entry, Jacqueline Wells (later Julie Bishop) was Roy's leading lady.

Elements of the early days in the Republic of Texas were included in this fabricated tale in which Sam Houston was part of the heroics. Davison Clark (initially uncredited) was Houston. Among the actor's roles were two more in the Houston filmography–1942's *Down Rio Grande Way* and 1952's *Lone Star.*

Of the Roy Rogers Westerns on video, *The Ranger and the Lady* is included.

8 *Down Rio Grande Way*

Columbia Pictures / 1942 / 58 minutes / Black and White

CREDITS: William Berke (director); Jack Fier (producer); Milton Carter (assistant director); Irving Briskin (executive producer); Paul Franklin (screenplay); George Meehan (photography); Mel Thorsen (editor); Lionel Banks (art director). Song: "Texas," words and music by Johnny Marvin.

CAST: Charles Starrett (Steve Martin), Russell Hayden (Lucky Haines), Britt Wood (Britt Haines), Rose Anne Stevens (Mary Ann Baldridge), Norman Willis (Mack Vandall), Davison Clark (Col. Elihu Baldridge), Joseph Eggenton (Judge Henderson), Lee Prather (Van Norden), Ed Peil Sr. (Adams), and Paul Newlan (Sam Houston).

SYNOPSIS: In Texas, Sam Houston's efforts to make the republic a state in the Union are thwarted. Van Norden and Judge Henderson are among those who are opposed because of Texas' proslavery stand. Yet their actions are illegal.

Norden works secretly with newspaper publisher Elihu Baldridge to sabotage the efforts to promote Texas. To stir up trouble among the ranchers, tax agent Mack Vandall is sent to impose unjust assessments.

A Texas Ranger, Steve Martin, is dispatched by Houston to confront the problems. Pretending to be a rancher, Steve's real identity is further known just to the newspaperman.

After his cattle are stampeded by Vandall's gang, rancher Lucky Haines retaliates and a gang member is killed. Steve soon realizes that Baldridge has revealed his identity to Vandall.

With Lucky, Steve finds where Vandall is hiding. In the ensuing gun battle, Baldridge is taken prisoner and both Vandall and Judge Henderson are killed.

Texas is admitted into the Union.

NOTES: In April 1942, Columbia Pictures released *Down Rio Grande Way.* Like *The Ranger and the Lady* before it, the film was a "B" Western; instead of Roy Rogers as star, Charles Starrett was the heroic Texas Ranger this time around.

Supporting Starrett was Paul Newlan as Sam Houston. A long acting career for Newlan included work in both film and television. He was in 1937's *Wells Fargo* and 1956's *Davy Crockett and the River Pirates.*

Jack Fier produced and William Berke directed *Down Rio Grande Way.* During production in late 1941, it was called *After the Alamo.*

The script by Paul Franklin was another fictional treatment of Texas trying to become a state. Unlike the previous picture, which was set in 1836, this one was set in the last days that Texas was still actually a republic.

9 *Men of Texas*

Universal Pictures / 1942 / 82 minutes / Black and White

CREDITS: Ray Enright (director); George Waggner (producer); Fred Frank (assistant director); Harold Shumate (screenplay);

Richard Brooks (additional dialogue); Milton Krasner (photography); Clarence Kolster (editor); Jack Otterson (art director); R.A. Gausman (set decorator); Vera West (gowns); Edward Ward (music director). Song: "Dixie," words and music by Daniel Decatur Emmett.

CAST: Robert Stack (Barry Conovan), Broderick Crawford (Henry Clay Jackson), Jackie Cooper (Robert Houston Scott), Anne Gwynne (Jane Baxter Scott), Ralph Bellamy (Major Lamphere), Jane Darwell (Mrs. Scott), Leo Carrillo (Sam Sawyer), John Litel (Col. Colbert Scott), Janet Beecher (Mrs. Sam Houston), Rex Lease, Bob Barron (Ranchers), Lane Chandler, Kernan Cripps (Telephone Operators), and William Farnum (The Ghost of Sam Houston).

SYNOPSIS: Following the Civil War, newspaper correspondent Barry Conovan and photographer Sam Sawyer travel by stagecoach to Huntsville, Texas. Among the folks they encounter on the trail are Jane Baxter Scott and later Henry Clay Jackson, the latter claiming to be her fiancé.

In Huntsville, Sam and Barry are welcomed by Major Lamphere. Jane also learns that her father, Col. Colbert Scott, although thought dead is very much alive.

The bank is robbed by raiders and Jane's brother, Robert Houston Scott, is recognized as one of them. Robert is a member of a gang led by Henry Jackson, who is bent on making Texas again into a republic.

Jackson leads an attack on an Indian agency which a picture taken by Sam later proves. For romancing Jane, Barry is shot by Jackson. She then realizes she loves the correspondent as he recovers at the Scott home. However, the anti–American views of Colbert force Barry to leave.

Along with Sam, Barry is captured by Jackson. Helping Barry to escape, Robert is killed by Jackson, and the murder is blamed on Barry and Sam.

But Major Lamphere arrests Jackson

for the murder. For his own behavior, Colbert seeks counsel at the gravesite of an old friend, Sam Houston. Confronting an about to be executed Jackson, Houston's ghost tells him that justice will be served.

NOTES: William Farnum, who portrayed Sam Houston in 1917's *The Conqueror*, appeared as his ghost in *Men of Texas*. Universal Pictures released the film on July 3, 1942. It was also known as *Men of Destiny*. Alternate titles during production were *Bad Men of Texas* and *Deep in the Heart of Texas*.

Harold Shumate earlier shared a story credit on *Man of Conquest*; now he was credited for this scenario. Additional dialogue was written, however, by Richard Brooks. Ray Enright directed while George Waggner produced.

The leading man was Robert Stack (who 33 years later portrayed Sam Houston in a television special). Broderick Crawford lent vigorous support as the villain. Appearing as Houston's wife, Margaret, was Janet Beecher.

The Encyclopedia of Western Movies called *Men of Texas* "an entertaining, minor film." Neither it nor *Down Rio Grande Way* are available on video.

10　*Pulitzer Prize Playhouse*

ABC Television / 1950–52 / Episodes, 60 minutes / Black and White

NOTES: The television series, *Pulitzer Prize Playhouse*, was broadcast by ABC over two seasons. The first was from October 6, 1950, to June 29, 1951. The second season, from January 2, 1952, to June 4, 1952, alternated with another series called *Celanese Theatre*.

While the latter series showcased various presentations from prominent playwrights, the former had programs based on writings from Pulitzer Prize–winning authors. Each series also cast known performers.

On November 10, 1950, *Pulitzer Prize Playhouse*, aired "The Raven." It was based on the 1929 prize-winning book by Marquis James on the life of Sam Houston.

Although Zachary Scott was labeled by *Variety* as giving a "fine" performance as Houston, it also found the biography "fragmentary" and thus "difficult to follow its story." The title was the meaning of the Indian name of Co-lon-neh, which had been bestowed upon Houston.

Actor Scott's work included roles in motion pictures and television. He was in the 1950 film *Colt 45*, as well as a 1961 episode of the *Rawhide* television series.

11 *Lone Star*

Metro-Goldwyn-Mayer Pictures / 1952 / 94 minutes / Black and White

CREDITS: Vincent Sherman (director); Z. Wayne Griffin (producer); Borden Chase (screenplay); Harold Rosson (photography); Ferris Webster (editor); Cedric Gibbons, Hans Peters (art directors); David Buttolph (music). Based on a magazine story by Borden Chase and screen story by Howard Estabrook.

CAST: Clark Gable (Devereaux Burke), Ava Gardner (Martha Ronda), Broderick Crawford (Thomas Craden), Lionel Barrymore (Andrew Jackson), Beulah Bondi (Minniver Bryan), James Burke (Luther Kilgore), Ed Begley (Anthony Demmett), William Farnum (Tom Crockett), Lowell Gilmore (Captain Elliott), Russell Simpson (Maynard Cole), William Conrad (Mizette), Victor Sutherland (Anson Jones), Trevor Bardette (Sid Yoakum), Rex Lease, Davison Clark (Senators), and Moroni Olsen (Sam Houston).

SYNOPSIS: The Texas Revolution is long over. Andrew Jackson wants Texas to become part of the United States. To find and convince Sam Houston, the former president assigns the task to cattleman Devereaux Burke.

Concealing his real identity, Burke helps impresario Tom Craden battle hostile Indians. Craden opposes any plans for annexation and the war with Mexico that would result; instead he plans to rule things in the independent Texas. Although Craden later tries to have Burke killed once his identity is revealed, Dev escapes.

Dev Burke had found Houston in friendly Indian territory and then given a letter supporting annexation. In Austin, Dev also met and fell in love with Martha Ronda, the newspaper editor regarded as Craden's girl. Loving Dev, and learning the truth of Houston's support, Martha prints the story.

In another effort to stop annexation, Tom Craden gathers men to fight Burke and his supporters. Sam Houston rides in and order is restored, but not before Burke and Craden fight with fists and knives.

After his defeat by Dev, Tom joins him and the other men as Houston lets them march against Mexico over the annexation of Texas.

NOTES: Metro-Goldwyn-Mayer's *Lone Star* was released in February 1952. Z. Wayne Griffin produced the Western film with the studio's zeal for lavish productions. Nonetheless, it seemed somewhat of a conventional Western under Vincent Sherman's direction.

A screen story from Howard Estabrook and magazine story by Borden Chase supplied the inspiration for the actual script written by Chase. While both Andrew Jackson and Sam Houston were historically for the annexation of Texas, ingredients were added for more flair. Also included in the film and true was Houston's feigning to not want annexation after the U.S. had earlier denied it.

Clark Gable gave his customary solid and strong performance as the fictitious cattleman mixed up with Houston and Jackson. Although sharing star billing, the beautiful Ava Gardner seemed to be relegated to supporting the robust action on hand.

In yet another sturdy villainous role, Broderick Crawford now had the chance to redeem himself by film's end (unlike *Men of Texas*). Lionel Barrymore and Moroni Olsen were both charismatic in their respective roles as Jackson and Houston.

Past historical film roles for Olsen also included Buffalo Bill Cody in 1935's *Annie Oakley* and Robert E. Lee in 1940's *Santa Fe Trail*. In fact, with his beard and buckskins in *Lone Star*, the actor resembled Cody. Former Sam Houstons William Farnum and Davison Clark were seen as senators in the film.

It can be found on video.

12 *The Man from the Alamo*

Universal-International Pictures / 1953 / 79 minutes / Technicolor

NOTES: In 1953's *The Man From the Alamo*, fictional character John Stroud is mixed up with Davy Crockett, Jim Bowie and Sam Houston. As with the Crockett filmography, this entry was the first one with Houston in color.

Howard Negley was seen as the Texas general, who raises a militia against Santa Anna after learning the Alamo is besieged. At the film's end, Stroud rides off to join Houston in the fight between the Texans and Mexicans at San Jacinto.

Another 1953 film, *Shane*, had Negley in a supporting role. An especially rewarding roster of television Westerns included appearances in two episodes during 1956 of *The Roy Rogers Show*.

Main information is in the Crockett filmography. Additional notes are in the Bowie filmography.

13 *The Last Command*

Republic Pictures / 1955 / 110 minutes / Trucolor

NOTES: At the conclusion of the 1955 motion picture *The Last Command*, Jeb

Lacey brings to Sam Houston a letter from Jim Bowie at the Alamo. But the request for help is too late as the fortress has fallen to the Mexican soldiers under Santa Anna. Houston reads the names of the courageous souls who have sacrificed their lives.

Cast as Houston was Hugh Sanders. An even more impressive list of television Western roles were reflected in Sanders' career than the previous actor to portray the Texan, Howard Negley. Between 1953 and 1955 alone, Sanders was in six episodes of *The Long Ranger* series. He was also in a 1959 episode of the *Lawman* series (which starred John Russell, who played Lieutenant Dickinson in *The Last Command*).

Main information is in the Bowie filmography. Additional notes are in the Davy Crockett filmography.

14 *The First Texan*

Allied Artists Pictures / 1956 / 82 minutes / Technicolor / CinemaScope

CREDITS: Byron Haskin (director); Walter Mirisch (producer); Bud Brill, Edward Morey Jr. (assistant directors); Daniel B. Ullman (screenplay); Wilfred M. Cline (photography); George White (editor); David Milton (art director); John McConaghy (set decorator); Emile LaVigne (makeup); Roy Webb (music). From a story by Daniel B. Ullman.

CAST: Joel McCrea (Sam Houston), Felicia Farr (Katherine Delaney), Jeff Morrow (Jim Bowie), Wallace Ford (Henry Delaney), Abraham Sofaer (Don Carlos), Jody McCrea (Lieutenant Baker), Chubby Johnson (Deaf Smith), Dayton Lummis (Stephen Austin), Rodolfo Hoyos Jr. (Colonel Cos), William Hopper (Bill Travis), Roy Roberts (Sam Sherman), David Silva (Santa Anna), Frank Puglia (Pepe), Salvador Baguez (Juan Veramendi), James Griffith (Davy Crockett), Nelson Leigh (Colonel Hockley), Lane Chandler (Jim Fannen), and Carl Benton Reid (Andrew Jackson).

Joel McCrea's Houston in action in *The First Texan*.

SYNOPSIS: Crossing the Red River, Sam Houston enters Texas. At first his intentions are just to practice law and to avoid politics after a past scandal back in the United States. But President Andrew Jackson gives him orders to fight to free Texas from the domination of Mexico.

Becoming a leader in the movement for Texas' independence, Houston is unable to prevent the Alamo's destruction at the hand of Mexican leader Santa Anna. The deaths of Jim Bowie, Davy Crockett and the other defenders who perished there are avenged by Sam and his army.

The force of Texans that Houston whips into shape defeat Santa Anna's troops at San Jacinto. Texas is liberated and Sam Houston becomes president of the new Republic.

NOTES: Joel McCrea made many fine Western films over the years. *The First Texan*, unfortunately, was not regarded as one of them despite his appreciation for the famed frontiersman he portrayed, Sam Houston.

Allied Artists, which released the picture on June 22, 1956, presented a rather too clean viewpoint to be wholly satisfying or successful. Walter Mirisch produced and Byron Haskin directed from a scenario by Daniel B. Ullman that, while earnest, was also considered cliched.

Perhaps *The Encyclopedia of Western Movies* summed it up best by stating, "McCrea's performance as the lawyer turned hero is simply too respectful and Haskin's direction is equally quiet."

The fight at San Jacinto was filmed in the San Fernando Valley of California. Wide-screen movies were then in vogue and *The First Texan* was made in the popular CinemaScope process.

Sam Houston (Joel McCrea, center) leading his troops in *The First Texan*.

Besides playing Houston, Joel Mc-Crea's various roles included other famous Western figures. He was Buffalo Bill in the 1944 film of the same name, Wyatt Earp in 1955's *Wichita* and Bat Masterson in 1959's *Gunfight at Dodge City*.

While *The First Texan* is not available on video, it is in the Library of Congress.

Additional notes are in the Bowie and Crockett filmographies.

15 *The Adventures of Jim Bowie*

ABC Television/Desilu Productions / 1956–58 / 76 Episodes / Each 30 minutes / Black and White

NOTES: During the first season of the television series *The Adventures of Jim Bowie*, a pair of episodes featured Sam Houston. They were "A Horse for Old Hickory" on 1/4/57 and "Master at Arms" on 1/25/57.

While Peter Mamakos was seen as Jean Lafitte in both, Denver Pyle played Houston. Scott Forbes, of course, was Jim Bowie.

Gambler Thimblerig of 1960's *The Alamo* was one of Pyle's film roles. The versatile character actor appeared in a regular or recurring role in a host of television shows. Among his television roles was gunman Ben Thompson during the 1955-56 season of *The Life and Legend of Wyatt Earp*.

Main information is in the Bowie filmography. Additional notes are in the Crockett filmography.

16 *Telephone Time*

CBS Television (1956-57) / ABC Television (1957-58) / Episodes 30 minutes / Black and White

NOTES: *Telephone Time* was a dramatic anthology series seen initially on CBS-TV from April 8, 1956, to the end of March 1957. During that time its programs were based on short stories written by John Nesbitt, who was also the host of the series.

In April 1957, the series, including Nesbitt, switched over to the ABC network. By then the shows featured works by other writers. Nesbitt left the series in September and was replaced as host by Dr. Frank Baxter. He in turn hosted until the final show on April 1, 1958.

The various programs on *Telephone Time* alternated between historical and modern. On December 10, 1957, the episode "Sam Houston's Decision" aired with Don Taylor in the title role.

The story was set in Texas at the time the Alamo was under siege by Santa Anna. Houston had to decide to fight the Mexican troops with his own smaller army or retreat and fight another day.

Taylor was a very visible actor during the 1950s. He played Elizabeth Taylor's husband in *Father of the Bride* in 1950 and its

Richard Boone as Houston in 1960's *The Alamo*.

1951 sequel, *Father's Little Dividend*. He later became a major film director.

17 *The Alamo*

Batjac Productions/United Artists / 1960 / 202 minutes / Technicolor / Todd-AO

NOTES: Main information is in the Davy Crockett filmography. Additional notes are in the Jim Bowie filmography.

"Richard Boone is a definite standout in his two scenes as General Sam Houston–a sincere, meaningful slice of acting." This praise came from *Variety*'s 1960 review of *The Alamo*.

Star and character actor in many film and television roles over the years, Boone was always a forceful presence; whether as villain or hero it didn't matter. He became very popular for his heroic portrayal of Paladin in the television Western series of 1957–63, *Have Gun, Will Travel*.

His portrayal of Houston was right on the mark, and Boone's final moment in the film reflected an unforgettable image. Wearing a magnificent leather jacket, he shares his tough yet heartfelt concern for the sacrifice the men in the Alamo are making to buy him time to raise an army. His last words are "I hope Texas remembers."

Both Texas and Sam Houston remembered.

Along with being on video, *The Alamo* is available on DVD.

18 *Temple Houston*

NBC Television / 1963-64 / 26 Episodes / Each 60 minutes / Black and White

EPISODES/AIR DATES:
1 "The Twisted Rope" (9/19/63)
2 "Find Angel Chavez" (9/26/63)
3 "Letter of the Law" (10/3/63)
4 "Toll the Bell Slowly" (10/17/63)
5 "The Third Bullet (10/24/63)
6 "Gallows in Galilee" (10/31/63)
7 "The Siege at Thayer's Bluff" (11/7/63)

8 "Jubilee" (11/14/63)
9 "Thunder Gap" (11/21/63)
10 "Billy Hart" (11/28/63)
11 "Seventy Times Seven" (12/5/63)
12 "Fracas at Kiowa Flats" (12/12/63)
13 "Enough Rope" (12/19/63)
14 "The Dark Madonna" (12/26/63)
15 "The Guardian" (1/2/64)
16 "Thy Name Is Woman" (1/9/64)
17 "The Law and Big Annie" (1/16/64)
18 "Sam's Boy" (1/23/64)
19 "Ten Rounds for Baby" (1/30/64)
20 "The Case for William Gotch" (2/6/64)
21 "A Slight Case of Larceny" (2/13/64)
22 "Last Full Moon" (2/27/64)
23 "The Gun That Swept the West" (3/5/64)
24 "Do Unto Others, Then Gallop" (3/19/64)
25 "The Town That Trespassed" (3/26/64)
26 "Miss Katherina" (4/2/64)

NOTES: Jeffrey Hunter starred in the series *Temple Houston* during its one season (1963-64) on NBC-TV. The 1963 pilot episode was called "The Man from Galveston." The series was derived from the life of Sam Houston's youngest child born in 1860.

In this scenario, Temple was a dashing lawyer making the rounds of the circuit courts in the American Southwest of the 1880s. Traveling along with him was a U.S. marshal named George Taggart, played by Jack Elam.

To compete with the other Western television shows, Temple was also proficient with the six-gun. The real Temple Houston supposedly competed with Bat Masterson and others in shooting contests.

Actor Hunter in 1956 costarred in films with each of the most famous Davy Crocketts. He was with Fess Parker in *The Great Locomotive Chase* and John Wayne in *The Searchers*.

Jeffrey Hunter and an unidentified actress in *Temple Houston.*

19 *The Great Adventure*

CBS Television / 1963-64 / 26 Episodes / Each 60 minutes / Black and White

EPISODE 16: "The Testing of Sam Houston" (Aired 1/31/64)

CAST: Robert Culp (Sam Houston), Victor Jory (Andrew Jackson), Mario Alcaide (Too-Chee-La), Katherine Crawford (Eliza Allen), Robert Emhardt (Stanbery), Kent Smith (William Carroll), David White (John C. Calhoun), Ralph Moody (Do-Loo-Techka), Tom Palmer (Tom Allen), and June Vincent (Mrs. Allen).

NOTES: Additional notes on *The Great Adventure* series are in the Daniel Boone and Kit Carson filmographies.

This CBS-TV anthology series was reflective of early chapters in American history. "The Testing of Sam Houston" was aired in January 1964.

Robert Culp played Houston when he served with Andrew Jackson as a lieutenant against the Creek Indians. Also reflected were portions of Sam's early political life and his relationship with his first wife, Eliza Allen.

An earlier television Western series, *Trackdown* (1957–59), starred Culp as a Texas Ranger. But he became especially identified for the adventure series *I Spy* (1965–68), in which he costarred with Bill Cosby as agents working for the American government.

20 *Profiles in Courage*

NBC Television / 1964-65 / 26 Episodes / Each 60 minutes / Black and White

EPISODE 5: "Sam Houston" (Aired 12/13/64)

CAST: J.D. Cannon (Sam Houston), Warren Stevens (Lt. Gov. Edward Clark), Peggy McCay (Margaret Houston), Slim Pickens (William Rogers), Noah Keen (Throckmorton), and John Hoyt (Finchley).

NOTES: John F. Kennedy wrote the book *Profiles in Courage* in 1956; the following year it won him the coveted Pulitzer Prize. At the time a Massachusetts senator, Kennedy honored with individual chapters the courage against adversity of eight American senators. Included was Sam Houston.

In 1854, the Kansas-Nebraska Bill was supported by all the southern senators but John Bell from Tennessee and Houston from Texas. Houston voted against the bill because it repealed the Missouri Compromise of 1820, which had balanced out the northern anti-slavery states and the southern pro-slavery states.

The territories in the new bill were above the line of latitude originally set by the Missouri Compromise to separate the North and South. Kansas chose to be anti-slavery but this still created bloodshed with neighboring pro-slavery Missourians. Houston's prediction of civil war over the bill and later secession came true. And in both instances he was persecuted for his opposition by many of his peers and constituents.

Kennedy's book gave credence to Houston's firm actions against the Kansas-Nebraska Bill and secession, as did an episode of the NBC television series *Profiles in Courage*, based on the book. The episode "Sam Houston" was first aired in December 1964. It can be found on video.

Seven of John Kennedy's senators were in fact included in the series, which ran from November 8, 1964, to May 9, 1965, (as were five more political leaders represented in a single chapter of the book). An additional 14 scripts made up the 26-part television series and all were supposedly given approval by then President Kennedy before his 1963 assassination.

Houston was portrayed by J.D. Cannon in the television show. Recalled from his Senate seat during the drama to run for governor, he opposes support of the Confederacy in Texas. In reality, Sam Houston finished out his last Senate term to 1859 after losing an initial gubernatorial race two years earlier; he was replaced when governor in 1861.

Among Cannon's acting credentials were roles in two Burt Lancaster films, 1971's *Lawman* and 1973's *Scorpio*. He was the police chief in the popular 1970–77 television series *McCloud*, starring Dennis Weaver.

21 *The Honorable Sam Houston*

ABC Television/David L. Wolper Productions / 1975 / 60 minutes / Color

CAST: Robert Stack (Sam Houston), Lynn Carlin (Margaret Houston), Charles Aidman (Wilson), Robert Symonds (Roberts), Jim Antonio (Chilton), Ted Eccles (Sam Houston Jr.), Jewel Blanch (Nancy Houston), and Norman Alden (Wilfred Brown).

NOTES: On January 22, 1975, ABC and

An advertisement for television's *The Honorable Sam Houston*, starring Robert Stack.

David L. Wolper Productions telecast the *American Heritage* special *The Honorable Sam Houston*. Stan Margulies was the producer, Richard T. Heffron the director, and Jean Holloway wrote the script.

Varity deemed Robert Stack "excellent" as Houston, the governor of Texas fighting a lost campaign to avoid secession just before the Civil War. Yet the drama was felt to not have explained fully the reasons Houston did so.

Historically, Sam Houston was opposed to secession because of his strong Union bond. He believed Texas fought too hard becoming part of the United States to secede. Houston also believed that Union ties were stronger than any individual northern or southern loyalties.

After his 1861 president inauguration, Abraham Lincoln offered Houston 50,000 Federal troops to help keep Texas in the Union. But the state had already seceded just a month earlier in February; realizing that the troops would create bloodshed among his fellow Texans, Houston declined.

Actor Stack had a distinguished film and television career. For the 1956 motion picture *Written on the Wind*, he was nominated for an Academy Award as best supporting actor; and he won the 1959-60 Emmy Award for outstanding performance by an actor (lead or support). The latter win was for his memorable role as crimefighter Eliot Ness in his popular 1959–63 television series, *The Untouchables*.

22 *Houston: The Legend of Texas*

CBS Television/J.D. Feigelson Productions/Taft Entertainment / 1986 / 180 minutes / Color

CREDITS: Peter Levin (director); Frank Q. Dobbs (producer); J.D. Feigelson (executive producer); John Binder (writer); Frank Watts (photography); Mike Eliot, Paula Sanburn (editors); Mort Rabinowitz (production design); William Strom (art director); Amy Broad, Bobby Bernhardt (set decorators); Joe Hutchinson (costumes); Ken Horn (makeup); Dennis McCarthy (music). Based on a story by John Binder and Frank Q. Dobbs.

CAST: Sam Elliott (Sam Houston),

Michael Beck (Jim Bowie), Claudia Christian (Eliza Allen), Devon Ericson (Tiana Rogers), Michael C. Gwynne (Mosley Baker), Bo Hopkins (Sidney Sherman), Donald Moffat (John Allen), Ned Romero (John Jolly), William Russ (William Travis), John P. Ryan (David Burnet), James Stephens (Stephen Austin), G.D. Spradlin (Andrew Jackson), Richard Yniguez (Santa Anna), James Monroe Black (Fannin), Blue Deckert (Thomas Rusk), Peter Gonzales Falcon (Juan Seguin), Robert F. Hoy (Burleson), John Nixon (Joe), Ivy Pryce (Deaf Smith), John Quade (Stanbery), Katharine Ross (Woman at Alamo), John B. Wells (Kuykendall), and William Schallert (Narrator).

SYNOPSIS: On the night before the Battle of San Jacinto, Gen. Sam Houston and his Texas army contemplate the impending fight with Santa Anna. Houston reflects too on the past events in his life.

In 1829, Houston is the governor of Tennessee when he marries teenaged Eliza Allen. She then admits to loving someone else, having been pressured into the marriage by her ambitious father. Sam ends the marriage and the scandal makes him resign as governor.

On a riverboat, a depressed Houston almost gets into a fight during a card game. His foe turned friend is Jim Bowie, who then tries to persuade Sam to journey on to Texas and seek his fortune. Houston declines, opting instead to return and live among the Cherokee Indians on the Arkansas River.

Sam is welcomed by his adopted Indian father, John Jolly, who years earlier gave him the nickname of the Raven. While Sam marries John's cousin, Tiana Rogers, his drinking consumes him with rage.

The Cherokee are paid for their Tennessee land by the U.S. government with script instead of the promised gold. During 1832, Houston goes to Washington, D.C., and confronts both Congressman Stanbery and President Andrew Jackson over the Indian dilemma. Tried before Congress for beating Stanbery with a cane, Houston uses his forceful oratory skills to get acquitted.

A plan for Houston to look into the vast opportunities in Texas is approved by the president. Traveling there, Sam bids farewell to Tiana.

Sam Houston practices law in Nacogdoches. In San Felipe, he meets colonizer Stephen Austin and becomes a Catholic to secure land under the Mexican law.

By 1835, revolution becomes a certainty between the Texans and dictator Santa Anna. The Texans, including Jim Bowie, take San Antonio and the Alamo away from the Mexicans. As commanding general of the Texas forces, Houston feels the fortified Alamo is a deathtrap but is unable to get Bowie and William Travis to blow it up.

While Houston and others are trying to form an independent government for Texas, at Washington-on-the-Brazos, word arrives that the Alamo is under attack by Santa Anna's huge forces. Called a coward, by political antagonist David Burnet, for not rushing blindly to the Alamo's defense, Sam rides instead to Gonzales to recruit soldiers. There he learns of the Alamo's fall.

As Texans flee from Santa Anna, Houston is again accused of cowardice although he is desperately trying to organize his own army. Word reaches Houston that the Texans at Goliad, under Colonel Fannin, have been captured and killed. Sam also learns that David Burnet has been chosen president of the new independent government.

At San Jacinto in 1836, Houston deploys his men against part of Santa Anna's troops. While wounded in the leg, General Houston is victorious and over 600 enemy soldiers are killed.

Santa Anna is found hiding in the

Sam Elliott in *Houston: The Legend of Texas* (also known as *Gone to Texas*).

rector. When later placed on video and DVD, the title than became *Gone to Texas.*

The strongest visual of the film was the tragic aftermath of the Alamo battle. Yet conveyed with visual excitement was the fighting at Goliad, where the Mexicans chase down and kill their prisoners; and also at San Jacinto, where the Texans get their revenge.

While *Variety* felt "Sam Elliott makes an imposing if tedious Houston," the actor indeed cut a splendid figure. Elliott's finest moments, however, were in the rage and anguish revealed.

1982's *Seguin* is not listed separately in the Sam Houston filmography, but it is mentioned here. For Juan Seguin was certainly part of Houston's army at San Jacinto. Peter Gonzales Falcon portrayed him in *Houston: The Legend of Texas.*

A good many of the actual people in Houston's life were given their moments in the film. Before he became a Texas legend, there were his wives, Eliza Allen (Claudia Christian) and Tiana Rogers (Devon Ericson); and his mentors, Chief John Jolly (Ned Romero) and President Jackson (G.D. Spradlin). In Texas, Sam must not only contend with rival general Santa Anna (Richard Yniguez) and the Mexican forces, but with his political rival David Burnet (John P. Ryan) and the Texas forces.

The film was made entirely in Texas, including at the Sam Houston Park in Houston. A riverboat called the *Landing Queen* doubled for the *Yellowstone.* Supposedly Houston was initially denied entry on it by Burnet just as in the film. When it reached Galveston, the real Sam Houston

woods and ordered to have his remaining troops in Texas surrender and return to Mexico. Texas is free, but President Burnet relieves Sam of his command. Sam Houston is taken away on the riverboat, the *Yellowstone,* for medical attention. Yet he will return to Texas and become a long and enduring presence.

NOTES: *Houston: The Legend of Texas* was originally telecast over the CBS-TV network on November 22, 1986. It was a joint effort with J.D. Feigelson Productions and Taft Entertainment Pictures. Frank Q. Dobbs produced and also wrote the story with John Binder. Peter Levin was the diwas not allowed to travel on any government vessels to New Orleans and receive the medical care needed for his injury suffered at San Jacinto. He had to take a commercial schooner, the *Flora*.

In Westerns both on television and in the movies, Sam Elliott presented a stellar image. He was Virgil Earp in the 1993 film *Tombstone*. In a few television movies, Elliott had roles based on stories by Louis L'Amour; these included 1979's *The Sacketts* and 1982's *The Shadow Riders*.

Additional notes are in the Jim Bowie and Davy Crockett filmographies.

23 *The Alamo, 13 Days to Glory*

NBC Television/Briggle-Hennessy-Carrothers Productions/The Finnegan Company/Fries Entertainment / 1987 / 180 minutes / Color

NOTES: Main information is in the Bowie filmography. Additional notes are in the Crockett filmography.

Lorne Greene might have been a great Sam Houston as an older statesman fighting against secession just before the Civil War. But as a younger Houston during the Texas Revolution, he was too old for the part.

To this fine actor's advantage, his single scene is set at night in Indian territory and he is seen in the shadows. James Bonham (Jim Metzler) rides into Houston's camp looking for help to come to the Alamo. When Houston refuses, not having the manpower then to help, Bonham calls him a coward.

Never to be forgotten will be Lorne Greene as patriarch Ben Cartwright in *Bonanza*. One of television's most popular series, the Western enjoyed a long run from 1959–73.

24 *Sam Houston: Man of Honor*

Grace Products Corporation Presentation / 1993 / 31 minutes / Color

CREDITS: Fred Holmes (director, editor); Greg Vaughn (producer); James Daniels (writer); Joe Cantu Jr. (photography); Jerry Clardy (art director); Joe Riley (makeup). Song: "Beautiful Dreamer," piano arrangement by Stephanie Rocker.

CAST: James Daniels (Sam Houston), Holley Vaughn (Holley Vaughn), and Fred Holmes (Fred the Cameraman).

NOTES: *Sam Houston: Man of Honor* was an informative 1993 video from Grace Products Corporation. Geared for schools, past and present magically come together as Sam is interviewed in modern times; he relates his life's experiences to Holley Vaughn, a journalist student.

Holley Vaughn played herself, while James Daniels was Houston and also the writer of the video. Daniels contributed a humorous and feisty portrayal in the short time allotted.

The director and editor was Fred Holmes, who was also the unseen cameraman accompanying Holley. Greg Vaughn was the producer.

Utilized were landmark locations in Texas. Included was a distant shot of the Alamo at Happy Shahan's AlamoVillage in Brackettville; along with the battlefield at San Jacinto Memorial Park and Monument in Houston, and the Sam Houston Memorial Museum in Huntsville.

Special thanks to the Alamo Village was given in an earlier 1992 educational video from Grace Products Corporation. In color and 40 minutes long, *The Cost of Freedom* depicted a schoolgirl using her imagination in a mysterious old library to go back in time to the Alamo siege and battle.

She then meets William Travis and witnesses his drawing of the line in the sand. His black servant, Joe, is the first to cross in this account. From Travis, the girl learns that freedom is worth dying for to make a better world.

Davy Crockett and Jim Bowie are not actually seen, but they are mentioned by actor Lou Diamond Phillips in the introduction. Sam Houston is also mentioned in the film.

Portraying Travis was Benton Jennings and Joe was played by David King. Holley Vaughn, from the Houston video, was the schoolgirl. While Kevin Young coordinated the reenactors in the Alamo footage, a number of the same crew were on hand as well. Included were Greg Vaughn as producer and Fred Holmes as director, editor and writer.

25 *James A. Michener's Texas*

ABC Television/Spelling Television / 1995 / 2 parts / 360 minutes / Color

CREDITS: Richard Lang (director); Howard Alston (producer); Aaron Spelling, E. Duke Vincent, John Wilder (executive producers); Sean Meredith (writer); Neil Roach (photography); John A Martinelli (editor); John Frick (production design); Adele Plauche (art director); Ron Talsky (costumes); Lee Holdridge (music). Based on the novel by James A. Michener.

CAST: Maria Conchita Alonso (Lucia), Benjamin Bratt (Benito Garza), Fred Coffin (Zave), Patrick Duffy (Stephen Austin), Chelsea Field (Mattie Quimper), Anthony Michael Hall (Yancy Quimper), Stacy Keach (Sam Houston), David Keith (Jim Bowie), John Schneider (Davy Crockett), Rick Schroder (Otto MacNab), Grant Show (William B. Travis), Randy Travis (Sam Garner), Daragh O'Malley (Finley MacNab), Lloyd Battista (Santa Anna), Roland Rodriguez (Juan Seguin), Deborah Nunce (Josephina Garza), Lanell Pena (Maria Trinidad Garza), Lonnie Schuyler (James Bonham), Russ McCubbin (Panther Komax), Esteban Powell (Young Yancy), Sully Ross (Young Otto), and Charlton Heston (Narrator).

SYNOPSIS: In 1821, impresario Stephen F. Austin has a mandate from the Mexican government to bring American settlers into Texas. Among the settlers are Mattie Quimper and her stepson, Yancy.

Others have visions of Texas land like Finley MacNab and his son, Otto; and Jim Bowie, who kills a man in a knife fight in Tennessee. Sam Houston is the Tennessee governor.

When his political career falls apart, Houston is tossed out of an establishment for being a drunkard. Houston meets Bowie and they talk about Texas.

Mattie defends Austin's honor against some of the settlers who oppose his wishes to follow the Mexican laws. She is in love with Stephen.

Finley and Otto come to Texas and meet Benito Garza, the Mexican who rounds up wild mustangs. To acquire more land under the Mexican law, Finley and a friend, Zave, marry Garza's sisters.

When Mexico restricts further American emigration, Austin must deal with the dilemma. Men like William Travis speak out against the oppression.

Sam Houston arrives in Texas with a declaration from President Andrew Jackson to help the settlers. Jim Bowie is also there and helps Benito when he is accused of being a thief by some Anglo troublemakers. Realizing that Stephen Austin will never have the time to love her, Mattie succumbs to the affections of Garza.

During these years, Otto and Yancy become young men. The friction between Texas and Mexico continues. While Houston is for a separate government for Texas, he promises Austin not to advocate any violence as long as he is opposed to the fighting.

But Stephen is imprisoned by the Mexicans for bringing his concerns to bear. After he is freed, Austin admits to Houston that warfare is the only recourse.

As Mexican leader Santa Anna marches with his forces to put down the revolt, Benito Garza joins him. Mattie cares for Austin when he is stricken with pneumonia.

Rebels under the command of William Travis, including Bowie and Davy Crock-

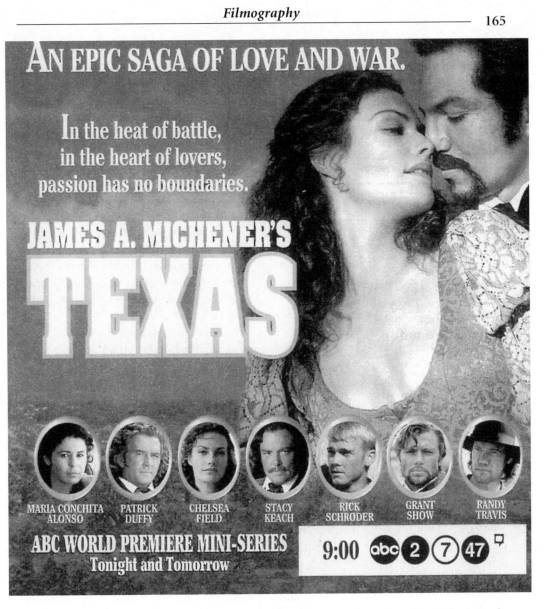

An advertisement for the TV miniseries *James A. Michener's Texas.* Despite the emphasis on the romance between Chelsea Field and Benjamin Bratt, Stacy Keach's Houston stole the show.

ett, make a defense at the Alamo against Santa Anna. Tejano Juan Seguin makes a plea in Gonzales for reinforcements; among those who then join Travis are Zave and Finley.

Santa Anna's troops, including Garza, wipe out the Alamo's defenders in 90 minutes after a long siege. Otto MacNab witnesses the aftermath.

Before the Alamo fell, a new Texas Re-

public was formed. As Houston organizes an army to fight Santa Anna, the Mexicans kill Colonel Fannin and his Texans at Goliad.

Having tried to rally support in the United States, Austin is sent by Houston to blow up Mattie's ferry barge to keep it out of enemy hands. Garza arrives with soldiers, who mistakenly kill Mattie.

General Houston's army attacks Santa

Anna's camp at San Jacinto. Among Sam's men are Otto, Yancy and Sam Garner; also fighting with the Texans is Juan Seguin.

Wounded, Houston still wins the battle. When Santa Anna tries to escape, a cowardly Yancy takes credit over Otto for his capture. Otto saves Garza's life.

With Santa Anna's promise to leave Texas, Sam Houston is elected president of the Texas Republic. He appoints Stephen Austin to a post in his cabinet. But Austin's pneumonia reoccurs and he soon dies.

The Texas Rangers are formed to stop the border raids by the Comanche Indians and Benito Garza, who is now a bandit. With him is his mistress, Lucia. Sam Garner and Otto MacNab are part of the rangers.

A senator in Texas, Yancy Quimper wants to accept a premature treaty for annexation to the United States. Yet Houston feels the time is not ready and forces the conniving Yancy to leave Texas.

Although the rangers cannot cross the border into Mexico to chase Garza, Otto nonetheless goes after him. In a gunfight, Otto is wounded and is forced to kill both Lucia and Benito.

The flag of the Texas Republic is lowered in 1846. But Sam Houston raises a new one–the flag of the United States of America.

NOTES: Stacy Keach's Sam Houston was the biggest role in *James A. Michener's Texas*. Michener's novel of the same title was the basis for the script by Sean Meredith. A 1994 video release initially, the miniseries followed on ABC-TV on April 16 and 17, 1995. Howard Alston was the producer and Richard Lang the director.

Fictitious incidents and characters coexisted with historical events and figures for an epic entertainment. Yet *Variety* felt "most Texans will find the heavy-footed version of only a part of their history routine and predictable."

As a colorfully garbed Tennessee governor, Houston is first seen by David Keith's Jim Bowie. A humorous exchange is soon shared between them while in an intoxicated state that uses the Bowie knife as a phallic symbol.

Stephen Austin and Sam Houston actually shared leadership of the rebel forces during the Texas Revolution (initially in October 1835, Austin was in charge with Houston becoming officially the commander in short order). While they had their differences over the course of command taken, an especially sympathetic relationship is emphasized in *Texas*. Patrick Duffy's Austin was the first major role undertaken in a film by the man Houston eulogized as "the Father of Texas."

Following Stephen Austin's death in history, Houston, as Texas president, had 23-gun salutes at all the military posts to represent each one of the then republic's counties. But Austin's heirs believed Sam had reneged on an earlier promise never to oppose Austin for the presidency.

Like *Houston: The Legend of Texas*, the action at San Jacinto is excitingly presented. In *Texas*, General Houston's leading his men into battle and being wounded in the process is even visualized in slow-motion.

Again, as with the earlier film, *Texas* dramatizes the destiny of Sam Houston with an eagle soaring overhead. It is seen as he rides across the Red River into Texas and before his monumental victory at San Jacinto.

Besides the famous Alamo Village, other Texas sites were utilized. Included were the Devil's River Ranch and Rancho Rio Grande.

Other historical film roles, besides Houston, were done by Stacy Keach. He was gunman Doc Holliday in 1971's *Doc* and outlaw Frank James in 1980's *The Long Riders*. His versatility and charisma shone through in all.

Additional notes are in the Bowie and Davy Crockett filmographies.

26 *True Women*

CBS Television/Craig Anderson Productions/Hallmark Entertainment / 1997 / 2 parts / 170 minutes / Color

CREDITS: Karen Arthur (director); Lynn Raynor (producer); Craig Anderson (executive producer); Christopher Lofton (writer); Tom Neuwirth (photography); Corky Ehlers (editor); Rodger Maus (production design); Christa Munro (art director); Barbara Haberecht (set decorator); Vicki Sanchez (costumes); Bruce Broughton (music). Based on the book *True Women*, by Janice Woods Windle.

CAST: Dana Delany (Sarah McClure), Annabeth Gish (Euphemia Ashby), Angelina Jolie (Georgia Lawshe), Tina Majorino (Young Euphemia), Rachael Leigh Cook (Young Georgia), Michael York (Lewis Lawshe), Jeffrey Nordling (Peter Woods), Salli Richardson (Martha), Tony Todd (Ed Tom), Julie Carmen (Cherokee Lawshe), Terrence Mann (Captain Haller), Michael Greyeyes (Tarantula), Khadijah Karriem (Tildy), Anne Tremko (Matilda Lockheart), Irene Bedard (Tobe), Powers Boothe (Bartlett McClure), Charles Dutton (Josiah), and John Schneider (Sam Houston).

SYNOPSIS: Young Euphemia Ashby is visiting Georgia Lawshe, a playmate on a Georgia plantation, when she receives word of her father's death. Having also lost her mother, she then goes to Texas to live with pregnant sister Sarah, who is married to Bartlett McClure.

News of the fall of the Alamo is brought to the McClures by Sam Houston. As Bartlett joins Houston's army, Sarah leads 2,000 Texas women and children toward the Louisiana border from the advancing Mexican forces of Santa Anna. During the journey, Sarah loses a little son to sickness and her baby is stillborn.

On a distant ridge overlooking San Jacinto, the women and children witness the battle ranging between Houston and Santa Anna. The Texas men win the fight and return to their waiting families.

With President Andrew Jackson ordering the removal of the Indians from her own homeland, young Georgia witnesses the persecution the Indians must endure. She must bear the secret that she is part Indian.

In the years ahead, Indians fight against the Texans. Georgia finally moves to Texas with her doctor husband, Peter Woods. Now a Texas Ranger, Bartlett dies in a horse fall.

Euphemia marries horse rancher William King and both she and Georgia have children. Yet the childhood friends are divided over the slavery issue, with Georgia using slaves on her cotton plantation. Their husbands fight in the Civil War as rebels, as does another son of Sarah's.

Reconstruction following the war means the end of slavery, but a killing is committed by Georgia to protect a daughter from a Yankee captain named Haller. During the ladies suffrage movement, Georgia helps Euphemia fight for their right to vote.

Georgia's husband and Euphemia are at her side when she later dies from an illness. As old women, sisters Sarah and Euphemia look back at their lives in Texas.

NOTES: *True Women* was initially a two-part miniseries which aired on CBS television on May 18 and 20, 1997. It is on video. Lynn Raynor produced and Karen Arthur directed the epic filmed in Texas. The scenario from Christopher Lofton was based on the book by Janice Woods Windle.

Dana Delany as Sarah, Annabeth Gish as Euphemia, and Angelina Jolie as Georgia gave remarkable performances. Equally notable were Tina Majorino and Rachael Leigh Cook, who respectively played Euphemia and Georgia as children.

The trials and tribulation of these formidable females was, as *TV Guide* noted, "inspired by a real family history." Perhaps the strongest moments of the film were the Texans fleeing from Santa Anna (the Runaway Scrape), and the Creek Indians forced from their homes (the Trail of Tears).

Early in the story, Sam Houston is seen riding magnificently on his white horse, Saracen; the scene is reminiscent of Richard Boone's arrival on horseback in the earlier *The Alamo*. John Schneider's work as the colorful Texan in *True Women*, while brief, makes one want to see more of him in the proceedings, just as it did when he played Davy Crockett in *James A. Michener's Texas*.

The fight at San Jacinto is seen here as a nighttime battle from afar. Historically, while the Mexicans were sleeping, it was a siesta for Houston attacked Santa Anna in late afternoon.

27 Two for Texas

TNT Presentation/Bleecker Street Films Production / 1998 / 96 minutes / Color

CREDITS: Rod Hardy (director); Dennis Bishop (producer); Lois Bonfiglio (executive producer); Larry Brothers (writer); David Connell (photography); Michael Ornstein (editor); Cary White (production design); Edward Vega (art director); Barbara Haberecht (set decorator); Dan Moore (costumes); Lee Holdridge (music). Based on the novel by James Lee Burke.

CAST: Kris Kristofferson (Hugh Allison), Scott Bairstow (Son Holland), Irene Bedard (Sana), Tom Skerritt (Sam Houston), Peter Coyote (Jim Bowie), Victor Rivers (Emile Landry), Thomas Schuster (Alcide Landry), Rodney A. Grant (Iron Jacket), Marco Rodriguez (Santa Anna), Karey Green (Susannah Dickinson), Richard Jones (Deaf Smith), and Gatlin Boone Smith (Baby Dickinson).

SYNOPSIS: Convicts Hugh Allison and Son Holland escape from a Louisiana prison camp. Intent on joining Sam Houston's army, they enter the Mexican state of Texas. Trying to recapture them is a gunrunner for Santa Anna, Emile Landry.

Stealing horses, the convicts trade them to Choctaw Indians for food, shelter and a slave woman named Sana. She was captured from another Indian tribe.

Mexican soldiers try to renege on a deal with the Choctaw leader, Iron Jacket, over a herd of stolen horses. Both Hugh and Son help the Indians against the soldiers. As payment, the convicts are given six horses which they take when they leave along with Sana.

Young Holland hates Indians because his family was killed by drunken Shawnee. Yet he falls in love with Sana, although she is made to leave since he must join up with General Houston.

Chased into Houston's camp with Son by Emile Landry, Allison is reacquainted with his old friend Jim Bowie. Once learning of the reasons why Son and Hugh were made prisoners–Son was falsely accused of stealing a purse, while Hugh killed a cardsharp–Houston lets them stay.

Bowie soon leaves to join the rebel forces already at the Alamo. When Houston receives word that it is besieged by Santa Anna's soldiers, Allison and Holland go there. They find the Alamo's defenders dead, and Hugh takes Bowie's knife as a keepsake.

After retreating from Santa Anna, Sam Houston faces him in battle at San Jacinto. Ordered to blow up a bridge to keep the enemy from escaping, Son and Hugh also kill Landry.

Hugh rides north following the battle, giving Son Jim Bowie's knife. Son finds Sana to begin a new life together on 640 acres of land given to him by Houston.

NOTES: On January 18, 1998, Turner Network Television (TNT) first presented *Two for Texas*. It is also on video. James Lee Burke's novel was the source for the script by Larry Brothers. Rod Hardy directed while Dennis Bishop produced. Fine scores were composed by Lee Holdridge for both this film and *James A. Michener's Texas*.

In contrast to the past few Houston entries, this one was indeed much shorter. Still included was the Battle of San Jacinto and Santa Anna's surrender to Sam Houston. Mainly focused on, however, were the fictitious title protagonists played well by Kris Kristofferson and Scott Bairstow. Irene Bedard, who played an Indian hanged by racists in *True Women*, was the leading lady.

Peter Coyote's Jim Bowie has long hair and a beard, and Tom Skerritt's Sam Houston has a Lincolnesque beard in *Two for Texas*. Both actors contributed laid-back performances for the most part, although each had their spirited moments–Bowie when he shows off his knife-throwing skills, and Houston when he rallies his fellow Texans with the battle cry to "Remember the Alamo" before their victory at San Jacinto.

Like Coyote's memorable appearance in *E.T.*, Skerritt played an unforgettable part in another science fiction classic. He was the space team leader in 1979's *Alien*.

Additional notes are in the Bowie filmography and Davy Crockett is included here. While not seen, Crockett is mentioned a few times during *Two for Texas*–most vividly when Karey Green's Susannah Dickinson tells Kristofferson and Bairstow that the frontiersman was hacked to death with a few of his comrades.

28 *The Alamo*

Touchstone Pictures/Imagine Entertainment / 2004 / 137 minutes / Technicolor

CREDITS: John Lee Hancock (director); Mark Johnson, Ron Howard, Brian Grazer (producers); Todd Hallowell, Philip Steuer (executive producers); Leslie Bohem, Stephen Gaghan, John Lee Hancock (screenplay); Dean Semler (photography), Eric L. Beason (editor); Michael Corenblith (production design); Lauren Polizzi, Dan Webster (art directors); Carla Curry (set decorator); Daniel Orlandi (costumes); Stephen L. Hardin (historical consultant); Carter Burwell (music).

CAST: Dennis Quaid (Sam Houston), Billy Bob Thornton (Davy Crockett), Jason Patric (James Bowie), Patrick Wilson (William Travis), Jordi Molla (Juan Seguin), Emilio Echevarria (Santa Anna), Marc Blucas (James Bonham), Castulo Guerra (Manuel Castrillon), Afemo Omilami (Sam), Edwin Hodge (Joe), Leon Rippy (William Ward), Tom Davidson (Green Jameson), Kevin Page (Micajah Autry), Joe Stevens (Mial Scurlock), Stephen Bruton (Almeron Dickinson), Laura Clifton (Susanna Dickinson), Ricardo Chavira (Gregorio Esparza), Lanell Pena (Ana Esparza), Estephania LeBaron (Juana), Emily Deuschanel (Rosanna Travis), Nathan Price (Charlie Travis), Blue Deckert (Colorado Smith), Turk Pipkin (Issac Millsaps), Brandon Smith (J.C. Neill), W. Earl Brown (David Burnet), Stewart Finlay-McLennan (James Grant), Tommy G. Kendrick (T.J. Rusk), Tom Everett (Mosley Baker), Rance Howard (Governor Smith), Michael Crabtree (Deaf Smith), Nick Kokich (Daniel Cloud), Lynn Mathis (James Hackett), and Safia Gray (Ursula Veramendi).

SYNOPSIS: The Alamo has fallen to Santa Anna's Mexican army. At a distant campsite, Sam Houston and his own Texian army receive the terrible news. Houston then reflects back one year.

At that earlier time in Washington, D.C., Houston shares the prospects for acquiring land in the Mexican province of Texas. Among his listeners is Congressman David Crockett. While attending a play derived on his exploits as a frontiersman, Crockett shares his celebrity with all those present.

A drunken Houston faces down his political detractors back in San Felipe,

Texas, who wish to relieve him as general. The Texian politicians are at odds over whether or not to make Texas a republic in the war against the Mexican government. But Col. James Bowie comes to Sam's defense brandishing his famous knife.

Also in San Felipe is Lt. Col. William Travis, who is signing the divorce papers with his wife, Rosanna. Taking custody of their son, Charlie, Travis soon leaves the little boy in the care of others when he is ordered to go to the Alamo in San Antonio de Bexar.

At the Alamo, Travis learns from its commander, J.C. Neill, that the mission turned fortress is being used to keep the advancing army of Santa Anna from passing and attacking the Texas settlements. Called away on a personal matter, Neill turns over command of the Alamo to Travis.

With Houston and Bowie both drunk, Sam receives Jim's promise to go and blow up the Alamo to keep it out of enemy hands. Houston believes that using it as a fort is not the best way to fight Santa Anna.

But once in Bexar, Bowie changes his mind after visiting his home, ravaged in the struggles between the Texians and Mexicans. The memory of his deceased wife, Ursula, and their love shared there prove overwhelming.

Although Travis and Bowie agree that the Alamo should remain fortified, there is friction between them over command. After his arrival, and now a former congressman, Davy Crockett acts as a mediator to settle their differences. With Bowie then commanding the volunteers, Travis commands the regular army.

Several thousand Mexican soldiers soon besiege the Alamo under Santa Anna. When Bowie tries to arrange a truce, only surrendering at discretion is first offered.

After Travis fires off a cannon, Santa Anna has a red flag flown, meaning death to all who oppose him. But also in the Alamo are women, children, even slaves owned by Bowie and Travis.

When Bowie is stricken with consumption and bedridden, he is cared for by his sister-in-law, Juana. William Travis then becomes the sole commander, showing strong leadership during the ongoing cannon bombardment against the Alamo.

Testing the Alamo's strength, a group of Mexican soldiers use the surrounding jacales as cover to attack. They are driven back, however, and Crockett leads a small party to burn down the jacales. During the siege, Davy also fires a shot at Santa Anna. Crockett's fame as a frontiersman is even known to the Mexicans.

Mexican native Juan Seguin, who supports those in the Alamo, is sent by Travis to inform Sam Houston of their dilemma. In Gonzales, Sam is trying to raise an army to successfully confront Santa Anna's own forces; some 30 Texicans from the town have gone to the Alamo's defense already. Seguin is ordered to stay with Houston, who realizes many more men besides his own 124 and the 189 in the Alamo are needed.

Santa Anna allows any of the native Mexicans inside the Alamo to leave, hoping it will cause the other defenders to try and escape. Some of the Mexicans do depart with their families, and Jim Bowie lets his slave, Sam, go with them.

None of the others in the Alamo try to leave as, encouraged by Crockett, Travis gives a speech in the courtyard reminding them all of their life-and-death stake in Texas. Bowie hears the words from his sickbed.

One of Santa Anna's officers, Manuel Castrillon, urges him to wait for the bigger

Opposite page: Poster Art for 2004's *The Alamo.* Despite its ad-line, the film was not a box office success.

cannons to arrive to break down the Alamo's walls. But Santa Anna refuses, showing little regard for the lives of his men in planning a massive assault.

During the early morning hours following the 13-day siege, Santa Anna attacks the Alamo with his soldiers. Travis is shot in the forehead and killed instantly. While the Alamo defenders put up a heroic defense, they are soon overpowered by the 2,500 men sent against them over the walls. Bowie fires off two pistols before the Mexicans breaking into his room kill him with their bayonets.

Driven back from their post at the palisade, Crockett and a few comrades make a last stand in the Alamo church. Captured and bound, Davy seems to be the last defender alive. Before he is killed by the enemy's bayonets, Crockett wants Santa Anna to surrender.

Juana and other women and children do survive. Their lives are spared, as is Joe, Travis' slave.

As the story returns to Sam Houston in the aftermath of the Alamo's fall, he is leading a great tide of Texians as they flee from Santa Anna. Although his men want him to fight, Sam is prepared to run until he feels the time is right.

The time comes after learning that Santa Anna's forces are divided. On the vast field at San Jacinto, Houston and his now-large army attack the Mexican leader, wiping out part of his army in 18 minutes. With Houston's victory, Santa Anna is captured and Texas is liberated.

Juan Seguin returns to the Alamo and buries the remains of its defenders. The spirit of Davy Crockett is seen atop its hallowed walls.

NOTES: Additional notes are in both the Crockett and Bowie filmographies.

Throughout 2004's *The Alamo*, Dennis Quaid's Sam Houston is seen as the central force caught between bringing relief to the Alamo or waiting in order to save Texas. Houston's resiliency to overcome all obstacles–whether fellow Texans, Santa Anna, even his own heavy drinking–ultimately proved his worth as a great man.

This is admirably conveyed in the film. While there are moments where Quaid perhaps has his jaw clenched too firmly, nonetheless the strong determination of the commander of the entire Texas forces is fully realized.

The real Sam Houston was wise in feeling Santa Anna could not be stopped by forting up at the Alamo. This was proven when the Mexican forces became divided and Santa Anna was defeated on the open battleground that was San Jacinto.

Substituting for San Jacinto in the film was an 840-acre ranch near Batrop, Texas. Beautifully recreated is Houston's battle cry to "Remember the Alamo," and leading his men on his white horse, Saracen.

Variety reflected that this climactic battle "possesses a sense of anxiety, urgency and impending tilt in the balance of history largely missing from the rest of the film."

Both Jordi Molla's Juan Seguin and Emilio Echevarria's Santa Anna also figured prominently in the final passage, as they did earlier on in *The Alamo*.

On December 16, 2003, Dennis Quaid hosted a two-hour program on television's History Channel called *Remember the Alamo* (which was later rebroadcast). The documentary was yet another examination of the actual story of the battle at the Alamo.

Reenactments and personal stories of its key figures were included in the attempt to bring forth a balanced account. Also revealed was the information that some of its defenders may have actually survived the battle.

Five

JIM BRIDGER

Biography and Overview

James Bridger was born on March 17, 1804, near Richmond, Virginia. It was in a tavern owned by his father whom he was named after. His mother was Chloe Tyler Bridger.

When both the tavern and the family farm near Fredericksburg failed, the Bridgers moved on to Six Mile Prairie in 1812. Right across the Mississippi River was St. Louis, Missouri.

After five years living in Missouri, Jim's mother died from an undiagnosed illness, and in short order so did his father and a brother. Jim was 13 years old at the time. He and a younger sister were then cared for by an aunt who came to live with them.

An additional five years would pass with Jim Bridger working as an indentured servant to a blacksmith named Phil Creamer. The work was hard but young Bridger was up to it as he grew to be a muscular 6-footer.

Jim had never learned to read but was informed of an advertisement in a St. Louis newspaper from March 20, 1822. It was placed there by William H. Ashley, who was lieutenant governor of Missouri and brigadier general of the state militia.

The advertisement, which would forever change James Bridger's life, called for 100 men to journey up the Missouri River on a fur-trapping expedition. The time frame was between two to three years.

On April 3, when the first of two keelboats departed, an 18-year-old Bridger was aboard; he was the youngest member. Many of the others were runaway slaves, army deserters, even downright criminals. Yet also with Jim was Mike Fink, the legendary river king, and Jedediah Smith came along as a hunter with the second keelboat.

An elderly Jim Bridger and Mike Fink are part of the adventures of a 1977 television movie. It is called *The Incredible Rocky Mountain Race* (NBC).

William Ashley's business partner, Maj. Andrew Henry, led the first keelboat of adventurers, including Bridger. The other keelboat followed in May, but it sank en route and was replaced.

Meanwhile, Major Henry's keelboat had reached the Platte River. Over the summer, Assiniboine Indians stole horses from Henry that were being driven along inland. The 1,800-mile journey took four and a half months to reach its destination at the junction of the Missouri and Yellowstone Rivers. This was the same waterway Lewis and Clark took years earlier.

By the middle of September, a trading post was built called Fort Henry; and the men proceeded to set up trap lines to catch mountain beaver. In October, General Ashley and the second keelboat arrived with additional horses and men (for some recruits had earlier deserted). Jim Bridger's previous blacksmith skills were then put to good use at the fort, although he preferred to be out trapping with the other men.

As they became confined to the fort and the area over the cold winter, restlessness set in among the trappers. During the prior journey, Mike Fink and a friend named Carpenter had entertained them by shooting tin cups of whiskey off each other's head. Now Mike and Carpenter were embroiled in a winter long argument that ended tragically in April 1823.

While testing their sharpshooting skills once again with the tin cups, Mike shot Carpenter in the forehead with his rifle, killing him. Supposedly it was not an accident, at least to the thinking of another trapper, Talbot. As Mike Fink hurried to reload his rifle, Talbot shot him dead through the heart with a pistol.

The following month, both the Arikara and Blackfeet Indians began fighting with the fur trappers for intrusion into their territory. It was during the initial conflict with the Arikara that Jim Bridger first began to admire Jed Smith, who was only five years older, for his great bravery.

Smith had gone down river to meet William Ashley, who was returning with some new keelboats, when fighting broke out in the Arikara village. Over a dozen trappers were killed, but Jed, thick in the danger, rallied the men. He then further risked his life getting word to Andrew Henry, as Ashley was escaping down river.

With some 50 men, including young Bridger, Henry went to join his partner by traveling in dugouts down the Missouri River and passing the Arikara village without incident. The trappers then went further down river, eventually ending up at Fort Kiowa, an outpost of the rival French Fur Company.

By August, the United States government, to safeguard its interests in the Northwest, had sent 230 soldiers to confront the Arikara with the help of Sioux Indians and the fur trappers. Col. Henry Leavenworth's command of this body of men proved ineffective, for while negotiating a truce, the Arikara were allowed to escape.

Of the 80 trappers now with the Ashley-Henry company, about 29 were willing to venture on after this situation. As Jed Smith led 16 of the men further west from Fort Kiowa in September 1823, Major Henry took a group back up toward the Yellowstone; the plan was for both groups to meet in the land of the Crow Indians. Although Bridger was mighty tempted to return to St. Louis, he went on with Henry's party.

Accompanying Smith's party were Bill Sublette and Tom Fitzpatrick, both who would have close ties with Jim Bridger in the years ahead. Meanwhile, Jedediah Smith was attacked by a grizzly bear, and the torn scalp and ear that resulted were stitched back on.

Among the 13 trappers with Major Henry, and 200 miles from Fort Kiowa on their inland trek to reach the Yellowstone, was hunter Hugh Glass. While out hunting for fresh meat with Black Harris that same September of Smith's bear attack, Glass was attacked by a mother grizzly with two yearling cubs.

Glass shot at the big grizzly but to no immediate effect. As the bear horribly mauled the hunter, Harris was forced to kill one of the yearlings to protect himself.

After hearing his screams, the other trappers with Henry rushed to help Glass. More shots were fired and both the rampaging grizzly and her other yearling were brought down. Like Smith, Glass suffered a torn scalp; yet his injuries were more extensive and included heavy bleeding, crushed ribs and a broken leg.

A variation of this encounter is included among the 18 entries in the Jim Bridger filmography. It is a 1971 motion picture called *Man in the Wilderness* (Warner Brothers).

While his various wounds and broken bone were tended to, Hugh Glass was barely conscious and all his comrades felt that death would come soon. An attempt was made to move him but this proved a slow undertaking. So as not to risk all their lives in the hostile Arikara territory where they still were, Major Henry asked for volunteers to remain behind with Glass until he died.

Only James Bridger came forward to stay with Hugh. Finally an older man than Jim, John Fitzgerald, agreed to stay as well when Henry promised them $40.00 each as compensation.

They stayed with the seemingly dying Glass for five days when Fitzgerald convinced the teenaged Bridger to leave the man because of the ongoing threat of Indian attack. Fitzgerald also took the hunter's rifle and knife.

Yet Hugh Glass fully regained consciousness, crawling to the river to drink. Eating roots, berries, even raw meat from a buffalo calf brought down by hungry wolves, he struggled back to Fort Kiowa. It took him six weeks.

Supposedly Glass joined a trading party going upriver and that November they came under attack by the Arikara. Glass

and another, Toussaint Charbonneau, survived but soon separated. The next month Glass reached Fort Henry, only to learn from Sioux Indians that Henry and his men had gone on to make another post near the Big Horn River, an outlet off the Yellowstone.

When he reached this post, Glass wanted to kill both Bridger and Fitzgerald. The latter man wasn't there, having quit the company, and Henry convinced Glass that Jim had to be excused for he was still a boy. This humiliated Jim even more and he felt it was a cowardly thing that he did. But Hugh Glass forgave Jim Bridger.

In the first weeks of 1824, Major Henry sent some of his men to trade with the Crow Indians. Jim was with the small detachment led by John Weber at the Indian village where the Big Horn and Wind Rivers met. The Crow fondly called Bridger by the name of Casapy (meaning Chief of the Blankets) because he guarded the blankets so well from being stolen.

Other white men were in the Crow village, including Jed Smith and the trappers he led earlier from Fort Kiowa. When the Crow gave Smith directions to find a wealth of beaver streams just west of the mountains, Bridger was in the group of around 11 men that went along.

From the Wind to the Popo Agie and Sweetwater Rivers, Smith and his party took a pass through the Rocky Mountains. It was part of the Continental Divide, which separated the waterways flowing east toward the Atlantic and west toward the Pacific.

This was the South Pass, which in the years ahead became a popular wagon trail for emigrant families heading west. The trappers reached it on March 17, 1824, Jim Bridger's 20th birthday.

Beyond the mountain gateway was a river the Indians called Siskadee Agie. Proving indeed to be a rich source for beaver, to the trappers it was the Green River.

That spring, beaver traps were set all along the Green; soon over two dozen more men with John Weber, having left the post by the Big Horn, followed Smith's trail. After crossing the Green River Valley, Bridger joined Weber for a fall hunt on the Bear River as Smith and others went up the Green.

From the initial Ashley-Henry outposts on the Yellowstone and near the Big Horn River (in present-day Montana), Bridger was part of that influx of fur trappers ultimately opening the way through the South Pass and to the Green River (also in present-day Wyoming). Now they were preparing for a winter camp on the Bear in today's Idaho.

Speculation soon stirred among the men as to where the Bear River led downstream. Jim Bridger was chosen to find out. In November 1824, he built a small round craft called a bullboat (made from willow hoops and buffalo skins secured with rawhide and tallow).

Young Jim then went over rapids and through canyons on his boat to a large body of salt water. He thought at first it might be part of the Pacific Ocean. But it was the Great Salt Lake in today's Utah, and Bridger was given the recognition of being the first white man to see it.

By the time of the first rendezvous in the summer of 1825, Major Henry had left the fur-trapping business and returned to St. Louis. Jed Smith was offered a partnership then by General Ashley. Over 100 trappers, or mountain men (from more than just one fur company), gathered at the rendezvous on a tributary of the Green River called Henry's Fork. It took place on July 1 and may have lasted but a single day, unlike the gatherings in the years ahead; those lasted far longer and were attended by both trappers and Indians, where a carnival atmosphere of both frolic and business went on.

Earlier on, trapper Tom Fitzpatrick

and two companions made it to St. Louis after an arduous trek with a cache of furs. Ashley then brought a supply caravan back to the rendezvous, inland along the South Platte River, and crossing the Continental Divide not at the South Pass but along an edge of the desolate desert known as the Great Divide Basin.

The competition was so strong that Ashley was able to buy beaver skins for low prices as did others. A rival, Etienne Provost (who claimed to have seen the Great Salt Lake two months before Jim Bridger), paid Ashley only $2.50 a pound.

William Ashley realized all too well that more money was to be found in supplying the outfits than in the actual trapping. In the course of buying, selling and trading, when he returned to St. Louis it was with over $40,000 in beaver furs.

After taking another caravan of supplies to the next year's rendezvous in Cache Valley off the Bear River, Ashley had become a rich man. He then sold his interest in the company to Jed Smith, David Jackson and Bill Sublette.

The summertime rendezvous is boldly featured as part of this filmography in a 1978 television miniseries. It is included in the second episode of *James A. Michener's Centennial* (NBC) called "The Yellow Apron."

During the winter of 1825-26, Bannock Indians had made off with 80 horses belonging to the Ashley and Smith company of trappers. It happened at their base camp in the Great Salt Lake Valley. Jim Bridger and 40 fellow trappers gave chase; included was a mulatto spending his first winter in the mountains named James Beckwourth.

The mountain men divided into two groups to attack the Indian camp. Bridger was made a captain of one and Tom Fitzpatrick of the other. Six Indians were killed and 120 stolen horses were recovered.

Jim joined a group of his comrades led

by Bill Sublette for a fall hunt in 1826. As the men made their way up Wyoming's Snake River and then to the Teton Range of the Rockies, they were pitted against hostile Blackfeet Indians.

However, Sublette and his men struggled on until they came upon a strange land smelling of sulfur, with boiling pools of water and mud, and water and steam shooting furiously into the air. Just as trapper John Colter did, some 19 years earlier when first seeing this place, Bridger also called it hell.

And like Colter, Bridger's stories of the bizarre terrain were disbelieved for years. It wasn't until 1871 that the stories were vindicated when a U.S. Geological Survey team went there under Dr. Ferdinand Hayden. In time this place became known as Yellowstone National Park.

While Sublette, Bridger and their comrades were exploring the wonders of Yellowstone, Jed Smith took the first white men into California from the interior of the country. The journey was filled with hardship; finally leaving most of his party there to camp, Smith with two others crossed over the Sierra Nevada Mountains and went to Bear Lake, east of the Great Salt Lake. Arriving there as the third summer rendezvous was underway, Smith soon returned to his party with further provisions for a fall hunt.

At that same rendezvous, the trappers discovered the Blackfeet had made a truce. James Beckwourth, Bridger and another, Pierre Tontavantogan, went then to the Indian village to trade.

Getting into a fight with the Blackfeet, Bridger was taken captive. He escaped as did Beckwourth when the truce collapsed. But old Pierre was killed by the Indians.

When Sublette took the company's beaver furs to sell in St. Louis in 1828, he assigned Jim Bridger as guide to a trapper brigade under Robert Campbell. This was to Crow country east of the Great Divide,

and Jim also served as interpreter. Beckwourth went along; in January 1829, and tired of being a trapper, he began living with the Crow Indians.

Jed Smith had rejoined both his partners, Jackson and Sublette, by the summer of 1829 at Pierre's Hole (between the Snake River and the Tetons in Wyoming). Soon piloting a brigade of men under Smith was Jim Bridger as they trapped beaver on a number of rivers that fed off the Yellowstone River, including the Powder and Big Horn.

By the following spring, Smith was calling Bridger by the sobriquet Gabriel because of the solemn expression he wore. The nickname became Old Gabe and mountain men remembered Jim by it for years.

The summer rendezvous of 1830 was held near the mouth of the Popo Agie, off the Wind River. There, Smith, Sublette and Jackson sold their fur company for $16,000 (the same price at which they bought it from William Ashley).

The new owners called themselves the Rocky Mountain Fur Company. They were Bill Sublette's brother, Milton; Tom Fitzpatrick; Henry Fraeb; Jean Baptiste Gervais and James Bridger.

After selling out, Smith and his partners took over $84,000 worth of accumulated beaver furs to St. Louis. They invested then in the Santa Fe trade market. In May 1831, on the Santa Fe Trail in southwest Kansas, Jedediah Smith was killed by Comanche Indians. He was 32 years old.

Having eliminated a good bit of its competition already, in 1830 the bigger American Fur Company began going after the Rocky Mountain Fur Company. Initially organized by John Jacob Astor, the American Fur Company was being directed now by others, including Kenneth McKenzie. In the background loomed the British-controlled and even bigger Hudson's Bay Company.

Both the American and Rocky Mountain Fur Companies raced to get their supply caravans to rendezvous in 1832. Bill Sublette, who continued to supply his former company, reached the designated site at Pierre's Hole first. By the time the rival caravan showed up the rendezvous was over. Not only did the Rocky Mountain Fur Company benefit from dealing with Sublette, but so did free trappers and friendly Indians.

Despite this victory, after two years Jim Bridger and his partners were facing serious financial woes due in no small way to the fierce competitiveness and depletion of beaver in many areas. Tom Fitzpatrick even offered to divide the trapping areas between both companies. The American Fur Company refused the offer at that time.

Kenneth McKenzie had sent William Henry Vanderburgh with a group of trappers to dog Bridger's trail to the best beaver streams. It then became necessary to hunt in Blackfeet Indian country when the other trapping locations were depleted.

The Indian danger thus was continuous. Frustrated by Vanderburgh's persistence, Bridger went into the hostile terrain knowing his rival would follow. Unfortunately for Vanderburgh and his trappers, they came across some 100 warriors in October 1832. Vanderburgh and another man were both killed.

With his own men, including Tom Fitzpatrick, Bridger was still in Blackfeet country (off Madison Fork in Montana) when they ran into an entire Indian village migrating. Jim approached the chief on horseback; his Hawken rifle was pulled from his grasp as two arrows struck him in the lower backside.

Bridger managed to get back to the safety of his trappers, who were rushing to his aid. For the rest of the day both sides exchanged fire until the Blackfeet withdrew during the night. Three trappers and nine Indians lost their lives.

The following morning, Fitzpatrick pulled one arrow free and only the broken shaft of the other. An arrowhead too deeply embedded remained stuck in Bridger's back.

That spring of 1833 found Fitzpatrick and Bridger trapping along what would one day be the Wyoming and Colorado border. It was here that Jim learned that old Hugh Glass, who had allied himself with the American Fur Company, was fatally shot and scalped by Arikara Indians off the Yellowstone River. It was near that company's post called Fort Union (up by the North Dakota and Montana border).

Jim Beckwourth, once an ally of Bridger's, was also associated with the American Fur Company. In September 1833, Beckwourth supposedly deployed around 100 Crow Indians against Fitzpatrick trapping on the Tongue River (which ran off the Yellowstone in Montana).

The Indians stole from Fitzpatrick's camp, including furs and horses. His threats to have Bridger come after them worked to some degree, as the Indians returned the horses if not the beaver pelts. They were later sold by the Crow at another American Fur Company post. Beckwourth afterward denied any part in the matter.

Following the 1832 rendezvous, Bill Sublette and his then business partner, Robert Campbell, began building trading posts along the Missouri River to compete with those of the American Fur Company. One, Fort William, was near Fort Union.

But by early 1834, due in part to a scandal forcing Kenneth McKenzie to depart over the building of an illegal still at Fort Union, the American Fur Company reached an agreement with Sublette. And he was apparently helped in this by none other than William Ashley, now a U.S. congressman representing Missouri.

Sublette and Campbell, by the agreement, would sell all their trading posts to the American Fur Company. In return, the

American Fur Company would withdraw from the Rockies for a year. In that time Sublette expected the Rocky Mountain Fur Company would go under financially.

While this was transpiring, Tom Fitzpatrick had already arranged for an independent trader, Nathaniel Wyeth, to bring out the supply caravan to the summer rendezvous of 1834 and charge half of what Sublette would. Discovering this, Sublette actually beat Wyeth with his own caravan to the rendezvous off Ham's Fork (a tributary of Wyoming's Green River).

As Sublette had been empowered by Fitzpatrick with the company's debts two years earlier, the Rocky Mountain Fur Company had to exchange the harvest of beaver furs for Bill Sublette's supplies. The exchange did not liquidate the debts accrued by the company; so the prior arrangement made by Sublette and the American Fur Company remained binding.

Nathaniel Wyeth didn't care for the way he was ousted and was able to collect a $500 default fee from the Rocky Mountain Fur Company. In time Wyeth sold his accumulated supplies and a trading post to the Hudson's Bay Company.

During that 1834 rendezvous, Henry Fraeb and Jean Baptiste Gervais sold out to their partners for horses and trade goods. Fitzpatrick, Jim Bridger and Milton Sublette remained partners and merged with Lucien Fontenelle and Andrew Drips, both of whom had been allied with the American Fur Company.

The Rocky Mountain Fur Company then became Fontenelle, Fitzpatrick and Company. Over the following winter of 1835, the new company and the American Fur Company made an alliance.

With John Jacob Astor officially retired, Pratte, Chouteau and Company took over the Rockies for the American Fur Company in the year after the agreement with Bill Sublette. An agreement was now reached with Bernard Pratte Sr., Pierre

Chouteau Jr. and Fontenelle, Fitzpatrick and Company which enabled them all to share the mountains.

While Lucien Fontenelle brought the supply caravan in 1835 halfway to the rendezvous on the Green River, Tom Fitzpatrick brought it the rest of the way. Part of Jim Bridger's brigade of trappers at that summer rendezvous included a smaller but equally tough mountain man. His name was Kit Carson.

Film adventures shared by Bridger and Carson are included here. They are reflected in three motion pictures–the 1928 silent *Kit Carson* (Paramount); then 1940's *Kit Carson* (United Artists), and 1947's *Along the Oregon Trail* (Republic).

Television entries with the legendary frontiersmen are also included. They are a television movie and two miniseries— *Bridger* (ABC) in 1976; then *Kit Carson and the Mountain Men* (NBC) in 1977, and *Dream West* (CBS) in 1986.

Two other milestones were part of James Bridger's life at the rendezvous of 1835. He married an Indian woman whom he called Cora. She was the daughter of Insala, chief of the Flathead Indians. Jim also met the missionary doctor Marcus Whitman (and the following year his missionary wife, Narcissa).

Now as curious Indians and trappers gathered around them, Dr. Whitman extracted the 3-inch arrowhead still embedded in Bridger's back. When Whitman wondered how infection hadn't set in, Jim made a jovial remark to the effect that meat doesn't spoil in the mountains.

Continuing to trap beaver, it often seemed more of Jim's time was spent fighting Blackfeet Indians. In February 1837, he and about 60 men, including Kit Carson, held off over 1,000 braves up in the Yellowstone country.

The mountain men had built a 6-foot barricade and behind it were their frightened families. Jim's wife was there with a new daughter, Mary Ann, born in 1836. The Blackfeet, however, stopped fighting, supposedly because the aurora borealis lit up part of the sky which the Indians took to be a bad omen.

Conflicts with other Indian tribes continued as well. During the 1837 spring hunt, trapper Joe Meek, with Bridger, shot down a Crow warrior. The Indian had slapped Joe's Shoshone wife. The violence escalated until the Indians fled and Bridger moved out of Crow country.

By the next springtime, Jim Bridger had no choice but to penetrate deeply into Blackfeet country; the beaver were again becoming scarce. Both Carson and Meek were among his trappers. Fighting did occur with one village, but another would not fight because smallpox had broken out among the Indians.

While the Blackfeet blamed white men for the disease, Bridger blamed Jim Beckwourth for stealing infected blankets from St. Louis and thereby exposing the Indians. Most likely this wasn't true, but Bridger was still upset that Beckwourth could have been behind the Crow's robbing of Tom Fitzpatrick's camp earlier on.

Bridger left his family in the care of the Flathead Indians in 1839 as he visited St. Louis for business reasons. It was the first time Jim had seen the growing town in 17 years and he actually got lost there.

Pratte, Chouteau and Company were now just Pierre Chouteau and Company, but Jim managed to secure contracts over the next few years for trading and trapping. An earlier partner of Jim's, Henry Fraeb, was again a partner for a while.

In 1840, there was a last rendezvous held on the Green River. Bridger and Fraeb assisted Andrew Drips with the final caravan of goods. The market was collapsing for the once-popular beaver hats and coat collars back east and overseas. Silk hats were instead the fashion.

Buffalo hides were also proving profitable. In the summer of 1841, Fraeb was off on a buffalo hunt with 20 men (on Battle Creek, in south central Wyoming near the Colorado border) when 500 Cheyenne and Sioux warriors attacked. Four hunters were killed, including Henry Fraeb.

Included in the Bridger filmography is a variation on the death of Fraeb and the last days of the fur trappers. It is a 1980 film called *The Mountain Men* (Columbia).

In December 1841, near the Great Salt Lake, a son was born to Cora and James Bridger named Felix Francis. Like the buffalo hunting, guiding early emigrant wagon trains west was another way to make a living for men like Kit Carson and Tom Fitzpatrick.

On one such trek, Bridger had Fitzpatrick take daughter Mary Ann to live with the Whitmans at their Waiilatpu Mission in Oregon. In 1848, Joe Meek brought word to Jim that a Cayuse Indian attack on the mission (in November 1847) resulted in the death of Narcissa, Marcus and 12 others. Included was Meek's own daughter, Helen; supposedly Mary Ann was taken captive and died shortly afterward.

Another daughter, Mary Josephine, had been born to the Bridgers in 1846. Yet soon after giving birth, Cora died and it might have been from the bite of a rabid wolf.

Three years before, in 1843, Jim found another business partner, Louis Vasquez, and built a trading post off Black's Fork (another Green River tributary in today's Wyoming). Not forgetting his boyhood trade, Jim set up a blacksmith shop at the new post called Fort Bridger.

But Jim wasn't always found at Fort Bridger, for his wanderlust would take him back to the mountain wilderness he loved. In one excursion, in 1844-45, he led 30 men to explore and trap beaver in California.

Involving Jim Bridger in 1846 was a controversy even more unsettling than the

Hugh Glass episode with the bear. An emigrant wagon train westward bound, known as the Donner-Reed Party, stopped at Fort Bridger and inquired about a shorter route to the Sierra Nevadas. Later claiming to have advised against it, due to a 40-mile stretch without water among other problems, Bridger told them of a shortcut over the Great Salt Desert to their mountain range crossing.

The emigrants nonetheless used the route although it took much longer than anticipated. Late getting into the mountains, they became trapped there when heavy snows closed off the trails. Among the hardships faced was starvation, and cannibalism occurred. Forty of 82 people perished.

In June 1847, Bridger was on a trail, west of the Little Sandy River in Wyoming, when he came across another group of emigrants. This 73-wagon train called itself the Pioneer Party and was led by Brigham Young.

Jim Bridger has a supporting role in a 1940 motion picture about the Mormon leader. Included here, the title is simply *Brigham Young— Frontiersman* (20th Century-Fox).

Fleeing from religious persecution in Illinois, the Mormons were looking for their promised land. Bridger was supposedly invited to dine with Young and shared the prospects of the Great Basin region and the Great Salt Lake for settlement.

A friendly bet may have been made by Bridger to Young that crops wouldn't grow in that arid terrain. But the following month Young and his Pioneer Party did begin to settle there; in a year's time some 3,000 Mormons migrated to join their leader.

A religious wagon train of settlers is also part of the scenario in another Bridger film entry. It is a 1933 movie, *Unknown Valley* (Columbia).

Other movies are included too about wagons rolling west. They are the 1923

silent *The Covered Wagon*, and a 1931 sequel of sorts, *Fighting Caravans* (both for Paramount).

In the winter of 1847-48, Jim Bridger led his friends, the Shoshones, on a raid against their enemies, the Ute Indians. A Ute squaw was taken who became Jim's wife. But she died in July 1849 giving birth to their daughter, Virginia Rosalie.

Gold was discovered in California in 1848, and in the year ahead trading post partners Bridger and Vasquez handled the supply demands of thousands of people seeking their fortunes. With Jim busy at Fort Bridger, Louis set up an advance post to catch the fortune hunters coming through the South Pass.

The tragedy of the earlier Donner-Reed Party brought the United States Corps of Topographical Engineers, under Capt. Howard Stansbury, to seek out Bridger. That ill-fated shortcut, whose passage included the desert crossing, was called the Hastings Cutoff (after Lansford Hastings who wrote a rather misguided book, *The Emigrant's Guide to Oregon and California*). Apparently it was the Hastings description of the cutoff which James Frazier Reed and brothers George and Jacob Donner had inquired from Bridger then followed with their wagon train.

Jim's assistance was required by Stansbury's engineers to help select a better trail for wagons to take to California. On a buffalo hide and with a piece of charcoal, Bridger drew a detailed map. Thus traveling northwest of Fort Bridger to Fort Hall on the Snake River, wagons could then move easily along the Snake to the Humboldt River. The rivers divided, with the Humboldt going toward California and the Snake toward Oregon.

With his children being cared for by the Shoshone, Jim took another Indian wife in 1850. She was the daughter of Shoshone chief Washakie, and her name was Little Fawn.

James Bridger was then 45 years old. According to legend, he had to fight to the death for Little Fawn's hand against a younger Indian rival, Ear of the Fox. As each man charged the other on horseback, their mounts fell to the ground. The men rose and fought with knives until Bridger was able to kill his adversary.

The first entry in this filmography is called *Jim Bridger's Indian Bride* (Kalem). It is a silent film from 1910.

Little Fawn and Jim were remarried in a Christian ceremony in 1851 by missionary Father Pierre-Jean de Smet. It took place at Fort Laramie (in today's North Platte valley of Wyoming), and Jim then called his wife Mary Washakie. The year before, a son, John, was born to them. Two more children followed–Mary Elizabeth in 1853 and William in 1857.

Jim had brought his father-in-law's Shoshone braves to a treaty council held at Fort Laramie at the time of the remarriage. Old friend Tom Fitzpatrick, who died of pneumonia three years later, was an Indian agent trying to secure the peace treaty at the council involving various tribes. When the Sioux Indians present threatened violence, Bridger had his own Indians display the percussion cap rifles he had armed them with to deter any aggression.

During 1852, while Jim's then youngest children, John and Virginia, remained with him, six-year-old Mary Josephine and 10-year-old Felix went to Father de Smet's mission school in St. Louis. Felix and Mary Josephine were temporary wards of Robert Campbell. Bill Sublette, Campbell's one-time partner in the fur trade, had died in 1845 from tuberculosis.

When Utah became a U.S. territory in 1850, Brigham Young was recognized as governor. He felt free to then impose his will over the inhabitants of the Green River country (which apparently was still part of Utah at that time). This included the residents of Fort Bridger.

Thirty thousand Mormons had followed Young west by 1853. When they set up charters to take over the commerce on the Green River, conflicts arose with the current ferrymen there who were once mountain men.

The Mormons blamed Bridger for instigating this resistance and the killing of four Mormon men that summer. They also were against Jim supplying his Indian allies with rifles.

Thus, Governor Young ordered Jim Bridger out of Utah and sent a 150-man militia force to get him at Fort Bridger. Jim eluded capture, but property and livestock at the fort were confiscated. Part of the force, which called itself the Nauvoo Legion, also attacked the Green River ferrymen, supposedly killing three of them.

Chief Washakie wanted to strike against the Mormons with 1,200 warriors. But Bridger refused their help knowing that Young, if attacked, could then demand protection from federal troops. Jim realized he just had to bide his time until Young was legally removed from the governorship.

After a stay at Fort Laramie, Bridger took his family to live in western Missouri by the summer of 1854. This was in Jackson County on 640 acres of land, and near the community of Westport.

In the care of his old mountain men friends, Jim had constructed a ferry crossing called simply enough, Bridger's Ferry. Safe from Brigham Young's wrath, it was located off the North Platte River (and near Orin Junction in Wyoming).

While checking on the ferry, that same summer Mary and the children settled into their new home. Jim met at Fort Laramie an Irish nobleman named George Gore. Bridger was hired as guide to the large hunting party Gore had assembled and so wintered at the fort.

In the spring of 1855, Bridger guided the Gore expedition to the Powder River, and continued on to other areas in Wyoming over that summer and fall. The winter of 1855-56 was spent with Gore along the Tongue River.

The hunting ended that coming spring in the Yellowstone country. During the long hunt, Gore and his party brought down a large portion of the wildlife–included were some 40 bears and 2,500 buffalo.

Pierre Chouteau and Company, Jim's old outfit (which remained in a business capacity on the frontier until 1865), offered to buy Gore's stock at Fort Union. But George Gore, upset over the pricing, gave his oxen and horses away to Indians and his own employees.

When Jim was occupied on the long hunt, the Mormons had purchased Fort Bridger in August 1855. Neither Bridger or former partner Louis Vasquez were present. Vasquez, running another trading post for the Mormons near their city by the Great Salt Lake, undoubtedly supported the transaction. A Mormon, H.F. Morrell, forged both signatures. Actually an X was made by Jim's name since he couldn't write.

A trip to Washington protesting Young's actions was made by Bridger soon after the March 1857 presidential inauguration of James Buchanan. Jim discovered that he wasn't alone in having trouble with the Mormons. Federal officials had been ousted from their posts in Utah too.

President Buchanan had Brigham Young replaced as governor by Alfred Cumming, a non–Mormon. This was used by Young as a way to unite his followers against their opposition. On September 15, war was declared against the United States.

Earlier that same month, emigrants passing through Utah were confronted by the Mormon war fervor. Allied with Paiute Indians, or perhaps disguised as Indians, Mormons commanded by Young's foster son, John Doyle Lee, attacked them.

At Mountain Meadows, 120 emigrant men, women and children were massacred.

Afterward, Young disclaimed any part in the tragedy. Yet it would hang over his head for 20 years until Lee was brought to trial, found guilty, and put to death by the Mormons.

Jim Bridger guided eight federal companies of the 10th Infantry to the Green River 12 days after the Mormon declaration of war. Initially the U.S. troops were commanded by Col. E.B. Alexander, who proved an ineffective leader, not even putting up a defense when Young had men attack the army supply trains. Alexander was replaced by Col. Albert Sidney Johnston.

Taking Bridger's advice, Johnston wintered at what was left of Fort Bridger after the Mormons got through with it earlier on. Chief Washakie again offered to ally his Indian braves with Jim and the soldiers.

In November 1857, not only was Jim appointed chief guide of Johnston's troops, with the rank of major, but the U.S. government made him a deal for the use of Fort Bridger. As the prior sale to the Mormons was deemed illegal, the army began leasing the fort from him for $600 a year.

Although Brigham Young had 6,000 men then making up the Nauvoo Legion, by the spring of 1858 the Mormons agreed to a peaceful end to their standoff. Government envoys even promised the Mormon leader a full pardon.

When Bridger guided the U.S. troops into Salt Lake City, on June 26, 1858, Young and the other Mormons living there had temporarily vacated it. Shortly thereafter, Jim received a discharge and returned home to his family in Missouri.

While Jim was away on his quest against the Mormons, Mary gave birth to son William. When he returned, it was to learn that complications from the birth had taken her life.

Back in 1850, Jim successfully helped Captain Stansbury and the U.S. Corps of

Topographical Engineers find a trail through the Rocky Mountains for the Union Pacific Railroad to follow. Ironically, once the Union Pacific crossed the Continental Divide, it helped put Bridger's Ferry out of business.

Less successful with the Corps of Engineers was an excursion between 1859 and 1861 under Capt. W.F. Raynolds. The captain was persistent in finding a trail leading from the headwaters of the Wind River to the Yellowstone, although Jim knew such a pathway didn't exist. Still Bridger guided the expedition on until it was turned back by a canyon wall.

As a guide, Jim's services were always in great demand. The spring of 1862 had him taking a military escort of two judges

A depiction of Jim Bridger at age 62.

into Utah; later that summer Jim guided to the Green River another detachment working on telegraph lines.

As the Civil War unfolded, Jim had leased the Westport home and acquired another in the same community. George London and his wife took care of the place and Bridger's children. While son John may have died at age five, Felix was a soldier in the war with the 2nd Missouri Artillery.

During 1864, Bridger led an emigrant wagon train to the Montana gold fields. En route in Wyoming, and just before the Big Horn River, an Indian camp was sighted in the distance. Jim thought it might be hostile Sioux but it was the Shoshone out on a buffalo hunt. Reunited with Chief Washakie, Jim told him of his daughter's passing.

Troubles with the Sioux Indians are reflected in the Jim Bridger filmography. Three films are included — 1951's *Tomahawk* (Universal-International), 1953's *Pony Express* (Paramount), and 1955's *The Gun That Won the West* (Columbia).

Following the November 1864 massacre of a Cheyenne Indian village by a former missionary named John Chivington, all hell broke loose on the western frontier. Not only did the Cheyenne nation retaliate but so did the Sioux and Arapaho.

Jim Bridger was home with his family in early 1865 when a call for his services as a scout in the ensuing Indian conflicts came. It was from the commander of the entire western army, Gen. Grenville Dodge.

The 11th Ohio Infantry was guided by Bridger in its military campaign against the Indians. In July, Jim was made chief of scouts under Gen. Patrick Connor. An Arapaho village along the Tongue River was then attacked; although driven away, the Indians tried in vain to recapture over 1,000 ponies.

Thousands of Sioux and Cheyenne Indians attacked Bridger and the soldiers in the Powder River area as they rescued a detachment of road builders. All fell back to the safety of a frontier outpost, Fort Connor, as the Indians pursued them.

When outpost Fort Philip Kearney was officially dedicated in October 1866, Jim Bridger was present. Two months later he was inside the fort when Lt. Col. William Fetterman disobeyed orders and chased after Sioux Indians instead of just going to the aid of a wagon train of woodcutters. The Indians decoyed Fetterman and 80 soldiers, killing them all.

Fighting between the U.S. Army and the Indian tribes continued for years. Serving at one point under Bridger as an assistant scout was none other than Jim Beckwourth. Legend has it that Indians later poisoned Beckwourth because they still believed that he brought the smallpox to the mountains.

On July 21, 1868, Bridger was given a permanent discharge as a frontier scout. It was at Fort D.A. Russell near Cheyenne, Wyoming. He was 64 years old, and medical problems were bothering him such as rheumatism and failing eyesight.

With Jim home in Missouri, he was surprised when he had to wage his own campaign against the U.S. government. It was proving his title to Fort Bridger was legitimate so he would receive the lease payments from the army. His own surviving children helped to resolve the matter after he was gone and received a recompense of $6,000.

In 1871, Jim had moved back to his first Westport home after selling the second one. As Daniel Boone had done over 50 years earlier with his grandchildren, Jim enjoyed surrounding himself with the neighborhood children and telling them stories. With his dry wit and deadpan expression, he had always been a good storyteller.

One of his favorite yarns to the children was how he had been boxed into a canyon by fierce Indians, with his guns empty and his knife missing. When the children asked him what happened then, Jim replied that he was killed and scalped.

Felix Bridger spent some time in the Rocky Mountains and even scouted for George Armstrong Custer. But in 1876, Felix took ill and died, some five years before his father.

By 1875, Jim had gone totally blind. Daughter Virginia, who was married to a military man, Lt. Albert Wachsman, gave her father a gentle horse to get around on. Sometimes Jim got lost on his own property.

Jim Bridger passed away on July 17, 1881. He was 77.

In 1904, his remains were disinterred from a little roadside graveyard near his home and moved to Kansas City's Mount Washington Cemetery. This was at the request of General Dodge, who had great respect for the old scout who had been involved in hundreds of military patrols.

Perhaps President Franklin D. Roosevelt paid Jim his greatest tribute in 1941. For among the places which bear his name, none stands out more than Bridger-Teton National Forest in Wyoming. The memory of his deeds may have dimmed, but his mountain wilderness remains forever.

Jim Bridger Filmography

1 *Jim Bridger's Indian Bride* 1910
2 *The Covered Wagon* 1923
3 *Kit Carson* 1928
4 *Fighting Caravans* 1931
5 *Unknown Valley* 1933
6 *Brigham Young — Frontiersman* 1940
7 *Kit Carson* 1940
8 *Along the Oregon Trail* 1947

1 *Jim Bridger's Indian Bride*

Kalem Company / 1910 / 1,000 feet / Silent / Black and White

NOTES: *Jim Bridger's Indian Bride* was released on November 18, 1910. Kalem distributed this now lost silent picture as well as the following year's release of *Daniel Boone's Bravery.*

No other information was found for this 12-minute entry in the Bridger filmography. The title could refer to any of the actual frontiersman's three Indian wives.

It was not uncommon for mountain men and Indian women to be companions. The mountains could be a lonely, harsh environment and the trappers making a living there often found a deep contentment among the Indians. Their women were referred to as squaws and they were squaw men.

Both Jim Bridger and Kit Carson were included in this group.

2 *The Covered Wagon*

Paramount Pictures/Famous Players-Lasky Corporation / 1923 / 10 Reels (98 minutes) / Silent / Black and White

CREDITS: James Cruze (director, producer); Adolph Zukor, Jesse L Lasky (presenters); Jack Cunningham (adaptation); Karl Brown (photography); Dorothy Arzner (editor); Hugo Riesenfeld (music arranger). Based on the novel by Emerson Hough.

CAST: J. Warren Kerrigan (Will Banion), Lois Wilson (Molly Wingate), Alan Hale (Sam Woodhull), Ernest Torrence (Bill Jackson), Tully Marshall (Jim Bridger), Charles Ogle (Jesse Wingate), Guy Oliver (Joe Dunstan), Ethel Wales (Mrs. Wingate), and Johnny Fox (Jed Wingate).

SYNOPSIS: It is May 1848 at Westport Landing (since called Kansas City). A massive emigrant wagon train, captained by Jesse Wingate, is set to embark on a 2,000-mile journey to Oregon.

Molly, Wingate's daughter, is engaged to his first lieutenant, Sam Woodhull. Yet she is uncertain about their wedding plans.

Another wagon train soon joins the Wingate train led by Will Banion. With Banion is trail guide Bill Jackson.

Informing Jesse that Will lost his army commission, Sam is then given command over Banion's wagons. Will is given the task of guarding the stock in the rear.

As the wagon trains begin their trek across the Valley of the Platte, Will and Molly take a shine to each other. Along the way, an argument between Sam and Will nearly ends in gunplay before Jackson stops it. Later Will does beat Sam in a fight.

Some emigrants head back home, finding the trail just too tough. Disheartened, the remaining wagoners are cheered up by Banion and Jackson. But Jesse tells Will to stay away from Molly once Woodhull relates Will's commission was lost for stealing cattle.

Reaching the North Fork of the Platte River, the wagon train cannot cross over the deep water. Indians run a ferry barge but the $10 charge per wagon is too high for most of the emigrants. Only Woodhull crosses and then kills an Indian.

Following Banion's lead, the Wingate wagons travel upriver and cross at a better point. Bill Jackson is reluctant to help Sam after he is attacked by the Indians.

Trader Jim Bridger, returning to his home at Fort Bridger, is reunited with old friend Jackson. En route, much-needed meat for the emigrants comes from a buffalo hunt. Although Will is unaware of it, Woodhull fires a shot at him.

All the wagons enter a canyon below Fort Bridger in October 1848. Frontiersman Joe Dunstan informs Jim that Will has been exonerated by the army for he took the cattle to feed a starving detachment of soldiers.

Yet after drinking with both Dunstan and Jackson, Bridger forgets to tell Will the good news. Will soon pulls out with his wagons intending to try his luck in California with the recent discovery of gold.

As Molly prepares to marry Sam Woodhull, Jim finally remembers the message about Will. Molly then stops the wedding just as Indians attack, wounding her in the shoulder.

Will Banion and his wagoners return to help drive the Indians away. In the fighting, Jim Bridger is badly hurt.

Not allowed to see Molly because of a promise made to Woodhull, Will again heads out for California. Bill Jackson stays behind to help care for Bridger.

When Jim is recovered, Bill follows Banion to the gold fields. Setting out with the others for Oregon, Molly bids Bridger farewell and asks Jackson to have Will join her there. At a crossroad, Woodhull and some followers break off from the main body and go to California as well.

The Wingates and their own followers do finally reach Oregon. Back in California, in the spring of 1849, Jackson kills Woodhull to save Will's life. Will then goes to Oregon and is reunited with Molly.

NOTES: *The Covered Wagon* has the distinction of being called the first epic Western film. A great success in its day, many a Western that followed drew inspiration from its tale of emigrants moving west over the Oregon Trail.

Available on video, this famous silent had its New York premiere on March 16, 1923. A general release by its distributor, Paramount Pictures, followed in September 1924. It was presented by pioneer filmmakers Adolph Zukor and Jesse L. Lasky.

Back in 1916, Zukor and Lasky had merged their respective motion picture companies and formed the Famous Players-Lasky Corporation. Two years later, Paramount became a partner.

Given the task of helming *The Covered Wagon*, as producer and director, was James Cruze. Utilized was a hefty production cost for its day of $782,000 to bring to the screen elements of the 1922 novel by Emerson Hough. Jack Cunningham adapted the story.

Among the locations used was Snake Valley, Nevada, with some 400 covered wagons deployed. Under the supervision of future cowboy star Tim McCoy, 3,000 Indians were supposedly in the film from a number of reservations.

While the romantic subplot, with hero J. Warren Kerrigan and villain Alan Hale competing over heroine Lois Wilson, was considered a bit trite, the panoramic vistas of the exodus of wagons were simply stunning. Karl Brown's camera work was the single most memorable aspect of the film.

But the most memorable performances in *The Covered Wagon* came from the frontiersmen played by Ernest Torrence and Tully Marshall. Their colorful interpretations of respectively Bill Jackson and Jim Bridger added a combination of heroics and comic flair that were delightful.

"With Torrence he takes much of the picture and makes it go," said the *New York*

Times referring to Marshall. *Variety* added that the latter's scenes "lent an admirable touch."

Marshall's Bridger doesn't come into the story until about the halfway point. But Torrence's Jackson calls him "the best scout in the Rockies."

Soon Jim is seen jumping on a running buffalo and killing it with only his knife. At Fort Bridger, he is living with a pair of Indian wives–Blast Yore Hide and Dang Yore Eyes–treating them both affectionately.

Included in *The Covered Wagon* is a takeoff on the infamous episode involving Mike Fink and his friend Carpenter where they shot whiskey cups off the other's head. Here Bridger and Jackson amusingly engage in just such a contest; ironically their shots are so clean that the cups don't even fall off their heads.

While there might have been no Bill Jackson in the actual life of Jim Bridger, there was one Dave Jackson. He was 34 years old to Bridger's 18 when they were first part of the William Ashley-Andrew Henry expedition into the mountains in the early 1820s. And Dave, for whom Jackson Hole in Wyoming was named, was partner to Bill Sublette and Jedediah Smith when Ashley's interests in the fur trade were bought out later in that decade.

Both Tully Marshall and Ernest Torrence reprised their roles in another entry in the Bridger filmography. It is the forthcoming *Fighting Caravans*.

Additional notes can be found in the Kit Carson filmography, as well as main information on an entry which credits Marshall playing Jim Bridger. This latter title is the 1933 serial, *Fighting with Kit Carson*.

3　*Kit Carson*

Paramount Pictures / 1928 / 8 reels / Silent / Black and White

NOTES: Fred Thomson had the title role in this Paramount release. In a smaller part, Nelson McDowell was cast as Jim Bridger.

McDowell's impressive list of Western film credits includes both silents and talkies. He was Windy Bill Sharp in 1925's *Kit Carson Over the Great Divide*.

Main information on *Kit Carson* can be found in the frontiersman's filmography.

4　*Fighting Caravans*

Paramount Pictures / 1931 / 91 minutes / Black and White

CREDITS: Otto Brower, David Burton (directors); Edward E. Paramore Jr., Keene Thompson, Agnes Brand Leahy (scenarists); Lee Garmes, Henry Gerrard (photography); William Shea (editor); Robert Odell (art director); John Leipold, Oscar Potoker, Emil Bierman, Max Bergunker, Emil Hilb, Herman Hand, Karl Hajos, Sigmund Krumgold, A. Cousminer (music). Based on the novel by Zane Grey.

CAST: Gary Cooper (Clint Belmet), Lily Damita (Felice), Ernest Torrence (Bill Jackson), Fred Kohler (Lee Murdock), Tully Marshall (Jim Bridger), Eugene Pallette (Seth Higgins), Roy Stewart (Couch), May Boley (Jane), Eve Southern (Faith), James Farley (Amos), Frank Campeau (Jeff Moffitt), and Charles Winninger (Marshal).

SYNOPSIS: In Missouri, during the Civil War, a wagon train is preparing to set out for California. Old frontiersmen Bill Jackson and Jim Bridger are the trail scouts, along with their younger protege, Clint Belmet.

When Clint is arrested for disturbing the peace, his partners persuade a French girl named Felice, going along on the wagon train, to pretend she is married to him so the marshal will let him go. The ruse works only too well as soon Clint tries without success to take advantage of his phony marriage to Felice.

Along the trail, Clint and Felice become honestly attracted to each other; much to the chagrin of Bill and Jim who don't want to lose him yet to an actual marriage. Ultimately, they do advise Clint to settle down with her.

Another member of the wagon caravan, Lee Murdock, is afraid of any encroachment on his fur trade. He then works with hostile Indians to betray his fellow travelers.

Fighting breaks out with Lee and the Indians against the wagoners. Bridger is shot and killed by Lee. Jackson is mortally wounded by an Indian arrow, but is able to kill Murdock to avenge his friend's death. Clint helps drive the Indians away by spilling kerosene from one of the wagons into the river and setting the water ablaze.

As the wagon train continues its journey westward, Clint is now the sole guide. But Felice is at his side.

NOTES: Zane Grey's 1929 novel was the source of the 1931 motion picture, *Fighting Caravans.* Yet clearly paralleled was the ear-

Ernest Torrence (left) and Tully Marshall in *Fighting Caravans.*

lier *The Covered Wagon*, after its New York premiere by Paramount that January. This was most astutely felt with the return of Tully Marshall's Jim Bridger and Ernest Torrence's Bill Jackson.

The tale was set in the 1860s instead of the 1840s, and in the interim the frontiersmen had helped raise a fledgling scout. Embodied engagingly by Gary Cooper, who was at the beginning of his big-screen career in the sound film era, his character quickly turns into a fine frontiersman. Like a son, he is dear to the hearts of the old scouts.

Visualized once again were some

amusing antics like the trademark shooting at cups on their heads. And the *New York Times* said, "there are some good dramatic episodes, notably when Jim Bridger and Bill Jackson are killed."

Two directors, Otto Brower and David Burton, and three writers, Edward E. Paramore Jr., Keene Thompson and Agnes Brand Leahy, tried valiantly to give the film the same epic scope of *The Covered Wagon*. Yet it failed to duplicate that earlier success, at least to the same extent.

So much footage was filmed for *Fighting Caravans* that Paramount used it for a remake three years later called *Wagon*

Wheels. Randolph Scott had the Cooper role of Clint Belmet, while Raymond Hatton and Olin Howland played the older scouts albeit with different last names. Howland's Bill O'Meary is killed in the Western but Hatton's Jim Burch survives.

Fighting Caravans is available on DVD. At one point, the title was changed to *Blazing Arrows* when it was shown on television.

5 *Unknown Valley*

Columbia Pictures / 1933 / 64 minutes / Black and White

CREDITS: Lambert Hillyer (director, screenplay); C.C. Coleman (assistant director); Al Siegler (photography); Clarence Kolster (editor). From a story by Donald W. Lee.

CAST: Buck Jones (Joe Gordon), Cecilia Parker (Sheila O'Neill), Wade Boteler (Elder Crossett), Frank McGlynn (Head Elder Debbs), Ward Bond (Elder Snead), Arthur Wanzer (Tim), Alfred P. James (Pop Gordon), Bret Black (Shad O'Neill), and Edward LeSaint (Jim Bridger).

SYNOPSIS: Crossing a desert, ranger Joe Gordon searches for his missing father. Residing in a hidden valley is a secret village, survivors of a religious wagon train.

Brother and sister Shad and Sheila O'Neill are in the valley when they see Joe collapse in the distant desert. A guard, Tim, then summons the village elders; the intent is to keep Joe there with them.

Falling in love with Sheila, Joe plans on escaping with her, Shad and Tim. However, finding that elders Crossett and Snead have entrapped an old man in a mine, Joe tries to help him. While Tim is killed, Joe is put into the mine with the old man who turns out to be his father.

With his father and the O'Neills, Joe escapes back into the desert. Snead and Crossett are taken into custody by the other elders.

It is agreed by Joe and his companions to keep the valley a secret from the outside world.

NOTES: Columbia's 1933 "B" Western, *Unknown Valley*, was helmed by Lambert Hillyer. He was the director of the aforementioned *The Return of Daniel Boone* and *The Son of Davy Crockett*. The writing for this latest entry was shared by Hillyer with Donald W. Lee.

And this all-but-forgotten film starred one of the great cowboy stars, Buck Jones, from the silent 1920s and the talking 1930s. The brave stance Jones gave to his Western film persona was sadly echoed in an attempt to rescue people from the 1942 nightclub fire which took his life.

As *Unknown Valley* is not available on video, no further insight on Edward LeSaint's participation as Jim Bridger could be found. Initially, the actor went unbilled.

However, LeSaint was a very prolific Western player of the '30s. In the last year of that decade alone, he was in at least 10 Westerns, including *Overland with Kit Carson*.

6 *Brigham Young—Frontiersman*

20th Century-Fox Corporation / 1940 / 113 minutes / Black and White

CREDITS: Henry Hathaway (director); Darryl F. Zanuck (producer); Otto Brower (second unit director); Lamar Trotti (screenplay); Arthur Miller (photography); Robert Bischoff (editor); William Darling, Maurice Ransford (art directors); Thomas Little (set decorator); Gwen Wakeling (costumes); Fred Sersen (special effects); Alfred Newman (music). From Louis Bromfield's story.

CAST: Tyrone Power (Jonathan Kent), Linda Darnell (Zina Webb), Dean Jagger (Brigham Young), Brian Donlevy (Angus Duncan), Jane Darwell (Eliza Kent), John Carradine (Porter Rockwell), Mary Astor (Mary Ann Young), Vincent Price (Joseph Smith), Jean Rogers (Clara Young), Ann

Todd (Mary Kent), Moroni Olsen (Doc Richards), Marc Lawrence (Prosecutor), Tully Marshall (Judge), and Arthur Aylesworth (Jim Bridger).

SYNOPSIS: During the 1840s, vigilantes from Carthage, Illinois, attack a Mormon family and their friends. Killed are the fathers of Jonathan Kent and Zina Webb. Although she is not a Mormon, Zina is cared for by Jonathan and his mother, Eliza.

When Mormon prophet Joseph Smith urges his followers to bear arms, he is arrested for treason. Despite a passionate speech on his behalf from follower Brigham Young, Joseph is found guilty. Vigilantes then murder him.

Another Mormon, Angus Duncan, urges compromise as he has business dealings with the townsfolk who are against their religious beliefs. Yet Brigham, realizing the Mormons will all be attacked, leads them across an icy river into Iowa. Alerted by Angus, townsmen shoot at the fleeing Mormons, wounding Eliza Kent.

On the trail westward, some of the Mormons are reluctant to follow Brigham's plan to leave the United States because of the persecution. But he does keep them united.

Past Missouri, Brigham Young leaves the main body of Mormons at Council Bluffs to grow a crop. Preparing to push on with a large group of his followers, Brigham learns of Eliza's death.

At Fort Bridger, as Young's party rests, he meets Jim Bridger. Angus arouses the Mormon men, including Jonathan, with talk about gold in California.

Continuing west, Brigham falls into a coma from a fever. When he awakens, it is with a revelation about the new land the Mormons will settle on. Although Angus points out it is a desert, Brigham does have crops planted and homes built there in the Great Salt Lake region of Utah.

Brigham sends his scouts Jonathan and Porter Rockwell to bring back the rest of the Mormons at Council Bluffs. Before he goes, Jonathan proposes marriage to Zina.

The winter is extremely hard and Brigham orders everyone on rations. When Jonathan returns that spring, he finds Zina sick from hunger. He becomes angry with the Mormon leader.

Hordes of crickets swarm down from the mountains and attack the wheat fields. Attempts to drive them off prove futile, and the Mormons blame Young for their misfortune. He has his own misgivings on his leadership. However, sea gulls fly in from the lake to devour the insects and faith is restored for all.

NOTES: 20th Century-Fox's 1940 motion picture *Brigham Young — Frontiersman* was a most sympathetic portrayal of its subject (and was premiered in Salt Lake City on August 23). Tyrone Power and Linda Darnell were top billed, but it was Dean Jagger who held the biggest part in the title role. It just might be his greatest performance.

Integrated into the main character was a powerful sense of humanity. Lamar Trotti's script, from a story by Louis Bromfield, conveyed elements of the Mormon exodus with both fact and fancy.

Although Jim Bridger's reference to Young about the possibility to settle by the Great Salt Lake is ignored in the film (in favor of a revelation), he is seen in two sequences. At Fort Bridger, sitting by a well, he and Brigham introduce themselves. Jim is a bit excited when a reference to the Mormon having 12 wives is made (historically, Brigham surpassed 30). The other scene with Arthur Aylesworth's Bridger is with John Carradine's Porter Rockwell where they have a frog jumping contest.

Aylesworth does an amusing, pleasant turn as this frontiersman. He even bears a resemblance to the likeness of Bridger at age 62. The actor was in another frontier adventure that year, *Northwest Passage*.

Spencer Tracy, the star of that film, was initially considered to play Brigham Young.

The issue of polygamy was handled with discretion in *Brigham Young — Frontiersman*. Following Young's death in 1877, having more than one wife would be stopped by the Mormon Church of Jesus Christ of Latter-day Saints; the U.S. government otherwise wouldn't have made Utah a state in 1896.

Producer Darryl F. Zanuck and director Henry Hathaway lent considerable prestige to the film, although it still was not a box office success. Otto Brower, who shared direction in *Fighting Caravans*, directed the second unit. Especially impressive were the wagon train trekking sequences, which included location filming in Kanab, Utah.

The film, with an original title card of *Brigham Young* (without *Frontiersman* added), can be found on video.

7 *Kit Carson*

United Artists/Edward Small Productions / 1940 / 97 minutes / Black and White

NOTES: Main information is in the Carson filmography.

In 1940's *Kit Carson*, actor Raymond Hatton, according to the *Motion Picture Guide*, had "some memorable scenes as the legendary trailblazer Jim Bridger." Seen in the film's title role was Jon Hall.

Hatton had a particularly distinguished film career making Westerns. Two famous series bear his mark as part of a Western trio — as one of The Three Mesquiteers (with John Wayne and Ray Corrigan), and as one of The Rough Riders (with Buck Jones and Tim McCoy). He was also a sidekick to Johnny Mack Brown in some 45 films.

8 *Along the Oregon Trail*

Republic Pictures / 1947 / 64 minutes / Trucolor

CREDITS: R.G. Springsteen (director); Melville Tucker (associate producer); Earle

Snell (screenplay); Royal K. Cole (additional dialogue); Alfred S. Keller (photography); Arthur Roberts (editor); Fred Ritter (art director); John McCarthy Jr., Helen Hansard (set decorators); Adele Palmer (costumes); Mort Glickman (music). Songs: "Along the Wagon Trail" and "Oregon," words and music by Foy Willing.

CAST: Monte Hale (Himself), Adrian Booth (Sally Dunn), Clayton Moore (Gregg Thurston), Roy Barcroft (Jake Stoner), Max Terhune (Himself), Will Wright (Jim Bridger), LeRoy Mason (John Frémont), Wade Crosby (Tom), Kermit Maynard (Marshal), and Forrest Taylor (Kit Carson).

SYNOPSIS: In Missouri during the 1840s, trail guide Monte Hale's mentor is Kit Carson. Monte is congratulated by Kit for helping put an outlaw named Jake Stoner behind bars. However, Stoner escapes with the help of his cronies.

Needed as guides for Lt. John Frémont's expedition to Oregon, Monte and Kit cannot chase after Stoner. But along the trail west, at Fort Bridger, Stoner is in cahoots with Gregg Thurston, aide to Jim Bridger.

In an attempt to rob Bridger's wagon train of its rifles, Thurston uses Stoner and their gang. Unbeknownst to Thurston, his own fiancee, Sally Dunn, is with the wagons; and the outlaws are driven off by Monte.

Bridger entrusts Monte with a key to the fort's storeroom. The only other key belongs to Thurston, who has Stoner steal the stored rifles with Monte failing to stop it.

Following Thurston to a cave, Monte discovers his plans on manipulating the Indians to get control of the territory. Overpowered, Monte is left tied up in the cave.

Sally overhears Thurston plotting to kill Frémont and Bridger. Captured by Stoner, she soon escapes, as does Monte.

At the Indians' village, Monte and

Stoner have a gun duel in which the outlaw is killed. Frémont and his men stop Thurston from taking over Fort Bridger. Thurston is then shot down by Monte in another gunfight.

NOTES: Cowboy star Monte Hale, cast as himself, headlined Republic's "B" Western *Along the Oregon Trail*. Released in September 1947, it featured as the main villain Clayton Moore, just a couple of years away from riding the Western trail into legend as the Lone Ranger.

An amiable if average Western film, it was directed by R.G. Springsteen and the associate producer was Melville Tucker. Earle Snell wrote the scenario, while Royal K. Cole supplied additional dialogue.

Like Tully Marshall in *The Covered Wagon*, graybeard Will Wright enacted the part of Jim Bridger as a much older man; the frontiersman was actually only 45 years old by the end of the 1840s, the decade which was the time frame in both films. And both Marshall and Wright were in their late 50s during filming. In their respective 1940 entries playing Bridger, Arthur Aylesworth was 52 and Raymond Hatton 48.

Western roles for Wright included work in movies and series television. He was in Burt Lancaster's first Western film in 1950, *Vengeance Valley*, as well as a television episode of *The Lone Ranger* in 1955.

Not available on video, *Along the Oregon Trail* is the initial entry in the filmographies for both Bridger and Carson in color. Additional notes are in the latter.

9 *Tomahawk*

Universal-International Pictures / 1951 / 82 minutes / Technicolor

CREDITS: George Sherman (director); Leonard Goldstein (producer); Silvia Richards, Maurice Geraghty (screenplay); Charles P. Boyle (photography); Marvin W. Spoor (additional photography); Danny B. Landres (editor); Bernard Herzbrun, Richard H. Riedel (art directors); Russell A. Gausman, Oliver Emert (set decorators); Bill Thomas (costumes); Hans J. Salter (music). Suggested from Daniel Jarrett's story.

CAST: Van Heflin (Jim Bridger), Yvonne DeCarlo (Julie Madden), Alex Nicol (Lt. Rob Dancy), Preston Foster (Colonel Carrington), Jack Oakie (Sol Beckworth), Tom Tully (Dan Castello), John War Eagle (Red Cloud), Rock Hudson (Cpl. Burt Hanna), Susan Cabot (Monahseetah), Arthur Space (Captain Fetterman), Ann Doran (Mrs. Carrington), and Stuart Randall (Sergeant Newell).

SYNOPSIS: In 1866 Wyoming, at the Laramie Conference, frontier scout Jim Bridger tries to convince U.S. government representatives not to use the Bozeman Trail. Instead he urges them to use the Bridger Trail, since it is not on Sioux Indian land and would not infringe on the buffalo hunting grounds.

But Chief Red Cloud overhears Bridger speak of the trail and of Fort Phil Kearney, already built in the Indian territory. The conference is ended, and Bridger realizes that if any Indian blood is shed, it will escalate into warfare.

Colonel Carrington, the fort's army commander, offers Jim and his friend Sol Beckworth jobs as scouts. Initially refusing, Jim accepts when another friend, Cheyenne maiden Monahseetah, suspects Lt. Rob Dancy as having attacked her family a few years earlier.

On a mail detail, Dancy escorts traveling performers Dan Castello and Julie Madden to the fort. Dancy tells her about a preacher named Chivington whose militia he was once part of against the Indians.

En route to Fort Kearney, Dancy kills a Sioux boy trying to steal the horses. A small group of Indians then attack Dancy's party, wounding Dan with an arrow. Bridger and his friends accompany Dancy to the fort.

Van Heflin as Jim Bridger in 1951's *Tomahawk.*

At Julie's urging, Jim removes the arrowhead from Dan, thus saving his life. But a jealous Dancy tells Julie he thinks Bridger is a spy for the Sioux and that Monahseetah is his squaw.

Scouting, Jim sees that the Indians are preparing for war and several troopers are killed. Despite this, Julie goes out riding and is chased by a war party. Jim is forced to kill an Indian brave to protect her.

Julie learns that Jim was married to Monahseetah's sister, who was killed with a baby son in a raid by Chivington's militia. She later confirms that Dancy was part of it.

An army detachment under Captain Fetterman is deployed by Carrington to help a woodcutting detail against the Sioux. Fetterman, at Dancy's prompting, disobeys orders not to go beyond a distant ridge and the Indians nearly annihilate his command.

Bridger chases down a fleeing Dancy, who confesses to killing his wife and child. Another Sioux boy kills Dancy with an arrow.

Scout Beckworth arrives with breechloading rifles, which are used by the rest of Carrington's soldiers against Red Cloud's warriors. The Indians are all but annihilated.

However, a new treaty is signed two years later in favor of the Sioux. The army abandons Fort Kearney.

NOTES: Like the groundbreaking *Broken Arrow* the year before, 1951's *Tomahawk* cast a sympathetic view on the American Indian. Yet after its February release by Universal-International, the *New York Times* said the film "is nothing exceptional in the cavalry and Indians line, outside of its generous intimation of pro–Indian sentiment."

Although the *Times* also felt Van Heflin's portrayal of Jim Bridger "doesn't inspire great excitement or admiration," it was a strong depiction of a rugged individualist. Sharply conveyed as well was a man caught between opposing sides, with loyalties to both the army under Colonel Carrington (Preston Foster) and to the Indians under Chief Red Cloud (John War Eagle).

Silvia Richards and Maurice Geraghty based their script on a story suggested by Daniel Jarrett. This first feature-length film to star Bridger was produced by Leonard Goldstein and directed by George Sherman.

Interlaced throughout were elements of fancy and fact. Particularly fanciful was the frontier scout's involvement with the females in the film. There was no actual Julie Madden (Yvonne De-Carlo) or Monahseetah (Susan Cabot), let alone a marriage to a Cheyenne Indian. The part of scout Sol Beckworth (Jack Oakie) appears to be a variant on fellow scout and trapper James Beckwourth.

Van Heflin's Bridger in action in *Tomahawk*.

Other characters, however, were clearly derived from their real-life counterparts: Red Cloud, Carrington and Captain Fetterman (Arthur Space).

Historically, Bridger, when he led emigrants to Montana in 1864, competed with John Bozeman for a better trail west. The Bridger Trail, which was west of the Big Horn Mountain Range of the Rockies (and the Bozeman Trail east), actually was only longer by a few days' travel. While Bridger's avoided Sioux county, Bozeman's nonetheless became the established route.

Fort Philip Kearney was one of the frontier outposts along the Bozeman Trail and under the command of Col. Henry Carrington. Bridger and Carrington were present at the fort that December 1866 when the Indians massacred Lieutenant Colonel Fetterman's detachment. Among Red Cloud's warriors was a young Crazy Horse, destined to become one of the most famous of all Indians.

The Fort Laramie Treaty of 1868, which concludes *Tomahawk*, did close down Fort Kearney and other forts in the Powder River Basin. Peace prevailed until George Custer sparked military intervention on Sioux land with a reported gold strike. Even after Custer was wiped out at the Little Big Horn in 1876, Chief Red Cloud wanted peace. He died on the Pine Ridge Reservation in South Dakota in 1909.

Included in *Tomahawk*, which is available on video, is a reference that the film's title is the meaning of the Sioux name for

Jim Bridger. Seen in a small role was a young Rock Hudson, just prior to his attaining film stardom. He was the corporal in charge of the wood detail which precipitates the rescue attempt by Fetterman and Lieutenant Dancy (Alex Nicol).

Ironically, Van Heflin, unlike the previous actors seen as Bridger, was considerably younger than the role's actual place in history. The frontier scout was in his early 60s in 1866–68. Both *Shane* in 1953 and *3:10 to Yuma* in 1957 are classic Westerns which boast heroic turns as well from Heflin.

10 *Pony Express*

Paramount Pictures / 1953 / 101 minutes / Technicolor

CREDITS: Jerry Hopper (director); Nat Holt (producer); Charles Marquis Warren (screenplay); Ray Rennahan (photography); Eda Warren (editor); Hal Pereira, Al Nozaki (art directors); Sam Comer, Bertram Granger (set decorators); Edith Head (costumes); Wally Westmore (makeup); Paul Sawtell (music). Based on a story by Frank Gruber.

CAST: Charlton Heston (Buffalo Bill Cody), Rhonda Fleming (Evelyn Hastings), Jan Sterling (Denny Russell), Forrest Tucker (Wild Bill Hickok), Michael Moore (Rance Hastings), Porter Hall (Jim Bridger), Richard Shannon (Barrett), Henry Brandon (Cooper), Stuart Randall (Pemberton), Lewis Martin (Sgt. Russell), and Pat Hogan (Yellow Hand).

SYNOPSIS: Buffalo Bill Cody is riding across the prairie when he is attacked by Indians. Although his horse is killed, Cody holds the Indians at bay. On foot, he catches a ride on a passing stagecoach.

Aboard the stage as well are a brother and sister, Rance and Evelyn Hastings. At a way station, Cody learns that they want California to secede from the Union. He inadvertently disrupts their plans.

The stage reaches St. Joseph, Missouri, and Cody is greeted by tomboy Denny Russell who has an unrequited love for him. Buffalo Bill also engages in a shooting contest with his friend, Wild Bill Hickok.

The Hastings' plot with stage owner Joe Cooper to stop Cody and Hickok from opening a faster line of communication to Sacramento, California. The enterprise is called the Pony Express.

Evelyn feels that California is just too far from Washington, D.C., to be an effective part of the United States. Cooper simply doesn't want another business to interfere with his stage line.

Helping to finance the Pony Express is Denny's father, with money to buy needed ponies from the Indians. Cody has selected the relay stations for the express riders from Fort Bridger west to Sacramento, and Hickok the stations east of the fort to St. Joseph. Denny is assigned the task of following Evelyn and Rance.

Ponies are bought from Cody's nemesis, Yellow Hand, and the frontiersman knows the other Indians will then buy guns from Cooper. When Hickok saves Cody from a Cooper accomplice, it is seen by a man named Pemberton; and the latter is really an agent for California's secession traveling with Denny and the Hastings' toward Sacramento.

En route, the stage is waylaid by Yellow Hand's Sioux braves using Cooper's rifles. All aboard are trapped in a cabin along with Hickok and Cody. After Buffalo Bill is captured and then kills Yellow Hand in a tomahawk duel, the other Sioux stop fighting.

Confronting Cooper, Cody shoots him down as he tries to escape. Meanwhile, the stage stops at Fort Bridger.

Upon realizing Pemberton would have killed Cody earlier on, Evelyn remains at the fort not able to condone murder for secession. Her brother leaves with Pemberton.

Cody and Hickok share drinks with Jim Bridger at the fort. He also shares their enthusiasm for the forthcoming Pony Express.

Evelyn's allegiance is now switched to Cody, with whom she has fallen in love. With Denny, she goes on to Sacramento to keep tabs on Rance and Pemberton. Soon enough, Hickok and Cody arrive there too.

The Pony Express begins its trek westward from St. Joseph. All the riders are committed and even risk their lives to deliver the mail dispatches within the 10-day schedule of the 2,000-mile journey.

Finding their adversaries destroying the relay stations, Cody and Hickok use their guns to good effect. Wild Bill then chases down Rance, killing him, as Cody becomes the last express rider into Sacramento.

When Pemberton and his gang try to kill Cody, Denny sacrifices her life to save him. Cody kills Pemberton as Hickok rides in to help finish off the gang. Moved by Denny's death, Buffalo Bill then sets out to keep the return trip on schedule for the Pony Express.

NOTES: Paramount's 1953 motion picture, *Pony Express*, was produced by Nat Holt and directed by Jerry Hopper. Somewhat loosely patterned on a 1925 silent film of the same name (from *The Covered Wagon*'s same team), the story by Frank Gruber was fashioned into a script by Charles Marquis Warren. The result, while cliched, still made for an exciting Western.

Throughout the Western were bits of fact on the actual Pony Express, which did deliver the mail in 10 days' time between St. Joseph and Sacramento. And some 190 relay stations and 80 riders were deployed from April 1860 to October 1861.

The company of Russell, Majors and Waddell initially financed the operation (but only Russell is mentioned in the film with Buffalo Bill Cody and Wild Bill Hickok as partners). For the remaining six months of its 18-month duration, the Pony Express was subsidized by the U.S. government. The service was disbanded with the formation of the faster transcontinental telegraph.

William F. Cody was only 15 years old at the time, with James Butler Hickok in his early 20s. James Bridger was 56–the U.S. Army was then leasing Fort Bridger, which was one of the relay stations used for the express riders. And despite his youth, Buffalo Bill was given credit for the longest ride at over 300 miles.

Pony Express seemed a better film than it was actually due to the incredible energy supplied by Charlton Heston as Cody and Forrest Tucker as Hickok. At Fort Bridger, the frontier legends drink whiskey and laugh with a third legend in one of the film's lighthearted moments.

Flanked by his costars, Porter Hall as Jim Bridger lacks the imposing physical stature they have (as well as the real Bridger). Yet conveyed amusingly was the spirit of the man, the self-induced humor being reminiscent of both Arthur Aylesworth and Tully Marshall's past outings in the role.

Hall's first Western film was the famous Hickok-Cody adventure, *The Plainsman*, in 1936. He was nasty Jack McCall who shot Gary Cooper's Wild Bill in the back.

Despite any shortcomings of *Pony Express*, it is worth seeing (and can be found on video) just for the crackerjack performances of Tucker and Heston.

11 *The Gun That Won the West*

Columbia Pictures/Clover Productions / 1955 / 69 minutes / Technicolor

CREDITS: William Castle (director); Sam Katzman (producer); James B. Gordon (screenplay); Henry Freulich (photography); Al Clark (editor); Paul Palmentola (art director); Sidney Clifford (set decora-

Dennis Morgan (left) and Richard Denning in 1954's *The Gun That Won the West.*

tor); Ross DiMaggio (music). From a story by James B. Gordon.

CAST: Dennis Morgan (Jim Bridger), Paula Raymond (Maxine Gaines), Richard Denning (Jack Gaines), Chris O'Brien (Sgt. Timothy Carnahan), Robert Bice (Red Cloud), Roy Gordon (Col. Henry Carrington), Michael Morgan (Afraid of Horses), Howard Wright (Gen. John Pope), Dick Cutting (Edwin M. Stanton), and Howard Negley (Gen. Carveth).

SYNOPSIS: Jim Bridger and Jack Gaines were once scouts for Col. Henry Carrington's 18th Cavalry. After Jim helps a drunken Jack with his struggling Wild West show, they are rehired as scouts. Their new assignment is to assist the colonel erect a series of forts along the Bozeman Trail.

The forts are to protect the railroad workers from the Indians. Jim is concerned that Chief Red Cloud and his Sioux might cause trouble. But Jack's wife, Maxine, hopes the venture will turn her husband's life around.

New Springfield rifles are on the way to aid the army. Meanwhile, Sioux warrior Afraid of Horses leads a war party against Bridger and Gaines. Jim keeps Jack from killing the Indian in an attempt to secure peace with Red Cloud.

When the chief does arrive at Fort Laramie, Jack is again drunk and tries to scare him with talk of the rifles. Yet this only makes Red Cloud want to attack the army. Jack is arrested by Carrington over the matter, and Maxine, thinking Jack no longer loves her, plans on leaving him.

The Sioux and Cheyenne unite to try

Richard Denning (left), Dennis Morgan, and Paula Raymond in *The Gun That Won the West.*

and stop the building of the railroad. With Maxine and a scouting party with him, Bridger holds off the attacking Indians until Colonel Carrington can assist with troops from the fort.

The Big Horn Mountain Range provides a temporary haven from the Indians. Jim and Maxine share an attraction there to each other, although he stops it from going any further.

Afraid of Horses wants to attack the fort as it is not at full strength. But Jack has sobered up and demonstrates the newly arrived rifles to try to discourage any conflict. However, Jack is captured by the Indians.

After escaping from Red Cloud, Jack prevents the Indians from killing Carrington. Riding for help, Jim brings General Pope with more soldiers and the rifles.

With the new weapons, the soldiers defeat the Indians. In a fight to the death, Afraid of Horses is drowned by Bridger.

Still in love, Maxine and Jack leave the fort to begin life on a ranch. Jim remains a frontier scout.

NOTES: A Columbia release, *The Gun That Won the West* was Jim Bridger's second starring vehicle. Premiered in Hollywood in July 1955, it was directed by William Castle and produced by Sam Katzman. The James B. Gordon scenario was adapted from his own story.

Although Technicolor was utilized, so was stock Indian footage from past films. This gave the film some unmatched grains and tints.

Seemingly just another routine Western, however, the Indians were accorded a less sympathetic treatment than the earlier *Tomahawk.* Racism was a key figure here.

Still, story elements similar to *Toma-*

hawk were evident. Especially so with the new army rifles being used to battle the Indians. Roy Gordon was Colonel Carrington this time around and Robert Bice portrayed Red Cloud.

Topping the cast were Dennis Morgan and Richard Denning respectively as scouts Jim Bridger and Jack Gaines (with the latter a fictional character). *Variety* reflected that the pair "are as good as parts will allow."

A talented performer, Morgan was also a notable singer whose film work included musicals and Westerns. One in the latter category was as outlaw Cole Younger in 1941's *Bad Men of Missouri*.

The Gun That Won the West is listed on DVD.

12 *Man in the Wilderness*

Warner Brothers/Sanford Howard-Limbridge Productions / 1971 / 105 minutes / Technicolor

CREDITS: Richard Sarafian (director); Sanford Howard (producer); Jack DeWitt (screenplay); Gerry Fisher (photography); Geoffrey Foot (editor); Dennis Lynton Clark (production design, costumes); Gurnersindo Andres (art director); Richard M. Parker (special effects); Johnny Harris (music).

CAST: Richard Harris (Zachary Bass), John Huston (Capt. Filmore Henry), Henry Wilcoxon (Indian Chief), Percy Herbert (Fogarty), Dennis Waterman (Lowrie), Prunella Ransome (Grace), Norman Rossington (Ferris), James Doohan (Benoit), John Bindon (Coulter), Manolo Landau (Zachary as a Boy), and Peggy the Bear.

SYNOPSIS: In the American Northwest during 1820, Captain Henry's trapping expedition is traveling overland with a keelboat of furs. The boat is being pulled by 22 mules and the men are trying to reach the Missouri River.

Zachary Bass and young Lowrie are hunting for fresh meat for their comrades.

Suddenly a big bear attacks Bass, viciously mauling him.

Afraid, Lowrie rushes to get help. The bear is then killed by the other trappers. Although seemingly near death, the unconscious Zach's wounds are treated.

Captain Henry decides to leave two men behind to bury Zach when he's dead. Feeling guilty, Lowrie volunteers and so does another man named Fogarty. They are given orders by the captain to kill Bass in the morning if he hasn't died by then.

As Zach lies comatose, memories of his childhood return including being orphaned. When Indians approach in the morning, instead of killing Bass, Fogarty and Lowrie race off just leaving him in the wilderness.

The Indian chief lets Bass alone in the belief that he will not survive. But Zach does come to after the Indians have left and drinks from a nearby stream. He remembers his pregnant wife, Grace.

Catching up to Henry, Lowrie and Fogarty relate that they didn't kill Bass. Lowrie is willing to go back to him with help, but the captain will not risk the lives of his men.

From a dying buffalo calf brought down by wolves, Bass continues to find nourishment. Yet he is still so weak he can only crawl.

Later, Zach scavenges through the remains of an Indian attack and finds a spearhead. He uses it to help light a fire and to hunt. Finally he can walk with the aid of a makeshift crutch and journeys over the mountains.

In the wilderness, Zach witnesses an Indian woman giving birth. After his own wife had earlier died in childbirth, Zach did not want to be with their son. The child was left in the care of her mother.

Both Henry and Fogarty are fearful that Bass is coming after them for revenge. Thinking it is Bass, Fogarty mistakenly shoots Lowrie dead.

When Zach does catch up to the keelboat, it is stuck fast in the mud. The Indians attack Henry and his men. But the fighting is ended when the chief recognizes Bass.

Confronting Henry, Zach asks for his rifle and starts out for home and to be with his boy. Leaving the boat behind and its furs, the other trappers follow.

NOTES: Warner Brothers released *Man in the Wilderness* in November 1971. Like another film the year before, *A Man Called Horse*, it was a frontier adventure which was produced by Sanford Howard, written by Jack DeWitt and starred Richard Harris.

Both films reflected on the survival of its protagonists–the earlier one an English lord captured by the Sioux, and this entry a trapper mauled by a grizzly bear. Richard Sarafian directed the latter which was clearly patterned on the real-life mishap of Hugh Glass in 1823. Actor Harris is called, however, by the fictional name of Zachary Bass.

While fictionalized, several other members of the cast were also based on real men. John Huston's leader is called Captain Henry (although Filmore is his first name in the film and not actually Andrew). Percy Herbert's Fogarty and Dennis Waterman's Lowrie were derived from respectively John Fitzgerald and Jim Bridger.

Harris and Waterman both contributed thoughtful performances–conveyed by Harris was the desire to live beyond the vengeance sought initially for being abandoned; and there was genuine remorse by Waterman for leaving his comrade (and a Bible is even left at his side).

In *Man in the Wilderness*, Richard Harris plays a character based on Hugh Glass, who was abandoned by a young Jim Bridger.

Despite its splendid locations (filmed in Spain), the film was a bit slow moving.

Hugh Glass never did harm Bridger, Fitzgerald or Henry. While Jim was there with the captain at Fort Henry, following the mauling and the return of Glass, Fitzgerald was not. Later in 1824, Glass found him a U.S. soldier at Fort Atkinson on the Missouri River. As retribution, Hugh accepted from Fitzgerald a new rifle, horse and saddle.

Man in the Wilderness is available on video.

13 *Bridger*

ABC Television/Universal / 1976 / 120 minutes / Color

CREDITS: David Lowell Rich (director, producer); Merwin Gerard (writer); Bud Thackery (photography); Asa Boyd Clark (editor); Lloyd S. Papez (art director); Elliot Kaplan (music).

CAST: James Wainwright (Jim Bridger), Ben Murphy (Kit Carson), Sally Field (Jennifer Melford), Dirk Blocker (Joe Meek),

John Anderson (Andrew Jackson), William Windom (Daniel Webster), Margarita Cordova (Shoshone Woman), Tom Middleton (Doctor), and Keith Evans (Presidential Aide).

SYNOPSIS: In the 1830s, Jim Bridger receives a commission from President Andrew Jackson to open a trail for the U.S. to the Pacific Northwest. The territory is from the Rocky Mountains to California.

To accomplish this task, Jim is given only 40 days. If he fails, Senator Daniel Webster will succeed in having England take possession of the land in exchange for fishing rights in Newfoundland.

Along on the Bridger expedition are fellow frontiersmen Kit Carson and Joe Meek. Numerous obstacles abound–snow, desert, Indians and dangerous wildlife–yet all are met with fortitude.

Bridger is ultimately victorious. Senator Webster accepts that it is perhaps the best thing for the United States after all.

NOTES: *Bridger*, a joint effort from ABC and Universal, was initially televised as a two-hour movie on September 10, 1976. The action content apparently was criticized due to the predictability of a cliched story line and its characters.

Meriting thus scant faith from the network, a later rerun was edited down to fill a 90-minute length. The film is not on video.

David Lowell Rich functioned as both its producer and director. The fanciful teleplay was by Merwin Gerard.

During the time of the story's setting with Andrew Jackson president of the United States, Jim Bridger was pathfinding in the Rocky Mountain domain to trap beaver. Yet, at the same time, Daniel Webster was being outspoken against the push by the U.S. to the Pacific coast.

In the film's title role, James Wainwright was nonetheless a strong, formidable presence. Seen as Kit Carson was Ben Murphy. Along for the ride as well was Sally Field, just a few years away from winning her first best actress Oscar for 1979's *Norma Rae.*

Previous roles for Wainwright included motion picture and television work. He had the recurring role of Cully (during 1969-70) alongside Fess Parker in the *Daniel Boone* series and in a 1972 film, *Joe Kidd,* he menaced Clint Eastwood.

Additional notes are in the Kit Carson filmography.

14 *Kit Carson and the Mountain Men*

NBC Television/Walt Disney / 1977 / 2 parts / 120 minutes / Color

NOTES: *Kit Carson and the Mountain Men* was made for the *World of Disney* television show. It aired over the NBC network in 1977.

Starring as Carson was Christopher Connelly. Gregg Palmer had the supporting role of Jim Bridger.

A familiar Western player, Palmer appeared in movies and on television. Several John Wayne films bear his presence, including *Big Jake* in 1971 and *The Shootist* in 1976. His own big frame made him a perfect foil for the Duke.

Main information is in the Carson filmography.

15 *The Incredible Rocky Mountain Race*

NBC Television/Schick Sunn Classics / 1977 / 120 minutes / Color

CREDITS: James L. Conway (director); Robert Stabler (producer); Tom Chapman, David O'Malley (writers); Henning Schellerup (photography); John F. Link II (editor); Charles Bennett (art director); Cheryl Beasley (wardrobe); Dennis Marsh (makeup); Bob Summers (music).

CAST: Christopher Connelly (Mark Twain), Forrest Tucker (Mike Fink), Larry

Storch (Eagle Feather), Jack Kruschen (Jim Bridger), Mike Mazurki (Crazy Horse), Parley Baer (Farley Osmond), Whit Bissell (Simon Hollaway), Bill Zuckert (Calvin Mercer), Don Haggerty (Sheriff Benedict), and John Hansen (Bill Cody).

SYNOPSIS: In St. Joseph, Missouri, the leading citizens are tired of the feud between reporter Mark Twain and river man Mike Fink. A plan is hatched to get rid of the pair by having a race to California.

Fink immediately takes off with a stagecoach, not knowing that Twain is riding on the boot. A list of items have to be collected along the way; and at a train station both collect the first, a conductor's hat from the Union Pacific.

A Pony Express mailbag is next up for grabs. Although getting to it ahead of Fink, Twain is tied up by express rider Bill Cody. So Mike makes off with it instead.

Still bound, Twain is left in the wilderness by Fink. Kidnaped by Indians, Mark is soon rescued by mountain man Jim Bridger.

The third and fourth items needed for the race are Chief Crazy Horse's moccasins and some eagle feathers. Sneaking into the Indian village, Mark makes off with the moccasins and Mike the feathers. Both men are then captured.

An attempt by Fink and Twain to escape fails. Once again, intervention from Bridger saves the day, but a brave called Eagle Feather is sent after the moccasins.

Arguing, Mike and Mark rip the mailbag apart. They each end up with half of it.

In Virginia City, Nevada, the pair steal the last item needed–a menu from Delmonico's Restaurant. For wrecking the place, Mike is jailed and sentenced to hang.

Eagle Feather tags along with Twain and helps rescue Fink. After trading Mark a feather for one moccasin, Mike continues the race.

Twain and Eagle Feather chase after Fink in canoes. When the Indian is trapped beneath a broken tree in the Trinity River, Mike stops to free him.

All then arrive together at their California destination near the Pacific Ocean. Unknown to Mike, Mark throws the contest allowing the river man to be declared the winner.

NOTES: A lighthearted romp through history, *The Incredible Rocky Mountain Race* presented a perspective that never existed. With some familiar names tossed around, it all seemed like one big tall tale.

Set decades after the real Mike Fink's death (when he was middle age and Jim Bridger a teenager), the story was shared by Tom Chapman and David O'Malley. James L. Conway directed, while Robert Stabler produced the television movie for Schick Sunn Classics. It was aired by NBC on December 17, 1977, and is available on video.

Embarrassingly silly, the film nonetheless brought out the most exuberant energies of some of its old-timers. Especially so with Forrest Tucker's Fink and Jack Kruschen's Bridger.

Suffering from memory loss, Jim is so loud and wild that even the Indians call him loco. Yet he does have a couple of opportunities to be heroic.

More subdued in their roles were Christopher Connelly as Mark Twain and Larry Storch as Eagle Feather. If *The Incredible Rocky Mountain Race* did nothing else, it reunited Storch and Tucker, who were a funny duo earlier (1965–67) on the television Western comedy series *F Troop*.

Kruschen's own past film work included a best supporting Oscar nomination for 1960's *The Apartment*, and a role in 1963's comedy-flavored Western, *McLintock!*, with Duke Wayne.

16 *James A. Michener's Centennial*

CHAPTER 2: "THE YELLOW APRON"

NBC Television/Universal Pictures/John Wilder Productions / 1978 / 120 minutes / Color

CREDITS: Virgil W. Vogel (director); Howard Alston (producer); John Wilder (executive producer, writer); Duke Callaghan (photography); Howard S. Deane (editor); Jack Senter (production designer); Mark Mansbridge (art director); Helen Colvig (costumes); John Addison (music). Based on the novel *Centennial*, by James A. Michener.

CAST: Robert Conrad (Pasquinel), Richard Chamberlain (Alexander McKeag), Raymond Burr (Herman Bockweiss), Sally Kellerman (Lise Bockweiss), Barbara Carrera (Clay Basket), Chief Dan George (Old Sioux), Stephen McHattie (Jacques Pasquinel), Kario Salem (Marcel Pasquinel), David Janssen (Narrator), and Reb Brown (James Bridger).

SYNOPSIS: During the early 1800s, Pasquinel and Alexander McKeag are trappers in the Colorado wilderness. Clay Basket is Pasquinel's Indian wife; and they have two sons, Jacques and Marcel. However, an unspoken love is felt between Clay Basket and Alexander.

In St. Louis, Missouri, silversmith Herman Bockweiss finances Pasquinel's trapping for beaver to share the profits. Herman's daughter, Lise, is also married to Pasquinel; and they have a baby daughter named Lisette. In time, both Lise and Clay Basket become aware of each other.

When Pasquinel is at a fort with his Indian family and McKeag, young Jacques is badly scarred by a drunken soldier with a knife. Jacques is hurt again back in the wilderness by attacking Indians. Both incidents embitter him.

As a troubled youth, Jacques attacks Alexander with a knife. Hurt and angry, McKeag then leaves Pasquinel and Clay Basket to trap beaver alone.

Years pass when trapper Jim Bridger rides by McKeag's cabin with his comrades. Told of the rendezvous on Bear Lake where they are headed, Alexander joins them to sell his beaver pelts.

At the rendezvous, Alexander and Pasquinel are briefly reunited. McKeag removes an arrowhead from an old wound on Pasquinel's back.

Alexander finds Lisette a young lady when he goes to St. Louis. Lise urges him to return to Pasquinel and reveal the love he still feels for Clay Basket.

Near his wilderness home, Pasquinel finally finds the gold that for so long has been an obsession. But Indians attack him; mortally wounded, he dies in the returning McKeag's arms.

With her sons now grown and gone, Clay Basket is able to consummate her love with Alexander. He will raise her small daughter, Lucinda, as his own as they journey on to begin a new life together.

NOTES: *James A. Michener's Centennial* was a 12-chapter, 26-hour miniseries originally broadcast between October 1978 and February 1979 by NBC-TV. "The Yellow Apron," the second chapter, aired on October 8.

Executive producer John Wilder (whose production outfit allied itself with Universal Pictures) also wrote the teleplay from Michener's mammoth novel. Blended with historical events were the fictitious characterizations and setting; the title referred to the made-up Colorado town of Centennial. Four directors were utilized for the entire saga, including Virgil W. Vogel. It can be found on video.

Along with Robert Conrad as Pasquinel and Richard Chamberlain as Alexander McKeag, a long list of stars contributed with marvelous performances. Yet Chamberlain and Conrad just may have been the most memorable.

Sharing a few scenes with the pair was the historical figure of Jim Bridger. Embodied amiably by Reb Brown, the mountain man's fine physical stature was especially notable. As with David Keith's Jim Bowie in *James A. Michener's Texas*, it is a charismatic performance.

At the depicted rendezvous in *Centennial*, the so-called yellow apron is seen first on fellow mountain man James Beckwourth, when he and Bridger share a wild and woolly dance. McKeag then dons the apron and dances with Pasquinel.

The incident which follows, with Alexander extracting the arrowhead from his friend, is clearly a variation on missionary doctor Marcus Whitman's removal of the barb from Bridger at the 1835 Green River rendezvous.

Brown, whose acting credits included the role of superhero Captain America in a couple of television movies a year later, is last seen here placing a blanket over Pasquinel following his surgery.

Charlton Heston (left) and Brian Keith in *The Mountain Men*. Their characters were drawn from the exploits of Jim Bridger.

17 *The Mountain Men*

Columbia Pictures/Martin Ransohoff Productions / 1980 / 100 minutes / Metrocolor

CREDITS: Richard Lang (director); Martin Shafer, Andrew Scheinman (producers); Fraser Clarke Heston (screenplay); Michael Hugo (photography); Eva Ruggiero (editor); Bill Kenney (production design); Rick T. Gentz (set decorator); Thomas S. Dawson, Kathleen McGregor (costumes); Lon Bentley, Del Armstrong (makeup); Michel Legrand (music).

CAST: Charlton Heston (Bill Tyler), Brian Keith (Henry Frapp), Stephen Macht (Heavy Eagle), Victoria Racimo (Running Moon), John Glover (Nathan Wyeth), Seymour Cassel (La Bont), David Ackroyd (Medicine Wolf), Cal Bellini (Cross Otter), Bill Lucking (Jim Walker), Ken Ruta (Fontenelle), and Victor Jory (Iron Belly).

SYNOPSIS: It is the 1830s. Fur trapper Bill Tyler is coming out of the Rocky Mountains when he is joined by another trapper, Henry Frapp. Both realize the beaver is nearly trapped out.

Along with merchant Nathan Wyeth, Frapp and Tyler travel to the rendezvous by the Popo Agie River. En route, Crow Indians try to steal their horses; but when Blackfeet Indians attack, led by Heavy Eagle, all join forces to drive them off.

During the fight, Heavy Eagle's woman, Running Moon, is captured. Although Tyler releases her, she follows him. At the rendezvous, a wild time is had by all the mountain men. Tyler sells his beaver pelts for a lower price than anticipated–for the market has turned from beaver to silk.

An old Crow chief, Iron Belly, tells Bill about the secret Wind River Valley still swarming with beaver. As Nathan sets out with emigrants heading west, Tyler, Frapp and Running Moon search for the valley in Blackfeet country.

The Indians attack several times. Henry is scalped by Heavy Eagle and left for dead. Bill is forced to flee for his life.

In time, Running Moon and Bill fall in love. Yet the Blackfeet are relentless, capturing them both. Believing she is dead, Tyler is chased by Heavy Eagle and his braves. Bill escapes down a raging river and over a waterfall.

In the frozen wilderness, Bill finds Henry still alive and well. They learn that Running Moon is also alive.

Fellow trappers La Bont and Jim Walker go along with Tyler and Frapp, hoping to find the beaver valley. Bill instead goes after the still-captive Running Moon. In the ensuing conflict, Walker, La Bont and Henry are killed by the Indians.

To rescue Running Moon, Bill fights Heavy Eagle. She is forced to kill the warrior to save Tyler.

Having given Henry Frapp an Indian burial, Bill Tyler and Running Moon journey on looking for the beaver valley.

NOTES: Although Jim Bridger is not actually seen in 1980's *The Mountain Men*, his spirit is felt throughout. He is asked about by Charlton Heston's Bill Tyler near the beginning, and is told by Brian Keith's Henry Frapp that he is in the Santa Fe country. A mention is made later by the pair about "Old Gabe" losing stock to the Indians.

Two prominent moments in the film, while historically accorded to Bridger, were given to Frapp and Tyler. The first is the humorous story related by Henry of being trapped by Indians and killed; and the other is in the final fight between Bill and Stephen Macht's Heavy Eagle over Victoria Racimo's Running Moon. As in Bridger's legendary battle with an Indian brave over Little Fawn, Tyler and his antagonist charge

each other on horseback and then fight with knives.

Like Richard Chamberlain and Robert Conrad in *Centennial*, an endearing quality is shared between Keith and Heston, whose trappers in *The Mountain Men* were a composite of several actual names, including Bridger and his last trapping partner, Henry Fraeb.

But this movie was edited so heavily for its action content that the story and characters received harsh criticism. The screenplay, originally titled *Wind River*, was written by Fraser Clarke Heston, Charlton's son.

To be fair, this Columbia release may have suffered too under its novice director, Richard Lang, despite an earnest depiction of the last days of the Rocky Mountain fur trappers. While authentic, the bawdy language and extreme violence hurt its box office potential with a wider audience. Martin Shafer and Andrew Scheinman were also responsible as the producers.

The finest attributes of *The Mountain Men*, which is available on video, are the beautiful backgrounds. Location filming was done in both Shoshone and Bridger-Teton National Forests.

Incidentally, Jim Bridger's spirit is nicely felt in 1962's film, *How the West Was Won*. Fictitious mountain man Linus Rawlings (James Stewart) tells a tale of how he and Bridger were climbing up the Rockies one time and ran into an angel with a harp.

18 *Dream West*

CBS Television/Sunn Classic Pictures / 1986 / 3 parts / 420 minutes / Color

NOTES: In the CBS-televised miniseries of 1986, *Dream West*, Richard Chamberlain starred as notable explorer John Charles Frémont. Portraying the formidable frontiersmen Kit Carson and Jim Bridger were, respectively, Rip Torn and Ben Johnson.

One would have to look long and hard to find a performer with the tremendous body of Western film roles as Johnson. He made his debut for John Ford in 1948's *Three Godfathers*, and among Ben's unforgettable appearances were those in 1953's *Shane* and 1969's *The Wild Bunch*.

Main information is in the Carson filmography.

Six

KIT CARSON

Biography and Overview

Of Scottish-Irish descent, Kit Carson's ancestors traveled to the New World in the 18th century, settling in Lancaster County, Pennsylvania. His grandparents, William and Eleanor Carson, had six children including son Lindsey, their eldest. Eleanor would later remarry after William died apparently as a result from overheating while working.

Following the American Revolution, Lindsey journeyed to South Carolina where he married Lucy Bradley. With his wife and their four children, Lindsey Carson followed Daniel Boone's Wilderness Road to Kentucky. This was in 1793, and while another child was born there, Lucy died shortly afterward.

Lindsey remarried after two years to Rebecca Robinson. Ten children were born from this union — six in Kentucky and four in Missouri. The last, born in Kentucky, in their Madison County log cabin, was a son on December 24, 1809. Although named Christopher Houston Carson, he would be called Kit.

During 1811, when Kit was one and a half, Lindsey sold the Kentucky home and farm. With Kit riding in front of his mother on a horse, the family moved to Howard County, Missouri. Past St. Louis about 170 miles, they settled on a new home and farm by Boon's Lick.

One of Lindsey's now-grown sons with Lucy, also called William had married just the year before. His wife, Millie Boone, was Daniel Boone's grandniece. But Millie had died during childbirth. Having left the new baby daughter with his sister-in-law, William accompanied his father to Missouri.

Later on, William brought the child, Adaline, and sister-in-law, Cassandra Boone (whom he had married) to Missouri. Adaline became a favorite childhood companion to Kit.

The Carsons, along with other settlers, for a time had to live behind the protection of forts because of the ongoing threat of Indian attacks. In later years, Kit recalled (perhaps tongue-in-cheek) that his lack of a formal education was due to this danger. Seated in a classroom as a boy when an Indian warning was called, Kit threw down his spelling book, grabbed his rifle, and ran out, never going back.

Like Jim Bridger, Kit Carson was for the most part judged as illiterate. However, Kit did learn how to sign his own name.

In September 1818, when Kit was eight, his father was killed in a tragic accident. Lindsey was burning a tree to clear a field when one of the limbs broke off and struck him down. He was 64 years old.

Kit's mother, Rebecca, remarried four years later to Joseph Martin. Her oldest sons, including Kit, rebelled against this for they had become used to filling in for their late father's familial obligations. A particularly troublesome 13-year-old, Kit was even sent to live with stepbrother William's family.

At the age of 15, Kit was apprenticed to work for a saddler named David Workman in the town of Franklin. But in August 1826, Carson heard about an expedition heading west to the Rocky Mountains. Asking for his mother's permission to go along, she refused, wanting him to fulfill his contract with Workman.

Not caring for the saddlery trade, Kit instead disobeyed his mother and ran away from home. Kit was no doubt influenced by his other stepbrothers, Andrew and Moses, and by brother Robert, all of whom had shared with him tales of their own western adventures.

In a local Missouri newspaper, on October 6, Workman placed an ad offering a reward for Kit's return. But the reward was for only a cent as Workman, who went west the following year, clearly sympathized with young Christopher Carson.

And like Jim Bridger for 17 years, Carson would not return to Missouri for 16 years. In 1842, at 32, Kit returned there to find not one building in town that had previously stood.

The way west Kit now took, on a wagon train under William Wolfskill and Elisha Stanley, was along the Santa Fe Trail. The territories that the trail ran through in the southwest still belonged to Mexico.

Carson and the famed trail are part of at least three entries in his filmography. Two are silent films—Kalem's 1910 *The Cheyenne Raiders* (or *Kit Carson on the Santa Fe Trail*), and Arrow's 1923 serial *The Santa Fe Trail*. The third, from 1937, is another serial, Republic's *The Painted Stallion*.

By November 1826, Kit and his comrades had crossed the Raton Pass of the Rockies and had reached Santa Fe in the New Mexico territory. The caravan's goal all along had been to reach the town for trading.

During the journey, Kit had helped watch over the stock. And one of the men, Andrew Broadus (who was part of an 1825 surveying expedition with Robert and Andrew Carson), accidentally shot himself in the right arm. When the arm became gangrenous, it was amputated but Broadus survived.

After the trading party reached Santa Fe, Kit was there only a few days before going on with some of the traders to the town of Taos, further northeast in New Mexico. Carson wintered there at the home of another trader and local businessman, Mathew Kinkead.

Like Kit, Kinkead's family was from Boon's Lick. And David Kinkead, Mathew's father, had built the fort where the Carsons stayed when Kit was a little boy.

In the spring of 1827, Kit Carson was planning to return to Missouri back in the United States. He had even joined a caravan led by one Paul Ballio. Along the Arkansas River on the Kansas plains, he came across another caravan bound for Santa Fe. Kit decided then to go back to New Mexico with this wagon train, led by Ezekiel Williams.

Back in Santa Fe, Kit worked as a wagoner taking goods to El Paso in Texas. He then went to Taos and found work as a cook for William Wolfskill and Ewing Young. The pair had opened a store supplying trappers and it was Kit's intention to become a trapper. However, at this time his soft-spoken and diminutive characteristics just may have been held against him for such rugged work.

Another attempt to return to Missouri was made by Carson in the spring of 1828. Once more he met a caravan by the Arkansas River and went back to Santa Fe. Merchants William and Philip Trammel needed an interpreter in the Mexican city of Chihuahua. Despite not being able to read or write, Kit had managed to learn to speak Spanish and was hired.

Once this duty was finished, Carson found other work as a wagoner for businessman Robert McKnight. This was at a copper mine northwest of El Paso near the Gila River. But in August 1829, Kit was back in Taos just at the right time.

Ewing Young needed volunteers to help a wagon train, led by William and Charles Bent, that was besieged by Indians. Carson was among nearly 100 men that rode with Young and drove the Indians off. During this time, Young was so impressed by Carson's riding skills and courage that he made him a member of his forthcoming trapping expedition.

Fighting Indians takes place in many of the 30 entries that make up the Kit Carson filmography. Included are the initial two silents both titled *Kit Carson*—1903's film for American Mutoscope and Biograph, and 1910's film for Bison.

Forty men, including a 19-year-old Kit Carson, set out with Young that summer of 1829 to trap beaver. They headed north up the Rio Grande, feigning to trap in the beaver streams of the Colorado Rockies (which were part of the Louisiana Purchase by the U.S.). This was done to throw off Mexican officials because of the law against trapping in Mexico's rivers.

Yet this was exactly what Ewing Young's party did. Having gone north about 50 miles, they then veered back on another course through the southwest. In the then Mexican territory of Arizona they trapped beaver along the Salt River.

Aware that Apache Indians were close by, Young had most of the men conceal themselves in camp. When the Apaches attacked, they were then surprised by the hidden trappers. Some 15 to 20 Indians were killed.

Confronting the Apaches was one of the reasons why Young eschewed the Colorado Rockies. He wanted to avenge an Indian attack made on a trapping party he had earlier on sent to the southwest. Yet even after exacting his revenge, Young and his trappers had to contend with Apache harassment. This included stealing traps and killing stock.

The trappers nonetheless continued to trap for beaver. To replace the lost stock and traps, Young sent 22 of the men back to Taos with the pelts. With Carson and 17 others, he began moving further west despite the hardship of finding food and water in the arid country.

Actually heading northwest in Arizona, the party reached the Colorado River near the Grand Canyon and crossed the Mojave Desert into California (which was also then under Mexican rule). Much-needed nourishment and rest was received at the San Gabriel Mission. Before long, the trappers found a pass through the mountains of the Sierra Nevada.

Coming upon the San Joaquin Valley, Ewing Young and his trappers met those led by Peter Skene Ogden of the Hudson's Bay Company. Both parties briefly trapped what beaver could be found until they separated along the Sacramento River, with Ogden heading north.

Knowing that Young's trappers were

still there, the mission of San Jose requested their help in bringing back runaway Indians. Apparently various missions used captive Indians as servants.

Kit Carson and 11 other trappers were sent to aid mission-friendly Indians round up the runaways. But fighting broke out and after a whole day of it, the runaways fled and an Indian village was burned down. When further fighting was threatened, the runaway Indians returned to the mission.

With beaver furs the trappers had accumulated in California, Young made a sale to Don Jose Asero, a captain of a trading schooner. Horses were then purchased by Young of which 60 were stolen by Indians.

Again, Kit and 11 other men were sent out. Trailing the Indians into the Sierra Nevada mountain range, Carson's group recovered all but six of the horses. In the struggle to do so, eight Indians were killed.

The Mexican authorities in the town at Los Angeles demanded passports from Young and his men, which they did not have. Only their unpredictable, wild behavior kept the trappers from being arrested, for the authorities wanted no part of it.

Homeward bound, the trappers were camped along the Colorado River when, according to Kit, some 500 Indians rode in with the intent to do harm. While most of his comrades were out trapping with Young, Carson stood steadfast and gave the Indians an ultimatum in Spanish to clear out within 10 minutes or be shot. The Indians understood him and left, and thus was prevented any possible bloodshed.

Once the trappers reached Robert McKnight's copper mine in New Mexico, Ewing Young cached a ton of beaver furs there, not wanting them confiscated for the lack of a license. With Kit, Young went to Santa Fe and obtained a license to trade with the Indians along the Gila River. The pelts were then brought in as if they had been acquired from trading.

Thus ended, in April 1831, a 20-month adventure for Kit Carson which saw him for the first time as a fur trapper and fearless Indian fighter. He freely spent his first big pay from it of several hundred dollars.

By the fall of the year, Kit was trapping beaver with Tom Fitzpatrick, one of the partners of the Rocky Mountain Fur Company. Carson was actually one of 30 men with Fitzpatrick as they made their way north into the Wyoming territory. Among the paths traveled were along the North Platte River to the Sweetwater, and then to the Green through the South Pass.

While on the North Platte, Fitzpatrick had gone to St. Louis for supplies. Kit went then with one of Tom's partners, Henry Fraeb, onto the Green River and even further north to the Teton Range of the Rockies. Having spent a first winter with the Rocky Mountain Fur Company, Carson went with the outfit back along the Green in the spring of 1832.

Kit then joined a trapping party led by John Gantt in a rich beaver valley in Colorado called New Park. It was surrounded by the Park Range there and the Medicine Bow Range of Wyoming. Both ranges were part of the vast Rocky Mountains.

Soon Gantt and his men went south in Colorado to the Arkansas River where they trapped. Gantt went to Taos to dispose of their pelts; when he returned with needed supplies, they wintered there along the Arkansas.

In January 1833, 50 to 60 Crow Indians snuck into the camp one night and stole nine horses. With supposedly a pair of Cheyenne Indian scouts leading the way, a dozen trappers gave chase. Kit Carson was among them.

While the horses were recovered as the Crow slept, Kit and other trappers wanted to avenge the hardship of chasing after the Indians. The Indians suffered in the ensuing gunfire that broke out. Satisfied, the trappers returned to camp.

That spring, 400 pounds of beaver pelts were cached near the Arkansas by the trappers. They then made their way further north to trap along the South Platte River (still in Colorado). Here two men deserted with a few horses.

Carson and another trapper were sent after them by John Gantt, who suspected the deserters were headed for the buried cache. Sure enough, Kit found the pelts stolen. The deserters had escaped in a canoe the trapping party also secreted.

Gantt's partner, Jefferson Blackwell, brought Kit to their new campsite in South Park, between the Arkansas and South Platte Rivers. It was while scouting this terrain that Carson and a few others found themselves surrounded by about 60 Indians, yet they managed to get back to their camp. Only one trapper sustained a serious injury.

When Carson was waiting for Blackwell earlier on at the winter camp, he supposedly was part of a battle against Comanche Indians. Joe Meek told this tale of how he and a small group of trappers with the Rocky Mountain Fur Company came across Kit; some 200 Comanche were held off when the mules were killed to use as a barricade as they fired away with their rifles. The trappers escaped under the cover of darkness.

By October 1833, Kit, after trapping independently with a few comrades, went to Taos. There the beaver pelts they had accumulated were disposed of successfully.

Kit was again with Tom Fitzpatrick's trappers in March 1834. But Kit was soon trapping independently once more. Out hunting alone one day, near Wyoming's Laramie River, Carson was chased by a pair of grizzly bears. They fortunately never caught him, as he escaped up a tree and stayed there until they left. Despite his past encounters with Indians, Kit Carson found this one with the bears the most frightening.

The 1834 summer rendezvous on Ham's Fork and the Green River was Kit's first. He had ridden in with Fitzpatrick's good friend, and a partner in their outfit, none other than Jim Bridger.

Carson and Bridger also became very good friends. Six entries that include them both are part of each frontiersman's filmography.

Again they are, for television, 1986's *Dream West* (for CBS), 1977's *Kit Carson and the Mountain Men* (for NBC), and 1976's *Bridger* (for ABC). The theatrical films are *Along the Oregon Trail* in 1947 (for Republic), *Kit Carson* in 1940 (for United Artists), and the silent *Kit Carson* in 1928 (for Paramount).

After the rendezvous of 1834, Kit accompanied Bridger and his trapping brigade farther northwest. About 50 trappers wintered along the Snake River (which ran from Wyoming into the Idaho territory). Blackfeet Indians were on their trail.

The Indians stole 18 horses from the trappers in February 1835. Carson was among the 12 men sent after them. Although an attempt was made to parley, only five of the horses were offered back. Fighting broke out as a result.

Both Carson and a comrade, Mark Head, were under immediate return fire. Nonetheless Kit shot and killed the Indian aiming at Head. At the same time, another Indian fired a rifle at Carson; the ball hit him in the shoulder, passing through it.

Kit and his comrades retreated to make camp and where he suffered during the night from the wound. The following day, the trappers returned to their main campsite with the five horses initially offered by the Blackfeet. When 30 trappers rode back with Bridger, the Indians had already made off with the remaining 13 animals.

Jim Bridger was especially regretful about Kit's injury, although it healed. One of the stolen horses was Jim's own mount, Grohean.

At the 1835 summer rendezvous, held on Horse Creek and the Green River, both Bridger and Carson supposedly married Indian women. While Jim called his Flathead bride Cora, Kit's Arapaho wife was called Waanibe.

According to legend, Kit Carson fought a duel against a bullying trapper making advances on the Indian maiden. The trapper, known only as Shunar, was with the American Fur Company, which had aligned itself with Bridger's old Rocky Mountain outfit through Pratte, Chouteau and Company.

Both Shunar and Carson fired weapons at each other from horseback. Shunar's rifle ball just missed Kit's head, but Carson's pistol shot struck the other man in the arm. Thereafter, Kit had no further trouble with the man.

Carson is involved with Indian women in a pair of entries included in his filmography. Both are silent films—the aforementioned initial entry in 1903, *Kit Carson*, and Selig's 1911 *Kit Carson's Wooing*.

In September 1835, Kit rode with Jim Bridger's brigade to the Three Forks of the Missouri (in the Montana territory). Other trappers were also in the area, led by Joseph Gale, and they had been fighting with the Blackfeet. Among Gale's party was a wounded man named Dick Owens, who became a close friend of Carson's in the years ahead. Bridger had sent Kit with some others to seek out these men.

When 80 or so Indians attacked Gale's men again, Kit was caught in their camp. The Blackfeet set fire to the brush in an attempt to burn the trappers out. But Bridger's arrival with his main body routed the Indians and kept this from happening.

Under a mistaken notion that beaver were teeming at Mary's River, not far from Fort Hall in Idaho, Kit went there with Thomas McKay's brigade of trappers. They were part of the rival Hudson's Bay Company, yet Kit may have also been persuaded to join them because of their especial encouragement of wives coming along. Kit accompanied McKay to the summer rendezvous of 1836, which was at the same site as the year before on the Green River.

By the winter of 1837, Kit was again with Bridger on Montana's Yellowstone River and confronting the Blackfeet. Waanibe was apparently safe at Fort Hall while he was gone, with their baby daughter. She was named Adaline, after the niece of Kit's own childhood.

Waanibe and Kit were at the Green River rendezvous of 1837, although her lodge was not in Jim Bridger's camp but rather with the Arapahos. Many different Indian tribes attended that summer. Famous artist Alfred Jacob Miller was also there and painted his picture of Jim in a suit of armor.

Among the 110 mountain men was Kit Carson who went and trapped after the rendezvous in the Wyoming-Montana territories. And Bridger had led the way. Expecting trouble with the Blackfeet, when none came the trappers discovered that it was the smallpox ravaging the Indians that kept them away. Some 6,000 would die from this disease.

Supposedly Carson's last fight against the Blackfeet was provoked when he was with 40 of the trappers in April 1838. Not heeding Bridger's advice to simply trap, they instead rode against an Indian village. This may have been along the Madison River in Montana.

At first the Indians fled. Yet when the trappers ran low on ammunition, the Indians decided then to attack. One trapper, Cotton Mansfield, became pinned beneath a horse. Riding to his aid, Kit dismounted, killing an Indian and holding several more at bay. Mansfield managed to free himself and get away, but Carson's horse had galloped off, leaving him stranded. However, Kit was saved when another trapper named David White rode by, pulling Carson up behind him so they both could escape.

That summer's rendezvous in 1838 was far from the Green River. East of the Continental Divide, it was off the Popo Agie in Wyoming's Wind River Range. And it was the last one that Kit Carson attended although two more were held (in '39 and '40, again along the Green). The need for beaver had declined and the mountain men would have to find other ways to make a living on the frontier.

Yet trapping beaver was not completely abandoned. Kit continued to trap, among other places at Brown's Hole (on a bend of the Green River stretching into Colorado). A stockade was built there which came to be called Fort Davy Crockett.

After giving birth at Brown's Hole to another daughter, Waanibe soon died of fever. This may have been during the 1839-40 winter season at the fort. Sadly too, in 1843, the child was killed in Taos when she accidentally fell in a boiling kettle of soap.

Between these tragedies in Kit's life, he found work as a hunter for William Bent and Ceran St. Vrain. It was at their outpost, Bent's Fort, on the Arkansas River (in Colorado) during the fall of 1841. The pay was a dollar a day.

A Cheyenne, Making Out Road, became Kit's second wife during this time. Taking care of him and his children did not suit her and the marriage quickly dissolved. According to Indian custom, she simply placed Kit's belongings outside her lodge and it was over.

Following his tenure as a hunter at Bent's Fort, in April 1842 Kit went with a wagon train back to Missouri. This was the first visit there in 16 years. Daughter Adaline went with him to stay with her aunt, Kit's sister, Mary Ann Carson Rubey. When he was still employed at the fort, Kit managed to travel to Taos sometimes where he met Josefa Jaramillo, his future wife. She may have even been helping to care for his other daughter.

And after visiting his family and friends in Boon's Lick, Kit went on to St. Louis. Aboard a steamer heading up the Missouri River, Carson met a man who had as big an impact on his future as did Jim Bridger on his past. The man's name was John Charles Frémont.

Other than fighting Indians, Carson's adventures with Frémont make up the biggest part of this filmography with at least eight entries. The aforementioned *Dream West* (1986) and *Kit Carson and the Mountain Men* (1977) are two of the television entries. And they are joined by a couple of television shows—1960's *Destiny West* (for NBC), and a 1964 episode of *The Great Adventure* (for CBS).

Both 1947's *Along the Oregon Trail* and 1940's *Kit Carson*, already mentioned, are joined by two more films. They are a silent, 1925's *Kit Carson Over the Great Divide* (for Sunset), and 1939's *Mutiny on the Blackhawk* (for Universal).

John Frémont was just over three years younger than Carson. When they first met, Frémont was a lieutenant in the U.S. Corps of Topographical Engineers. He had married Jessie Benton the previous fall; she was the daughter of Missouri Senator Thomas Hart Benton. Initially the senator opposed the marriage, but quickly became Frémont's firm supporter in his future explorations into the West.

The first exploration that spring of 1842 was meant to pass through Kansas into Wyoming. The destination was supposed to have been the headwaters of the Sweetwater River. But in this scientific survey for the corps, which took into account the various plant and animal life, Frémont extended the orders to go beyond the Sweetwater to the South Pass and the Rocky Mountains.

Aware that Frémont was looking for a guide for the journey, Kit Carson offered his services aboard that steamer. Liking Carson immediately, Frémont still made inquiries on his abilities. Satisfied, Kit was hired for $100 a month.

The expedition may have consisted of as many as 25 members. While Kit also liked John, he realized that the man who would come to be called the Pathfinder did not always think things through properly. One instance early on occurred when Frémont loaded down a rubber boat so heavily with supplies that it overturned. Carson was one of the men who then had to swim after the items.

When Jim Bridger crossed trails with Kit, who was scouting ahead of Frémont, he reported a possible threat of a Sioux Indian attack. Fortunately none came. In fact, the Frémont party befriended a few hungry and weary Cheyenne by sharing their food and campsite.

Buffalo hunts were enjoyed during the expedition. One was upon reaching the Sweetwater that August. Both Frémont and Carson displayed their riding and shooting skills.

Once through the South Pass, Frémont decided to conquer what he believed was the highest mountain peak in the Rockies. It wasn't, nonetheless, there in the southern end of the Wind River Range, Kit led the way toward the summit the first day of climbing. The following day, August 14, the Pathfinder reached the summit which he named Frémont Peak.

Returning over the 1,000 miles of terrain, that September Kit took his leave from John Frémont at the Wyoming outpost of Fort Laramie. Kit went to Bent's Fort, where he perhaps hunted and trapped, until traveling south into New Mexico back to Taos.

The previous January 1842, Kit had been baptized into the Catholic faith in preparation for marrying Josefa. On February 6, 1843, they were married — the

bridegroom was 33 years old, the bride not quite 15. Yet the marriage was an enduring one, lasting the rest of their days.

Jessie Benton Frémont collaborated with her husband on a well-received Senate document about his first expedition. As John Frémont journeyed with Carson and the others, the path had been over a part of the already established Oregon Trail. Writing about it not only advanced the emigrant push westward but made Frémont famous.

With this early success in his army career with the corps, John embarked on another expedition with it in May 1843. Surveying the full Oregon Trail to the Pacific Northwest was the initial goal. A howitzer was even brought along as a precaution for any possible British takeover of the Oregon territory. Accompanying Frémont as scouts were both Tom Fitzpatrick and Kit Carson.

As Tom was head scout, Kit had to settle for a pay reduction to $70 a month. But instead of just a few months long, like the previous adventure, this one lasted Carson a year — covering some 3,500 miles. In that time, Josefa remained at their home in Taos.

The second expedition had in fact already set out when Kit heard about it. Catching up to Frémont along the trail, Carson then was part of the perhaps 40 members of the expedition heading west from Fort St. Vrain.

Like Bent's Fort, this latter Colorado outpost (situated farther north) was run by traders Ceran St. Vrain and William Bent. Kit had actually been working for them again when he linked up with the Frémont party.

As Fitzpatrick traveled along the Oregon Trail with most of the men and the supplies, Frémont with Kit and the others planned to join them later in Idaho at Fort Hall. Having crossed the southern end of the South Pass and gone on to Fort Bridger,

Frémont went to explore along Utah's Great Salt Lake.

Prior to reaching the lake that September, Kit was sent to Fort Hall for provisions. Tom and the main body, however, had not yet arrived. Carson's attempts to buy enough food supplies were in vain as an influx of emigrants had already done so and no more were currently available.

Kit was with Frémont's group when a rubber boat was taken to an island in the Salt Lake. Rowing back, a leak threatened as did an approaching storm. Their struggle to reach shore was also hampered by pounding waves nearly 10 feet high. But they made it.

Back at Fort Hall, Fitzpatrick was now waiting. Yet with the supplies they had, John Frémont was not certain there would be enough to sustain all of the men through the upcoming winter. Eleven of the party decided then not to go on and returned home.

By early November 1843, the Frémont expedition reached the Dalles, where a narrow channel ran along the Columbia River in the Oregon territory. With Kit overseeing the repairing of equipment there, Frémont and some of the men went west by boat on the Columbia to obtain supplies at Fort Vancouver.

Instead of this being the turning around point for the expedition, Frémont disobeyed orders by then going south with his men in Oregon along the Deschutes River. When they crossed into the Great Basin (which Frémont named) in the Nevada territory, it took 16 days or so to move over that desert terrain. It was by then just after Christmas.

The men, by the middle of January 1844, turned westward on a river Frémont labeled the Salmon Trout. Later called the Truckee River, it led toward the Sierra Nevada Mountains and California.

Both Kit Carson and Tom Fitzpatrick knew Frémont would have been wise to

winter east of the mountains. Yet loyal to the Pathfinder, they followed him in his haste to cross over them. Even the friendly Indians whom the expedition traded with warned them of the cold and deep snows waiting.

One wise decision was made by John Frémont. As he and his men made their way into the mountains that February, they abandoned the heavy howitzer already carried some 2,000 miles. It then took five weeks to struggle through the frozen wilderness. Half of their 67 horses and mules were lost. One comrade, Baptiste Derosier, wandered off and although he was found he had lost his mind.

Frémont and his men found their way to Sutter's Fort in the Sacramento Valley. While the California territory was still under Mexican rule, John Sutter, a Swiss emigrant, had been allowed to build his stockade. It served as a buttress between the friendly and unfriendly Indian tribes.

So at the junction of the Sacramento and American Rivers, the fort also served, for two weeks that March, as a point of recuperation for the weary expedition members. Yet Derosier again wandered off and was presumed dead until he turned up safe in Missouri a year later.

1936's *Sutter's Gold* (for Universal) is a motion picture depicting the life of John Sutter. It is part of the Carson filmography.

Beginning the trek home on March 24, 1844, the Frémont expedition found the snows still too deep the way originally taken. John Frémont then took the men south along California's San Joaquin River. Remembering this area, from his days with Ewing Young as a trapper, Kit Carson found a crossing over the southern edge of the Sierra Nevadas and to the Mojave Desert.

While Carson, Frémont and their companions were camped along the Mojave River, a Mexican man, Andreas Fuentes, arrived out of the desert with a boy in tow. It was later determined that the pair were the only survivors of an Indian attack which took the lives of the other four members of their party.

But Carson and fellow hunter Alexis Godey volunteered to help Fuentes retrieve his horses soon discovered stolen by the Indians. After a day's tracking, Kit and Alexis surprised the Indian camp the next morning as some of the horses were being eaten.

Guns blazing, Godey and Carson ran into the campsite, killing two Indians and scattering the rest. Kit guessed there were as many as 30 Indians. Some 15 horses were recovered and taken back to Fuentes.

While this action was attributed against the Paiutes, other Indian tribes plagued the expedition on its return journey. In May, Digger Indians were believed to have killed a member named Francois Tabeau.

Mountain man Joseph Walker crossed trails with Frémont and helped to guide his group over the Wasatch Range of the Rockies (in Utah). On July 1, the expedition arrived at Bent's Fort where it disbanded, with Carson going home to Taos and Frémont to the United States.

With wife Jessie, John Frémont collaborated on a second report about his wilderness adventures. Some 10,000 copies were sold to the public. The increased fame could only help in his promotion to brevet captain. But the Pathfinder's report this time also made another man famous—Kit Carson.

Congress authorized a third expedition for Frémont early in 1845. By June, 74 men may have been with him as they left St. Louis, including Alexis Godey and Basil Lajeunesse, the latter having been along on the past two expeditions. This new enterprise with the Topographical Corps was supposedly deployed to survey points west regarding their distance from Bent's Fort.

When the men with Frémont arrived at the fort that August, a messenger was sent into New Mexico to find Kit Carson. With Dick Owens, Kit had started a cattle ranch east of Taos in the Cimarron Valley. But when the messenger reached him, Kit then sold the ranch for half of its actual value. Both he and Owens went to Bent's Fort to join Frémont.

Twenty months would pass before Kit saw his wife Josefa. Then it was for only 10 days before he headed out again.

After crossing the Continental Divide in Colorado, Frémont with his party once again ran into Joseph Walker, who became a guide for them. They crossed over the Wasatch Mountains, as had the earlier returning expedition, but this time went north where they camped in October along the Great Salt Lake.

Determined to cross through the expanse of the Great Basin, John Frémont first sent Carson, Lajeunesse and a couple of others to scout ahead in that desert for water. When they found it, a smoke signal was to be sent up for the others to follow.

Kit and his companions traveled nearly 60 miles and reached a mountain where water was found. The signal was sent as was a rider to help bring the other men through. Frémont named the mountain Pilot Peak.

During November, Frémont and 10 men, including Carson, finished crossing the Basin. Walker and the rest proceeded further south along the Humboldt River (which Frémont also named) in Nevada. On the 24th, both parties met at Walker Lake with California their intended destination.

As provisions were low, the men split up once more with Walker guiding the main body south to cross the Sierra Nevada. Frémont, Carson, Owens and 13 others took an emigrant trail along the Truckee River to the mountains.

This time, with a crossing in December, there were no problems with deep snows. When Frémont's group came out of the mountains on the 9th, provisions were purchased at the Grimes Ranch on the way to Sutter's Fort.

Although an attempt was made to meet up with Walker's group, the latter hadn't turned up yet. On January 15, 1846, Frémont's group arrived at Sutter's Fort, where, with a passport issued by John Sutter, he was able to go on to Monterey and meet the American consul, Thomas Larkin.

Meanwhile, Dick Owens and Kit went to look for Walker, whom they found. Both groups were reunited at the Laguna Rancho near San Jose.

In early March, the men were at a hacienda in the Santa Clara Valley near Monterey, when Frémont received a message from Mexican Gen. Jose Castro ordering him and his men to leave California. The Mexican War was only a couple of months away; and Castro suspected that Frémont's true mission there was in a military role for the United States.

However, John Frémont refused to leave just then despite Consul Larkin advising him to do as ordered. Instead he took his men to make a stand at Hawk's Peak in the Gabilan Mountains.

While a group of Mexican soldiers made a halfhearted march against Frémont's men, no actual fighting transpired. Feeling Frémont was a coward for not fighting the Mexicans, Joseph Walker quit the expedition when it did go to Oregon.

On May 7, near Upper Klamath Lake, Frémont received another message. U.S. Marine Lt. Archibald Gillespie was coming to bring him important correspondence.

With a group of men the next day, including Kit Carson, Basil Lajeunesse and four Delaware Indians, Frémont intercepted Gillespie on the trail. One of the letters received was from John's father-in-law, Senator Benton. The Pathfinder interpreted

the letter to mean the U.S. was preparing to take over California.

As these men were camped that night, Klamath Indians attacked. Asleep, Kit was awakened by a groan from Basil, who was struck with a fatal tomahawk blow on the head. A Delaware was killed when enemy arrows tore into him. Another man was also slain.

Carson and two men fired their guns at a Klamath chief who came at them with a fury. Finally the chief fell and Kit would later claim that this was the bravest Indian he ever encountered.

The other Indians fired arrows into the camp in an attempt to recover their dead chief. But the firepower of the guns drove the enemy back. Later, at another campsite, the surviving Delaware Indians killed two of the enemy and took their scalps.

Then attacking the Klamath Indian village, Frémont saved Carson's life. Kit led the attack which routed and killed 20 more of the enemy. As one was aiming his arrow at Carson, Frémont, on horseback, sent the Indian sprawling. A Delaware finished him off.

On May 24, 1846 (11 days after the declaration of war by the U.S. against Mexico), Frémont's party reached Lassen's Ranch back in California. The ranch was on a tributary of the Sacramento River called Deer Creek; and Peter Lassen, the owner, once worked as a blacksmith for John Sutter.

While bivouacked at Lassen's in April, before venturing to Oregon, Frémont received a call of help from the local settlers against the Indian threat there. Perhaps 175 Indians, men, women and children, lost their lives in the path of destruction created by Frémont's attack. Carson, who was a participant, called it a butchery.

At Frémont's instigation that June, settler Ezekiel Merritt led 33 other settlers against the Mexican outpost at Sonoma, north of San Francisco. The Mexican commander there, Gen. Mariano Vallejo, was captured and confined at Sutter's Fort despite the protests of the act by Sutter.

Despite any disobeying of orders by still being in California, Frémont was promoted to lieutenant colonel. He even referred to himself as the U.S. military commander of the territory.

Warfare with the Mexicans is part of the Carson filmography. Among the films are a 1927 silent, *California* (for MGM), and 1961's *Frontier Uprising* (for United Artists).

On June 28, 1846, Kit Carson, apparently acting under Frémont's orders, had executed by firing squad three Mexicans who came ashore at San Pablo Bay. This was in retaliation for the earlier torturing to death of a pair of revolutionaries by other Mexicans.

When the U.S. Navy, under the command of Commodore John Sloat, arrived in California in July, Frémont's military authority came under question. But Robert Stockton replaced Sloat and had John Frémont recruit more men to form a unit called the California Battalion.

With word that his adversary, General Castro, had fled south to refit the Mexican troops, Frémont and his battalion followed aboard a U.S. warship. Carson became seasick during the voyage.

Both San Diego and Los Angeles surrendered to the Americans, although Castro evaded capture. Frémont, ironically, never battled the Mexican army during the war. Yet the same wasn't true for Kit Carson.

Dispatched to carry correspondence to Washington, D.C., Kit and a group of riders met Brig. Gen. Stephen Kearny on October 6 in Socorro, New Mexico. The general, with more men, was riding to take command of the American forces in California.

Although Kit protested — as he was determined to follow his orders and also spend a night together with Josefa in Taos — Kearny ordered him instead to guide them back to California. Tom Fitzpatrick, who had guided the general this far, was ordered to take the dispatches on to Washington.

Meanwhile, Los Angeles had been taken back by the Mexicans. Guided by Carson, Kearny became embroiled with the enemy in early December, northeast of San Diego in the San Pasqual Valley.

The Mexican troops were commanded by Gen. Andres Pico, who pretended to retreat only to turn and fight Kearny, Carson and some 110 men. The Americans were routed and General Kearny was wounded. Carson was nearly trampled to death by the galloping horses of his own comrades when he fell into their path.

During the night after the second day of fighting, Carson and Lt. Edward Beale volunteered to get help from Commodore Stockton in San Diego. Having to remove their shoes and crawl past the enemy sentries, the pair lost the shoes and had to continue barefoot over the rugged terrain.

Stockton was notified and 170 reinforcements were sent to Kearny's aid. While the Mexicans were then driven off, they suffered only a single fatality compared to the general's 21 men killed.

In Los Angeles, General Pico was defeated on January 8, 1847, by forces under the leadership of Kearny and Stockton. Kit Carson was among the 600 men who took part in the defeat.

Six days later, Kit was again part of John Frémont's command when the Pathfinder rode into Los Angeles with an additional 400 men. Upon Pico's earlier retreat from Stockton and Kearny, the Mexican commander actually surrendered to Frémont's advancing force. A treaty was even signed with Frémont ending the war in California.

But the Mexican government did not officially recognize any U.S. conquests until after Gen. Winfield Scott's successful invasion of Mexico. That was in September, and in February 1848 an official peace treaty was signed.

Less than a month before the treaty, Frémont was found guilty in a court-martial proceeding in Washington. Insubordination seemed to be the main charge brought by General Kearny against him. Earlier in California, John had failed to appreciate that the general was actually in command. Perhaps especially harmful was Frémont's handling of the treaty with Pico without even informing Kearny.

The court-martial verdict dismissed Frémont from the military, but President James Polk remitted the decision. Even so, John Frémont resigned a few weeks later.

In April 1847, Kit Carson had returned home to Taos in the aftermath of an even more devastating situation. Insurrectionists, among them Mexicans and Indians, violently rebelled that past January against the American control in New Mexico.

Charles Bent, the governor of the territory (and Kit's brother-in-law, married to Josefa's sister), was killed. So were an uncle and a brother of Josefa's, as well as others by the rebels.

Fortunately, the rebellion was put down by the time Carson arrived, although public hangings of the rebels still took place. Josefa was found by Kit safe but badly shaken from the ordeal which nearly took her own life.

Kit could stay with Josefa for only 10 days because he had to take dispatches from California on to Washington. Among the riders with him was Lieutenant Beale, who was still recovering from the rigors of that prior barefoot journey to bring help to the troops.

In Washington, Kit was warmly received in the homes of both Beale's mother and Jessie Benton Frémont. On June 7, he also met President Polk, who put forth an appointment for Carson in the U.S. Regular Army as second lieutenant.

Yet Kit found that Washington society and his own fame made him feel uncomfortable. He was only too eager to head west later in June with return dispatches. Jessie accompanied Kit's group to St. Louis to see her father and await further word of her husband (for John had yet to return from California). While in Missouri, Kit journeyed to Howard County to see his daughter Adaline.

As Kit passed through Santa Fe, Josefa was waiting there to spend a little time with him. He was able to take her home before venturing on to California.

When Carson arrived in Los Angeles that October, Kearny, Frémont and even Stockton had all gone east to Washington (for the inevitable court-martial). Kit then took his dispatches to Monterey to the acting governor, Col. Richard Mason. Prior to his leaving, Frémont had been appointed by Stockton to fill that role.

On May 4, 1848, Kit Carson was again carrying government correspondence eastward, this time with a group including Lt. Douglas Brewerton. Among the dispatches was news of the gold strike at John Sutter's mill in the Sacramento Valley.

Josefa and Kit were able to spend a few days together in Taos on his journey. In Santa Fe, he discovered that the appointment for second lieutenant had not been approved by the Senate. Apparently now just a private citizen without any military obligation, Kit still felt duty bound to go to Washington with the dispatches.

In Washington over the summer, Kit spent time with John and Jessie Frémont. He was at the baptism of their new baby son; unfortunately, the child was sickly and soon died.

Bound for Taos, Kit visited Adaline. She was entered by her father in Missouri's Howard Female Seminary.

As Kit returned home that fall of 1848, the Pathfinder was embarking on a fourth expedition. This one, privately financed, was to the San Juan mountain range of the Rockies (which covered areas in both New Mexico and Colorado). The goal was to find a breach in the mountains for a railroad crossing.

Carson, who did not go along, reportedly had warned Frémont against the undertaking at this time due to the expectant severe cold and heavy snows. A mountain man named Bill Williams acted instead as Frémont's guide.

The expedition ended horribly; no railroad passage was found and 10 of Frémont's party perished due to exposure and starvation. Some of the men, including Williams, were alleged to have cannibalized their dead comrades to survive.

To seek help, a pair of relief parties attempted to get back out of the mountains. Of the initial group, three out of four men survived. Frémont and Alexis Godey were among the other group of five who were guided out to safety by a Ute Indian, and found their way to Taos and to Kit Carson.

This was on January 21, 1849, and a rescue party was formed by Kit and another, Lucien Maxwell (a hunter with the first and third Frémont expeditions). As Kit and a pregnant Josefa nursed John back to health in their home, Godey returned to the mountains with the other rescuers. Fifteen more men were then saved.

After his recovery, John Frémont went overland to live in California, which would become part of the United States the following year. Wife Jessie and their six-year-old daughter traveled there on a sea voyage to join him.

The spring of 1849 found Carson and Maxwell starting a farm on Rayado Creek in New Mexico, south of Kit's earlier ranch with Dick Owens. The new place was across the Sangre de Cristos Range of the Rocky Mountains, and some 50 miles from Taos.

Soon a settlement was also started there with the help of others right on the Mountain Branch of the Santa Fe Trail.

But Josefa remained in Taos for another year or so because of the frequent Indian raids. A son, Charles, was born to the Carsons on May 1, but died from sickness within a year.

That October, Kit's services as a scout were acquired by the U.S. Army when Jicarilla Apaches attacked a wagon train of settlers. It happened on the Cimarron Cutoff of the Santa Fe Trail (in northeast New Mexico).

White it proved difficult to track the Indians since they often separated, after 10 or so days Kit located their campsite. A Mrs. White, her young daughter and a servant woman had been captured. Carson wanted then to rush the Indians, thereby surprising them. But Capt. William Grier, in charge of the army detail, called a halt for a parley.

This pause only enabled the Indians to escape after slaying Mrs. White. The servant and daughter remained captive.

The woman's death especially moved Kit for he felt she may have possibly been saved had the soldiers rushed the Indian camp. Another ironic twist was that Kit Carson found with her belongings a dime novel about his adventures fighting Indians.

Returning home to the Rayado, Carson experienced the worst snowstorm of perhaps his entire life. A member of his group died from exposure, as did many of the fleeing Apaches.

Again returning to the farm, in the springtime of 1851, Kit had a wagon train of provisions from St. Louis. Also along was Adaline, going to live with her father.

When Cheyenne Indians threatened Carson and the wagons, a runner was sent ahead to get help from the army. This time, Grier, promoted to major, wasted no time in dispatching a detail. The Indians became aware of it and did not attack.

Families heading west figure into the Kit Carson filmography. Included films are

1923's silent, *The Covered Wagon* (Paramount); 1931's *West of the Rockies* (Road Show); and 1974's *Seven Alone* (Doty-Dayton).

During the fall of 1850, Kit had helped another army detail. He guided the 1st Dragoons, commanded by Lt. Oliver Taylor, to chase down a former soldier turned outlaw. The culprit's name was Fox, and he was supposedly bent on murdering two travelers, Elias Brevoort and Samuel Weatherhead, for the gold they carried.

Fox was captured and arrested; a gang he had formed was then driven off. For his help, Weatherhead and Brevoort sent Kit a pair of silver-mounted Colt pistols.

Carson's adventures with outlaws and gold are part of the filmography. Included are a pair of serials and feature films.

The serials are 1933's *Fighting with Kit Carson* (Mascot), and 1939's *Overland with Kit Carson* (Columbia). The features are 1942's *Lawless Plainsmen* (also Columbia), and 1945's *Trail of Kit Carson* (Republic).

For old times' sake, in 1852, Carson

A daguerreotype of Kit Carson between 1850 and 1854.

went on a final beaver-trapping expedition. In October, Josefa gave birth to another son named William. And Adaline, about 14 years old that year, took a husband.

His name was Louis Simmons, and he was almost 20 years older than Adaline. The marriage, however, would end in divorce or with Simmons just leaving her.

With Lucien Maxwell and a few others, Kit went into the sheep business in 1853. That February, Carson rounded up some 6,500 sheep south of Santa Fe, costing only 50 cents or so a head.

The animals were herded into three groups and taken to Sacramento, California. At $5.50 a head, they were sold to Samuel Norris.

Adaline and Louis accompanied Kit to California when he brought in a group of the sheep in September. It would be the last time he saw his daughter, as she remained there when he returned home to the Rayado. She died in 1860.

When Congress appointed him an Indian agent upon his return from California, Kit's initial duties were to administer to the needs of the Mohuache Utes. But other tribes came under his jurisdiction, including the Jicarilla Apaches and Pueblo Indians.

Wresting peace from the Indians was a difficult task. Kit often found himself serving as guide or scout on military campaigns against them. Men on both sides were killed in the struggles.

As time went on, Kit became regarded as a fair-minded agent. He especially earned the trust of Mohuache chief Ka-ni-ache. At the same time, Pueblo chief Blanco distrusted all white men, including Kit Carson. Ka-ni-ache might just have saved Kit's life by pulling a gun aimed at him from Blanco's grasp.

Not being literate created problems for Kit as a government agent. He then utilized several clerks over time to help him. One clerk, John Mostin, actually wrote down his memoirs in 1856 as they were being dictated by Kit. The memoirs were thought lost until they turned up nearly 50 years later, of all places, in Paris, France.

Kit Carson resigned as Indian agent on May 24, 1861. The Civil War had broken out and he soon joined the New Mexico Volunteers as a lieutenant colonel. A commission for a full colonelcy came through that fall. New Mexico was officially only a territory then of the United States (becoming a state in 1912), but its allegiance was to the Union.

Josefa and the children (included with William was a daughter, Teresina, born in 1855, and son Christopher in 1858) all joined Kit for a period at military headquarters in Albuquerque, New Mexico. A fourth son had been born there in August; the Carsons also called him Charles, in memory of their departed first-born.

As the country was initially torn by war, Kit found a great pleasure in simply playing with the children. Hiding candy in his pockets, he would let them jump all over him to find it. Kit and Josefa adopted a three-year-old Navajo boy in 1862 and named him Juan.

Col. E.R.S. Canby, Kit's commanding officer, led him and their assembled troops against the advancing Confederate soldiers. From Texas, the enemy was led by Gen. H.H. Sibley. Fighting broke out that February 1862 when both sides met at Valverde, south of Albuquerque along the Rio Grande.

Although Carson was able to gain ground against the enemy with his immediate command, the majority of the Union troops were not as fortunate. A retreat was then sounded by Canby.

Killed in the battle were 68 Union soldiers and 40 Confederate. Sibley's army continued north, planning to take the capital at Santa Fe.

Other Union forces from Colorado soon stopped the Confederates, driving

A photograph of Kit Carson in 1865.

them back to Texas. One of the Colorado leaders was Col. John Chivington. While Canby headed north to help, Carson was sent to protect Fort Craig near Valverde from any possible danger when the enemy soldiers were being rerouted.

Not yet realizing that New Mexico was free of this threat, Maj. Gen. James Carleton arrived with over 2,300 men, the California Volunteers, to quell any invasion. That September, Carleton took over as commander in the territory after Colonel Canby went to Washington.

With no Confederate threat to face, Carleton's attentions were drawn to putting down Indian attacks generated by the Navajos and Mescalero Apaches. Kit Carson became a key player on that path.

The 52-year-old frontiersman resisted his superior officer's orders, which were to crush the Apache resistance by killing all the men and imprisoning the women and children until a complete surrender was made. When another officer, Capt. James Graydon, was accused of needlessly killing at least 11 Apaches, Carson succeeded in moving forward that November for the man's resignation.

But Graydon died the same month from an earlier injury sustained in a fight with Kit's former military surgeon, J.W. Whitlock, who initiated the accusation against the captain. Graydon's own company murdered Whitlock over the matter.

Many of the Apaches began surrendering and were sent by Major General Carleton to a reservation called the Bosque Redondo. It lay 140 miles or so southeast of Santa Fe on the Pecos River. A new military outpost, Fort Sumner, was built over the next year to oversee the reservation.

In February 1863, Kit Carson wanted to resign. Instead Carleton sent him, after an extended leave with his family, to put down the Navajo resistance. A party of Ute

A painting of Kit Carson as an old and sick man. He had lost a great deal of weight.

Indians, led by Chief Ka-ni-ache, joined Carson against the Navajos that summer. But the Utes left when it was realized that they couldn't continue to keep any of the horses nor captives taken.

A 1925 silent film, *The Vanishing American* (Paramount), is about the Navajo Indians. It is included in this filmography.

The orders for Kit Carson with the Navajo were the same as those with the Apache — annihilation and captivity — unless they surrendered. While he tried to keep the killing down, the methods used were devastating to the Indians.

Between the summer and fall of 1863, Navajo homes and crops were destroyed, and their grain and livestock were taken. Over 700 soldiers were deployed in this military action.

The Canyon de Chelly, in northeast Arizona, became the refuge for some 300 Navajos during the winter if 1864. Conflicting stories grew that most of the Indians, atop a mountain fortress, either surrendered to Carson's soldiers or kept them at bay until their departure. A small number of the Indians were hit with ricocheting bullets off the rocks.

Thousands more of the Navajos did surrender. Journeying from Fort Canby (the new name for Fort Defiance, in the Arizona territory) to the Bosque Redondo, many died of starvation and exposure. The 400-mile journey was called the Long Walk.

Even on the reservation, starvation persisted. Carson's pleas for more supplies were never enough. Although the Apaches and Navajos lived separately there, they still fought among themselves. In time, most of the Apaches escaped, as did 1,000 of the Navajos.

The Bosque Redondo was abandoned when a treaty was signed on June 1, 1868. The Navajo people were able to return to their tribal lands to live on a new reservation. Yet Kit Carson did not live long enough to see this all happen.

Kit suffered from an aneurysm, attributed to a hunting accident in the San Juan Mountains during 1860. Having fallen from his horse at the time, he became entangled in a lead rope and was dragged across rough ground. The aorta was damaged which resulted in his eventual death.

After other Indian campaigns in the Colorado territory, he finally resigned from the army in July 1867. Carson held the title of brevet brigadier general of volunteers.

Another daughter, Rebecca, had been born in 1864. Between Kit's resignation, Josefa gave birth to two more daughters— Estefana in December 1866, and Josefita in April 1868. Just a couple of weeks after the birth of their eighth child, Josefa succumbed to fever and died.

The loss of his wife devastated Kit, completely weakened beyond hope by his condition. A month later, on May 23, 1868, he too died. It was at Fort Lyon in Colorado. He was 58 years old. The children were cared for by family members.

Earlier on, Kit had sold his share of the Rayado farm (and another home in Taos). Before being laid to rest with Josefa, near their Boggsville, Colorado, home, he received a military funeral. Held at Fort Lyon, it included flying the American flag at half-staff and the sounding of taps.

Kit and Josefa's remains were disinterred the following year and taken to Taos, the place they actually loved the most. Where he formerly lived was eventually turned into a museum. In 1990, protesters against Kit's treatment of the Indians vandalized the tombstones located in what is Kit Carson State Park.

Three additional entries are part of his filmography. One is a 1985 Italian film, *Tex Willer e il signore degli abissi* (or *Tex and the Lord of the Deep*). Another is a 2000 educational video, *Explorers of the World*.

But the third is the most memorable entry of all. It is the syndicated television series of the 1950s, appropriately called *The Adventures of Kit Carson*.

Kit Carson Filmography

1 *Kit Carson*   1903
2 *The Cheyenne Raiders*   1910
3 *Kit Carson*   1910
4 *Kit Carson's Wooing*   1911
5 *The Santa Fe Trail*   1923
6 *The Covered Wagon*   1923
7 *Kit Carson Over the Great Divide*   1925
8 *The Vanishing American*   1925
9 *California*   1927
10 *Kit Carson*   1928
11 *West of the Rockies*   1931
12 *Fighting with Kit Carson*   1933
13 *Sutter's Gold*   1936
14 *The Painted Stallion*   1937
15 *Overland with Kit Carson*   1939
16 *Mutiny on the Blackhawk*   1939

17 *Kit Carson*   1940
18 *Lawless Plainsmen*   1942
19 *Trail of Kit Carson*   1945
20 *Along the Oregon Trail*   1947
21 *The Adventures of Kit Carson*   1951–55
22 *Destiny West*   1960
23 *Frontier Uprising*   1961
24 *The Great Adventure*   1964
25 *Seven Alone*   1974
26 *Bridger*   1976
27 *Kit Carson and the Mountain Men*   1977
28 *Tex Willer e il signore degli abissi*   1985
29 *Dream West*   1986
30 *Explorers of the World*   2000

1 *Kit Carson*

American Mutoscope and Biograph Company / 1903 / 10 parts / 1,186 feet / Silent / Black and White

CREDIT: Wallace McCutcheon (camera).

PARTS:
1 "Morning in the Wilderness"
2 "Indians Find the Trail"
3 "In Camp For the Night"
4 "The Night Attack"
5 "Over the Log"
6 "The Canoe Chase"
7 "Arrival of the Indian Scout"
8 "Attack on Canoe and Second Capture"
9 "In the Indian Camp"
10 "The Home in the Wilderness"

SYNOPSIS: Awakening in the forest, Kit Carson and another trapper soon leave their campsite. Hostile Indians are following their trail.

Another camp is made by the two trappers that evening. The Indians attack, killing Kit's comrade and capturing him.

The Indians take their prisoner through the forest. But Kit escapes after jumping off a log and into a stream.

Before long, Kit is in a canoe being chased on the river by Indians in other canoes. Scouting ahead, one Indian alerts his tribesmen of Carson's approach. Kit is then taken prisoner once more.

Tied to a tree in the Indian camp, Kit is tortured. A sympathetic Indian maiden secretly frees him.

Kit Carson returns to his wilderness home. His wife and children warmly greet him.

NOTES: The American Mutoscope and Biograph Company released *Kit Carson* in October 1903. This was the same outfit that also made the first Daniel Boone entry three years later, *Attack on Fort Boonesboro*.

For the initial silent Carson entry, Wallace McCutcheon was credited as cameraman. Utilized were locations in New York's Adirondack Mountains— September 3 to 8 were the actual production days.

"The brief film incorporates semidocumentary scenes of Indian life," related *A Guide to Silent Westerns*. While the real Kit Carson fought various Indian tribes over the years, his adventures here are fictitious. The canoe chase seems more inspired by the heroics of James Fenimore Cooper's literary frontiersman, Natty Bumpoo.

Also tied in with the film were a couple of even shorter 1903 films from American Mutoscope and Biograph. Footage was included in *The Pioneers* from this adventure. And *Kit Carson #6 Panorama* (also shot at the same time in the Adirondacks by McCutcheon) was apparently made as a separate entity. But the latter was cited by the American Film Institute as being abandoned.

The Library of Congress, however, includes 1903's *Kit Carson* as part of its collection.

2 *The Cheyenne Raiders*

Kalem Company / 1910 / 950 feet / Silent / Black and White

NOTES: *The Cheyenne Raiders* was released by Kalem on June 24, 1910. An alternate title was listed as *Kit Carson on the Santa Fe Trail*.

The Kalem Company put out *Jim Bridger's Indian Bride* that same year, and *Daniel Boone's Bravery* was released the next.

None of the three silent films are available on video.

3 *Kit Carson*

Bison Films/Motion Picture Distributors and Sales Company / 1910 / 990 feet / Silent / Black and White

NOTES: Bison's silent film, *Kit Carson*, was released on August 26, 1910. This was a year after the company's involvement on the first Crockett entry, *Davy Crockett — In Hearts United*. Both are unavailable on video.

A Guide to Silent Westerns felt this Carson adventure "offers little insight into the life of the famous frontiersman or frontier life in general." Indians are again on the warpath in the story, this time against settlers in a stockade.

4 *Kit Carson's Wooing*

Selig Polyscope / 1911 / Silent / Black and White

CREDITS: Frank Boggs, Hobart Bosworth (directors); Lannier Bartlett, Hobart Bosworth (screenplay).

CAST: Hobart Bosworth, Betty Harte, Tom Mix, and Tom Santschi.

NOTES: Like the very first Carson film, an Indian maiden helps to save his life in 1911's *Kit Carson's Wooing* for Selig. Kit marries her in this one, yet later leaves her to return to a settlement of white people who need him.

Historically, Kit Carson was married to two Indian women at different times. He left neither of them by his own accord; the first one, Waanibe, died, and the second, Making Out Road, ended their union.

Different sources cite either Frank Boggs and Lannier Bartlett as respectively director and writer, or star Hobart Bosworth handling those dual chores. The latter was not only involved with *Kit Carson's Wooing*, but also with Selig's silent films about Boone (*The Chief's Daughter*, also in 1911) and Crockett (*Davy Crockett* in 1910).

This trilogy of frontier adventures is also unavailable on video.

5 *The Santa Fe Trail*

Arrow Film Corporation / 1923 / 15-Chapter Serial / Silent / Black and white

CREDITS: Ashton Dearholt, Robert Dillon (directors); Robert Dillon (screenplay).

CAST: Jack Perrin, Neva Gerber, Jim Welch, Elias Bullock, Wilbur McGaugh, Clark Coffey, Joe de la Cruz, Maria Laredo, and Ned Jarvis.

CHAPTERS:
1 "Mystery of the Trail"
2 "Kit Carson's Daring Ruse"
3 "Wagon of Doom"
4 "The Half-Breed's Treachery"
5 "The Gauntlet of Death"
6 "Ride for Life"
7 "Chasm of Fate"
8 "Pueblo of Death"
9 "The Red Menace"
10 "A Duel of Wits"
11 "Buried Alive"
12 "Cavern of Doom"
13 "Scorching Sands"
14 "Mission Bells"
15 "End of the Trail"

NOTES: Eight years after it began producing films, Arrow made the 15-chapter serial *The Santa Fe Trail*. Robert Dillon wrote the scenario for the silent and shared directing duties with Ashton Dearholt. It could not be found on video. Jack Perrin was credited with starring as Kit Carson.

From silents to talking motion pictures, Perrin played in many Westerns. Two other serials he was in were 1937's *The Painted Stallion* (as Davy Crockett), and 1938's *The Lone Ranger*.

6 *The Covered Wagon*

Paramount Pictures/Famous Players-Lasky Corporation / 1923 / 10 Reels (98 minutes) / Silent / Black and White

NOTES: Main information is in the Jim Bridger filmography.

Several cast listings found for *The Covered Wagon*, 1923's silent epic, cite Guy Oliver as portraying frontiersman Kit Carson. One source at least, along with the dialogue captions in the video version, refers to him instead as a character named Joe Dunstan.

At Fort Bridger in the film, Oliver's Dunstan is an old friend and boisterous drinking companion to Tully Marshall's Jim Bridger and Ernest Torrence's Bill Jackson. When they bid Dunstan farewell, he is sitting backwards on his horse in a happy-go-lucky drunken state.

In the forthcoming 1925 silent for Paramount, *The Vanishing American*, Oliver actually does play Carson.

7　*Kit Carson Over the Great Divide*

Sunset Productions/Aywon Film Corporation / 1925 / 6 Reels / Silent / Black and White

CREDITS: Frank S. Mattison (director, screenplay); J.C. Hull (titles); Bert Longenecker (photography).

CAST: Roy Stewart (Seaton Maurey), Henry B. Walthall (Dr. Samuel Webb), Marguerite Snow (Norma Webb), Sheldon Lewis (Flint Bastille), Earl Metcalfe (Basil Morgan), Charlotte Stevens (Nancy Webb), Arthur Hotaling (Lt. John C. Frémont), Nelson McDowell (Windy Bill Sharp), and Jack Mower (Kit Carson).

NOTES: In 1921, Sunset Productions was formed by producer Anthony J. Xydias. *Kit Carson Over the Great Divide* became the company's initial film in a series of silents dealing with historical frontier figures. Aywon Film Corporation distributed the Carson silent in September 1925.

The other silent films in the series were *Daniel Boone Thru the Wilderness*, *Davy Crockett at the Fall of the Alamo*, *Buffalo Bill on the U.P. Trail*, and *General Custer at Little Big Horn*. These four were all in 1926. The last silent in the series, a year later, was *Sitting Bull at the Spirit Lake Massacre*.

Jack Mower played Kit in the very first adventure for Xydias. And it was written and directed by Frank S. Mattison, who also shared directing credit on the Daniel Boone film. Starring as Boone was Roy Stewart, top billed in the Carson film as a character named Seaton Maurey.

Mower was top billed in the 1923 serial *In the Days of Daniel Boone*. Like Jack Perrin in 1923's *The Santa Fe Trail*, Mower made the transition from silents to talkies. He appeared in a number of Errol Flynn Westerns; including the historical epics *Santa Fe Trail* (which was not about Kit Carson) in 1940, and *They Died with Their Boots On* (about George Armstrong Custer) in 1941.

With Kit Carson Over the Great Divide was used as well as a title of this early entry concerning the frontiersman's life. While no video version was found, apparently the film dealt with episodes, albeit fictitiously, in both the lives of Carson and explorer John Charles Frémont (Arthur Hotaling).

8　*The Vanishing American*

Paramount Pictures/Famous Players-Lasky Corporation / 1925 / 10 Reels (109 minutes) / Silent / Black and White

CREDITS: George B. Seitz (director); Adolph Zukor, Jesse L. Lasky (presenters); Ethel Doherty (screenplay); Lucien Hubbard (adaptation); C. Edgar Schoenbaum, Harry Perry (photography). Based on Zane Grey's novel *The Vanishing American*.

CAST: Richard Dix (Nophaie), Lois Wilson (Marion Warner), Noah Beery (Booker), Malcolm McGregor (Earl Ramsdale), Nocki (Indian Boy), Shannon Day (Gekin Yashi), Charles Crockett (Amos Halliday), Bert Woodruff (Bart Wilson), Bernard Siegel (Do Etin), and Guy Oliver (Kit Carson).

SYNOPSIS: Nophaie, a Navajo Indian, clashes with an Indian agent named Booker. It is over Marion Warner, a white schoolteacher whom the Indian loves.

Escaping Booker's wrath, Nophaie flees into the hills. But the Navajo returns and saves the life of army agent Earl Ramsdale, who is also in love with Marion.

When the Indians prepare for war, Nophaie warns the white community. During the fighting he is mortally wounded, as is Booker. The dying Nophaie is comforted in Marion's arms.

NOTES: *The Vanishing American*, based on the story by legendary western writer Zane Grey, was premiered in New York City on October 15, 1925. Lucien Hubbard's adaptation of the book was turned into a script by Ethel Doherty for director George B. Seitz.

Produced and released by the triumvirate behind *The Covered Wagon*, this silent motion picture starred Richard Dix as the noble Indian caught between two worlds. Dix would star in 1931's *Cimarron*, the first Western to win an Academy Award for best picture (and, of course, he was Sam Houston in 1939's *Man of Conquest*).

Guy Oliver played Kit Carson in the silent version of *The Vanishing American* (as there was a later sound version in 1955, without Carson, starring Scott Brady). While the silent was set in the early 20th-century American West, a prologue depicted the prior struggles of the Navajo Indians.

The real Carson was certainly involved with the military campaign which led to the Navajo removal to the Bosque Redondo Reservation. Called initially by the Indians the Rope-Thrower for the tricks he could perform, unfortunately the sobriquet became a bitter one to imply how Kit helped to round up the Indians for the U.S. Army.

Leonard Maltin's Movie and Video Guide lists 1925's *The Vanishing American* as being available on both video and DVD.

9 *California*

Metro-Goldwyn-Mayer Pictures / 1927 / 5 Reels / Silent / Black and White

CREDITS: W.S. Van Dyke (director); Frank Davis (screenplay); Marian Ainslee, Ruth Cummings (titles); Clyde De Vinna (photography); Basil Wrangell (editor);

Eddie Imazu (sets). Based on a story by Peter B. Kyne.

CAST: Tim McCoy (Capt. Archibald Gillespie), Dorothy Sebastian (Carlotta del Rey), Lillian Leighton (Duenna), Edwin Terry (Brig. Gen. Stephen W. Kearny), Frank Currier (Don Carlos del Rey), and Fred Warren (Kit Carson).

NOTES: Tim McCoy had worked behind the scenes on both *The Covered Wagon* and *The Vanishing American*. By the time of 1927's *California*, he was a star player in a series of silent Westerns for MGM.

This particular film was directed by W.S. Van Dyke and scripted by Frank Davis from a story by Peter B. Kyne. McCoy was cast as Capt. Archibald Gillespie, who historically delivered the message to John Frémont which supposedly shared the desire of the United States to wrest the California territory from Mexico. At that time, Gillespie was actually a lieutenant.

The Mexican War and the U.S. conquest of the territory in *California* revolved around a fabricated romance between the American Gillespie and a Mexican senorita, Carlotta del Rey. She was played by Dorothy Sebastian.

Adventuring with the real Frémont, whose path was changed by that message from exploration leader to military leader, was Kit Carson. He was enacted by Fred Warren in the film.

Warren's Western films, while not an extensive list, were still interesting. Among the films were the same year's *Sitting Bull at the Spirit Lake Massacre*, and 1929's *In Old Arizona* (for which Warner Baxter won a best actor Oscar as the Cisco Kid).

California could not be located on video.

10 *Kit Carson*

Paramount Pictures / 1928 / 8 Reels / Silent / Black and White

CREDITS: Alfred L. Werker, Lloyd Ingraham (directors); Paul Powell (screenplay); Frederick Hatton (titles); Mack Stengler (photography); Duncan Mansfield (editor). Based on a story by Frank M. Clifton.

CAST: Fred Thomson (Kit Carson), Nora Lane (Josefa), Dorothy Janis (Sings In The Clouds), Raoul Paoli (Shuman), William Courtright (Old Bill Williams), Raymond Turner (Smoky), and Nelson McDowell (Jim Bridger).

SYNOPSIS: Kit Carson and a man named Shuman are Indian agents for the United States government. In Taos, they get into a fight over a Spanish dancer.

On a mission further north to procure peace with the Blackfeet Indians, Kit saves the life of a chief's daughter from a bear attack. Her name is Sings In The Clouds.

For his heroic action, Kit is able to help sustain peace. Yet Shuman nearly ruins things when he attacks the Indian maiden. Kit forces him to flee.

However, Sings In The Clouds is again attacked by Shuman. This time she is killed and the peace is threatened.

Going after her killer, Carson fights with Shuman on a cliff. When Shuman falls to his death, the peace with the Indians is restored.

NOTES: While Kit Carson was indeed an Indian agent for the U.S. government, his duties did not involve the Blackfeet Indians. His trials and tribulations with those Indians were as a hunter and trapper.

Yet the fanciful 1928 silent *Kit Carson* captured the legendary prowess of the frontiersman better than any other silent film. Paramount brought out the adventure on June 23, with directing duties shared by Alfred L. Werker and Lloyd Ingraham. Frank M. Clifton's story was the basis for Paul Powell's screenplay.

A major factor in this being such a splendid depiction of Carson's heroics went beyond the script or direction. The robust performance of the film's star, Fred Thomson, just may be the true force here.

Sadly, Thomson died the same year as his *Kit Carson* was released. A prior series of Western silents (including the title role in the previous year's *Jesse James*) were taking him down the same memorable trail as perhaps the greatest of all Western silent stars, Tom Mix.

Thomson's own brand of daredevil athleticism especially made the comparison to Mix possible. While a copy of *Kit Carson* could not be found, *America on Film* does give a video listing.

11 *West of the Rockies*

Road Show / 1931 / 60 minutes / Black and White

CREDITS: Ray Johnston (director); Lew Gater, Al Dezer (producers); King Gray, H.H. Brounell (photography).

CAST: Ben Lyon (Matthew), Marie Prevost (Arleta), Russell Simpson (Gunner Bill), Anders Randolph (Jim Vance), Gladys Johnson (Sylvia), and James Mason (Tony).

NOTES: Possibly made as a silent film, *West of the Rockies* was given a dubbed soundtrack for its 1931 release. This all but forgotten little Western, from an outfit called Road Show, is not available on video. Lew Gater and Al Dezer were the producers, and the director was Ray Johnston.

Sources cast its star, Ben Lyon, as either a character named Matthew or Kit Carson. The plot has to do with the hero leading an emigrant wagon train into the Rocky Mountains. Along the way, there are the usual dangers, including hostile Indians.

An alternate title was *Call of the Rockies*.

12 *Fighting with Kit Carson*

Mascot Pictures / 1933 / 12-Chapter Serial / Black and White

CREDITS: Armand Schaefer, Colbert Clark (directors); Nat Levine (producer);

Jack Natteford, Barney Sarecky, Colbert Clark, Wyndham Gittens (screenplay).

CAST: Johnny Mack Brown (Kit Carson), Betsy King Ross (Joan Fargo), Noah Beery Sr. (Kraft), Noah Beery Jr. (Nakomas), Edmund Breese (Matt Fargo), Robert Warwick (Dark Eagle), Edward Hearn (Morgan), Lafe McKee (Foster), Lane Chandler (Sergeant), Jack Mower (Carter), and Tully Marshall (Jim Bridger).

CHAPTERS:

1 "The Mystery Riders"
2 "The White Chief"
3 "Hidden Gold"
4 "The Silent Doom"
5 "Murder Will Out"
6 "The Secret of Iron Mountain"
7 "The Law of the Lawless"
8 "Red Phantoms"
9 "The Invisible Enemy"
10 "Midnight Magic"
11 "Unmasked"
12 "The Trail to Glory"

Kit (Johnny Mack Brown) and his Indian friend (Noah Beery Jr.) in *Fighting with Kit Carson.*

SYNOPSIS: Army scout Kit Carson is leading a caravan carrying a gold shipment to California military posts. When an outlaw gang, known as the Mystery Riders, strikes and steals the gold, Carson is the only one in his party to escape.

With a cavalry detachment, Kit captures the gang except for the leader. Suspecting a man named Kraft as the ringleader, Carson also uses his friends, Joan Fargo and the Indian Nokomas, to help find the gold.

Kit and the troopers disguise themselves as the Mystery Riders, hoping Kraft will reveal the hideout where the gold is hidden. Instead Kraft, realizing the ruse, booby traps a fake hideout with explosives.

Warning Kit of the danger, Joan has also discovered the real hideout. Kraft is then exposed and the gold is recovered.

NOTES: *Fighting with Kit Carson* was the first serial for Western film great Johnny Mack Brown. Carson is again embodied as the vigilant hero, although the actual action content was felt to be a bit slow moving.

Nat Levine and his Mascot Pictures made the serial in 1933. Sharing the director's chores were Colbert Clark and Armand Schaefer. Wyndham Gittens, Barney Sarecky, Jack Natteford and Colbert Clark all shared in the screenplay.

Brown gave many a stalwart performance, ranging from star status to supporting roles, in a multitude of Western adventures. This included his performances as Kit Carson and the pioneer inspired by Daniel Boone in 1931's *The Great Meadow*.

In 1947, the Carson entry was reissued as a feature film called *The Return of Kit Carson*. It is available on video under its original title.

13 *Sutter's Gold*

Universal/Edmund Grainger Productions / 1936 / 94 minutes / Black and White

CREDITS: James Cruze (director); Edmund Grainger (producer); Jack Kirkland, Walter Woods, George O'Neill (screenplay); George Robinson, John P. Fulton (photography); Philip Cahn (editor); Albert S. D'Agostino (art director); Franz Waxman (music). Based on a biography by Blaise Cendrars and a story arrangement by Bruno Frank.

CAST: Edward Arnold (John Sutter), Lee Tracy (Pete Perkin), Binnie Barnes (Countess Elizabeth Bartoffski), Katherine Alexander (Anna Sutter), Addison Richards (James Marshall), Montagu Love (Captain Kettleson), John Miljan (Juan Batista Alvarado), William Janney (John Sutter Jr.), Morgan Wallace (General Frémont), and Harry Carey (Kit Carson).

SYNOPSIS: In 1833, Johann (John) Sutter flees Switzerland because of a false murder charge. Yet in doing so, he leaves his family behind.

Sutter first finds work in New York, where he is injured in an altercation with strikebreakers. He then embarks on a journey west with his friend Pete Perkin.

Eventually they end up on a ship bound for California. John and Pete become part of a mutiny against the ship's captain and help to free a cargo of slaves.

In the Mexican territory of California, Sutter is given a vast land grant and starts an empire called New Helvetia. He falls in love with a countess from Russia, Elizabeth Bartoffski.

After gold is discovered on Sutter's land in 1848, an onslaught of prospectors stake their claims on the property and Elizabeth leaves him. John's family arrives, yet the misfortune continues as his wife, Anna, dies from fever.

California becomes part of the United States of America. As the years pass, son John Jr. tries in vain to have the claims returned to his father. For his efforts, the son is killed in the rioting which breaks out.

An embittered old man by 1880, John Sutter is in Washington, D.C., still trying to get his land back. He dies on the steps of the Capitol.

NOTES: For Universal's 1936 film release, *Sutter's Gold*, liberties were assuredly taken with the life of Johann Augustus Sutter. Not the least was the fabricated romance with a Russian countess. Reviews at the time were divided on Edward Arnold's performance as the immigrant who made and lost a fortune in America. Perhaps the best description was "earnest."

The lavish production values accorded the film only hastened a financial decline at Universal once it was deemed a box office failure. However, the success that same year of the musical *Show Boat* saved the studio from bankruptcy.

Sutter's Gold initially was to have been a vehicle for Russian director Sergei Eisenstein. When that fell through, Howard Hawks became the director in the early stages of the Edmund Grainger production. But Hawks was replaced by *The Covered Wagon*'s James Cruze, who in turn received the sole directorial credit.

Three writers worked on the screenplay — George O'Neil, Walter Woods and Jack Kirkland. It was derived from a story arrangement by Bruno Frank and the Blaise Cendrars biography.

Kit Carson was portrayed by Harry Carey in the film and rides into the action to confront the Mexican forces at Sutter's Fort. With him is John Frémont (Morgan

Wallace)— a general rather than the lieutenant colonel he was at the time of the Mexican War depicted. This sequence was also fictitious, for Carson and Frémont never actually battled any enemy forces together in the war.

At the end of this conflict in California, Kit did join Frémont and his army when they marched into Los Angeles. While Frémont and Carson would again see each other over the years, this was the last time they ever rode together.

One of the most endearing of all Western players, Carey was a true pioneer in early motion pictures. His rich body of work included a silent series of Cheyenne Harry adventures, and the role of Hawkeye in 1932's serial version of *The Last of the Mohicans*.

Although not released on video, the Library of Congress lists *Sutter's Gold* in its collection.

14 *The Painted Stallion*

Republic Pictures / 1937 / 12-Chapter Serial / Black and White

CREDITS: William Witney, Alan James, Ray Taylor (directors); J. Laurence Wickland (associate producer); Morgan Cox, Ronald Davidson, Winston Miller, Barry Shipman (screenplay); Edgar Lyons, William Nobles (photography); Murray Seldeen, Helene Turner (editors); John Victor Mackay (art director); Morris Braun (set decorator); Raoul Kraushaar (music). From ideas by Hal G. Evarts.

CAST: Ray Corrigan (Clark Stewart), Hoot Gibson (Walter Jamison), Sammy McKim (Kit Carson), LeRoy Mason (Alfredo Dupray), Duncan Renaldo (Zamorro), Gordon De Main (Governor), Jack Perrin (Davy Crockett), Hal Taliaferro (Jim Bowie), and Julia Thayer (The Rider).

CHAPTERS:
1 "Trail to Empire"
2 "The Rider of the Stallion"
3 "The Death Leap"
4 "Avalanche"
5 "Volley of Death"
6 "Thundering Wheels"
7 "Trail Treachery"
8 "The Whistling Arrow"
9 "The Fatal Message"
10 "Ambush"
11 "Tunnel of Terror"
12 "Human Targets"

SYNOPSIS: During the 1820s, U.S. agent Clark Stewart is traveling to negotiate a trade treaty in New Mexico. He joins a wagon train led by Walter Jamison, which is bound for Santa Fe with trade goods. Among the other travelers are Jim Bowie and young Kit Carson.

But Alfredo Dupray wants to control the territory by sabotaging the treaty; henchman Zamorro uses his gang and Indians to try to destroy the wagons and even kill Stewart. These attempts fail due to a mysterious rider on a painted stallion, who uses her whistling arrows to warn of the danger.

At the same time, Stewart's trade authorization papers are stolen by the gang. Going on to Santa Fe, Stewart finds another ally in Davy Crockett.

In the fight at their hideout, Zamorro and Dupray are killed by Stewart and his supporters. Joining in as well is the mystery rider.

Thus the new treaty is signed, establishing trade relations in the Mexican territory.

NOTES: Of the entries in the Carson filmography, 1937's Republic serial, *The Painted Stallion*, is the only one to feature Kit as a boy. He is played by Sammy McKim, also seen in other Westerns including *Annie Oakley* in 1935, and *The Great Adventures of Wild Bill Hickok* in 1938.

Although the adventures on display with Kit, Jim Bowie and Davy Crockett are fictitious, the real Kit Carson was a teenager

The young Kit Carson (Sammy McKim) being held by Hoot Gibson as Ray Corrigan (in white hat) looks on in *The Painted Stallion*.

when he first journeyed to Santa Fe. And it was aboard a wagon train.

Ray Corrigan and Hoot Gibson were the actual stars on hand. Three directors—William Witney, Alan James, Ray Taylor—and four writers—Barry Shipman, Winston Miller, Ronald Davidson, Morgan Cox—teamed up to make this one of the best action-packed serials of its day.

The Painted Stallion can still be enjoyed on video. Additional notes are in both the Bowie and Crockett filmographies.

15 *Overland with Kit Carson*

Columbia Pictures / 1939 / 15-Chapter Serial / Black and White

CREDITS: Sam Nelson, Norman Dem-ing (directors); Jack Fier (producer); Joseph F. Poland, Morgan Cox, Ned Dandy (screenplay); Benjamin Kline, George Meehan (photography); Lee Zahler (music).

CAST: Bill Elliott (Kit Carson), Iris Meredith (Carmelita Gonzales), Richard Fiske (David Brent), Bobby Clark (Andy Gardner), James Craig (Tennessee), LeRoy Mason (John Baxter), Hal Taliaferro (Jim Stuart), and Trevor Bardette (Arthur Mitchell/Pegleg).

CHAPTERS:
1 "Doomed Men"
2 "Condemned to Die"
3 "Fight for Life"
4 "The Ride of Terror"
5 "The Path of Doom"

6 "Rendezvous with Death"
7 "The Killer Stallion"
8 "The Devil's Nest"
9 "Blazing Peril"
10 "The Black Raiders"
11 "Foiled"
12 "The Warning"
13 "Terror in the Night"
14 "Crumbling Walls"
15 "Unmasked"

SYNOPSIS: With his infamous Black Raiders, mysterious outlaw Pegleg envisions an empire west of the Mississippi River. But frontiersman Kit Carson is persuaded to put an end to the outlaw's reign.

In the process, Kit takes a shine to Carmelita Gonzales, heading west on a wagon train. One of the Black Raiders is captured, but he is killed by his own leader to keep from informing.

The attempt to attack a frontier post by the outlaws is deterred by Carson and his allies. A trader at the post, Arthur Mitchell, is revealed as Pegleg. Trying to escape, he falls beneath his horse and is killed.

NOTES: Like the later-released films *The Return of Daniel Boone* and *The Son of Davy Crockett*, 1939's serial, called *Overland with Kit Carson*, was from Columbia Pictures. All three of these entries were given a real boost, despite being ordinary oaters, by the sturdy presence of star Bill Elliott.

Morgan Cox, who had been one of the writers on *The Painted Stallion*, collaborated on this one with Joseph F. Poland and Ned Dandy. While Jack Fier was the producer, Sam Nelson and Norman Deming collaborated on the directing.

Elliott made a whole passel of Westerns at Columbia before moving on to Republic Pictures. There, in 1944, he began his popular Red Ryder series with the film *Tucson Raiders*.

Overland with Kit Carson is not available on video.

16 *Mutiny on the Blackhawk*

Universal Pictures / 1939 / 67 minutes / Black and White

CREDITS: Christy Cabanne (director); Ben Pivar (associate producer); Michael L. Simmons (screenplay); John W. Boyle (photography); Maurice Wright (editor); Jack Otterson (art director); R.A. Gausman (set decorator).

CAST: Richard Arlen (Capt. Robert Lawrence), Andy Devine (Slim Collins), Constance Moore (Helen Bailey), Noah Beery Sr. (Captain), Guinn Williams (Mate), Thurston Hall (Sam Bailey), Sandra Kane (Tania Bailey), Francisco Maran (General Romero), Charles Trowbridge (Gen. John Frémont), and Richard Lane (Kit Carson).

SYNOPSIS: To fight the slave trade in the Sandwich Islands, United States officer Robert Lawrence investigates a ship called the *Blackhawk*. He begins by stowing away on the vessel.

Slim Collins, a crew member, joins Lawrence to help free the cargo of slaves. A mutiny against the ship's captain and first mate is successful.

Following the mutiny, those involved look for shelter at Fort Bailey in the California territory. The fort's leader Sam Bailey, is hard pressed to protect the American settlers in the area from the Mexican control.

Sam's daughter, Helen, wants her father to aid the mutineers. In doing so, Lawrence decides to fight with the settlers against the Mexican forces. Her mother, Tania, opposes the rebellion, instead siding with the enemy army under General Romero.

Discovering from Kit Carson that Gen. John Frémont is nearby with American troops, Lawrence goes for help. When Romero's soldiers attack, they are repelled by Frémont and his men.

Leaving California afterward, Lawrence is joined by Helen.

NOTES: Christy Cabanne, who directed *The Martyrs of the Alamo* in 1915, helmed this August 1939 release from Universal. Footage for *Mutiny on the Blackhawk* was lifted from the studio's earlier *Sutter's Gold*. Michael L. Simmons' scenario was based on a story by Ben Pivar, who was also the film's associate producer.

A *New York Times* review at the time reflected that the film "is probably the first double feature to be combined into a single bill." This was undoubtedly a reference to the separate segments which begin and close the movie — one at sea, the other land bound — in which fighting breaks out.

The Mexican War setting in the latter portion was yet another fictionalized treatment of John Frémont's role in the struggle. He was played by Charles Trowbridge, while Richard Lane had the supporting role of Kit Carson. The actual stars were Richard Arlen and Andy Devine, who teamed for 11 films with Universal.

A relatively short list of Western films were credited to Lane. But there were at least two notable ones — *The Outcasts of Poker Flat* in 1937 and *Union Pacific*, also in 1939.

A video listing for *Mutiny on the Blackhawk* could not be found.

17 *Kit Carson*

United Artists/Edward Small Productions / 1940 / 97 minutes / Black and White

CREDITS: George B. Seitz (director); Edward Small (producer); John Burch (assistant director); George Bruce (screenplay); John Mescall, Robert Pittack (photography); Fred Feitshans Jr., William Claxton (editors); John DuCasse Schulze (art director); Edward Boyle (set decorator); Edward Lambert (costumes); Don Cash (makeup); Edward Ward (music). From a story by Evelyn Wells. Songs: "Sail Along Prairie Schooner," "With My Concertina," words by Chet Forrest, Bob Wright and music by Edward Ward.

CAST: Jon Hall (Kit Carson), Lynn Bari (Dolores Murphy), Dana Andrews (Capt. John C. Frémont), Harold Huber (Lopez), Ward Bond (Ape), Clayton Moore (Paul Terry), Renie Riano (Genevieve Pilchard), Rowena Cook (Alice Terry), Harry Strang (Sergeant Clanahan), C. Henry Gordon (General Castro), Lew Merrill (General Vallejo), Edwin Maxwell (John Sutter), William Farnum (Don Miguel Murphy), and Raymond Hatton (Jim Bridger).

SYNOPSIS: Riding to Fort Bridger, frontier scout Kit Carson and his comrades, Lopez and Ape, are attacked by Shoshone Indians. Yet the three men are able to make their escape to the fort.

Wagon master Paul Terry then asks Kit to guide a wagon train on to California. Feeling the journey is too dangerous, Kit initially refuses until Capt. John Frémont and his cavalry decide to ride along and give the travelers further protection.

Both Carson and Frémont soon become rivals over the attentions of Dolores Murphy, one of the passengers on the wagon train. She is going to the hacienda of her father, Don Miguel, in Monterey.

Friction develops in California between the Mexican and American people there over the land. General Castro, the Mexican governor, uses the Indians to try to stop the advancing wagons.

Frémont's insistence to bring his troops through a canyon, with Carson and the wagon train taking another route, causes a backlash. Indians dynamite the canyon pass, trapping Frémont and his men. Fortunately, Kit manages to open the pass and rescue the soldiers despite his own troubles with the Indians. They go after the wagons.

Having reached the Murphy hacienda, the wagon train comes under attack again from Castro's own soldiers. In the fighting, both Ape and Lopez are killed.

Kit Carson once more uses his skills, and with Frémont's help, the enemy forces

Kit (Jon Hall, left) helps John Frémont (Dana Andrews) in 1940's *Kit Carson.*

are defeated. Afterward, Kit is made a colonel in the U.S. Army. Dolores, having decided she favors Kit, watches him ride out for further adventures.

NOTES: Although there were reservations about 1940's *Kit Carson*, they mainly stemmed from the romantic interludes and an apparent lack of a big budget. Yet it proved a lively actioneer, and perhaps the very best of all the frontier hero's motion pictures, following its opening on August 26 in Denver, Colorado.

Despite any slights against its economies, United Artists and producer Edward Small included one of the most famous of all backgrounds in film history, namely Monument Valley. George B. Seitz directed the George Bruce script (from a story by Evelyn Wells) with a firm tongue-

in-cheek style that only enhanced the legendary status of Kit Carson.

Jon Hall cut a handsome and dashing figure in the title role. And Dana Andrews lent fine support as John Frémont. Their appeal was not diminished by the fabricated romantic triangle with the film's heroine, played by Lynn Bari.

Fabrications abounded throughout this Western adventure. Kit was never a colonel during the Mexican War (and an actual commission as second lieutenant never materialized). Once again, Carson and Frémont's fighting Mexicans together never happened, although Jose Castro, the Mexican general, did make a haphazard effort in history against them. Castro was portrayed in the film by C. Henry Gordon.

While the *New York Times* correctly

Lynn Bari and Jon Hall in 1940's *Kit Carson*.

stated that "the film is hardly a character study of our buckskin hero and only very incidentally history," it nonetheless conveyed better than any other big-screen treatment the myth behind the man. The *Motion Picture Guide* called *Kit Carson* "an excellent action film with marvelous cinematography that captures the splendor of the Old West."

In more than simply a small way was Hall's charismatic persona a factor to any success the film enjoyed. The actor's popularity over the years was reinforced in exotic adventures such as the 1944 film *Ali Baba and the Forty Thieves*, and that television series of the 1950s, *Ramar of the Jungle*.

Apparently *Kit Carson* has been colorized from its original black and white photography by John Mescall and Robert Pittack. The Western is available on video and is part of the collection at the Library of Congress.

Additional notes are included in the Jim Bridger filmography.

18 *Lawless Plainsmen*

Columbia Pictures / 1942 / 59 minutes / Black and White

CREDITS: William Berke (director); Jack Fier (producer); Luci Ward (screenplay); Benjamin Kline (photography); William Lyon (editor); Lionel Banks (art director).

CAST: Charles Starrett (Steve Rideen), Russell Hayden (Lucky Bannon), Luana Walters (Baltimore Bonnie), Cliff Edwards (Harmony Stubbs), Raphael Bennett (Seth McBride), Gwen Kenyon (Madge Mason),

Frank LaRue (Bill Mason), Stanley Brown (Tascosa), Carl Mathews (Keller), Nick Thompson (Ochello), and Forrest Taylor (Kit Carson).

SYNOPSIS: Driving a herd of cattle to Arizona is Steven Rideen, the foreman on a Texas ranch. Lucky Bannon, the son of his boss, accompanies him. At a cow town along the way, Steve finds friend Bill Mason leading a wagon train bound for Tucson.

Seth McBride secretly robs the safe of his ex-wife, saloonkeeper Baltimore Bonnie. His accomplice, Keller, causes a diversion in which Lucky is hurt. But he is tended to back at the wagons by Mason's daughter, Madge.

After losing her money and then being accused by Keller of cheating, Bonnie is forced to leave town. She joins the wagon train; so does townsman Harmony Stubbs, who becomes Steve's ally, and both Keller and McBride.

Trying to steal from Mason, McBride shoots at him and causes him to fall to his death off a cliff. Steve feels he is to blame, not realizing yet McBride's dirty work, and leads the wagon train on.

Apache Indians, in cahoots with McBride, attack the wagons but are routed. By the time a friendly Pima Indian, Tascosa, is killed by McBride, his past actions are exposed by Keller. In self-defense, Steve shoots McBride dead.

Having sent Lucky to bring help back from Fort Grant against the Apaches, Steve is now captured by the vengeance seeking Pima Indians. Crossing trails with Kit Carson, who volunteers to go to the fort, Lucky returns to help free Steve.

After the 7th Cavalry arrives from the fort to drive away the Indians, the wagon train goes on to Tucson. Madge and Bonnie open a store, while Steve and Lucky return to Texas.

NOTES: The Charles Starrett-Russell Hayden duo were part of a series of "B" Western films previously produced by

William Berke. Columbia's 1942 release, *Lawless Plainsmen*, was apparently the first one Berke directed with the pair. This routine adventure was produced by Jack Fier and scripted by Luci Ward.

Kit Carson, as enacted by Forrest Taylor, is again placed in a supporting role, albeit a heroic one. During his frontier days, Kit rode against many an Indian threat.

His last fight against Indians was in November 1864 at Adobe Walls in the Texas Panhandle. As leader of a military field command, Carson and 259 men (soldiers and Ute and Apache Indian allies) routed over 1,200 Comanches and Kiowas with superior firepower. Three of Kit's men were killed, and, according to him, 60 of the enemy.

Taylor played the frontiersman once more in the forthcoming *Along the Oregon Trail*. His Western credits were legion, extending from the silent era to television. Included was a role in the 1942 Sam Houston entry, *Down Rio Grande Way*, which featured the same director, producer and stars as *Lawless Plainsmen*.

No video release could be found for the latter.

19 *Trail of Kit Carson*

Republic Pictures / 1945 / 55 minutes / Black and White

CREDITS: Lesley Selander (director); Stephen Auer (associate producer); Jack Natteford, Albert DeMond (screenplay); Bud Thackery (photography); Ralph Dixon (editor); Fred Ritter (art director); George Milo (set decorator); Richard Cherwin (music director). From a story by Jack Natteford.

CAST: Allan Lane (Bill Harmon), Helen Talbot (Joan Benton), Tom London (John Benton), Twinkle Watts (Peggy Bailey), Roy Barcroft (Dr. Charles Ryan), Kenne Duncan (Trigger Chandler), Jack Kirk (Sheriff Buffalo Bailey), Bud Geary (Red

Snyder), and Robert J. Wilke (Dave Mac-Roy).

SYNOPSIS: Bill Harmon journeys from Texas to California to help his friend, Dave MacRoy, with a gold mine. But Bill learns that Dave supposedly sold the mine to Dr. Charles Ryan and was accidentally killed in cleaning his gun when it discharged.

Suspecting foul play, Bill begins an investigation. Among the things which only make the job harder is Sheriff Buffalo Bailey revealing that a check from Ryan was with Dave's belongings.

Later on, Bill discovers the check was for a gambling debt owed by Ryan and not for any mine sale. Bill breaks into Ryan's office to find more incriminating evidence.

Gunman Red Snyder, actually hired by Ryan to kill Dave for the gold, is sent to get rid of Bill. When the attempt fails, another Ryan accomplice, Trigger Chandler, kills Snyder and Bill is blamed.

Although Bill is then jailed, witness John Benton, a miner, is prepared to testify on his behalf. When Trigger injures John, Bill escapes from jail and forces Dr. Ryan to save him.

The sheriff finally realizes the truth. As Trigger tries to expose Ryan, the doctor shoots him down. Apprehended, Ryan is soon sentenced to die for his past crimes.

NOTES: According to the *American Film Institute Catalog*, "Kit Carson is not a character in this film, and there is no mention of a trail established by the noted frontiersman."

Another irony of *Trail of Kit Carson* is one source does list Robert J .Wilke as playing the role; instead of his actual part of Dave MacRoy. Cowboy film star Allan Lane starred as the Texan searching for his pal's killer.

Republic released this "B" Western movie in 1945. The director was Lesley Selander. Both Albert DeMond and Jack Natteford worked on the screenplay from the latter's own story. Natteford was also one of the writers on the earlier *Fighting with Kit Carson* serial.

Wilke first began offering stalwart support in Westerns in 1939. Among his own legion of credits over the next few decades were roles in motion pictures and television. Memorable film roles included as one of the four badmen against Gary Cooper in 1952's *High Noon*, and as the cowboy who fights James Coburn (gun against knife) in 1960's *The Magnificent Seven*. His television work included parts in *The Adventures of Jim Bowie* and Fess Parker's *Daniel Boone*.

Trail of Kit Carson is unavailable on video.

20　*Along the Oregon Trail*

Republic Pictures / 1947 / 64 minutes / Trucolor

NOTES: Main information is in the Jim Bridger filmography.

Five years after *Lawless Plainsmen*, Forrest Taylor reprised the role of Kit Carson for Republic Pictures in *Along the Oregon Trail*. The frontier scout is mentor to the 1947 film's leading character.

Included in the action this time around is John Frémont, who is played by LeRoy Mason, that dastardly villain from Republic's earlier *The Painted Stallion*. Both Kit and his protege (Monte Hale) are guides for Frémont.

And while Carson actually filled that role historically on three expeditions with Frémont (two to Oregon), this shared adventure was a fabrication.

21　*The Adventures of Kit Carson*

Syndicated Television/Revue Productions / 1951–55 / 102 Episodes / Each 30 minutes / Black and White

CREDITS: Richard Irving (producer); Derwin Abbott, John English, Richard Irving, Lew Landers, Norman Lloyd (directors); Maurice Tombragel, Luci Ward (writers).

CAST: Bill Williams (Kit Carson), Don Diamond (El Toro), and Hank Peterson (Sierra Jack).

EPISODES/AIRDATES:

Season 1 (1951-52)
 1 "California Outlaws" (8/11/51)
 2 "Prince of Padua Hills" (8/18/51)
 3 "The Road to Monterey" (8/25/51)
 4 "The Padre's Treasure" (9/1/51)
 5 "The Murango Story" (9/8/51)
 6 "Riders of Capistrano" (9/15/51)
 7 "Enemies of the West" (9/22/51)
 8 "Law of the Six Guns" (9/29/51)
 9 "The Devil of Angel's Camp" (10/6/51)
10 "Law of the Frontier" (10/13/51)
11 "The Road to El Dorado" (10/20/51)
12 "Fury at Red Gulch" (10/27/51)
13 "The Outlaws of Manzanita" (11/3/51)
14 "The Desperate Sheriff" (11/10/51)
15 "The Hero of Hermosa" (11/17/51)
16 "A Ticket to Mexico" (11/24/51)
17 "The Return of Trigger Dawson" (12/1/51)
18 "The Teton Tornado" (12/8/51)
19 "Bad Man of Briscoe" (12/15/51)
20 "Spoilers of California" (12/22/51)
21 "Feud in San Filipe" (12/29/51)
22 "The Trap" (1/5/52)
23 "Border Corsairs" (1/12/52)
24 "Curse of the Albas" (1/19/52)

Season 2 (1952-53)
25 "Snake River Trapper" (8/2/52)
26 "Baron of Black Springs" (8/9/52)
27 "Danger Hill" (8/16/52)
28 "Wild Horses of Pala" (8/23/52)
29 "Trail to Ft. Hazard" (8/30/52)
30 "War Whoop" (9/6/52)
31 "Outlaw Paradise" (9/13/52)
32 "Powdersmoke Trail" (9/20/52)
33 "Trouble in Tuscarora" (9/27/52)
34 "Trail to Old Sonora" (10/4/52)
35 "Road to Destiny" (10/11/52)
36 "Border City" (10/18/52)
37 "Roaring Challenge" (10/25/52)
38 "Range Master" (11/1/52)

39 "Thunder Over Inyo" (11/8/52)
40 "Pledge to Danger" (11/15/52)
41 "Golden Snare" (11/22/52)
42 "Singing Wires" (11/29/52)
43 "Mojave Desperados" (12/6/52)
44 "Highway to Doom" (12/13/52)
45 "Hide-out" (12/20/52)
46 "Broken Spur" (12/27/52)
47 "Venutre Feud" (1/3/53)
48 "Bad Men of Marysville" (1/10/53)
49 "Claim Jumpers" (1/17/53)

Season 3 (1953-54)
50 "Outlaw Trail" (8/1/53)
51 "Savage Outposts" (8/8/53)
52 "Hawk Raiders" (8/15/53)
53 "Widow of Indian Wells" (8/22/53)
54 "Law of Boot Hill" (8/29/53)
55 "Trouble at Fort Mojave" (9/5/53)
56 "Powdersmoke Law" (9/12/53)
57 "Secret Sheriff" (9/19/53)
58 "Outlaw Army" (9/26/53)
59 "Lost Treasure of Panamint" (10/3/53)
60 "Frontier Mail" (10/10/53)
61 "Open Season" (10/17/53)
62 "Renegade Wires" (10/24/53)
63 "Ambush" (10/31/53)
64 "Gunsmoke Justice" (11/7/53)
65 "Challenge to Chance" (11/14/53)
66 "Marshal of Guntown" (11/21/53)
67 "Uprising at Pawhuska" (11/28/53)
68 "Army Renegades" (12/5/53)
69 "Badman's Escape" (12/12/53)
70 "The Haunted Hacienda" (12/19/53)
71 "Gunsmoke Valley" (12/26/53)
72 "Warwhoop" (1/2/54)
73 "Dry Creek Case" (1/9/54)
74 "Copper Town" (1/16/54)
75 "Counterfeit County" (1/23/54)
76 "The Cache" (1/30/54)

Season 4 (1954-55)
77 "Trails Westward" (7/31/54)
78 "Stampede Fury" (8/7/54)
79 "Bullets of Mystery" (8/14/54)
80 "The Wrong Man" (8/21/54)
81 "The Gatling Gun" (8/28/54)
82 "Powder Depot" (9/4/54)

Bill Williams in *The Adventures of Kit Carson.*

83 "The Hermit of Indian Ridge" (9/11/54)
84 "Riders of the Hooded League"
        (9/18/54)
85 "Frontier of Challenge" (9/25/54)
86 "Trail to Bordertown" (10/2/54)
87 "No Man's Law" (10/9/54)
88 "The Missing Hacienda" (10/16/54)
89 "Renegades of Rejo" (10/23/54)
90 "Ghost Town Garrison" (10/30/54)
91 "Eyes of the Outlaw" (11/6/54)
92 "Valiant Outlaw" (11/13/54)
93 "Judge of Black Mesa" (11/20/54)
94 "Frontier Empire" (11/27/54)
95 "Trouble in Sundown" (12/4/54)
96 "Outlaw's Justice" (12/11/54)
97 "The Golden Ring of Cibola" (12/18/54)
98 "Overland Stage" (12/25/54)
99 "Devil's Remedy" (1/1/55)
100 "Phantom Uprising" (1/8/55)
101 "Mission to Alkali" (1/15/55)
102 "Incident at Wagontire" (1/22/55)

NOTES: Ironically sources cite 104 television episodes of *The Adventures of Kit Carson*; yet only 102 actual titles were found. The same irony implies to its western setting. While one source relates that the action takes place in the 1840s, for another it is the 1880s (with the latter period being quite a feat even for the fabled frontiersman since he died in 1868).

Kit Carson was just a few months shy of becoming the first historical western figure to be portrayed on a television series. That distinction went instead to James Butler Hickok for *The Adventures of Wild Bill Hickok*. Both programs were prone, however, to use stories far removed from the actual lives of their real-life counterparts. Still, garbed in their terrific buckskin outfits, Hickok and Carson never looked better.

Bill Williams, who played Kit, had co-starred with Hickok's Guy Madison in the 1946 film *Till the End of Time*. While their respective television Westerns earned them their most fame, Williams wanted to distance himself from his role by the time of his 1957 television situation comedy, *Date with the Angels* (which lasted less than a season compared to *Kit Carson*'s four).

Nonetheless, Bill's heroics helped to brighten the lives of many children (including this author as a boy), as the series was geared that way with all the good-guy-against-bad-guy shoot-em-ups. Episodes can still be enjoyed on video.

Between 1951 and 1955, Revue Productions originally made the shows for syndication. Filming was done at both Republic Studios and Gene Autry's Melody Ranch.

Only a partial listing of all the folks who worked on the series is presented. Sources mention Richard Irving as both a producer and director. Another director was Lew Landers, who worked with actor Williams on radio in 1949. One of the regular writers, Luci Ward, had worked earlier on the screenplay for *Lawless Plainsmen*.

The *Adventures of Kit Carson*, like many of the Westerns on television at the time, benefitted from having a sidekick ride along with the hero. For Kit, it was Don Diamond's El Toro, who fancied himself quite the fellow with the ladies. For others like Wild Bill Hickok, it was Andy Devine's Jingles; or for the Lone Ranger, it was Jay Silverheels as Tonto. The combinations all contributed to make the various Westerns even more popular.

22 *Destiny West*

NBC Television / 1960 / 60 minutes / Color

CREDITS: Jack Smight (director); Mildred Freed Alberg (producer); William Altman (writer).

CAST: Jeffrey Hunter (John Charles Frémont), Susan Strasberg (Jessie Benton Frémont), Howard St. John (Thomas Hart Benton), and James Daly (Kit Carson).

NOTES: On January 24, 1960, NBC-TV aired *Destiny West*, which was part of a series of specials under the *Our American Heritage* banner. Mildred Freed Alberg produced, Jack Smight directed and William Altman wrote the teleplay. The subject was John Charles Frémont.

As portrayed by *Temple Houston*'s Jeffrey Hunter, Frémont's life is unfolded with apparently an overemphasis on the romance shared with Jessie Benton Frémont (Susan Strasberg) during the first half. The remainder of the hour program was then left to focus (with less than satisfactory results) on one of the Pathfinder's expeditions to California.

But at least one really positive note

Bill Williams rides in *The Adventures of Kit Carson.*

was sounded by *Variety*. "The only member of the cast who came out as a credible personality was James Daly," it said, "in the role of the backwoods scout, Kit Carson."

Daly was a distinguished dramatic actor during the Golden Age of Television in the 1950s, whose work included a number of anthology shows and a series called *Foreign Intrigue*. His acting skills served him well throughout his career; viewers may especially remember him from the series *Medical Center* (1969–76).

23 *Frontier Uprising*

United Artists/Zenith Pictures / 1961 / 68 minutes / Black and White

CREDITS: Edward L. Cahn (director);

Robert E. Kent (producer); Owen Harris (screenplay); Maury Gertsman (photography); Kenneth Crane (editor); Serge Krizman (art director); James Roach (set decorator); Paul Sawtell, Bert Shefter (music). From a story by George Bruce.

CAST: James Davis (Jim Stockton), Nancy Hadley (Consuela), Ken Mayer (Beaver), Nestor Paiva (Montalvo), Don O'Kelly (Kilpatrick), Stuart Randall (Ben Wright), and Herman Rudin (Chief Taztay).

NOTES: As with *Trail of Kit Carson*, the famous scout doesn't appear as a character in 1961's *Frontier Uprising* either. Nor is there a video listing for the latter film.

However, George Bruce's short story, called *Kit Carson*, was the basis for the script written by Owen Harris. Robert E. Kent produced and Edward L. Cahn directed this adequate Western fare from United Artists. The production values were deemed better than the actual story and screenplay.

Starring as scout Jim Stockton (who apparently was patterned after Carson) was Jim Davis. This was not that long after his television exposure as a regular on the *Rescue 8* series, but still years away from the *Dallas* series. In between, his other television work included several episodes of *Daniel Boone*.

Conveying his customary ruggedness in *Frontier Uprising*, Davis' frontiersman is bent on helping the Americans win California from the Indians and Mexicans. *Variety* noted the actor plays the role "agreeably and heroically."

24 *The Great Adventure*

CBS Television / 1963-64 / 26 Episodes / Each 60 minutes / Black and White

EPISODE 20: "The Pathfinder" (Aired 3/6/64)

CAST: Rip Torn (Lt. John C. Frémont), Carroll O'Connor (Johann Sutter), Arthur Batanides (Gomez), Joe De Santis (General Vallejo), Don Dubbins (Jason Chiles), David White (Benton), Noel Drayton (Buchanan), and Channing Pollock (Kit Carson).

NOTES: Main notes on *The Great Adventure* television series are in the Daniel Boone filmography. Additional notes are in the Sam Houston filmography.

"The Pathfinder" was episode 20 of the series; and it initially aired in March 1964. Like the earlier television broadcast, *Destiny West*, its subject was John Frémont.

Portraying the famous explorer this time was Rip Torn, who 22 years later played Kit Carson, alongside Richard Chamberlain's Frémont, on television's *Dream West* miniseries. Sharing the earlier adventure west with Torn was Channing Pollock as Carson. Also seen as Johann (John) Sutter was Carroll O'Connor in his pre–Archie Bunker days.

While Pollock's Western credits were few, they also included a 1966 episode of the *Daniel Boone* series. Along with episodes of *The Great Adventure* involving Carson, Boone and Houston, another one (No. 12), with Lloyd Bridges in the title role, was called "Wild Bill Hickok — The Legend and the Man."

None of these episodes from the series could be found on video.

25 *Seven Alone*

Doty-Dayton Productions / 1974 / 97 minutes / Color

CREDITS: Earl Bellamy (director); Lyman D. Dayton (producer); Eleanor Lamb, Douglas Stewart (screenplay); Robert W. Stum (photography); Dan Greer (editing); Ray Markham (production design); Robert O. Ragland (music). Based on the book *On to Oregon*, by Honore Morrow.

CAST: Dewey Martin (Henry Sager), Aldo Ray (Dr. Dutch), Anne Collings (Naome Sager), Stewart Petersen (John Sager),

James Griffith (Billy Shaw), Dehl Berti (White Elk), Bea Morris (Sally), and Dean Smith (Kit Carson).

SYNOPSIS: In 1843, Henry and Naome Sager leave their Missouri farm, with their children, and join a wagon train bound for Oregon. Along on the 2,000-mile journey is Dr. Dutch, who helps the family when needed.

Henry's oldest son John, a mischievous teenager, is robbed by an Indian. Kit Carson, riding by, then helps the family as well. There is fighting and a few Indians are killed.

Taking ill, Henry dies and so does Naome. John takes charge of his six siblings, including an infant, and they continue the journey west. Despite all hardships, the children stay together.

NOTES: A Doty-Dayton production, *Seven Alone* was first released in December 1974. Lyman D. Dayton produced and Earl Bellamy directed the film. Screenwriters Eleanor Lamb and Douglas Stewart based their work on Honore Morrow's book, which supposedly was drawn from a true story.

During the trek along the Oregon Trail in the film, the Sager children, both before and after they are orphaned, cross trails with assorted characters. Included is Kit Carson.

While Dewey Martin (Disney's Daniel Boone) was featured as Henry, the children's father, Kit was played by Dean Smith. A few John Wayne Western films were part of the latter's resume, including 1967's *El Dorado*, as was the 1972 Burt Lancaster Western *Ulzana's Raid*.

Strongly geared for family viewing (and boasting Wyoming locations), nonetheless *Seven Alone* was felt by *Motion Picture Guide* to "be bland and uninteresting for children as well as adults." Yet it apparently can be obtained on both video and DVD.

26 *Bridger*

ABC Television/Universal / 1976 / 120 minutes / Color

NOTES: Main information is in the Bridger filmography.

During the 1830s, Jim Bridger and Kit Carson shared a strong friendship. As mountain men together, they undoubtedly swapped yarns around a campfire, trapped beaver in cold streams and fought Indians tooth and nail.

Although the time frame remained the same, there was no shared adventure like the one depicted in 1976's television movie, *Bridger*, where Jim (James Wainwright) and Kit (Ben Murphy) race against time to save the Rockies from British intervention. Yet this herculean feat could have just as easily been believed with these bigger-than-life frontiersmen around.

Carson and Bridger were regarded as the greatest of the mountain men. Another of their ilk, Joe Meek (Dirk Blocker), shares

Ben Murphy as Kit Carson in *Bridger*.

in the television adventure as well; historically, he was a comrade and all were not above risking their lives for each other.

Murphy in 1968, and Wainwright in 1969, had each appeared in an episode of that popular 1960s' television Western series, *The Virginian*. As Kid Curry (alias Thaddeus Jones), Ben was a star of the comedy Western series, *Alias Smith and Jones* (1971–73).

27 *Kit Carson and the Mountain Men*

NBC Television/Walt Disney / 1977 / 2 parts / 120 minutes / Color

CREDITS: Vincent McEveety (director); Winston Hibler (producer); Harry Spalding (writer); Andrew Jackson (photography); Bob Bring (editor); John B. Mansbridge, Frank T. Smith (art directors); Charles R. Pierce (set decorator); Chuck Keehne (costumes); Robert J. Schiffer (makeup); Buddy Baker (music). Song: "Kit Carson," by Jay Livingston, Ray Evans, Buddy Baker.

CAST: Christopher Connelly (Kit Carson), Robert Reed (Capt. John C. Frémont), Gary Lockwood (Bret Haskell), Ike Eisenmann (Randy Benton), Emile Genest (Basil Lejeunesse), Richard Jaeckel (Ed Kern), Joaquin Martinez (Renni), Nick Ramus (Tioga), and Gregg Palmer (Jim Bridger).

SYNOPSIS: Following a winter of fur trapping, Kit Carson and a group of mountain men head into the Green River Valley. Delaware Indians called Renni and Tioga, and hunter Basil Lejeunesse, are with him.

In the valley, a shooting contest is held to choose the 10 finest marksmen. Carson is among those who then join Capt. John Frémont on a surveying expedition to California.

Frémont's young brother-in-law, Randy Benton, disobeys orders to stay behind. During the journey, Kit finds himself being idolized by Randy. They must contend with others trying to sabotage the expedition.

NOTES: *Kit Carson and the Mountain Men* was a two-part show broadcast on the *World of Disney* television series. The original airdates on the NBC network were January 9 and 16, 1977. No video listing could be found.

Vincent McEveety was the director and Winston Hibler the producer of this fictionalized treatment based on the expeditions shared by Kit Carson and John Frémont in the 1840s. Harry Spalding wrote the teleplay. Filming took place in California's Inyo National Forest.

Carson was portrayed by Christopher Connelly, who that same year was also seen in NBC's showing of *The Incredible Rocky Mountain Race*. Robert Reed, the father on television's *The Brady Bunch* series (1969–74), played Frémont.

Other actual members of the Frémont expeditions were featured in *Kit Carson and the Mountain Men*. They included Randolph Benton and Basil Lejeunesse, played by Ike Eisenmann and Emile Genest respectively.

Historically, 12-year-old Randolph accompanied brother-in-law John on the first expedition through the Rockies; the youngster's very first watch while camped was with Kit. Basil, who was actually closer to Frémont than Carson, was killed by Indians during the third expedition.

Additional notes are in the Jim Bridger filmography.

28 *Tex Willer e il signore degli abissi*

Italian Film Production / 1985 / 90 minutes / Color

CREDITS: Duccio Tessari (director); Giorgio Bonelli, Giovanni L. Bonelli (writers); Francesco Paolucci, Gaetano Paolucci (special effects).

CAST: Giuliano Gemma (Tex Willer),

William Berger (Kit Carson), Carlo Mucari (Tiger Jack), Isabel Russinova (Tulac), Aldo Sambrell (El Dorado), Giovanni L. Bonelli (Indian Sorcerer), Flavio Bucci (Kanas), and Riccardo Petrazzi (Lord of the Deep).

SYNOPSIS: After the Civil War, western hero Tex Willer and his Indian sidekick, Tiger Jack, are chasing after bootleggers selling liquor to the Indians. They come across Kit Carson, who leads them to where renegade Indians are bent on creating trouble.

An Indian is captured and it is discovered that there is a movement underfoot by various tribe members to take control of the country. The Indians try to do so with the help of supernatural forces, including a green rock with the power to turn all their enemies into mummies.

But Tex, Tiger Jack and Kit join forces in a rousing fight to prevent this threat. They are victorious.

NOTES: *Tex Willer e il signore degli abissi* was a 1985 film from Italy. This unconventional Western, with its English title of *Tex and the Lord of the Deep*, was directed by Duccio Tessari. It is listed on video.

The writing, credited to Giorgio Bonelli and Giovanni L. Bonelli, was derived from either an Italian comic strip or cartoon (depending on the source) about the incredible adventures of Tex Willer in the American West. Combined in the film were those very elements of wild Western action and fantasy found in both.

Guiliano Gemma starred as the heroic Tex, always ready for a good fight against the insurmountable odds of winning. He was more than evenly matched by William Berger's Kit Carson, who uses exploding arrows to even the odds in their efforts together.

Among the film credits for Berger over the years were other Italian Westerns. He was in on the action with Lee Van Cleef in 1970's *Sabata*.

29 *Dream West*

CBS Television/Sunn Classic Pictures / 1986 / 3 parts / 420 minutes / Color

CREDITS: Dick Lowry (director); Hunt Lowry (producer); Evan Hunter (writer); Jack Wallner, Bob Baldwin (photography); Byron Brandt, Jack Fegan, Dennis Mosher, Anita Brandt-Bergoyne (editors); Dena Roth, Gregg Fonseca (art directors); Linda Pearl (production design); Fred Karlin (music). Based on the novel by David Nevin.

CAST: Richard Chamberlain (John Charles Frémont), Alice Krige (Jessie Benton Frémont), F. Murray Abraham (Abraham Lincoln), Rene Enriquez (General Castro), Ben Johnson (Jim Bridger), Jerry Orbach (John Sutter), G.D. Spradlin (Stephen Watts Kearny), Fritz Weaver (Thomas Hart Benton), Anthony Zerbe (Bill Williams), Claude Akins (Tom Fitzpatrick), John Anderson (Brigadier General Brooke), Lee Bergere (Papa Joe Nicollet), Jeff East (Tim Donovan), Michael Ensign (Charles Preuss), Mel Ferrer (Judge Elkins), Burton Gilliam (Martineau), John Harkins (George Bancroft), Gayle Hunnicutt (Maria Crittenden), Matt McCoy (Louis Freniere), Cameron Mitchell (Robert Stockton), Noble Willingham (James Polk), Bill Campbell (Lieutenant Gaines), Jonathan Frakes (Lieutenant Gillespie), Kip Niven (John Crittenden), Timothy Scott (Ezekial Merritt), Nikki Creswell (Lily Frémont), and Rip Torn (Kit Carson).

SYNOPSIS: In the late 1830s, John Charles Frémont is a member of a U.S. Topographical Corps surveying expedition. Papa Joe Nicollet is the team's leader.

Upon his return to Washington, John falls in love with Jessie Benton, the teenaged daughter of Senator Thomas Hart Benton. The senator disapproves when they marry.

In time, Benton acknowledges the union and even supports John's own expedition in 1842. Frémont's vision of making the way west accessible to all is shared by both Jessie and her father.

Partaking in the journey west with Frémont are others, including his mapmaker, Charles Preuss, and guide, Kit Carson. The goal is to survey and map the Oregon Trail.

In the next several years, the push westward by Frémont extends to both the Oregon and California territories. Hunting buffalo, going down rapids on a raft, and confronting Indians are part of the adventures shared. Kit, meanwhile, has become John's most trusted friend.

The war between the United States and Mexico in 1846 reaches California, involving Frémont and his followers. Jessie continues to support her husband's vision despite his long absences from their Washington home.

Alice Krige and Richard Chamberlain as the Frémonts, good friends of Kit Carson, in the 1986 television miniseries *Dream West.*

In Los Angeles, John Frémont is placed under arrest for refusing to recognize Gen. Stephen Watts Kearny as his superior officer. Soon enough, Frémont is forced to endure a court-martial.

Unable to obtain Kit's services for an expedition into the San Juan Mountains, John instead uses Bill Williams as a guide. But the winter weather traps Frémont's group of men and some perish.

Frémont becomes the first Republican candidate to run for U.S. president in the 1850s. During the Civil War, as a Union commander, John angers President Abraham Lincoln when he oversteps his authority.

All the trials and tribulations in Frémont's life have taken a toll. Yet Jessie remains John's most ardent supporter over the passage of time.

NOTES: CBS and Sunn Classic Pictures collaborated on the epic television miniseries about the life of John Frémont. Called *Dream West*, it was broadcast in three parts on April 13, 14, and 15, 1986. Dick Lowry was the director and Hunt Lowry the producer.

Evan Hunter based his teleplay on the equally epic David Nevin novel of the same title. While undoubtedly there were distortions of history, and weighty romanticism, no previous film or show captured the essence of the Pathfinder as well. Ironically, no video listing could be found.

Then known as "King of the Miniseries," for his fine television roles, Richard Chamberlain surely added another one with his portrayal of Frémont. Showcased was the great ambition that made the explorer both fearless and reckless in history.

Conveying an equally ambitious spirit was Alice Krige in the role of Jessie Frémont. Their romantic interludes may be overstated, but her chemistry with Chamberlain was enthralling. They also appeared together the year before in the NBC miniseries, *Wallenberg: A Hero's Story.*

Many of the historical figures in the actual lives of the Frémonts were reflected upon in *Dream West*, while filming included locations in Arizona, Colorado and Wyoming. Among the names were President Lincoln (F. Murray Abraham), Senator Benton (Fritz Weaver), Commodore Stockton (Cameron Mitchell), General Kearny (G.D. Spradlin), Tom Fitzpatrick (Claude Akins), and Charles Preuss (Michael Ensign).

Perhaps the most endearing support, however, came from Rip Torn's Kit Carson. *Variety* may have brushed it off as "good sidekick stuff," but the frontiersman's friendship with Frémont is the stuff of legends. Torn even bore a bit of a resemblance to the real Carson.

Much earlier, in 1964, Torn had played John Frémont on *The Great Adventure* series. But not long before *Dream West*, in 1983, the noted actor was nominated for a best supporting Oscar for the film *Cross Creek*.

Historically, Frémont's mapmaker on three of his own expeditions was Charles Preuss (including the ill-fated fourth one which both were fortunate to survive). While later living in California, Frémont was the first Republican to be nominated in a presidential election (in 1856; he lost to Democrat James Buchanan).

In the winter of 1868 (and just a few months before his death), Kit Carson saw John Frémont for the last time in Washington. Kit traveled there with an Indian delegation. John was greatly concerned about the weakened state brought on by Carson's damaged aorta.

Frémont, himself, died in 1890 after his appendix burst. At the time he was away from Jessie in New York City. He was 77 years old.

Additional notes are in the Jim Bridger filmography.

30 *Explorers of the World*

Issembert Productions/Schlessinger Media / 2000 / 23 minutes / Color

CREDITS: Yves Gerard Issembert (director, producer); Donald M. Cooper (writer); George Rosenberg (photography); Kristin Frascione (editor); Holly Beck (set design, wardrobe); Michael Sciuto (music).

CAST: Tim Marrone (Kit Carson), Ashley Hoffman (Jessica), Juan Albert (Roberto), and Laurie Ley (Ms. Durant).

SYNOPSIS: Two school students, Jessica and Roberto, encounter a portrait of frontiersman Kit Carson which comes to life. Kit then shares some adventures about other notable frontier figures from American history.

Included in Kit's stories are those about Daniel Boone, Zebulon Pike, Jedediah Smith, James Beckwourth, and John Charles Frémont.

NOTES: *Explorers of the World* was actually a video film series of 13 titles geared for young schoolchildren. It was made in collaboration by Schlessinger Media and Issembert Productions.

This one with Kit Carson was called "The American Frontier." Released in 2000, it was written by Donald M. Cooper; Yves Gerard Issembert acted as both producer and director.

Tim Marrone made a likeable and modest Kit Carson. Rather than telling about himself, he focused more on those others who made historic contributions.

APPENDIX:
VIDEO DOCUMENTARIES

Documentaries can be both enlightening and perplexing, just as any other motion picture or television entry. Stepping back into the past can fill the viewer with a sense of wonder at the different historical viewpoints realized.

While there will be some documentaries missing, a select group is listed and they are available on video.

1 *The Alamo*

A&E Entertainment / Video Release: October 19, 1996 / 2 Volumes / 100 minutes / Color/Black and White

This two-volume video set is narrated by Tom Berenger and presented by *American Heritage*. Many material sources are utilized, although they are not all mentioned here.

Volume 1 shows clips from John Wayne's *The Alamo*, as well as brief reenacted scenes during the siege with other actors. Included in the latter is Davy Crockett amusing his comrades with music, and Jim Bowie being cared for on his sickbed.

In Volume 2, pictures of Bowie reflect that he was so ill during the final battle that he perhaps fired only one pistol at the enemy. A reenactment of Crockett's death is seen as being brought before Santa Anna after his surrender and executed with six others.

There are also descriptive pictures of the Battle of San Jacinto. Sam Houston is made out as a procrastinator in each volume, and as not even believing that Santa Anna had such large forces at the Alamo.

A clip from *The Martyrs of the Alamo* is seen in the second volume as well.

2 *The Alamo: From Mission to Fortress*

Matson Multi-Media / Video Release: 1995 / Color

This video is part of a series called *Missions of Texas*.

The history of the Alamo is told from its beginnings as a mission in 1719 to its use as a fort by Bowie, Crockett and their comrades in 1836.

251

3 Battle of the Alamo

Discovery Channel Productions / 1996 / 55 minutes / Color

Made for cable television's Discovery Channel, this documentary is available on both video and DVD.

Hal Holbrook narrates as the 13-day siege and final battle at the Alamo are examined. Reenactments are also utilized based on actual journal entries from that period in history.

4 Boone and Crockett: The Hunter Heroes

A&E Home Video / Video Release: May 9, 2002 / 100 minutes / Color

Following its video release, this profile on Daniel Boone and Davy Crockett was broadcast on cable's History Channel in July 2003.

Reenactments and historical accounts, by authors and historians alike, are featured to help clear away the myths and get at the truth in the lives of the frontiersmen.

5 Carson and Cody: The Hunter Heroes

A&E Home Video / 2003 / 100 minutes / Color/ Black and White

Like *Boone and Crockett: The Hunter Heroes*, this video documentary was also broadcast on the History Channel.

The lives of Christopher "Kit" Carson and William "Buffalo Bill" Cody are explored to separate the men from their legends. This includes interviewing historians and showcasing collections found in the Smithsonian Institute.

6 Daniel Boone

A&E Entertainment / Video Release: February 7, 2000 / 50 minutes / Color

This is part of the *A&E Biography* series also broadcast on cable television.

It attempts to separate the factual Daniel from the fictional one by exploring his life and times. Period artwork and interviews contribute to the effort.

John Mack Faragher, author of *Daniel Boone: The Legend of an American Pioneer*, speaks about the frontiersman's many adventures.

7 Daniel Boone and the First American Pioneers

SVE & Churchill Media / Video Release: 1997 / 20 minutes

The events which brought Boone and other settlers into Kentucky are presented.

Reflected as well are the lifestyles of these pioneers in this video, which is part of a series called the *American Pioneering Experience*.

8 Daniel Boone's Final Frontier

Landmark Media / Video Release: 1995 / 22 minutes / Color

The journals of Daniel's children, Jemima and Nathan Boone, are the basis for exploring their father's last years living in Missouri.

Dramatic reenactments are also featured.

9 Davy Crockett: American Frontier Legend

A&E Entertainment / Video Release: February 7, 2000 / 50 minutes / Color

This too, like its *Daniel Boone*, is part of cable TV's *A&E Biography* series.

Davy's life and legends are explored to show how he became an American folk hero. This is accomplished with the help of artifacts, period art, and interviewing historians.

His life from his childhood to the Alamo are all accounted for, including his political career. It is pointed out that he may have never worn the coonskin cap which added to his fame in both films and television.

10 *Mountain Men*

A&E Home Video / Video Release: September 26, 2000 / 100 minutes / Color

Historical accounts and period art contribute to this glimpse into the lives of a number of the frontier figures who helped open the way west. Included are Jim Bridger and Kit Carson.

Robert M. Utley, author of *A Life Wild and Perilous*, is among those experts who separate the legends from the facts.

11 *Mountain Men and Gold Seekers*

SVE & Churchill Media / Video Release: 1997 / 20 minutes

This is part of the *American Pioneering Experience* series, like *Daniel Boone & the First American Pioneers*.

While the California gold rush is chronicled, also reflected are how the mountain men trapped in the various mountain ranges of the west.

Other titles about these hardy adventurers are part of earlier film series as well. They include 1979's *The Mountain Men* (for the *Growth of America's West* series), and 1992's *Mountain Men* (for the *American History* series).

12 *The Real West: The Battle of the Alamo*

A&E Home Video / Video Release: October 24, 1995 / 50 minutes / Color/Black and White

Part of a series called *The Real West*, this documentary is hosted by Kenny Rogers. Through a number of sources, including period accounts and authentic di-

aries, the ambitions and heroism of Davy Crockett, Jim Bowie and William Travis are examined.

Bowie is pictured as not being a strong factor during the battle because of his illness. Reports on Crockett reflect either his surrender and execution or fighting to the end.

13 *Remember the Alamo! Remember Goliad! Heroes of the Texas Revolution*

Matson Multi-Media / Video Release: 1995 / Color

Like *The Alamo: From Mission to Fortress*, this video is part of the *Missions of Texas* series.

Explored are the perspectives of the historical figures who played a part in the Alamo battle, the massacre at Goliad, and the San Jacinto battle.

There is also a 2004 video called *Remember the Alamo*, which emphasizes the Hispanic contribution to the Texas Revolution. It is narrated by Hector Elizondo (and was televised initially on PBS).

14 *Sam Houston and Texas: A Giant Man for a Giant Land*

AIMS Multimedia / Video Release: 1987 / 25 minutes

This documentary is reflective of *American Lifestyle Series II: Politics & the Military*.

Narrated by E.G. Marshall, a rich body of political and personal facts are given weight. Houston's military career is also explored, from being a soldier under Andrew Jackson to his role as a leader in the independence of Texas.

BIBLIOGRAPHY

Aaker, Everett. *Television Western Players of the Fifties*. Jefferson, NC: McFarland, 1997.

The Almanac of American History. Arthur M. Schlesinger, Jr., general ed. New York: G.P. Putnam's Sons, 1983.

Alter, J. Cecil. *Jim Bridger*. Norman: University of Oklahoma Press, 1962.

American Film Institute Catalog. Film Beginnings 1893–1910. Metuchen, NJ: Scarecrow, 1995. *Feature Films 1911–1920*. Berkeley and Los Angeles: University of California Press, 1988. *Feature Films 1921–1930*. New York: R.R. Bowker, 1971. *Feature Films 1931–1940*. Berkeley and Los Angeles: University of California Press, 1993.

The American Heritage Encyclopedia of American History. John Mack Faragher, general ed. New York: Henry Holt, 1998.

Baugh, Virgil E. *Rendezvous at the Alamo: Highlights in the Lives of Bowie, Crockett, and Travis*. Lincoln: University of Nebraska Press, 1960.

Blair, Walter. *Tall Tale America: A Legendary History of Our Humorous Heroes*. New York: Coward-McCann, 1944.

Braff, Richard E. *The Universal Silents: A Filmography of the Universal Motion Picture Manufacturing Company 1912–1929*. Jefferson, NC: McFarland, 1999.

Brooks, Tim, and Earle Marsh. *The Complete Directory to Prime Time Network TV Shows 1946–Present*. 3rd ed. New York: Ballantine, 1985.

Brown, Kelly R. *Florence Lawrence, the Biograph Girl: America's First Movie Star*. Jefferson, NC: McFarland, 1999.

Burke, James Wakefield. *David Crockett: The Man Behind the Myth*. Austin, TX: Eakin, 1984.

Buscombe, Edward, ed. *BFI Companion to the Western*. New York: Atheneum, 1988.

Caesar, Gene. *King of the Mountain Men: The Life of Jim Bridger*. New York: E.P. Dutton, 1961.

Calvert, Patricia. *Great Lives: The American Frontier*. New York: Atheneum, 1997.

Cameron, Kenneth M. *America on Film: Hollywood and American History*. New York: Continuum, 1997.

Carson, Kit. *Kit Carson's Own Story of His Life*. Blanche C. Grant, ed. Taos, NM: Santa Fe New Mexican, 1926.

Crockett, David. *The Autobiography of David Crockett*. With an introduction by Hamlin Garland. New York: Charles Scribner's Sons, 1923.

Davis, William C. *Three Roads to the Alamo: The Lives and Fortunes of David Crockett, James Bowie, and William Barret Travis*. New York: Harper Perennial, 1999.

DeBruhl, Marshall. *Sword of San Jacinto: A Life of Sam Houston*. New York: Random House, 1993.

Derr, Mark. *The Frontiersman: The Real Life and the Many Legends of Davy Crockett.* New York: Quill/William Morrow, 1993.

Draper, Lyman C. *The Life of Daniel Boone.* Edited by Ted Franklin Belve. Mechanicsburg, PA: Stackpole, 1998.

Dunlay, Tom. *Kit Carson and the Indians.* Lincoln: University of Nebraska Press, 2000.

Eickhoff, Randy Lee, and Leonard C. Lewis. *Bowie: A Novel of the Life of Jim Bowie.* New York: Forge, 1998.

Elliott, Lawrence. *The Long Hunter: A New Life of Daniel Boone.* New York: Reader's Digest, 1976.

Everson, William K. *The Hollywood Western.* Secaucus, NJ: Citadel, 1992.

Faragher, John Mack. *Daniel Boone: The Life and Legend of an American Pioneer.* New York: Henry Holt, 1992.

Frank, Sam. *Buyer's Guide to Fifty Years of TV on Video.* Amherst, NY: Prometheus, 1999.

Gaines, Ann Graham. *Jim Bowie: Hero of the Alamo.* Berkeley Heights, NJ: Enslow, 2000.

Garst, Shannon. *James Bowie and His Famous Knife.* New York: Julian Messner, 1955.

Gowans, Fred R. *Rocky Mountain Rendezvous: A History of the Fur Trade Rendezvous 1825–1840.* Layton, UT: Peregrine Smith, 1985.

Guild, Thelma S., and Harvey L. Carter. *Kit Carson: A Pattern for Heroes.* Lincoln: University of Nebraska Press, 1984.

Hardy, Phil. *The Encyclopedia of Western Movies.* Minneapolis: Woodbury, 1984.

Hine, Robert V., and John Mack Faragher. *The American West: A New Interpretive History.* New Haven, CT: Yale University Press, 2000.

Houston, Sam. *The Autobiography of Sam Houston.* Donald Day and Harry Herbert Ullom, eds. Norman: University of Oklahoma Press, 1954.

International Dictionary of Films and Filmmakers. Volume 2: Directors. 1984. *Volume 3: Actors and Actresses.* 1986. *Volume 4: Writers and Production Artists.* 1987. Detroit: St. James/Gale.

James, Marquis. *The Raven: A Biography of Sam Houston.* Austin: University of Texas Press, 1988. (From the 1929 Bobbs-Merrill edition.)

Kennedy, John F. *Profiles in Courage (Commemorative Edition).* New York: Harper Perennial, 1964 (first published in 1956).

Kilgore, Dan. *How Did Davy Die?* College Station: Texas A&M University Press, 1978.

Klepper, Robert K. *Silent Films, 1877–1996: A Critical Guide to 646 Movies.* Jefferson, NC: McFarland, 1999.

Konigsberg, Ira. *The Complete Film Dictionary.* 2nd ed. New York: Penguin, 1997.

Langman, Larry. *A Guide to Silent Westerns.* Westport, CT: Greenwood, 1992.

Lentz, Harris M. III. *Western and Frontier Film and Television Credits 1903–1995.* 2 vols. Jefferson, NC: McFarland, 1996.

Liebman, Roy. *From Silents to Sound: A Biographical Encyclopedia of Performers Who Made the Transition to Talking Pictures.* Jefferson, NC: McFarland, 1998.

Lofaro, Michael A., *The Life and Adventures of Daniel Boone.* Lexington: University Press of Kentucky, 1978.

_____, ed. *Davy Crockett: The Man, the Legend, the Legacy, 1786–1986.* Knoxville: University of Tennessee Press, 1985.

_____, and Joe Cummings, eds. *Crockett at Two Hundred: New Perspectives on the Man and the Myth.* Knoxville: University of Tennessee Press, 1989.

Lord, Walter. *A Time to Stand.* New York: Harper & Brothers, 1961.

Maltin, Leonard. *The Disney Films.* New York: Bonanza, 1973.

_____, ed. *Leonard Maltin's 2004 Movie & Video Guide.* New York: Signet, 2003.

Martin, Mick, and Marsha Porter. *DVD & Video Guide 2004.* New York: Ballantine, 2003.

Morton, Alan. *The Complete Directory to Science Fiction, Fantasy and Horror Television Series.* Peoria, IL: Other World, 1997.

The Motion Picture Guide. Silent Film 1910–1936. Robert B. Connelly, ed. Chicago: Cinebooks, 1986.

_____. *A–B, C–D.* 1985. *E–G, H–K, L–M, N–R.* 1986. *S, T–V, W–Z.* 1987. Jay Robert Nash and Stanley Ralph Ross, eds. Chicago: Cinebooks.

Nofi, Albert A. *The Alamo and the Texas War for Independence.* New York: Da Capo, 1994.

Osterberg, Bertil O. *Colonial America on Film and Television: A Filmography.* Jefferson, NC: McFarland, 2001.

Parish, James Robert, and Michael R. Pitts. *Great Western Pictures.* Metuchen, NJ: Scarecrow, 1976.

_____. *Great Western Pictures II.* Metuchen, NJ: Scarecrow, 1988.

Past Imperfect: History According to the Movies. Mark C. Carnes, general ed. New York: Henry Holt, 1995.

Pitts, Michael R. *Hollywood and American History: A Filmography of Over 250 Motion Pictures Depicting U.S. History.* Jefferson, NC: McFarland, 1984.

_____. *Western Movies: A TV and Video Guide to 4200 Genre Films.* Jefferson, NC: McFarland, 1986.

Ragan, David. *Who's Who in Hollywood.* Vols. 1 and 2. New York: Facts on File, 1992.

Rainey, Buck. *The Reel Cowboy: Essays on the Myth in Movies and Literature.* Jefferson, NC: McFarland, 1996.

_____. *Serials and Series: A World Filmography, 1912–1956.* Jefferson, NC: McFarland, 1999.

Richard, Alfred Charles, Jr. *The Hispanic Image on the Silver Screen: An Interpretive Filmography from Silents into Sound 1898–1935.* New York: Greenwood, 1992.

Roberts, David. *A Newer World: Kit Carson, John C. Frémont and the Claiming of the American West.* New York: Touchstone/ Simon & Schuster, 2000.

Roberts, Randy, and James S. Olson. *A Line in the Sand: The Alamo in Blood and Memory.* New York: The Free Press, 2001.

Rourke, Constance. *Davy Crockett.* New York: Harcourt, Brace & World, 1934.

Slide, Anthony. *The New Historical Dictionary of the American Film Industry.* Lanham, MD: Scarecrow, 1998.

Smith, Dave. *Disney A to Z: The Official Encyclopedia.* New York: Hyperion, 1996.

Thompson, Frank. *The Alamo: The Illustrated Story of the Epic Film.* New York: Newmarket, 2004.

_____. *Alamo Movies.* Plano, TX: Wordware, 1994.

_____. *Lost Films: Important Movies That Disappeared.* Secaucus, NJ: Citadel, 1996.

Utley, Robert M. *A Life Wild and Perilous: Mountain Men and the Paths to the Pacific.* New York: Henry Holt, 1997.

Watts, Steven. *The Magic Kingdom: Walt Disney and the American Way of Life.* New York: Houghton Mifflin, 1997.

Wiley, Mason, and Damien Bona. *Inside Oscar: The Unofficial History of the Academy Awards.* 4th ed. New York: Ballantine, 1993.

Williams, John Hoyt. *Sam Houston: The Life and Times of the Liberator of Texas, an Authentic American Hero.* New York: Touchstone, 1993.

Woolery, George W. *Animated TV Specials: The Complete Directory to the First Twenty-five Years, 1962–1987.* Metuchen, NJ: Scarecrow, 1989.

_____. *Children's Television: The First Thirty-five Years, 1946–1981. Part II.* Metuchen, NJ: Scarecrow, 1985.

INDEX

IFARW 791
.4365
2
A572

ANDREYCHUK, ED
    AMERICAN FRONTIERSMEN
    ON FILM AND TELEVISION
CENTRAL LIBRARY
05/06